ANALECTA BIBLICA

INVESTIGATIONES SCIENTIFICAE IN RES BIBLICAS

118

ABRAHAM MARIASELVAM

THE SONG OF SONGS AND ANCIENT TAMIL LOVE POEMS

POETRY AND SYMBOLISM

EDITRICE PONTIFICIO ISTITUTO BIBLICO – ROMA 1988

Vidimus et approbamus ad normam Statutorum

Pontificii Instituti Biblici de Urbe
Romae, die 16 mensis Decembris anni 1987

R. P. M. Gilbert, S.J.
R. P. M. Dhavamony, S.J.

ISBN 88-7653-118-1

Editrice Pontificia Università Gregoriana
Editrice Pontificio Istituto Biblico
Piazza della Pilotta, 35 - 00187 Roma

Dedicated
to
My Parents
Brothers and Sisters

ACKNOWLEDGEMENTS

The present study was presented and defended on 4-6-1987 as the dissertation for a Doctorate in Biblical Exegesis at the Pontifical Biblical Institute. With some modification, it now appears in the Analecta Biblica for the perusal of a wider circle of Biblical scholars and Tamil literary critics.

The thesis would not have seen the light and publication so fast and so well but for the Divine Providence and the protection of the Blessed Virgin Mary.

There are many who contributed in one way or other towards its completion. In the first place come my mother, brother and sisters. With their immense love, concern, encouragement and prayers they stood by me all along. But for their inspiration and insistence, this study would not have been undertaken.

My sincere thanks are due to my Archbishop Rt. Rev. V.S. Selvanather, D.D., D.C.L., for having permitted me to study for the Doctorate, and to Rev. Fr. D.S. Amalorpavadass, the Head of the Department of Christianity in the University of Mysore, for having sponsored my research programme. I thank also the authorities of the Sacred Congregation for the Evangelization of Peoples for the scholarship during the preparation of the thesis. I would like to express my appreciation to the Superiors, Sisters, Confrères and helpers in Collegio San Pietro, Rome, for what they were to me during my stay there.

I am very grateful to Fr. M. Gilbert, S.J. and Fr. M. Dhavamony, S.J., the moderators of the thesis. I went to them as a student, but they received me as a friend and treated me as a colleague.

In particular, I thank most sincerely, the Society of Missions Étrangères de Paris, and its Vicar General for their hospitality during my research in Paris and for their generous help towards the publication.

My most sincere and heart-felt thanks are due to the Society of the Precious Blood, the Moderator General and the team of his collaborators — the Fathers and Sisters — in the Generalate. I asked them just for a place to stay and work on the book. They offered me, in fact, a home to live in and a family atmosphere within to work. Everyone in the house made my stay pleasant and helped me with suggestions and support.

I am very grateful also to the Vicar General of the Archdiocese of Freiburg in Germany for giving me the possibility of doing pastoral work in the diocese for about two months.

I am thankful too, to the Institute of Missiology, Missio-Aachen and to the Kath Bibelwerk-Stuttgart for their aid for publishing this book.

I am deeply indebted to all my friends, well-wishers and benefactors at home and abroad who extended their support and help by word and deed for meeting the cost of the book. Their names are not printed here but are inscribed in my heart and cherished with grateful memory.

A. Mariaselvam

C.PP.S. Generalate,
Rome,
14th April 1988,
Anniversary of my Ordination.

LIST OF ABBREVIATIONS

A. BIBLICAL SECTION

1. *Journals*

AJSL	American Journal of Semitic Languages and Literature
Ann.Théo.	L'année théologique
BASP	Bulletin, American Society of Papyrologists
Bib	Biblica
BTB	Biblical Theology Bulletin
Bull.Secr.n.Chr.	Bulletin, Secretariatus pro non-Christianis
BZ.NF	Biblische Zeitschrift Neue Folge
CBQ	Catholic Biblical Quarterly
ClasQ	Classical Quarterly
ETL	Ephemerides theologicae lovanienses
Exp.T	Expository Times
Greg	Gregorianum
HTR	Harvard Theological Review
HUCA	Hebrew Union College Annual
Interpr	Interpretation
JAAR	Journal of the American Academy of Religion
JANES	Journal of the Ancient Near Eastern Society
JAOS	Journal of the American Oriental Society
JbAC	Jahrbuch für Antike und Christentum
JBL	Journal of Biblical Literature
JJS	Journal of Jewish Studies
JMEOS	Journal of the Manchester Egyptian and Oriental Society
JNES	Journal of Near Eastern Studies
JPOS	Journal of the Palestine Oriental Society
JQR	Jewish Quarterly Review
JRel	Journal of Religion
JSOT	Journal for the Study of the Old Testament
JSS	Journal of Semitic Studies
JTS	Journal of Theological Studies
MGWJ	Monatsschrift für Geschichte und Wissenschaft des Judentums
NKZ	Neue kirchliche Zeitschrift
NRT	Nouvelle revue théologique
Or	Orientalia
RB	Revue biblique
RSc.Phil.T	Revue des Sciences Philosophiques et Théologiques
RSR	Recherches de science religieuse
Script	Scripture

SR	Studies in Religion/Sciences Religieuses
TRu.NF	Theologische Rundschau Neue Folge
UF	Ugarit-Forschungen
VD	Verbum Domini
VT	Vetus Testamentum
VTS	Vetus Testamentum Supplement
ZAW	Zeitschrift für die alttestamentliche Wissenschaft
ZDMG	Zeitschrift der Deutschen Morgenländischen Gesellschaft
ZTK	Zeitschrift für Theologie und Kirche

2. *Other Abbreviations*

AB	Anchor Bible
AOAT	Alter Orient und Altes Testament
AnBib	Analecta Biblica
AnOr	Analecta Orientalia
BDB	Brown, F. - Driver, S.R. - Briggs, C.A., *A Hebrew and English Lexicon of the Old Testament,* Clarendon Press, Oxford 1979.
BHK	Biblia Hebraica (ed.) Kittel
BHS	Biblia Hebraica Stuttgartensia
BKAT	Biblischer Kommentar — Altes Testament
DBS	*Dictionnaire de la Bible, Supplément,* Paris, 1957
DTC	*Dictionnaire de Théologie Catholique,* Paris
HAT	Handbuch zum Alten Testament
IB	Interpreter's Bible
ICC	International Critical Commentary
IDB	*The Interpreter's Dictionary of the Bible,* 4 Vols. Nashville NY
IDBSup	*The Interpreter's Dictionary of the Bible Supplement Volume,* Nashville NY, 1976
Is.MEO	Istituto di Medio-Estremo Oriente, Roma
KHAT	Kurzer Handkommentar zum Alten Testament
NEB	New English Bible
PG	*Patrologia Graeca,* ed. J.P. Migne
RGG	*Die Religion in Geschichte und Gegenwart,* ed. J.C.B. Mohr Dritte Auflage, Tübingen, 1958
SBL	Society of Biblical Literature
UT	Gordon, C.H. *Ugaritic Textbook,* An.Or. - 38, PIB, Roma 1965. Reeditio Photomechanica, 1967
WuS	Aistleitner, J., *Wörterbuch der ugaritischen Sprache,* Akademie-Verlag, Berlin 1965

B. TAMIL SECTION

1. *Journals*

Ar.Or.	Archiv Orientálni
AUJRL	Agra University Journal of Research (Letters), Agra
Bull.ITC	Bulletin of the Institute of Traditional Cultures, Madras

JAU	Journal of Annamalai University, Annamalainagar
JRAS	Journal of the Royal Asiatic Society
JTamS	Journal of Tamil Studies, Madras
TC	Tamil Culture, Madras

2. *Other Abbreviations*

Aiṅ.	Aiṅkuṟunūṟu
Ak.	Akanāṉūṟu
Kuṟ.	Kuṟuntokai
Naṟ.	Naṟṟiṇai
Tol.	Tolkāppiyam
Por.	Poruḷatikāram
Akat.	Akattiṇaiyiyal
Puṟat.	Puṟattiṇaiyiyal
Kaḷ.	Kaḷaviyal
Kaṟ.	Kaṟpiyal
Por.	Poruḷiyal
Meyp.	Meyppāṭṭiyal
Uvam.	Uvamaviyal
Ceyy.	Ceyyuḷiyal
Marap.	Marapiyal
Cūt./sūt.	Cūtram or Sūttiram
CDIAL	A Comparative Dictionary of the Indo-Aryan Languages
DED	Dravidian Etymological Dictionary
IATR	International Association of Tamil Research
IFI	Institut Français d'Indologie
IITS	International Institute of Tamil Studies
NBCLC	National Biblical Catechetical Liturgical Centre
PFICSTS	Proceedings of the First International Conference Seminar of Tamil Studies, Kuala Lumpur - Malaysia - April 1966, Vol. I, IATR, Madras 1968. Vol. II, IATR, Madras 1969.
PSICSTS	Proceedings of the Second International Conference Seminar of Tamil Studies, Madras - India, January 1968, 3 Vols., (ed.) R. E. Asher, IATR, Madras 1971.
PTICSTS	Proceedings of the Third International Conference Seminar of Tamil Studies, Paris-July 1970, IFI, Pondichéry 1973.
PFifICSTS	Proceedings of the Fifth International Conference Seminar of Tamil Studies, Madurai, Tamilnad - India, January 1981, 3 Vols., IATR, Madras 1981.
SISSWPS	South India Saiva Siddhanta Works Publishing Society

A NOTE ON TRANSLITERATION

1. For the transliteration of Hebrew words, the method used in the *Jerome Biblical Commentary* has been adopted in our study with one slight change for *qameṣ* with *mater lectionis* which is represented by *āh*.

2. For the transliteration of Tamil words, the method followed is this:

a) When *citing* someone, his transliteration has been maintained.

b) Otherwise I have followed consistently the transliteration method used by the Tamil Lexicon, which has by now become more or less the standard one.

Vowels

a —	அ
ā —	ஆ
i —	இ
ī —	ஈ
u —	உ
ū —	ஊ
e —	எ
ē —	ஏ
ai —	ஐ
o —	ஒ
ō —	ஓ
au —	ஔ

Consonants

Hard:	k —	க
	c —	ச
	ṭ —	ட
	t —	த
	p —	ப
	ṟ —	ற
Soft:	ṅ —	ங
	ñ —	ஞ
	ṇ —	ண
	n —	ந
	m —	ம
	ṉ —	ன
Medial:	y —	ய
	r —	ர
	l —	ல
	v —	வ
	ḻ —	ழ
	ḷ —	ள

Āytam: ḵ — ஃ

A NOTE ON THE METHOD OF CITATIONS AND REFERENCES

I. As regards the original texts of Hebrew and Tamil love poems:

1. For the Song of Songs, the usual method is followed: e.g. SS 1:2-4. When the context is clear, the abbreviations SS may have been omitted.
2. For Tamil poems, the abbreviations of the anthology and the number of the poem are given. When needed, even the number of the line or lines is cited: e.g. Kuṟ. 3:4, i.e. Kuṟuntokai anthology, poem 3, line 4.
3. For the grammar Tolkāppiyam, the number indicates the number of cūtram or aphorism: e.g. Tol. Por. Kaḷ. 102, i.e. Tolkāppiyam, Poruḷatikāram, Kaḷaviyal cūtram 102.
4. Hebrew and Tamil words, when they occur in the text of the dissertation and have certain importance, are put in italics.

II. For books and articles cited or referred to:

1. For a book: In the first occurrence, sufficient details are given. In further occurrences, the first word or phrase of the title and the page are given.
2. For an article: In the first occurrence, details are given. Afterwards, only the name of the author, the abbreviation of the review, volume, the year and page are given.
3. For an article in a collected work or Festschrift: The first occurrence carries all the details. Afterwards, the author, the first word or phrase of the article in inverted commas, the first word or phrase or abbreviation of the collected work and the page are given. As for Festschrift, the *FS. & name,* are given.
4. In case of successive occurrences, Id. & Ead. refer to the author, and ib. to the work.

TABLE OF CONTENTS

PART TWO

Chapter 4: HISTORICAL INTRODUCTION TO THE CLASSICAL TAMIL LITERATURE

Chapter 5: LITERARY PRESENTATION OF AKAM POEMS

Chapter 6: POETRY AND SYMBOLISM

PART THREE

GENERAL INTRODUCTION

All will agree that a comparative study of two literatures helps to appreciate both of them in their commonness and specificity. On this ground will this present study on the Song of Songs and Ancient Tamil Love Poems be a welcome one, as it is useful to appreciate the poetry and symbolism of both of them.

From personal experience of teaching the Bible in Seminaries and other ecclesiastical institutions, I learnt the usefulness of the comparative study of the Bible and Tamil literature. The more I compared the Bible and its culture with the Tamil literature and culture, the more I felt at home with the Bible and the nearer the Bible seemed to the Tamil mind and culture. Among many stimulants which led me to this comparative study, special mention should be made of the thought provoking article of C. Rabin.[1] He relied for his comparative study on translations and selections of Tamil love poems, and only compared content and attitudes.[2] The comparative materials presented in his article are general and also not much. Here I have collected more materials to this effect. Another article by Peter C. Craigie turned the opinion of C. Rabin into a topic for scholarly discussion.[3] The question of historical connections and influence of Tamil poems on the SS was one of the main points of both these scholars. This question also interested me, although it is not the main scope of my comparative study here.[4]

The main scope of my study is to bring together two sets of literature on the same theme of Love, i.e. the Song of Songs and ancient Tamil love poems. Each of them, of course, has been studied quite elaborately and separately by many, but they were scarcely brought together for comparison and appreciation. It is useful, therefore, to bring together the results of studies from both sides and thereby introduce mutually the scholars of both literatures. As a matter of fact, the existence of a vast

---

[1] Rabin, C., "The Song of Songs and Tamil Poetry", *SR* 3:3 (1973/4), 205-219.

[2] C. Rabin, in his personal correspondence to the present writer, has mentioned this fact.

[3] Craigie, P. C., "Biblical and Tamil Poetry: Some further Reflections", *SR* 8 (1979), 169-175.

[4] The question has been formulated and focused in the Appendix on the "Possible Literary Dependence of SS on Tamil Akam Poetry?".

number of quite ancient love poems in Tamil is practically not known among scholars who have attempted comparative studies on the SS. Herein lies the chief contribution of the present work. This thesis, however, is not merely a comparative study. It also aims at using the indigenous rhetoric and literary categories for classifying and appreciating the poems in the SS. In this aspect, the present study goes further than other comparative studies on the SS.[5]

This thesis is meant to be a step forward in the line of inculturation. It is a new attempt and may appear a daring one. It is not, however, out of tune in the postconciliar era in which the theology and areas of inculturation are discussed and experimented. This new venture may be justified:

a) On the basis of the incarnational aspect of the Word of God in the word of man. The analogy between Incarnation and the scriptural inspiration may be extended and applied in the field of comparative study.[6]

b) On the basis of the guide lines of Vatican II on cultural exchange: The Pastoral Constitution *Gaudium et Spes* (nos. 44,58) affirms and explicates the many links between the Gospel and culture. The Constitution *Sacrosanctum Concilium* inculcates the need of cultural expression in the sphere of Liturgy (nos. 37-40). This recommendation may legitimately be put into practice in the campus of exegesis and hermeneutics too.[7]

To some extent, the Song of Songs has been the criterion for the limitation of the materials from Tamil love poems selected for comparison. From among the Tamil poems, only the love poems of the classical age are studied. Neither the so-called late classical poems, i.e. Kalittokai, nor the longer types of love poems found among the Ten Songs are taken for main study. Even among the love poems of the classical period, some poems do not come under direct discussion or comparison: e.g. the poems on love-quarrel between married couples. For in the SS, no poetical unit seems to pertain to love-quarrel.

---

[5] E.g. White, J. B., *A Study of the Language of Love in the Song of Songs and Ancient Egyptian Poetry*, SBL Dissertation Series - 38, Scholars Press, Missoula 1978. Stephan, S. H., "Modern Palestinian Parallels to the Song of Songs", *JPOS* 2 (1922), 199-278 – Palestinian love songs in Arabic are compared.

[6] For the analogy between the Incarnation and Inspiration, see Alonso Schökel, L., *The Inspired Word*: Scripture in the Light of Language and Literature, trans. F. Martin, Herder & Herder, 1965, 49-90.

[7] Roest Crollius, A. A., "Inculturation and Incarnation. On Speaking of the Christian Faith and the Cultures of Mankind", *Bull. Secr. n. Chr.* 38 (1978), 134-140. Amalorpavadass, D. S. (ed.), *Indian Christian Spirituality*, NBCLC, Bangalore 1982, 92-236. Dhavamony, M., "Problematica dell'Inculturazione del Vangelo oggi", *Stromata*, XLI (1985), 253-272.

Traditional instruments and methods are used for the basic and preliminary analysis of poetry and symbolism in SS and Tamil love poems. In this way, the results of the past studies on the poetry and symbolism of both corpora are well represented and reasonably applied. Only after taking stock of what has been achieved already, a new step forward can be dared. Thus the chapters on poetry and symbolism of the SS and of Tamil love poems are mainly, no doubt necessary, preparations for the following ones.

For the analysis, classification and appreciation of the literary features in the SS, the most ancient Tamil grammar extant, called Tolkāppiyam, is used. Now, Tolkāppiyam contains three parts and they are:

I. Treatise on phonetics (Eḻuttatikāram): This part with nine chapters deals with the number, pronunciation, position, combination, usage, etc. of the letters of the Tamil alphabet in 483 aphorisms or cūtrams.

II. Treatise on morphology (Collatikāram): It has nine chapters dealing with formation of words, cases, nouns, verbs, verbal suffixes, qualificatives, etc. of Tamil words in 463 aphorisms.

III. Treatise on literary study (Poruḷatikāram): This treatise also contains nine chapters which speak about the themes of literature and methods of literary appreciation. It contains altogether 665 aphorisms.

Obviously, the first two treatises of Tolkāppiyam on the phonetics and morphology of Tamil letters and words cannot be used in the study of the SS. The treatise on the literary study, on the other hand, can be used. The nine chapters of the third treatise of Tolkāppiyam are: [8]

1. Akattiṇai-iyal: Mutual love and love situations: 1-55.
2. Puṟattiṇai-iyal: Non-love situations: 56-91.
3. Kaḷavu-iyal: Premarital love: 92-141.
4. Kaṟpu-iyal: Wedded love: 142-194.
5. Poruḷ-iyal: Corollaries to aspects of love situations: 195-248.
6. Meyppāṭṭu-iyal: Exhibition of feelings and Dramaturgy: 249-275.
7. Uvamai-iyal: Treatise on simile: 276-312.
8. Ceyyuḷ-iyal: On Prosody and Rhetoric: 313-555.
9. Marapu-iyal: Tradition of literary usages and idioms: 556-665.

It should be clear that in our study, the principles laid down for portraying in literature the non-love situations (ch. 2) and the love life after marriage (ch. 4) are not applicable for the poems contained in the SS. For no poem in the SS refers to non-love situation and all of them

---

[8] Cf. Zvelebil, K., *The Smile of Murugan*, Leiden/Brill. 1973, 133, 154.

speak of premarital love affair. The principles and techniques in cc. 8 and 9 which are meant exclusively for Tamil language and poetry cannot also be used here. But the others, e.g. theories on mutual love and love situations, premarital love, corollaries to love situations, exhibition of feelings, and the treatise on simile, can very well be used for analyzing, classifying and appreciating the similes and metaphors, and the individual poems in the SS.

Another reason why Tolkāppiyam may be used in this study is that it offers principles on which speakers of love poems can be identified. In other words, Tolkāppiyam helps to recognize the speaker of a given love poem. Now the speakers of the different poems in the SS are not indicated in the original text itself and the first attempt to identify them is witnessed in the Codex Sinaiticus (ca. 400 AD). Tolkāppiyam, which represents centuries long tradition of literary criticism, can rightly be used for recognizing, identifying and assigning the speakers of different poems in the SS.

Quantitatively there is certainly a disproportion in the materials available for comparison – 28 smaller units or poems in the SS vis-à-vis more than 1000 Tamil love poems. In spite of this fact, the similarities between them on different levels and in various aspects are interesting and therefore worth explicating. It is hoped that this study will add something to the brilliance of the common theme of both these literatures – namely, the love between man and woman.

Part One

Chapter 1.

BRIEF SURVEY OF PREVIOUS STUDIES ON THE SONG OF SONGS

A minute and exhaustive history of interpretation is not our aim here, nor is it necessary for our purpose. Instead, a short survey is made only to state the different positions taken by commentators of the Song of Songs on such issues as the literary form, theories of interpretation, the date of the book and the number of smaller poetic units in it. The presentation is meant to be practical rather than critical, inasmuch as it serves as the point of departure for comparative study.[1] In the course of the exposition of these literary problems, the positive contribution of each different view will be pointed out and the position taken in this present study will be briefly indicated.

---

[1] For a somewhat exhaustive survey of the history of interpretation the following works are recommended: Ginsburg, C. D., *The Song of Songs*, NY 1970 (Rep. of 1857) 20-124: The author traces in pp. 20-60 in chronological order the Jewish exposition of the book from 328-246 BC to 1854 AD, and in pp. 61-102, the Chrisrian exposition, from Origen up to 1856. In pp. 102-124, he classifies and examines different theories of interpretation. Joüon, P., *Le Cantique des Cantiques*, Paris 1909², 9-58 (nn. 10-65): the history of interpretation; 96-110 (n. 121): annotated bibliography. Ricciotti, G., *Il Cantico dei Cantici*, Torino 1927, 53-157: examines different systems of interpretation. Kuhl, C., "Das Hohelied und seine Deutung", *TRu.NF* 3 (1937), 137-167; examines various theories of interpretation and concludes that no theory gives a satisfactory answer to the question of how the Song was taken into the Canon. Rowley, H. H., "The Interpretation of the Song of Songs", in *The Servant of the Lord and Other Essays*, London 1952, 182-234; revised ed., Oxford 1965, 195-246. References in this essay are to the edition of 1952. Lerch, D., "Zur Geschichte der Auslegung des Hohenliedes", *ZTK* 54 (1957), 257-277 treats about the very problem of how to classify the interpretations. Ohly, F., *Hohelied-Studien*, Wiesbaden 1958 – history of interpretation up to 1200 AD. Schonfield, H. J., *The Song of Songs*, The New American Library, New York 1959, 20-54. Robert, A.-Tournay, R.-Feuillet, A., *Le Cantique des Cantiques*, Paris 1963, 43-55: gives a short "histoire de l'interprétation." Gerleman, G., *Ruth/Das Hohelied*, BKAT, 1963, 43-51. Lys, D., *Le plus beau chant de la création*, Paris 1968, 31-50. Pope, M. H., *Song of Songs*, AB:7C. Garden City NY 1977, 89-229: elaborate, but somewhat confusing, survey of different theories of interpretation. White, J. B., *A Study*, 19-67: clear exposition of theories of interpretation. Mannucci, V., *Sinfonia dell'Amore Sponsale*, Torino 1982, 105-171: clear and elaborate exposition of different denominational interpretations, with a useful annotated bibliography.

A. **Literary Form of the Song of Songs**

Investigation into the literary form is necessary for the understanding and interpretation of any book — and all the more so, for the inspired books.[2] All students of the Bible agree that the determination of the literary forms influences the interpretation of Sacred Scripture. It may not be rash to say that a certain "caveat" is necessary in this exercise: "However necessary, not to say indispensable, is our determination of literary forms and interpretation according to their canons, we have to recognize that the determination and specification are really ours rather than the ancient writers'".[3] This caution is still more needed in dealing with poetical books: "Il existe un certain danger, celui d'exagérer l'importance des 'genres littéraires' pour la compréhension de l'oeuvre poétique. Ce danger existe spécialement lorsque à la sensibilité littéraire se superpose une soif technique de classifier...".[4]

1. *Classification Based on the Unity of Authorship*

The Classification of the literary form of the Song of Songs often depends on the positions taken by authors as regards the unity of the book. There are scholars who hold either explicitly or implicitly to the unity of authorship, and so consider the Song as the work of one author. These scholars classify the Song under one of the following genres:

a) *Drama*

Origen seems to have been the first to apply the designation "drama" to the Song of Songs.[5] The dramatic view has been presented in more than one form by various proponents. E. Renan, for instance, writes: "Deux points sont admis de tout le monde: c'est 1. que le poëme est en dialogue, bien que la distinction des personnages ne soit pas indiquée; et 2. qu'il se divise en parties distinctes, analogues à nos actes ou à nos scènes. Des espèces de refrains revenant assez regulièrement en certains endroits, ne laissent aucun doute sur ce second point."[6]

---

[2] Alonso Schökel, L., "Genera litteraria", *VD* 38 (1960), 3-15. Robert, A., "Littéraires (Genres)", *DBS*, Vol. V, cols. 405-421. Gelin, A., "Genres Littéraires dans la Bible", *DTC*, Tables I, cols. 1790-1794. Kuhl, C., "Formen und Gattungen", *RGG II*, cols. 996-999. Wellek, R.-Warren, A., *Theory of Literature*, Peng Books, 1970, 226-237 on "Literary Genres".

[3] Vawter, B., "Apocalyptic: Its Relation to Prophecy", *CBQ* 22 (1960), 33.

[4] Alonso Schökel, L., "Poésie hébraïque", *DBS*, Vol. VIII, col. 52.

[5] Origen writes: "Epithalamium libellus hic, id est nuptiale carmen, dramatis in modum mihi videtur a Salomone conscriptus", *PG*, Vol. XIII, 1862, col. 61.

[6] Renan, E., *Le Cantique des Cantiques*, Paris 1884[5], 3. Cf also pp. 4-5, 70-72, 76.

S. R. Driver considers that "the Song, as a whole, is of the nature of a *drama,* with dialogue and action, and character consistently sustained, constituting a rudimentary kind of plot..."[7] More recently, the dramatic view has been defended by G. Pouget et J. Guitton.[8] They present the Song in twelve dramatic scenes distributed to the characters: the Sulamite girl, Solomon, the Spouse and the choirs.[9] F. Delitzsch calls the Song "a dramatic pastoral." According to him, "the ancients saw in it a *carmen bucolicum mimicum.*"[10] Though in his commentary, F. Delitzsch presents the Song as a drama of six acts with two scenes each, he explicitly acknowledges that "the Song is certainly not a theatrical piece" but we see in it "the drama in process of formation from the lyric and narrative form of poetry."[11] The Song is classified by L. Cicognani as an ancient melodrama with four individual characters and five choruses.[12] He divides the Song "in otto parti corrispondenti a cantate, atti o scene o rappresentazioni."[13] A. Vaccari is almost at a loss to classify the Song of Songs. Though for practical purposes he divides the Song into six scenes, about its literary genre, this is what he says: "La *Cantica* è un dramma? È una lirica? È un pò di tutto questo; ma nulla che risponde esattamente alle nostre categorie letterarie. È un dialogo lirico accompagnato da qualche movimento drammatico."[14]

The view that classifies the Song as a drama has probably been inspired by the Codex Sinaiticus (ca. 400 AD). For the dialogue character of the Song has been explicitly recognized and textually indicated since the writing of that manuscript. Be it as it may, the scholars who take the Song to be a drama have seen the important (and according to them, the essential) rôle played by dialogue in the book. No one can deny the presence of dramatic dialogue in the Song. And the dialogue pattern, to some extent, seems to give a certain unity to the book.[15]

---

[7] Driver, S. R., *An Introduction to the Literature of the Old Testament,* Edinburgh 1913⁹, 443-444.

[8] In their commentary, after having examined the question of "Le genre littéraire du Cantique" in pp. 21ff, they conclude: "*le Cantique est un drame lyrique dont les trois personnages sont le roi Salomon, le berger, la Sulamite. L'intérêt de ce drame tient à ce que la Sulamite reste fidèle à son bien-aimé malgré les avances royales*", Pouget, G. et Guitton, J., *Le Cantique des Cantiques*, Paris 1948, 41.

[9] Cf. Ib., 64-66 & 150-179.

[10] Delitzsch, F., *Das Hohelied*: Leipzig 1851, 77-84: He entitles the chapter "Die dramatische Kunstform des Hohenliedes". The citation is from Delitzsch, F., *Commentary on the Song of Songs and Ecclesiastes*, trans. M. G. Easton, Edinburgh, 1877, 8.

[11] Delitzsch, F., *Commentary*, 8-9.

[12] Cicognani, L., *Il Cantico dei Cantici*: Torino 1911, 229; cf. 273.

[13] Ib. 244.

[14] Vaccari, A., *La Cantica*: La Sacra Bibbia: I Libri Poetici - 2, Firenze 1959, 113. For the division into six scenes, cf. 115-129.

[15] Cf. Murphy, R. E., "Towards a Commentary on the Song of Songs," *CBQ* 39 (1977), 488.

Perhaps this view sins *per excessum,* i.e. by attributing an essential character to this dialogue form and thus making the Song ultimately belong to the *genre of drama.* Drama has in its structure dialogues, but every dialogue need not necessarily be the part of a drama, since it is not impossible that a long monologue contains in itself a dialogue. At present, however, this view has not found serious supporters.[16] According to the present writer, this view no longer can be maintained.

b) *Idyl*

The Song of Songs has been classified by a few scholars as an idyl, i.e. "a composition describing pastoral or bucolic scenes." [17] The chief and elaborate exponent of this view is R. G. Moulton. He says that all must recognize that the Song of Songs is "dialogue of a dramatic character, with a story underlying it." [18] He describes it as a "lyric idyl" and for him, "the difference between Drama and Lyric Idyl is the difference between Opera and Oratorio ..." [19] D. Castelli had termed the Song of Songs, "an idyl in dialogue," [20] while C. Gebhardt regarded it as mime rather than drama: "Das Lied der Lieder ist Mimos. Es ist nicht Drama, bestimmt als Handlung auf irgendeiner Bühne dargestellt zu werden, und es ist auch nicht episches oder lyrisches Gedicht, bestimmt einfach gelesen zu werden, sondern es ist soweit Mimos, wie die mimischen Idylle Theokrits ... Es ist Hör-Spiel, nicht Schau-Spiel ..." [21]

---

[16] A number of objections are directed against the dramatic view. Here below are a few:

a) Impersonation is the first and cardinal element in drama which is essentially something to be interpreted by actors (cf. *Dictionary of World Literary Terms*, (ed.) J. T. Shipley, London 1970 under "Drama"). Stage directions or dialogue-assignments are to be provided by the author in the text itself. But such assignments are not found in the text of the Song of Songs, cf. White, J. B., *A Study*, 34; Childs, B. S., *Introduction to the Old Testament as Scripture*, Philadelphia 1982³, 572; Falk, M., *Love Lyrics from the Bible*, Sheffield 1982, 63; Feuillet, A., "Le Cantique des Cantiques et la tradition biblique", *NRT* 74 (1952), 706.

b) "There is no real conflict or catharsis in the Song", White, J. B., *A Study*, 34.

c) No literary evidence for the existence of dramatic plays produced among the Jews or among their neighbours: Schoville, K. N., "Song of Songs", in *Encyclopaedia Judaica*, (eds.) C. Roth & G. Wigoder, Jerusalem 1971, Vol. 15, col. 148; Phipps, W. E., "The Plight of the Song of Songs", *JAAR* 42 (1974), 83.

[17] Pope, M. H., *Song*, 36.

[18] Moulton, R. G., *The Literary Study of the Bible*, London 1896, 194. The same author says: "The term 'idyl' is descriptive of the matter of a poem: as to form it suggests nothing beyond fragmentariness or brevity", *Biblical Idyls*, London 1910, vii. But contrast Shipley, J. T., *Dictionary*, "Idyll".

[19] Moulton, R. G., *The Literary Study*, 195. Cf also 199-201.

[20] Apud Pope M. H., *Song*, 36. The original of D. Castelli was not available to the present writer.

[21] Gebhardt, C., *Das Lied der Lieder*, Berlin 1931, 21.

Those who classify the Song of Songs as idyl give due importance to the fact that the events of the poem(s) take place in the country side. This view explains sufficiently the sudden changes in the scenes and motifs in the Song: "In a lyric idyl... the story is not acted, but assumed and alluded to; and allusion can be made to the different parts of the story in any order."[22] Appreciation for the Song of Songs as lyric poetry is noteworthy in this view: "It must be remembered that lyric poetry is the most elastic medium of literature: a lyric poem may pass to and fro between epic description and dialogue presentation and purely lyric meditation, without at any point ceasing to be lyric."[23]

According to this view, the refrains by the chorus are meant to suggest "the transition from one scene to another" and are, therefore, not part of the dialogue.[24] Another insight of these scholars is that the incidents conveyed dramatically by the dialogue "cannot be part of scene in which they occur, but must, at that point, be a reminiscence."They are called technically "Dramatised Reminiscences."[25] The dramatised reminiscences explain in turn the free movement of lyric poetry between meditation and dramatic presentation in the Song of Songs.[26] This classification however does not explain all the parts of the SS, e.g. the scenes in chambers or city streets. It fits only partially.

c) *Cantata*

Combining both lyric and dramatic features in the Song of Songs, H. Ewald termed it a cantata, a term originally designating "a metrical narrative set to recitative."[27] In his later works, H. Ewald calls the Song of Songs a "Singspiel": "Es folgt aber aus alle dem dass man das HL am richtigsten ein *Singspiel* nennt."[28] K. Kohler calls the Song "Ein Jerusalemisches Singspiel" (operetta).[29]

d) *Midrash*

There are authors who classify the Song of Songs as a midrash. R. Bloch, for instance, writes about the Song of Songs: "La réference con-

---

22 Moulton, R. G., *The Literary Study*, 195.
23 Moulton, R. G., *Biblical Idyls*, viii-ix.
24 Moulton, R. G., *The Literary Study*, 196-197.
25. Ib. 197.
26 Ib. 199.
27 Pope, M. H., *Song*, 37.
28 Ewald, H., *Die Salomonischen Schriften*, Göttingen 1867, 349. In an earlier work, *Die poetischen Bücher des Alten Bundes*, Göttingen 1839, 45ff, he gives the division of the Song of Songs into five acts.
29 Apud Pope, M. H., *Song*, 37. K. Kohler's book was not available to the present writer.

stante aux données bibliques, la dramatisation et la réinterprétation des événements et des aspirations de l'époque qui suit Néhémie, montrent que nous sommes là, sans aucun doute, en face d'un pur midrash."[30] Recent studies by P. Trible have taken a more precise line of development.[31] According to her, "in many ways, the Song of Songs is a midrash on Genesis, 2-3. By variations and reversals it creatively actualizes major motifs and themes of the primeval myth... Whatever else it may be, Canticles is a commentary on Genesis, 2-3. Paradise Lost is Paradise Regained."[32] Genesis 2-3 is the hermeneutical key to the Song of Songs which "redeems a love story gone awry."[33] D. Lys has already said that "le Cantique n'est rien d'autre qu'un commentaire de Gen. 2," though he did not use the term "midrash."[34] According to F. Landy, "the Song constitutes an inversion of the Genesis narrative... The Genesis myth points outside the garden; the Song goes back to it. Their opposition conceals a hidden identity, for the Song is not merely a commentary on the garden of Eden, but a reenactment, almost a hallucination of it."[35] The Paradise that was lost still survives in the world through love (Genesis) and that Paradise can be rediscovered through love which is in fact a return to origins (the Song). Landy, however, does not apply the term "midrash" to the Song of Songs.[36]

The merit of this approach is *to understand and explain* the Song of Songs in the background of either the prophetical literature (R. Bloch) or Genesis 2-3 (P. Trible and F. Landy). The first trend uses the love-sentiments of the Song as a symbol and means for allegorical interpretation, while the efforts of Trible and Landy restore the pure human love to its original meaning and role in the primeval economy. However, whether the book as a literary product can be assigned to the *literary genre* of midrash, is still under dispute among the literary

---

[30] Bloch, R., "Midrash", in *DBS*, Vol. V, col. 1273. For a study of the literary form of Midrash, see Wright, A. G., "The Literary Genre Midrash", *CBQ* 28 (1966), 105-138 & 415-457: later in book form with the same title, (New York 1967). For a critical comment on this book of Wright, see Le Déaut, R., "À propos d'une définition du midrash", *Bib.* 50 (1969), 395-413; and "Apropos a Definition of Midrash", *Interpr.* 25 (1971), 259-282. For the definition of Midrash by R. Bloch, see *DBS*, Vol. V, cols. 1264-1265. Miller, M. P., "Midrash", in *IDBSup.* 593-597, treats the question elaborately.

[31] Trible, P., "Depatriarchalizing in Biblical Interpretation", *JAAR* 41 (1973), 30-48; Ead., *God and the Rhetoric of Sexuality*, Philadelphia 1978, 144-165.

[32] Trible, P., *JAAR* 41 (1973), 47. She adds a note saying, "I use midrash here to designate a type of exegesis, not a literary genre", ib., note 64.

[33] Trible, P., *God and the Rhetoric*, 144.

[34] Lys, D., *Le plus beau chant*, 52.

[35] Landy, F., *Paradoxes of Paradise*, Sheffield 1983, 183.

[36] Cf. Landy, F., "The Song of Songs and the Garden of Eden", *JBL* 98 (1979), 513-528, esp. 513.

critics.[37] The proponents themselves acknowledge the difficulty of defining and applying this term to the Song of Songs as literary genre.[38]

2. *Classification Based on the Unity of Structure*

There is a group of sholars who seem to maintain that the Song of Songs is a collection of love poems but possessing a *structural unity*. Minute analysis has been carried out by them to discover a unified structure or a definite pattern of arrangement among the poems. J. Angénieux in a series of three articles has attempted to establish a unified structure between the eight songs. After having formulated five methodological principles, he uses them to discover a literary structure in the Song.[39] J. C. Exum has also presented an elaborate structural analysis of the Song. According to her, the Song of Songs consists of six poems of which the first and last form an inclusion while the other four are placed in A B A' B' scheme. She even claims to have proved by her structural analysis the "unity of authorship with an intentional design."[40]

In a somewhat recent article R. E. Murphy arrives at the conclusion: "While a certain similarity is to be expected among any collection of love poems, the repetitions within the Song are striking enough to suggest a deliberate, contrived unity... It seems intrinsically more probable that one author has given a unity to his love poems by repeating certain words and motifs within them."[41]

---

[37] According to R. Le Déaut, "a satisfactory *definition* of midrash, in its general meaning and as a *literary* genre" is very difficult, nay almost impossible, to arrive at. Cf. *Interpr.* 25 (1971), 267-70.

[38] See P. Trible's note cited above in note 32.

[39] Angénieux, J., "Structure du Cantique des Cantiques", *ETL* 41 (1965), 96-142; "Les trois Portraits du Cantique des Cantiques", *ETL* 42 (1966), 582-596; "Le Cantique des Cantiques en huit chants à refrains alternants", *ETL* 44 (1968), 87-140. But his thesis is weakened by his own reconstruction of the Received Text in which he is obliged to have recourse to many transferences of portions according to his rigid principles.

[40] Exum, J. C., "A Literary and Structural Analysis of the Song of Songs", *ZAW* 85 (1973), 47-79. The quotation is from p. 78. See the comments of Murphy, R. E., *CBQ* 39 (1977), 487-488; esp. Falk, M., *Love Lyrics*, 65-67. Exum's own qualification of the phrase "unity of authorship" is very interesting, see p. 49, note 12. In another article, "Asseverative *'al* in Canticles 1,6?", *Bib.* 62 (1981), 416-419, she says explicitly: "I would not, however, argue so categorically for a unity of authorship. By unity of authorship I do not mean to suggest a de novo composition. Rather it seems to me a poet (perhaps poets/redactor[s]) may well have taken over love songs from oral tradition and, with additions of his or her own, worked them into an artistic whole", p. 418, note 19.

[41] Murphy, R. E., "The Unity of the Song of Songs", *VT* 29 (1979), 436-443; the citation is from p. 441. See also other studies by him: "The Structure of the Canticle of Canticles", *CBQ* 11 (1949), 381-391: implies unity of authorship and favours allegorical interpretation. "Recent Literature on the Canticle of Canticles", *CBQ* 16 (1954), 1-11: favours unity of theme and authorship. *The Book of Ecclesiastes and the Canticle of Canticles*, New York 1961: Collection of several songs, a certain unity given by the editor;

In the line of J. C. Exum, W. H. Shea has analyzed the Song and shows that "the Song of Songs is unified structurally," and that the "unified structure follows a chiastic pattern," i.e. A:B:C::C:B:A. According to him, the Song of Songs consists of "six lengthy units" of which each one is further "subdivided into approximately six smaller units."[42] E. C. Webster seems to defend a structural unity when he says that "Song of Songs is a medley of love song and banter set within a literary pattern."[43]

The merit of this view is to have shown that there exists in the Song of Songs a well designed *arrangement* of the poems. These scholars are not, however, so pronounced as regards the unity of authorship, though some of them would like very much to affirm so. While they are establishing the structural unity in the book, they are also aware of the presence of different poems in it.

3. *Classification Based on the Theory of Anthology*

The majority of scholars favour the opinion that the Song of Songs is a collection of love poems, and the unifying factor is the theme of love. Many are not explicit on the question of multiplicity of authorship. Some seem to imply it, while others state it.

a) *Love-Dreams*

Johann Leonhard von Hug seems to be the first to interpret the Song of Songs as a series of dreams. According to M. H. Pope, "Hug found the Song to be composed of thirty-eight disordered fragments, the disarray being a major argument in support of the dream sequence."[44] S. B. Freehof suggests that "the book is not the story of two lovers seeking each other in actual places, but in imaginary ... In other words, the book is a sequence of dreams."[45] He admits the possibility of the multiplicity of authorship.[46] Max N. Pusin seems to hold that "the Song proves to be a veritable Dream Book."[47]

---

cf. 52-53. He maintains the same position in his commentary on the Song in *Jerome Biblical Commentary*, and in "Form-Critical Studies in the Song of Songs", *Interpr.* 27 (1973), 413-422. The same stand continues, "Song of Songs", in *IDBSup.* and in *CBQ* 39 (1977), 482-496. In his latest articles, *VT* 29 (1979), 436-433 and "Interpreting the Song of Songs", *BTB* 9 (1979), 99-105, he admits many poems but single author.

[42] Shea, W. H., "The Chiastic Structure of the Song of Songs", *ZAW* 92 (1980), 378.

[43] Webster, E. C., "Pattern in the Song of Songs", *JSOT* 22 (1982), 74.

[44] Apud Pope, M. H., *Song, 132;* see bibliographical reference in p. 268. The pamphlets of von Hug were not available to me.

[45] Freehof, S. B., "The Song of Songs: A General Suggestion", *JQR* 39 (1948-49), 401.

[46] Ib. 401, he speaks of "several dreamers".

[47] Apud Pope, M. H., *Song*, 133-134. Pusin explained his work to M. H. Pope in a letter which the latter has cited in his book.

There is no doubt that there are pieces of dreams incorporated in the Song, e.g. 5:2-7 and probably also 3:1-4. The dream theory is right in emphasizing how the lovers indulge in fantasies and extravagant imaginations in their love-affairs, e.g. the so called waṣfs, 5:10-16 etc. The garden in 4:13-14 is more ideal than real.[48] But to make the whole of the Song of Songs into a collection of mere dreams and fantasies seems to go too far. At least a few pericopes seem to depict down-to-earth realities, e.g. 1:5-6.

b) *Wedding Feast Songs*

The view that the Song corresponds to the seven-day celebration of wedding in Palestine was first insinuated by Bossuet.[49] E. Renan, in his commentary, noted the similarities between the wedding ceremonies of Jewish marriage and the Song of Songs,[50] and his suggestion was confirmed by further study.[51] K. Budde suggested that the Song is a collection of poems sung at peasant weddings.[52] D. Buzy accepts this view and counts, apart from the prologue and nine isolated fragment-additions by the scribes, seven nuptial poems.[53] According to J. P. Audet, the Song, more precisely, is "l'échange du don de l'amour et de la promesse de fidélité." [54]

The contribution of this theory consists in defining more concretely the Sitz im Leben of these love poems in the social life of the Jews. SS 3:6-11 could be a song that might have been composed on the occasion of some royal wedding, if not on the occasion of one of Solomon's marriages to a foreign princess.[55] Some of the portions of the Song are probably reflections of marriage celebrations, e.g. 5:1.[56] It seems,

---

[48] Cf. Feuillet, A., "La formule d'appartenance mutuelle (II,16) et les interprétations divergentes du Cantique des Cantiques", *RB* 68 (1961), 12.

[49] "At postquam antiquos mores imitatus, pastoralem eclogam canere aggressus est (Salomon), eam in septem dies divisisse videtur...", Bossuet, J. B., *Libri Salomonis*, Venetiis 1732, 195.

[50] Renan, E., *Le Cantique*, 85-86.

[51] For details and bibliography, cf. Rowley, H. H., "Interpretation", *The Servant*, 209; Pope, M. H., *Song*, 141-143.

[52] Budde, K., "The Song of Solomon", *The New World*, III (Boston 1894), 56-77; "Was ist das Hohelied?", *Preussische Jahrbücher* 78 (1894), 92-117; *Die Fünf Megillot*, Das Hohelied erklärt: KHAT-XVII, Freiburg 1898, xvii-xxi.

[53] Buzy, D., "La composition littéraire du Cantique des Cantiques", *RB* 49 (1940), 172; Id. "Le Cantique des Cantiques", *L'Ann. Théo.* 8 (1947), 1-17. Id., *Le Cantique des Cantiques: La Sainte Bible*, (eds.) L. Pirot et A. Clamer, Paris 1951, 288-89.

[54] Audet, J. P., "Le sens du Cantique des Cantiques", *RB* 62 (1955), 213.

[55] Gordis, R., *The Song of Songs and Lamentations*, New York 1974, 20.

[56] Durable, A.-M., "L'amour humain dans le Cantique des Cantiques", *RB* 61 (1954), 67-86, esp. 82.

however, improbable to attribute the whole of the Song of Songs to the Sitz im Leben of wedding ceremonies.[57]

c) *Cultic Poems*

W. Erbt seems to have been the first one to speak of the Song of Songs as a collection of cultic poems. He suggests that the Song was a collection of poems of "Canaanitisch" origin, which celebrated the "Sonnengotthochzeit" and described the love of the sun-god Tammuz, called Dôd or Shelem, and the moon-goddess Ishtar called as Shalmith. These songs were taken over by the Israelites and used in their Passover Liturgy. Solomon in the Song, then, stands for the sun-god and the Shulammit for the moon-goddess.[58] The view that the Song is a collection of cultic poems or a ritual of the *hieros gamos* has been proposed in various forms and in different Sitz im Leben: e.g. the Babylonian Tammuz — Ishtar fertility cult;[59] the Egyptian Osiris — Isis spring time ritual;[60] and the Canaanite Baal — Astarte.[61]

Allusions to the myths are present in the Song of Songs, and descriptive words or phrases have been borrowed from the language of myths; e.g. the similes or metaphors in the waṣfs. But to affirm a fertility cult or liturgy as Sitz im Leben *in Israel* for the Song would be diametrically opposed to the Deuteronomic and prophetic movements which abhorred the pagan fertility cult.

d) Funeral Feast Songs

Most recently, M.H. Pope in his voluminous commentary has proposed a novel Sitz im Leben for the Song of Songs. Taking 8:6cd as "the climax of the Canticle and the burden of its message: that Love is the only power that can cope with Death,"[62] he goes on to show how

---

[57] H.H. Rowley says: "I am not persuaded that the marriage-week theory is soundly based, or that the songs had anything to do with a wedding occasion. They appear rather to be a series of poems in which a lover enshrined the love he gave and the love he received", "Interpretation", *The Servant*, 212. See also the objections of Falk, M., *Love Lyrics*, 63-64.

[58] Erbt, W., *Die Hebräer*, Leipzig 1906, 196-202.

[59] Meek, T.J., *The Song of Songs*: IB, Vol. V, Nashville 1956, 91-148, esp. 94-96. See also his previous articles: "Canticles and the Tammuz Cult", *AJSL* 39 (1922), 1-14; "The Song of Songs and the Fertility Cult", *A Symposium on the Song of Songs*, (ed.) W.H. Schoff, 1924, 48-79; Wittekindt, W., *Das Hohelied und seine Beziehungen zum Istarkult*, Hannover 1925, 179-217; Kramer, S.N., "The Biblical 'Song of Songs' and the Sumerian Love Songs", *Expedition* 5 (1962), 25-31: Dumuzi - Inanna cult theory.

[60] See Rowley, H.H., "Interpretation", *The Servant*, 215.

[61] Haller, M., *Die Fünf Megilloth*, HAT, Tübingen 1940, 21-22. For further details and refutation of this view, see Rowley, H.H., "Interpretation", *The Servant*, 213-230; Pope, M.H., *Song*, 145-153; White, J.B., *A Study*, 22-24.

[62] Pope, M.H., *Song*, 210.

sacred marriages, sacral meals with ritual drinking of intoxicating beverages, music, song, dance and sexual licence etc. were intimately connected with mortuary observances or funeral feasts. He suggests that "the occasion in question was a sort of Hallowmas, a feast for All Saints and Souls." He also suggests "that certain features of the Song of Songs may be understood in the light of the considerable and growing evidences that funeral feasts in the ancient Near East were love feasts celebrated with wine, women and song."[63] The conclusion seems to be implied, though not explicitly expressed, that the Song of Songs is one that was used in the cultic context of the funeral-love feasts.

At the most, Pope's investigation may show the application of an already existing text that can be used for different occasions, but does not and cannot explain its original context.[64]

e) *Love Songs*

The number of scholars, who classify the Song of Songs as an anthology of poems on human love, is steadily increasing. All are agreed that the language of the poems is simply the language of human love. The reasons for seeing in the Song a collection of different poems on the one theme of love are briefly the following:

1) Argument from the title: It is not improbable that the construct of the title – "the Song of Songs" – means "the Song composed of songs" and thus reveals the anthological nature of the book's content.[65]

2) Lack of continuous story: One cannot construct a logically continuous story from the Song. Hence the basic unity that is given by a single story is lacking in it.

3) Lack of logical climax or development in love: "The poem is as passionate and ardent in the beginning as in the end."[66] Nor is there a thematic continuity. The uneven sequence of thought has been recognized by commentators.[67] The whole book seems to be more an expression of mood than a carefully constructed theme.[68]

---

[63] Ib. 210-229.

[64] Landy, F., *Paradoxes*, 31. Besides, it is not at all sure that 8:6 gives the key to the understanding of the whole book. Even without that verse the burden of the book can be seen to be love. In fact there are critics who hold that this verse is a later addition by a wisdom writer. See Tromp, N. J., "Wisdom and the Canticle", in *La Sagesse de l'Ancien Testament*, (ed.) M. Gilbert, Leuven-Gembloux 1979, 89-92. Also Murphy, R. E., *Interpr.* 27 (1973), 416-417 and *BTB* 9 (1979), 100. See the critique of Gordon, C. H., *JAOS* 100 (1980), 355 and Gilbert, M., *NRT* 101 (1979), 422.

[65] Landy, F., *Paradoxes*, 281, note 17.

[66] Murphy, R. E., *CBQ* 15 (1953), 503.

[67] Cf. Murphy, R. E., *Book of Eccles. and the Canticle*, 52-53.

[68] Cf. Murphy, R. E,N *CBQ* 11 (1949), 383.

4) "The failure of any structural interpretation to impose itself" leaves us with the choice of concluding that the Song is an anthology.[69]

5) No one can deny the variety of audiences and speakers involved in the Song, though it is difficult to specify the different speakers.[70]

6) "Strange flights and sudden movements from place to place," [71] are indications of changes of localities of events or contexts of experiences that are described in the Song.

7) The variety of sentiments, and of tones and moods, call for different Sitz im Leben, and therefore for different poems.[72]

8) An argument of analogy can be drawn from Egyptian love poetry in which several collections have been preserved, and none among them really shows the unity of a consecutive work.[73]

The principles of arrangement of individual poems into a collection with a certain amount of unity seem to be: (a) the order based on catchwords; [74] (b) the *Stichwort* arrangement; [75] (c) the similarity of theme; [76] (d) a desire for literary balance or literary pattern.[77] Though authors do not agree upon the number of poems in the collection, they are all agreed that the Song belongs to the genre of anthology.[78]

---

[69] Murphy, R. E., *CBQ* 39 (1977), 487.

[70] Ib.; Falk, M., *Love Lyrics*, 4, 69.

[71] Freehof, S. B., *JQR* 39 (1948-49), 400.

[72] Cf. Falk, M., *Love Lyrics*, 69-70.

[73] Cf. Murphy, R. E., *CBQ* 39 (1977), 487.

[74] Cf. Eissfeldt, O., *The Old Testament: An Introduction*, trans. P. R. Ackroyd, New York 1976, 490.

[75] Cf. Gerleman, G., *Das Hohelied*, 59.

[76] Cf. Soggin, J. A., *Introduction to the Old Testament*, 1980, rev. ed., 400f.

[77] Cf. Webster, E. C., *JSOT* 22 (1982), 87.

[78] Cf. Gottwald, N. K., "Song of Songs", in *IDB*, Vol. IV, 420-426, esp. 424; Schoville, K. N., "Song of Songs", in *Encyclopaedia Judaica*, Vol. 15, cols. 144-150, esp. col. 144; Id., *The Impact of the Ras Shamra Texts on the Study of the Song of Songs*, Michigan 1972, 115-116; Albright, W. F., "Archaic Survivals in the Text of Canticles", in *Hebrew and Semitic Studies Presented to Godfrey Rolles Driver*, (eds.) D. W. Thomas & W. D. McHardy, Oxford, 1963, 1-7, esp. 1; Childs, B. S., *Introduction*, 572; Gordis, R., *The Song*, 16-18; Falk, M., *Love Lyrics*, esp. 66-68. R. J. Tournay says: "La critique moderne considère généralement le Cantique des Cantiques comme une anthologie de poèmes plus ou moins étendus, unifiés par un ou plusiuers rédacteurs", *Quand Dieu parle aux hommes le langage de l'amour*, Paris 1982, 21.

From the above observations, the folowing conclusions may be validly drawn:

1) It is not impossible that the different poems in the Song of Songs come from different regions of Palestine, mostly from the Northern region.[79] The predominance of northern geographical references in the Song seem to indicate the northern provenance.

2) It is possible that the poems belong to different periods and come from more than one author.[80] Linguistic variations argue in favour of plurality of authorship.

3) The minimum conclusion that has to be conceded is that the Song consists of many poems on different love-experiences belonging to different contexts of time and space, even if there had been only one author at their origin.[81]

4) The refrains and repetitions could be explained otherwise than by postulating the unity of authorship. In fact the refrains do not seem to belong to the poems as essential parts.[82]

As for the patterned arrangement or the so-called structural unity among the poems, the present writer finds an analogy in Akanāṉūṟu, one of the anthologies of Ancient Tamil Love Poems.

B. Theories of Interpretation

In this section, the aim is to give in a nutshell the main theories of interpretation of the Song. In some sense, the positions, discussed in the previous section, will influence the theories that come under review now. An attempt will be made to show the positive aspect of each theory of interpretation, and at the end of the section, the position taken in the present study will briefly be indicated.[83]

---

[79] Albright, W. F., "Archaic", *Fs.G.R.Driver*, 1; Schoville, K. N., *The Impact*, 53, note 51, and pp. 77, 80.

[80] Schoville, K. N., *The Impact*, 115-116.

[81] Cf. Murphy, R. E., *VT* 29 (1979), 441.

[82] Moulton, R. G., *The Literary Study*, 196-197; Landsberger, F., "Poetic Units within the Song of Songs", *JBL* 73 (1954), 203-216, esp. 212.

[83] Besides the works and articles cited in note 1 above, see also: Robert, A., "Le genre littéraire du Cantique des Cantiques", *RB* 52 (1943-44), 192-213, claims that allegorical interpretation is the only one which fits best. Buzy, D., "L'allégorie matrimoniale de Jahvé et d'Israël et le Cantique des Cantiques", *RB* 52 (1944), 77-90: favours allegorical interpretation; but later he opts for parabolic interpretation in "Le Cantique des Cantiques: Exégèse allégorique ou parabolique?", in *Mélanges Jules Lebreton I, RSR* 39 (1951-52), 99-114; Feuillet, A., *NRT* 74 (1952), 706-733, and *Le Cantique des Cantiques*, Paris 1953: defends allegorical method of interpretation. Dubarle,

1. *Historical Interpretation*

The basic presupposition of this theory is that the characters – at least the main ones – of the Song of Songs are historical persons, and the Song narrates an historical event. Thus those who hold this view try to identify the characters with persons who lived in Israelite history. As a rule, those who consider the Song as a drama or idyll or cantata lean toward this method of interpretation. While doing so, they also try to show the inner movement of the drama or poem, the tension between either two types of life (idyll) or two sets of persons (drama or cantata) and the way the tension is resolved. Thus according to Renan, the central characters were historically a maiden from the village of Sulem, in the tribe of Issachar, her lover, – a shepherd boy – and the King Solomon.[84] C.D. Ginsburg maintains that "this Song records real history of a humble but virtuous woman..."[85] Even among those who classify the Song as anthology (either of wedding songs or simply of love poems) there are authors who hold that the Song treats of historical Solomon.[86]

A. M., "Le Cantique des Cantiques", in "Bulletin de théologie biblique", *RSc.Phil.T.* 38 (1954), 92-102, a recension article on important commentaries since 1940 which propose various theories of interpretation; See also similar recensions by Tournay, R., *RB* 60 (1953), 414-417 and *RB* 62 (1955), 284-286. Murphy, R.E., *CBQ* 16 (1954), 1-11, examines the parabolic approach and the allegorical theory. Dubarle, A.M., *RB* 61 (1954), 67-86: a critique of allegorical view and a defence of naturalistic theory. Likewise, Audet, J.-P., *RB* 62 (1955), 197-221, naturalistic interpretation. Feuillet, A., *RB* 68 (1961), 5-38: examines minutely and refutes "les littéralistes" and gives further proofs and explanations of his allegorical theory. Also Cothenet, E., "L'interprétation du Cantique des Cantiques", *L'ami du Clergé* 73 (1963), 529-540 & 545-552: refutation of naturalistic approach and defence of allegorical view. Grelot, P., "Le sens du Cantique des Cantiques", *RB* 71 (1964), 42-56: a recension article which examines minutely and rejects the allegorical theory. He favours naturalistic interpretation. Cantwell, L., "The Allegory of the Canticle of Canticles", *Script.* 16 (1964), 76-93. Würthwein, E., "Zum Verständnis des Hohenliedes", *TRu.NF.* 32 (1967), 177-212: a recension of studies and commentaries that appeared for ca. 30 years before the writing of the article. He seems to favour naturalistic interpretation. Murphy, R.E., *CBQ* 39 (1977), 482-496: a recension article on commentaries; Id., *BTB* 9 (1979), 99-105: favours naturalistic view.

[84] Renan, E., *Le Cantique*, 71-72. R.G. Moulton identifies Solomon himself with the humble lover. He reconstructs the historical event as follows: "King Solomon, visiting his vineyard upon Mount Lebanon comes by surprise upon the fair Shulammite maiden; she flees from him, and he visits her disguised as a Shepherd and wins her love." *The Literary Study*, 194. According to S.R. Driver, "the poem, it is possible, may be constructed upon a basis of fact, the dramatic form and the descriptive imagery being supplied by the imagination of the poet", *An Introduction*, 450.

[85] Ginsburg, C.D., *The Song*, 11.

[86] For instance J.B. Bossuet held that the occasion of the Song was the marriage of Solomon with Pharaoh's daughter, cf. *Libri Salomonis*, 193. R. Gordis, who classifies the Song as an anthology (pp. 17f), is persuaded "*that we have here* (i.e. 3:6-11) *a song composed on the occasion of one of Solomon's marriages to a foreign princess* probably an Egyptian... All the references to Solomon in the book, aside from the title, are thus authentic, including the three references in this song (i.e. 3:7,9,11), which dates from Solomon's reign", *The Song*, 20.

This theory of interpretation gives full value to the dialogue form of the Song of Songs and tries to appreciate as well the possible, if not probable or certain, concrete historical context of at least some of the poetic units. In fact, this aspect contributes much for the appreciation of the poems as such, and of the cultural values of the poems.

2. *Typological and Parabolic Interpretation*

F. Delitzsch suggests that "the Song celebrates paradisiacal, but yet only natural love (*Minne*). It stands, however, in the canon of the Church, because Solomon is a type of Him of Whom it can be said, 'a greater than Solomon is here' (Mt 12:42). Referred to Him the antitype, the earthly contents receive a heavenly import and glorification..."[87] According to him, the Song has not only a historico-ethical, but also a typico-mystical meaning. He explains that "the typical interpretation proceeds on the idea that the type and the antitype do not exactly coincide; the mystical, that the heavenly stamps itself in the earthly, but is yet at the same time immeasurably different from it."[88]

According to some other exponents, the Song must be interpreted in the same way as a parable.[89] A. Vaccari adds another nuance to the parabolic approach to the Song: "L'azione della *Cantica* è una parabola e un contrasto; una parabola di fondo idillico, un contrasto fra due vite, fra due amori."[90]

The fact that the Song is found in the Canon seems to have called for an additional meaning for the Song. All exponents of this view will agree that this typological or parabolic sense *of the Song* is not the primarily intended meaning of the text by the original author.[91] Moreover, the typological or parabolic approach presupposes that the text is capable of multiple senses, besides, but not contrary to, the sense meant by the original author. The fact of inspiration is probably the ground for this presupposition. "The parabolic approach leads naturally and logically to Messianic interpretation of the Canticle."[92]

---

[87] Delitzsch, F., *Commentary*, 3.

[88] Ib., 6.

[89] See Murphy, R. E., *CBQ* 11 (1949), 381; Id., *CBQ* 16 (1954), 4-5.

[90] Vaccari, A., *La Cantica*, 111-113. It is good to remember that the typological or parabolic sense is different from the literal sense.

[91] The case of Jesus' parables is different. For there the parabolic sense coincides with the literal sense, and the speaker warns the hearer that he is "parabolizing". In the case of the SS, it is a superimposed meaning.

[92] Murphy, R. E., *CBQ* 16 (1954), 4.

3. *Allegorical Interpretation*

Apparently this interpretation seems to be the most ancient and traditional.[93] The proponents of allegorical interpretation claim that the Jews have always understood the Song as an allegory. In fact, the earliest witness of the allegorical interpretation is from the time of IV Esdras, V 24-26; VII 26 (alias II Esdras V 24-26; VII 26), which belongs between ca. 70-132 AD.[94]

Hippolytus (ca. 200 AD) seems to have been the first Christian to interpret the Song of Songs allegorically.[95] In recent times, Catholic scholars, particularly those from France, are well pronounced exponents of this theory. The names of P. Joüon, A. Robert, R. Tournay, A. Feuillet and many others are associated with this allegorical interpretation. A. Robert's thesis is that the Song "est une allégorie, développée avec une intensité lyrique extraordinaire, et avec un mouvement qui l'apparente au genre dramatique." [96]

Different shades of allegorical interpretation have been proposed. The most significant ones are the following:

a) *Historical Allegory*

According to this view, the Song in its literal sense speaks of the dealing of Yahweh towards Israel in history – the Lover being Yahweh and the Beloved being Israel;[97] e.g. P. Joüon distributes the Song as follows: Song 1:5-5:1 – the first covenant, i.e. from Exodus to the installation of the Ark in the city of David. Song 5:2-8:14 – the second covenant, i.e. from Exile to the rebuilding of the Temple.[98] Further development in this line of interpretation is as follows: Yahweh and Israel are replaced by Christ and Church; or Logos and human nature; or God and Mary;[99] or even the Messiah and Israel.[100]

---

[93] Cf. Pope, M. H., *Song*, 90.

[94] J. P. Audet is quick to remark that we are at least five centuries after the "composition" of the Writing and more than three centuries since the time of its inclusion in the Canon! Only since the time of Rabbi Akiba, the allegorical interpretation has been systematically and painstakingly carried out. One may ask, "how was the Song understood and used before the first century of our era?" See *RB* 62 (1955), 200ff.

[95] Hanson, R. P. C., *Allegory and Event*, London 1959, 116ff.

[96] Robert, A., *RB* 52 (1943-44), 211. See also *Le Cantique*, 43ff.

[97] For the interpretation of the Israelite history in the language of the Song, see Ginsburg, C. D., *Song*, 25-47.

[98] Joüon, P., *Le Cantique*, 15-20. In this he has only followed the Targum. See Gollancz, H., *The Targum to the Song of Songs*, London 1908.

[99] Pope, M. H., *Song*, 114ff.

[100] Ib., 141.

b) *Political Allegory*

Von Hug, who classified the Song as a collection of dreams, interprets it as a political allegory: For him, "the dreaming shepherdess represented the people of the ten Northern tribes, the people of Israel, and the burden of the dream is her longing to be reunited with the King of Judah in the formation of a new Solomonic state." [101]

c) *Sapiential Allegory*

The interpretation of the Song as a sapiential allegory has branched off in different lines: In the Jewish circle, for example, Joseph Ibn Caspi explains the Song "as representing the union between the active intellect and the receptive material intellect." [102] Don Isaac Abravanel "saw the protagonists of the Song of Songs as Solomon and Wisdom" and "it was necessary to regard only the Bride as an allegorical figure".[103]

d) *Spiritual Allegory or Mystical Marriage*

Origen was the first, it appears, to have initiated the mystical interpretation of the Song of Songs. Taking inspiration from his Jewish predecessors, he developed the interpretation of the Song in this way: In the historical level, the Bride is the Church replacing Israel and the Bridegroom is Christ in the place of Yahweh; but in the mystical level, the Bride is the individual soul and the Bridegroom the Logos, or Christ, or God.[104]

The principle behind this method of exegesis is to explain the Bible by the Bible. This method tries to interpret the Song from the point of view of the Heilsgeschichte, which in turn helps spirituality and mysticism. The view has rightly emphasized the marriage symbolism that is common to the prophetic literature and the Song of Songs. But to say that the Song of Songs is the result of the "méthode anthologique" of composition and that the symbolic language of the prophets has given rise to the whole gamut of the poems in the Song, seems to beg the question. For allegory is inspired by events and realities of experience, and allegorical language is, as a matter of fact, construed on the normal

---

[101] Apud Pope, M. H., *Song*, 132.

[102] Apud Ginsburg, C. D., *Song*, 47; cf. 47-49.

[103] Pope, M. H., *Song*, 110. See also Ginsburg, C. D., *Song*, 58. G. Kuhn identified the Bride with Wisdom but saw the Bridegroom as a type of the seeker after wisdom rather than as the historical Solomon: see "Erklärung des Hohenliedes", *NKZ* 37 (1926), 501-510 & 521-572.

[104] Cf. Origène, *Homélies sur le Cantique des Cantiques*, (ed.) O. Rousseau, Paris 1966², 21-23; see further Parente, P. P., "The Canticle of Canticles in Mystical Theology", *CBQ* 6 (1944), 142-158.

and literal use of language, and not vice versa. Besides, the greatest drawback of this theory is to insist that the allegorical sense is the literal sense or even the primary sense intended by the original author.[105] It is necessary to remember that anything beyond the literal sense is always an addition on theological grounds, be it the question of inspiration or canonicity, or on hermeneutical grounds, e.g. for the edification of the community or individual soul.[106] The chief objection against the allegorical interpretation is that nowhere *in the text itself* is it indicated that the author intends an allegorical meaning of the text.[107]

4. *Literal or Natural Interpretation*

The majority of scholars consider the Song as speaking of pure human love. "There is widespread agreement that the literal meaning of the Song is human love."[108] J.P. Audet[109] proves that the Song treats only of human love. He distinguishes two stages in the composition of the Song: (a) pre-literary stage in which the Song was a betrothal song; (b) literary stage in which the Song had become part of sapiential writings and thus "a text like other texts."[110] A.M. Dubarle holds that the obvious sense should be identified with the literal sense, and that in the case of the Song, the literal sense is the celebration of human love. He does not deny the openness of the text for further or "higher" meaning.[111] R.E. Murphy explains it as follows: "One begins with the fact that the community which accepted and preserved this work understood it in a sense that goes beyond the literal and historical meaning. In other words, the work grew in meaning as it grew in age within 'the people of the book'... It is a fact, recognizable within such a process, that a text has an after-life, and that meaning accrues to a text as

---

[105] The development of the different theories culminating in allegorical interpretation shows the danger of unconscious misemphasis: from historical to typological or parabolic, and finally to allegorical interpretation.

[106] For the critique of allegorical interpretation, see Audet, J.P., *RB* 62 (1955), 207ff; Murphy, R.E., *CBQ* 16 (1954), 5-6; Id., *CBQ* 39 (1977) 485-486 & 495; Childs, S.B., *Introduction*, 571-72; Falk, M., *Love Lyrics*, 63-64.

[107] Cf. Audet, J.P., *RB* 62 (1955), 207. He adduces Is. 5:1-7 which is an allegory, but indicated in the text itself at the end. Another typical example is Ps. 80 where the allegory of the vine is developed, but the author shows in a very subtle way that the vine stands for Israel: vv. 1-6 refer directly to the people and the allegory starts in v. 8 onwards. Verses 14ff pass over smoothly from allegory to reality. One more example from sapiential writings may be cited: Qoh. 12:1-8. The Classical example is Ez. 23 – an allegory about Israel and Judah.

[108] Murphy, R.E., *CBQ* 39 (1977), 486.

[109] Audet, J.P., *RB* 62 (1955), 197-221; Id., "Love and Marriage in the Old Testament", *Script.* 10 (1958), 65-83.

[110] Audet, J.P., *Script.* 10 (1958), 79.

[111] Dubarle, A.M., *RB* 61 (1954), 67-86.

it is handed down within a people... The traditional view is not the whole, nor the 'higher' meaning; it can simply be a valid meaning." [112]

According to Dubarle and Rowley, the celebration of human love is sacred, for it reflects God's sanction of human sexual love between a man and a woman and among the ancient Israelites there was no dichotomy between the sacred and profane. Hence the book deserves a place in the Canon, "for there is no incongruity in such a recognition of the essential sacredness of pure human love." [113]

The present study would agree with the natural or literal interpretation of the Song of Songs in the context of sapiential literature. "The primary meaning of the Song would then have to do with human sexual love – the expression of it, its delights, its fidelity, and its power." [114]

C. **Date**

There are various opinions as regards the date of the Song of Songs. Distinctions and specifications are made in the dating of the book as a whole or the individual units in the book. In general, the question of the date of the Song may be viewed in three ways:

1) Those authors who take the Song as a single literary work and as a composition by Solomon or about Solomon, date it either during or shortly after the reign of Solomon; e.g. those who give the Song the historical interpretation, – like Bossuet, F. Delitzsch, etc.[115] Because of the Solomonic humanism revealed in the Song, and the affinity of the Song to Egyptian love songs, G. Gerleman assigns a Solomonic date to the Song.[116]

2) Those who insist on late linguistic features such as Aramaisms, the relative particle *še* etc., bring the date of the Song down to the time after Exile.[117] There are even authors who date it in Hellenistic times; e.g. Pouget et Guitton give two lines of arguments:

---

[112] Murphy, R.E., *CBQ* 39 (1977), 495.

[113] Rowley, H.H., "Interpretation", *The Servant*, 234; Dubarle, A.M., *RB* 61 (1954), 67 & 81-86.

[114] Murphy, R.E., *Interpr.* 27 (1973), 422. Childs, B.S., *Introduction*, 574-575, says: "The writer simply assumes the Hebrew order of the family as a part of the given order of his society, and seeks to explore and unravel its mysteries from within".

[115] Cf. Bossuet, J.B., *Libri*, 195; F. Delitzsch says: "If not the production of Solomon, it must at least have been written near his time", *Commentary*, 11.

[116] Gerleman, G., *Das Hohelied*, 76-77. E. Renan places the composition of the Song, "peu de temps après le schisme, c'est-à-dire, vers le milieu du Xe siècle avant Jésus Christ", *Le Cantique*, 111. C.D. Ginsburg thinks that the Song was composed "about the time of Solomon", but not contemporary, *The Song*, 124f. L. Cicognani places the composition between 933-881 but the language has been later modernized, *Il Cantico*, 212.

[117] P. Joüon writes: "... nous pouvons conclure, avec une très grande probabilité, que le Cantique n'a pas été écrit avant l'exil", *Le Cantique*, 91.

a) Philological: i) Aramaisms
ii) Words belonging to late Hebrew
iii) The relative pronoun *še*
iv) Greek words

b) The spirit of the book: i) Political ideas
ii) Moral ideas.

They conclude "le *Cantique* aurait été composé entre 285 et 220, c'est-à-dire dans la première moitié du IIIe siècle." [118]

3) Finally there are those – esp. those who take the Song as an anthology of love poems – that strike a compromise. According to them, the earliest song, at least in its oral composition, could come from the time of Solomon.[119] R. Gordis admits that most of the songs in the collection have no historical allusions and are undatable. Judging from the few historical allusions to be found in some songs, he concludes that "the datable material in the Song spans five centuries. The period begins with Solomon's accession to the throne (ca. 960 B.C.E), includes the early days of the Northern Kingdom (c. 920-876), and reaches down to the Persian era (6th-5th century)." [120] K. N. Schoville is of opinion that the Song in its present form as anthology belongs to c. 400 B.C.E. "There are sufficient archaic elements in the book, however, to suggest that some of the songs are pre-Exilic." [121]

The present writer is of the opinion that the Song is an anthology of love poems, coming from different periods and from North and South Kingdoms, and the poems were collected and edited according to a certain pattern. There is a very great probability of a strong editorial activity to the extent of making the Song appear as one man's work, and of levelling some linguistic features. The final compilation and edition of the book took place ca. 400 BC.[122]

---

[118] Pouget, G.-Guitton, J., *Le Cantique*, 83. S. R. Driver assigns the Song to the age of Ptolemy Euergetes, 247-221 BC, cf. *An Introduction*, 450.

[119] E.g. SS. 3:6-11 is, according to R. Gordis, about one of Solomon's marriages, cf. *The Song*, 20.

[120] Ib., 24. Gottwald, N. K., *IDB*, Vol. IV, 420-424 agrees in essence to the position of R. Gordis. Several poems were composed in the North, before 722 BC but the book reached its final stage in 5th century BC. W. F. Albright denies any evidence for the frequently assumed Hellenistic date, and assigns fifth-fourth cent. BC., "Archaic", *Fs.G.R.Driver*, 1. He thinks that the oral sources of the contents were probably of North Palestine.

[121] Schoville, K. N., "Song of Songs", in *Encyclopaedia Judaica*, col. 150.

[122] For further discussions, see Pope, M. H., *Song*, 22ff. Cf. also Landy, F., *Paradoxes*, 18, 27, 283, note 31; & 290, note 68.

D. Poetic Units or Smaller Poems in the Song

The dictum "quot capita tot sententiae" is almost literally verified when one speaks of the number of smaller poems within the Song. In the same way, there is no unanimity at all as to the determination of the extent of individual poetic units. The following table is a sample to show the difference in the positions:

S. No.	*Author(s)*	*Units*	*Reference*
1.	A. Robert etc.	5	*Le Cantique*
2.	J.C. Exum	6	*ZAW* 85(1973), 77
3.	W.H. Shea	6($\times$6)	*ZAW* 92(1980), 378
4.	D. Lys	7	*Le plus beau chant*, 22-24
5.	D. Buzy	7(plus)	*RB* 49(1940), 172
6.	J. Angénieux	8	*ETL* 41(1965), 96-142; 42(1966), 582-96; 44(1968), 87-140
7.	R. Tournay	10	*Quand Dieu ...*, 28 note 7
8.	E.C. Webster	16	*JSOT* 22(1982), 84
9.	E. Bettan	18	*The Five Scrolls*, 10
10.	N. Schmidt	19	*The Message of the Poets*, 230
11.	L. Alonso Schökel	21	*El cantar de los cantares*
12.	K. Budde	23	*Die Fünf Megilloth*, xii-xxi
13.	O. Eissfeldt	ca. 25	*Introduction*, 490
14.	F. Landsberger	25(plus)	*JBL* 73(1954), 215-16
15.	M. Haller	26	*Die Fünf Megilloth*
16.	R. Gordis	28(plus)	*Song of Songs*, 35
17.	R.E. Murphy	30 (in 9 groups)	*CBQ* 39(1977), 489-93
18.	E. Würthwein	ca. 30	*Die Fünf Megilloth*, 25
19.	M. Falk	31	*Love Lyrics*, 4 et passim
20.	G. Gerleman	32	*Ruth/Das Hohelied*
21.	L. Krinetzki	52	*Bib.* 52(1971), 176-89, esp.185-87.

The present writer thinks that the SS is an anthology containing twenty-eight small poems. The delimitation of individual poems is based on such literary, stylistic and poetic criteria as:

a) Change of speaker(s)
b) Change of listener(s)
c) Change of concrete setting or place: e.g. landscape, etc.
d) Change of moods or sentiments
e) Change of imagery or groups of images
f) Certain insights into the life-setting revealed in the poem itself.

Either many or a few of these criteria have been taken into consideration for deciding the separate poems. These criteria may not convince individually every literary critic, but still their collective validity cannot be doubted. Each poem is seen as a self-contained piece and as revealing one complete aspect of love-sentiment: e.g. longing, admiration, etc.

Chapter 2.

POETRY OF THE SONG OF SONGS

There seems to be no extant work of Jewish antiquity on Hebrew Prosody and Rhetoric. All attempts on systematic study and exposition on Hebraw Poetry and Rhetoric are comparatively recent.[1] Consequently the research in these fields continues to grow and therefore differences in approach, treatment and conclusions are to be expected.

The Hebrew words denoting poetry, *hāgāh,* "to muse, to utter sounds," *zāmam,* "to consider," *maśśā'*, "utterance," all illustrate that for the Hebrews poetry is thinking aloud: *maśśā'* comes from the root *nāśa',* "to raise the voice and say." [2] It has been almost conclusively proved that the Hebrew poetry was originally oral composition.[3] Oral poetry necessarily involves "poet-audience" "sender-receiver" relationship.[4] Because the audience and its feed-back are involved, the oral poetry in the earliest times must have been antiphonal songs so that the audience might actively participate in the performance.[5] Oral poetry was either recited or chanted. Reduplication and antiphony helped and controlled the composition of oral poems.[6]

---

[1] For the history of the literary study of the Bible, i.e. poetry, rhetoric etc. see Alonso Schökel, L., *Estudios de Poética Hebrea*, (ed.) J. Flors, Barcelona 1963, 3-54 where a quick survey is given. This work is very useful for its annotated bibliography as well as for the sections on the treatment of the stylistics and imagery. The most recent work in English on Hebrew Poetry is that of W. G. E. Watson, *Classical Hebrew Poetry*: A Guide to its Techniques, JSOT - Supplement Series--26, Sheffield 1984. The latter work has been extensively used and followed in this study.

[2] Cf. Smith, G. A., *The Early Poetry of Israel in its Physical and Social Origins*: "The Schweich Lectures 1910", London 1912, 10. Compare the designation in Tamil, *akaval* for poetic metre, the root of which is *akavu*, meaning "to call, to sing"; cf. below on Akaval metre in Part Two Ch. 6.

[3] Cf. Yoder, P. B., "A-B Pairs and Oral Composition in Hebrew Poetry", *VT* 21 (1971), 470-489, esp. 588.

[4] Watson, W. G. E., *Classical*, 66-86 on oral poetry.

[5] Cf. Slotki, I. W., "Antiphony in Ancient Hebrew Poetry", *JQR* 26 (1935/36), 199-219, esp. 216. According to him, "it is this mode of recital of ancient Hebrew poetry that probably gave rise to parallelism and possibly also to strophe", ib., 216.

[6] Slotki, I. W., "Forms and Features of Ancient Hebrew Poetry", *JMEOS* 16 (1931), 31-49, esp. 37.

A. **Hebrew Metre**

Hebrew metre is one of the most disputed topics in the Old Testament studies.[7] Says G. B. Gray, "metre in Hebrew literature is obscure: the laws of Hebrew metre have been and are matters of dispute, and at times the very existence of metre in the Old Testament has been questioned."[8]

Metre in the strict sense of the term is defined as "a phonetic rhythm based on the alternation of long and short syllables."[9] According to W.G.E. Watson, metre is the measured use of such prominences as stress, loudness, pitch and length, grouping them regularly over segments of time.[10]

The problem of Hebrew metre arises from the fact that the Hebrew metrical system depends very much on the pronunciation and on the accented syllables. Now both the pronunciation and accent depend greatly on the system of Masoretic vowel-signs which are centuries later than the literary productions themselves![11] Hebrew metrics is made more complicated because of the problems of orthography, morphology etc. and it must have undergone even radical changes in a period of more than thousand years of its development.[12]

Among the metrists, three approaches to the problem are found, and these may be taken as three methods of metrical analysis of Hebrew poetry:

1. *Accentual or Stress Theory*

According to this theory, Hebrew metre is accentual, i.e. it "counts only *accented* syllables,"[13] and by means of counting the accents and noting its regularity of occurrence in the stichoi and the line, the metre was named.[14] C. A. Briggs based his theory of Hebrew metre on "words or word accents."[15] T. J. Meek,[16] I. W. Slotki,[17] and L. Krinetzki[18]

---

[7] For bibliography, reference may be made to Longman, T., "A Critique of Two Recent Metrical Systems", *Bib.* 63 (1982), 230-254, and Watson, W. G. E., *Classical*, 90-91 & 97.

[8] Gray, G. B., *The Forms of Hebrew Poetry*, New York 1972, 47.

[9] Robinson, T. H., "Hebrew Poetic Form: The English Tradition", *VTS* 1 (1953), 129.

[10] Watson, W. G. E., *Classical*, 87.

[11] Cf. Horst, F., "Die Kennzeichen der hebräischen Poesie", *TRu.NF* 21, Heft 2 (1953), 97-121, esp. 102-119.

[12] Segert, S., "Problems of Hebrew Prosody", *VTS* 7 (1960), 283-291, esp. 289.

[13] Longman, T., *Bib.* 63 (1982), 232. He calls this "syllable counting approach" or syllable count metre, cf. 231f. This designation does not seem to be clear.

[14] Albright, W. F., "The Earliest Forms of Hebrew Verse", *JPOS* 2 (1922), 69-86.

[15] Briggs, C. A., *The Book of Psalms*: Vol. I, ICC, Edinburgh 1907, xxxviii-xliii.

[16] Meek, T. J., "The Structure of Hebrew Poetry", *JRel.* 9 (1929), 523-550, esp. 538-540.

[17] Slotki, I. W., *JMEOS* 16 (1931), 36.

[18] Krinetzki, L., *Das Hohe Lied*, Düsseldorf 1964, 50-52.

accept and use this method. According to L. Krinetzki, "jede Zeile hat im HL zwei, drei oder auch vier Hebungen. Oft kommt die Verbindung von drei und zwei Akzenten (3+2) vor: das bekannte Klageliedvermass."[19] These accents are not simply ornamental, but often constitute also the rhythm and confer sound or rhythm-symbolism to the poem, e.g. SS 2:8.[20] The following are some examples for different metres occurring in the Song of Songs:

- Predominantly the *qînāh* metre: 3+2, e.g. 1:9
- Occasionally the reverse: 2+3, e.g. 1:12
- Sometimes there is: 2+2, e.g. 2:8
- Exceptionally is found: 3+3, e.g. 1:2-4, with its variant, i.e 3+3+3, as in 1:3.[21]

2. *Syllable-counting Theory*

The method consists in counting the number of syllables per line "without considering vowel length, or whether syllables are closed or open. It is, in effect, a mechanical reckoning of the number of vowels per colon."[22] This theory seems to be even earlier than the accentual or stress theory.[23] S. A. Geller claims that "it is becoming increasingly clearer that a syllabic approach to Hebrew (and Ugaritic) meter is the most useful one functionally; that is, parallel lines often display a syllable symmetry whose frequency cannot be due merely to the natural limitations imposed by the length of the Semitic word within the framework of parallelism. It must, therefore, be a conscious concern of the poet." He adds immediately, however, that "it cannot as yet be claimed that syllable symmetry is so pervasive that it clearly forms the chief determinant of Hebrew prosody."[24] S. T. Byington proposes a method in which accents, syllables and length of syllables are to be counted.[25] O. Loretz's method of counting the consonants is a further development of this syllable-counting theory.[26]

---

[19] Ib., 50.

[20] Ib., 51-52.

[21] For other authors who analysed the metre of the Song of Songs, cf. Pope, M. H., *Song*, 37-40. Segert's "alternating stress metre" theory may be included under this group. See Watson, W. G. E., *Classical*, 103 for exposition and rejection of the theory of Segert.

[22] Watson, W. G. E., *Classical*, 104.

[23] According to W. G. E. Watson, this theory was proposed as early as the 19th century by G. Bickell; cf. *Classical*, 105 note 61.

[24] Geller, S.A., *Parallelism in Early Biblical Poetry*, Harvard Semitic Monographs - 20, Missoula Mont. 1979, 9.

[25] Byington, S. T., "A Mathematical Approach to Hebrew Metres", *JBL* 66 (1947), 63-77, esp. 65.

[26] Loretz, O., *Das althebräische Liebeslied*, AOAT 14/1, 55ff.

Syllable counting method has been used further to discover some secondary metrical patterns, such as "double-duty modifier,"[27] "literary insertion,"[28] or "pivot pattern."[29] The principal drawbacks of the syllable counting theory are that it relies on reconstructing the vowels and that it ignores stress.[30]

3. *Word-sense-unit Theory*

This theory is represented by T.H. Robinson. He holds that "a metrical unit must always correspond to a sense unit. It has long been recognized that there can be no *enjambement* in Hebrew verse form. Where words run closely together in thought, they must be closely connected in metre; where there is a break in the sense, there must be also a break in the metre."[31] For this method, "the basic element of ancient Hebrew poetry is the word or thought unit irrespective of beats and stresses."[32] Two drawbacks may be detected in this theory: a) It assumes that there are a set number of 'word-feet' or word-units in every verse-line; b) It overlooks that metre is a phonological construct while 'word' is a grammatical element or a semantic component.[33]

The difficulties involved in finding one metrical theory that satisfies all, have led some scholars to scepticism and they are prone to think that Hebrew poetry does not yield to metric analysis.[34]

Any one theory, to the exclusion of the others, would not surely satisfy all the metrists. We can find a reasonable compromise in the use of the methods for understanding and appreciating Hebrew poetry: Word-sense-unit may serve as basis to distribute the stresses, while the syllable-counting may be used to analyse the word-clusters that have resulted from the orthography of Hebrew language.

---

[27] Dahood. M.J., "A New Metrical Pattern in Biblical Poetry", *CBQ* 29 (1967), 574-579.

[28] Tsumura, D.T., "Literary Insertion (AXB Pattern) in Biblical Hebrew", *VT* 33,4 (1983), 468-482.

[29] Watson, W.G.E., *Classical*, 214ff with bibliography in p. 221.

[30] Ib., 105.

[31] Robinson, T.H., "Some Principles of Hebrew Metrics", *ZAW* 54 (1936), 28-43, quotation is from p. 30.

[32] Kosmala, H., "Form and Structure in Ancient Hebrew Poetry (A New Approach)", *VT* 14 (1964), 423-445, quotation is from pp. 425-426. In this article the author explains his method. In *VT* 16 (1966), 152-180 under the same title, the author applies his method for some pericopes in Isaiah and a few Psalms.

[33] Watson, W.G.E., *Classical*, 104.

[34] Young, G.D., "Ugaritic Prosody", *JNES* IX (1950), 124-133, esp. 132-133 for the conclusion.

B. Parallelism

1. *Different Approaches to Parallelism*

Poetry is an art and the creative imagination of the poet is the chief source of poetry. With the Hebrews, poetry was an art with a purpose. Its aim is aesthetic and its appeal is to the emotions. Hence Hebrew poetry is characterized by a sense of beauty in its phraseology, in its verbal construction and melody.[35] That parallelism in Hebrew poetry contributes very much to this sense of beauty is accepted by all. But the origin of parallelism is explained differently by authors.

a) *Poet-Listener based Theory*: Parallelism implies "a rhythm, a balance, a regularity, not of sound but of thought. It was because the poet's mind ran in balanced ideas that his words balanced. When he had said a thing once, it was not enough; his instinct was to say it over again and it was saying it over again that made the poetic form."[36] In terms of communication technique, parallelism is based on the "expectation-fulfillment" correlation.[37] Thought-arrangement, and not word-arrangement, is the basis of the external form of Semitic versification. Parallelism is the norm and test of composition in verse. "But the balance of statement against statement in the progress of the theme is indispensable. It is the constitutive norm of poetry as such."[38] E.L. Greenstein explains parallelism from the speech perception aspect. When a listener perceives a sentence with a certain syntactic construction, this establishes in the listener a preference or expectation for the same syntax in the next sentence. The art of correlating similar or dissimilar syntactic constructions is called grammatical (or syntactic) parallelism.[39]

b) *Structural Approach*: This theory studies the question of parallelism on the basis of composition or structure of the line. Thus parallelism is defined as "balanced return of structure."[40] The emphasis is on the "balanced" and "structure." The presence or absence, return or quasi-return of the structure would give name to this art of composition called parallelism. The structure may be simply grammatical-syntactical or thought-structure. G.B. Gray's terminology, "complete parallelism" and "incomplete parallelism" (with or without compensation) comes

---

[35] Cf. Meek, T.J., *JRel.* 9 (1929), 523-525.

[36] Robinson, T.H., *ZAW* 54 (1936), 30.

[37] Robinson, T.H., "Basic Principles of Hebrew Poetic Form", in *Festschrift - Alfred Bertholet*, Tübingen 1950, 439; Id., *VTS* 1 (1953), 140; Meek, T.J., *JRel.* 9 (1929), 535.

[38] McClellan, W.H., "The Elements of Old Testament Poetry", *CBQ* 3 (1941), 208.

[39] Greenstein, E.L., "Two Variations of Grammatical Parallelism in Canaanite Poetry and Their Psycholinguistic Background", *JANES* 6 (1974), 87-105, esp. 87-89.

[40] Shipley, J.T., *Dictionary*: "Parallelism".

under this approach.[41] The recent study of J. L. Kugel on parallelism goes in the same line.[42] For him, "the parallelistic style in the Bible consists not of stringing together clauses that bear some semantic, syntactic, or phonetic resemblance, nor yet of 'saying the same thing twice', but of the sequence — / — // in which B is both a continuation of A and yet broken from it by a pause, a typically emphatic 'seconding' style in which parallelism plays an important part but whose essence is not parallelism, but the 'seconding sequence'."[43] J. L. Kugel's definition is quite elastic and not very precise, but it is concerned about the thought-structure. T. Collins' study, on the other hand, is centered around the grammatical-syntactical or word structure.[44] The boundaries of the semantic units figuring in the parallel cola have to be established before the examination of their grammatical-syntactical structure. In other words, the semantic field of the grammatical terms has to be determined.[45]

c) *Mathematical Concept Approach*: Proposed recently by W. G. E. Watson, [46] it is based on the mathematical (or rather geometrical) concepts of symmetry, asymmetry and parallelism. According to him, parallelism belongs within a larger group of mathematical analogues. He gives the following four analogues:

(i) Proper congruence (Parallelism): Same sequence and same sign: i.e. a′ a″ a‴ // a′ a″ a‴

(ii) Reflexive congruence (Mirror symmetry or chiasm): Same sign but opposite sequence: i.e. a′ a″ a‴ // a‴ a″ a′

(iii) Proper anticongruence: Same sequence but opposite sign: i.e. a′ a″ a‴ // –a′ –a′ –a‴

---

[41] Gray, G. B., *The Forms*, 59 & 74. "*Complete parallelism* may be said to exist when every single term in one line is parallel to a term in the other, or when at least every term or group of terms in one line is paralleled by a corresponding term or group of terms in the other. *Incomplete parallelism* exists when only some of the terms in each of two corresponding lines are parallel to one another, while the remaining terms express something which is stated once only in the two lines", p. 59. The qualificative "with compensation" or "without compensation" regards the number of terms in each line which are necessary for the balance of structure. The word-structure is in the upper stratum while the thought structure lies in a deeper level.

[42] Kugel, J. L., *The Idea of Biblical Poetry: Parallelism and its History*, Yale University Press, New Haven & London 1981, 51-55.

[43] Ib., 53-54.

[44] Collins, T., *Line-Forms in Hebrew Poetry*, Rome 1978, 23ff. For a brief exposition of T. Collins' position, see Watson, W. G. E., *Classical*, 119-120.

[45] Kaddari, M. Z., "A Semantic Approach to Biblical Parallelism", *JJS* XXIV (1973), 167-175, esp. 170-172. S. A. Geller has further studied the relationship between grammatical analysis and semantic parallelism, *Parallelism*, 6ff.

[46] Watson, W. G. E., *Classical*, 114-119.

(iv) Reflexive anticongruence: Reversed sequence and opposite sign: i.e. a′ a″ a‴ // –a‴ –a″ –a′

The author claims that this approach accounts for chiastic patterns as well as parallelism, and sets parallelism in its proper context.

All the three approaches have brought to lime light one aspect or other of parallelism: The poet-listener based theory gives importance to thought-content: hence semantic aspect. Structural approach appreciates the aspect of balance. And the geometrical concept approach gives prominence to the postition of thought-units in the poetical line.

L. Alonso Schökel's definition of parallelism seems to include the best points of these approaches: " Le parallélisme est une articulation binaire de propositions symétriques ou proportionées." [47] The formal factor is what is common to all parallelisms. As regards the content of the propositions or the articulated elements, there is certainly variety.

2. *Various Parallelisms found in the Song of Songs*

Here below some of the parallelisms with examples from the Song of Songs are listed and briefly explained:

a) *Gender-matched Parallelism*: "Gender-matched parallelism is a type of parallelism where the gender of the nouns involved is the basic component." [48] The main features of this gender-matched parallelism seem to be:

(i) the nouns should come in parallelism;

(ii) this parallelism is one of the types of synonymous parallelism.

Example: 4:8ef "From the dens (f) of lions (f),
From the hills (m) of leopards (m)."

- Synonymous parallelism
- Feminine nouns are balanced by masculine nouns.

---

[47] Alonso Schökel, L., "Poésie", in *DBS*, Vol. VIII, col. 68. Id., *Estudios*, 205ff for elaborate treatment.

[48] Watson, W. G. E., *Classical*, 123. The *genders* of the nouns in each colon *match* – masculine and feminine genders occurring in *parallel* lines – and this accounts for the designation "gender-matched parallelism." For various patterns of this parallelism and examples, see his article, "Gender-Matched Synonymous Parallelism in the OT", *JBL* 99 (1980), 321-341.

b) *Number Parallelism*: There cannot be, strictly speaking, a number parallelism since no number can have a synonym. A better designation would be "graded numerical sequence"[49] or "numerical ladder."[50] In Hebrew the occurrences of the n//n+1 pattern are many. There are a few variations of this pattern and one such is found in SS 6:8.

"*Sixty* queens are they,
Eighty concubines,
Maidens *no-number*."

c) *Staircase Parallelism*: "Staircase parallelism is a form of couplet (or tricolon) which proceeds in steps."[51] There are three components which make up the pattern: (i) the element that is repeated; (ii) the intervening element which may be an epithet or a vocative, etc.; (iii) the complementary element which resumes and completes the thought of the final line. This pattern is also called by some "repetitive parallelism."[52] Some others would call it "climactic parallelism,"[53] or "expanded colon."[54] The name "repetitive parallelism" does not coincide exactly with what is meant by staircase parallelism.[55] J. Muilenburg has pointed out various patterns of repetitive parallelism or staircase parallelism:[56]

Example: SS 4:8a-d: "Come from Lebanon, bride,
Come from Lebanon, set out;
Leap from the peak of Amana,
From the peak of Senir and Hermon."

---

[49] Haran, M., "The Graded Numerical Sequence and the Phenomenon of 'Automatism' in Biblical Poetry", *VTS* 22 (1972), 238-267. See also Roth, W. M. W., "The Numerical Sequence x/x + 1 in the Old Testament", *VT* 12 (1962), 300-311; Id., *Numerical Sayings in the Old Testament*, VTS Vol. XIII, Leiden 1965.

[50] Dahood, M. J., "Ugaritic Studies and the Bible", *Greg* 43 (1962), 77.

[51] Watson, W. G. E., *Classical*, 150.

[52] Albright, W. F., "Archaic", *Fs.G.R.Driver*, 4 on SS 5:9; Schoville, K. N., *The Impact*, 84-85.

[53] Krinetzki, L., *Das Hohe*, 53; Greenstein, E. L., *JANES* 6 (1974), 96ff.

[54] Loewenstamm, S. E., "The Expanded Colon in Ugaritic and Biblical Verse", *JSS* 14 (1969), 176-196, esp. 186-196 on Hebrew poetry. The last designation is rejected by W. G. E. Watson, *Classical*, 150, note 102.

[55] Watson, W. G. E., "A Note on Staircase Parallelism", *VT* 33 (1983), 510-512. J. L. Kugel seems to question the very existence of repetitive parallelism for that matter: see *The Idea*, 39.

[56] Muilenburg, J., "A Study in Hebrew Rhetoric: Repetition and Style", *VTS* 1 (1953), 97-111.

d) *Noun-Verb Parallelism*: Noun-verb parallelism is that pattern in which finite verbs can function as parallel members to nouns. According to D. Grossberg, there are many sub-types of noun-verb parallelism:

(i) *construct* + genitive//*construct* + finite verb
(ii) *preposition* + noun//*preposition* + finite verb
(iii) infinitive or participle in parallelism with a finite verb.[57]

He mentions also the following patterns:

(i) preposition + noun + noun//preposition + noun + verb
(ii) imperative + noun + noun//imperative + verb
(iii) adverb + verb + noun//adverb + verb + verb.[58]

To this last type belongs, SS 8:5def: [59]

"Under the apple tree I aroused you,
There conceived you *your mother,*
There conceived *she who bore you.*"

SS 3:4de represents yet another pattern: preposition + noun + noun (con) // preposition + noun + participle (constr) with object suffix:

"Till I brought him to the house of *my mother,*
To the chamber of *her who conceived me.*"

e) *Asymmetric Janus Parallelism*: The definition given by C.H. Gordon, is: "When a polyseme parallels what precedes it with one meaning, and what follows it with a different meaning, the phenomenon may be described as 'asymmetric Janus parallelism'." [60] SS 2:12 belongs to this type. In this verse, *zāmîr* parallels "blossoms" with its meaning "pruning," and parallels "the voice of the turtle-dove" with its meaning "song." [61]

---

[57] Grossberg, D., "Noun/Verb Parallelism: Syntactic or Asyntactic", *JBL* 99 (1980), 481-488; Watson, W.G.E., *Classical*, 157-158.
[58] Grossberg, D., *JBL* 99 (1980), 487-488.
[59] Ib., 488.
[60] Gordon, C.H., "Asymmetric Janus Parallelism", *Eretz-Israel* 16 (1982), 80-81 (English Summary), esp. 80; Watson, W.G.E., *Classical*, 159 simply calls it "Janus Parallelism".
[61] See Gordon, C.H., *JAOS* 100 (1980), 356. It was interpreted as such by him first in "New Directions", in *BASP* 15 (1978), Naphtali Lewis Festschrift, 59-66, esp. 59 for SS 2:12. To some extent, Janus Parallelism may be compared to the Tamil grammatical technique called *Ciṅka nōkku utti.*

f) *Synonymous Parallelism*: When the thought of the second member of the line expresses the thought of the first member in synonymous terms and thus makes a parallel to it, it is called synonymous parallelism. This parallelism is construed by the help of word-pairs which are semantically or rhetorically related as parallels in the two members of the line:

Example: SS 2:5ab: "*Sustain me* with raisin-cakes,
Support me with apples."

g) *Antithetic "Parallelism"*: There seems to be no case of antithetic parallelism in the Song of Songs in the strict sense of the phrase and definition.[62] But one may include here in a broad sense those antitheses which give great rhetorical effect: [63] e.g. expectation x disappointment, as in SS 5:6ab, and also such statements as are constructed with the help of antonymic word-pairs as "left" and "right": e.g. SS 2:6, though semantically they may not be antithetic statements: [64]

Example for antithesis: 5:6ab: "I opened to my Lover
But my Lover had turned away,
had gone!"

C. **Stanza and Strophe**

The stanza (from Italian, which means "pause": lit "room") may be described, rather than defined, as a subdivision of a poem – indeed a major subdivision – which comprises one or more strophes. The strophe (from Greek, meaning "turn" in the idea) is a group of one or more lines forming a subdivision of a stanza. It is possible that a poem consists of one strophe-stanza only. In such case, poem, stanza and strophe are all identified and are co-extensive.[65]

There are many stanza-markers which indicate the end of one stanza and the beginning of another: e.g. refrain, acrostic, certain particles

---

[62] Strictly speaking, "in antithetic parallelism, the situations represented and statements made about them are opposed, but the affirmations are made in such a way that each hemistich says approximately the same thing, for one implies the other (Prov. 3:5)": Fitzgerald, A., "Hebrew Poetry", in *Jerome Biblical Commentary*, London 1968, 13:16.

[63] In fact, L. Krinetzki considers such antithetic statements as antithetic parallelisms, cf. *Das Hohe*, 53.

[64] Watson, W. G. E., *Classical*, 130ff for different types of word-pairs used in parallelisms.

[65] Ib., 161-162.

[66] For details with examples, see ib., 163-165.

etc..[66] The change of speaker, for example, marks the stanza in SS 6:1;2-3. Certain stanzas are predetermined by their very nature: e.g. the description of beloved's body in SS 4:1-7.

Strophes follow certain patterns and they may at times coincide with what are called inter-linear parallelisms.[67] The strophic patterns are named monocolon, bicolon or couplet, tricolon etc. Some examples may be given: [68]

SS 2:10 – Introductory monocolon

SS 1:10 – Couplet with verbal ellipsis

SS 2:1 – Couplet with non-verbal ellipsis.[69]

SS 1:11 – A tricolon: a) ABA' type
b) a staccato tricolon
c) a tricolon with a longer final line

SS 2:16 – A staccato tricolon - two beats per line.

Strictly speaking there is no case of acrostic poem in the Song of Songs, although E.C. Webster claims one,[70] and S.M. Paul seems to suggest that there might be partial acrostics in SS 4:9-11.[71]

The so-called "expanded colon" may be considered also under this topic of strophic patterns.[72]

Some of the verse patterns that constitute strophes may be mentioned here:

1. *Chiasm*: This is a structural pattern based on the principle of "a series and its inversion" in the symmetrical cola. The components of such a series are the sub-units of the sentence, considered semantically or

---

[67] Cf. Fitzgerald, A., "Hebrew Poetry" in *Jerome Biblical*, 13:16 for the term "interlinear parallelism".

[68] These examples are taken from Watson, W.G.E., *Classical*, 171-178.

[69] Compare G.B. Gray's "Incomplete parallelism without compensation."

[70] Webster, E.C., *JSOT* 22 (1982), 85-86.

[71] Paul, S.M., "Mnemonic Devices", in *IDB Sup.*, 600-602: "To be noted also is the sequence of the three consecutive letters *lāmedh*, *mēm*, and *nûn* in Song of S 4:9-11", p.600 col. 2.

[72] On expanded colon, see Loewenstamm, S.E., *JSS* 14 (1969), 176-196; Avishur, Y., "Addenda to the Expanded Colon in Ugaritic and Biblical Verse", *UF* 4 (1972), 1-10.

grammatically.[73] The chiastic pattern[74] was not limited to nouns and verbs, but parallel identical pronominal suffixes, prepositions and particles could also play a part in the configuration.[75] This pattern is involved in word-plays.[76] It is especially true in the case of semantic-sonant chiasm.[77] Syntactic chiasm is commonly found in the Old Testament poetry:[78]

Examples: SS 1:6 Chiasm: The word-chiasm also symbolizes the reversal of the state.

For a merely syntactic chiasmus, one may cite 1:2b-3a in which, Adjective: Subject: Comparative element :: Comparative element: Subject: Adjective, are found, i.e. A B C // C B A.

SS 2:14cdef, is a very interesting combination of

a) Syntactic formal parallelism:

cd: Verb - Object // Verb - Object

ef: Subject - Complement // Subject - Complement

b) Chiastic pattern: Face: Voice :: Voice: Face

c) Anadiplosis: 14 de.

2. *Terrace Pattern*: The terrace pattern is a form of repetition where the last part of a line is repeated as the beginning of the next line.[79] This pattern is known also as anadiplosis,[80] epizeuxis,[81] chain

---

[73] Lundbom, J. R., *Jeremiah: A Study in Ancient Hebrew Rhetoric*, SBL Dissertation Series-18, Missoula 1975, 61-62; Ceresko, A. R., "The Chiastic Word Pattern in Hebrew", *CBQ* 38 (1976), 303-311; Kselman, J. S., "Semantic-Sonant Chiasmus in Biblical Poetry", *Bib.* 58 (1977), 219-223; Watson, W. G. E., *Classical*, 201ff with ample bibliography in p. 207ff.

[74] M. J. Dahood characterized chiastic structure as "A:B::B:A pattern": "Ugaritic - Hebrew Syntax and Style", *UF* 1 (1969), 25; F. M. Cross as "the Repetitive Chiasm": "Prose and Poetry in the Mythic and Epic Texts from Ugarit", *HTR* 67 (1974), 3-4; A. R. Ceresko as "Chiastic Word Pattern", *CBQ* 38 (1976), 303.

[75] Ceresko, A. R., *CBQ* 38 (1976), 305.

[76] Ib., 309-311.

[77] J. S. Kselman defines semantic-sonant chiasmus as one in which "one leg of the chiasmus is formed by a pair of words of similar meaning (the semantic pair), and the other leg is produced by a pair of words of similar sound (the sonant pair)", *Bib.* 58 (1977), 219.

[78] Cf. Lundbom, J. R., *Jeremiah*, 62.

[79] Watson, W. G. E., *Classical*, 208.

[80] Ceresko, A. R., "The Function of *Antanaclasis*. in Hebrew Poetry, Especially in the Book of Qohelet", *CBQ* 44 (1982), 564 on SS 3:2-3.

[81] Krinetzki, L., *Das Hohe*, 71.

figure,[82] epanadiplosis and epanastrophe.[83] The clearest example of a terrace pattern in the SS is 2:15: [84]

SS 2:15: Literal translation as in Hebrew is as follows:
"Catch for us *foxes,*
Foxes small;
Spoiling *vineyards,*
Vineyards of ours in blossom."

3. *Anaphora*: When two or more consecutive lines or cola begin with the same word or phrase, the pattern is called anaphora: [85]

Example: SS 1:7cd "*Where* do you pasture?
Where do you fold at noon?"

4. *Epiphora*: When two or more consecutive cola or lines end with the same word or phrase, the pattern is called epiphora: [86]

Example: There seems to be no occurrence of epiphora in the strictest sense of the term, but there is "epistrophe", i.e. repetition of a word or phrase at the end of two or more successive strophes; e.g. SS 8:1ad: *lî.*[87]

---

[82] Moulton, R. G., *The Literary Study*, 52-53.

[83] Casanowicz, I. M., *Paronomasia in the Old Testament*, Boston 1894, 33.

[84] In Tamil we have this pattern and is called *antātit toṭai*, i.e. the word which ends a line or a stanza starts the next line or next stanza.

[85] Watson, W. G. E., *Classical*, 276. He uses the designation "Repetition-initial." Compare in Tamil the *mutal maṭakku*, i.e. repetition of the initial word or phrase.

[86] Ib. He calls it "end-repetition", or "epistrophe", cf. ib., note 10. Compare our Tamil *kaṭai maṭakku*, lit. repetition of the end (word or phrase).

[87] Krintezki, L., *Das Hohe*, 69-70 cites SS 1:5bd; 4:8a9a10a11a; 8:7bc; 8:11d12c as cases of epiphora. It is doubtful whether one can speak of these cases as epiphora in the strict sense of the definition.

CHAPTER 3.

SYMBOLISM IN THE SONG OF SONGS

Symbolism in the Song of Songs is studied in this chapter under three sections: A. Sound element or sonority; B. Rhetorical devices; C. Imagery. Some of what will be said in this chapter may overlap with what has been seen under poetry of the Song of Songs.

Symbolism works out basically in the artistic and successful handling of the sound system of a language. The poetic or rather rhetorical devices serve at the level of words and phrases to build up symbolism. Then comes the symbolic language proper which consists in the use of simile and metaphor which are the essential elements of imagery.

A. **Sound Element or Sonority**

The sound element [1] in symbolism of any language depends very much on the pronunciation of the letters. Two points have to be kept in mind with regard to Hebrew: (i) There is no such thing as *the* pronunciation of Hebrew. For its pronunciation developed, evolved and also changed over the centuries. (ii) In spite of a certain levelling effect brought about by the collection of Hebrew poetry into the canon, relics of these language variations remain.[2]

Sound symbolism has two aspects: a) the symbolic use of the vowels; b) the symbolic use of the consonants: for example, where there is a prevalence of the use of vowels – especially long vowels – there is a predominance of sensuous emotions.[3] In the same way, the duplication of a root consonant in the verb gives to the verb an intensive or a factitive force. The Hebrew poet availed himself of this technique of doubled consonant for expressing emphasis and urgency, impression of weight

---

[1] For annotated bibliography, see Alonso Schökel, L., *Estudios*, 71-77; general considerations on phonetics and texts with ample bibliography in 77-86; specimen studies in Isaiah and some other prophets 86-110; general conclusions, 110-117. Smith, G. A., *The Early Poetry*, Lecture I, 1-25 on sound elements in Hebrew poetry. Watson, W. G. E., *Classical*, 222-250, quite a clear exposition with examples and bibliography. Krinetzki, L., *Das Hohe*, 59-61 application of the sound symbolism (Die Lautsymbolik) to the Song of Songs. Alonso Schökel, L., *El Cantar*, 105-107.

[2] Watson, W. G. E., *Classical*, 222.

[3] Casanowicz, I. M., *Paronomasia*, 6-9 with bibliography.

and mass, or for lingering melody.[4] The doubled consonant increases the staccato effect, gives the voice something to grip and roll upon. It may symbolize grief, scorn, or hate. It is used for the ringing forth of joy and triumph.[5] In short, the sound element of a language becomes the echo to the sense or emotion contained in the expression.[6] The sound factor translates the concrete thing.[7] The sound symbolism however belongs essentially to the original language and it is very difficult, if not impossible, to translate or reproduce it in the receptor language.[8] The sound element may also contribute for the general structure of the poem.[9]

1. *Assonance*

The simplest definition of assonance is that it is "a form of *vowel* repetition."[10] Assonance in the narrower sense is "the likeness of vowels without that of the consonants in the end syllables of words."[11] From the psychological point of view assonance is "an endeavour to reproduce by means of the close connection or juxtaposition of like sounding words that internal sensation of the Beautiful which is intended to affect the ear."[12] Since both assonance and alliteration are based on the principle of repetition, there is some lack of precision in the definitions given by authors.[13]

Assonance serves in the sound symbolism for the following purposes:

– Aesthetico-emphatic purpose.[14]

– Prevalence of long vowels â and ô in a verse may symbolize the grandeur, the majesty, the fulness or may evoke peace.[15]

---

[4] Smith, G. A., *The Early Poetry*, 5. Somewhat analogical features are found also in Tamil, e.g. *valittal vikāram*, i.e. hardening of soft consonants.

[5] Ib., 7.

[6] Cf. Casanowicz, I. C., *Paronomasia*, 7.

[7] Cf. Krinetzki, L., *Das Hohe*, 59.

[8] Cf. Alonso Schökel, L., *Estudios*, 113-117; Id., "Poésie", *DBS*, VIII, col. 57.

[9] Alonso Schökel, L., "Poésie", *DBS*, VIII, col. 59.

[10] Watson, W. G. E., *Classical*, 223.

[11] Casanowicz, I. M., *Paronomasia*, 3-4. This is equal to what W. G. E. Watson mentions in note 3, p. 223 as "final-vowel assonance" or "vocalic rhyme".

[12] Saydon, P. P., "Assonance in Hebrew as a Means of Expressing Emphasis", *Bib.* 36 (1955), 36-50 & 287-304. The definition is found in p. 37.

[13] E.g. compare the definition of P. P. Saydon with that of W. G. E. Watson. I. M. Casanowicz's idea of assonance is not clear in *Paronomasia*, 33 – he seems to include repetition of consonants in assonance. As W. G. E. Watson notes, "there is some overlap between alliteration (of consonants) and assonance (of vowels)". – Ib., 223.

[14] P. P. Saydon devotes both his articles for showing the emphatic purpose of assonance, see note 12 above.

[15] Alonso Schökel, L., "Poésie", *DBS*, VIII, col. 59.

– The final -a, can serve as the symbol of feminine nature.

– Sound symbolism is present in those cases where the sound of the keyword (Leitwort) becomes the key sound (Leitklang) of one or many verses.[16]

Example: SS 6:2a. The vowel sounds come so well that while pronouncing the three words, the sonority paints the picture of the Lover going down (*yārad*) and getting into his garden: The sequence of the sounds is: ô - î - ā - a - ĕ - a - ô: a movement through a valley. We may notice also the symmetrically sonorous phrases beginning with *lamedh* and ending in ô(2a) or ôt(2bc) or ōṭ(2d). SS 6:2cd is a very good example for assonance(i-ô), alliteration(l,š) and end-rhyme(îm).

2. *Alliteration*

We may define alliteration as the repetition or reproduction of the same consonant or juxtaposition of similar-sounding consonants within a unit of verse.[17] Some features of alliteration are:

– alliteration refers to *consonants,* not vowels.

– alliteration is taken in its wider sense of consonant repetition and is *not* confined to word-initial alliteration.

– near-alliteration is constituted by similar-sounding consonants considered to be equivalent.

– alliterative-clusters are also included under alliteration[18]

According to I. M. Casanowicz, the following consonants alliterate with each other:

– ʼ with ʻ
– **b** with **p**
– **q** with **g,k** and vice versa
– **d** with **ṭ,t** and vice versa
– **z** with **s,ś** and vice versa
– **s** with **ś,š** and vice versa
– **ḥ** with **k** - rarely.[19]

---

[16] Ib.

[17] Different definitions are attempted by authors. See Watson, W. G. E., *Classical,* 225 & 227; and Casanowicz, I. M., *Paronomasia,* 3.

[18] Cf. Watson, W. G. E., *Classical,* 225-226.

[19] Cf. Casanowicz, I. M., *Paronomasia,* 28-29.

The functions of alliteration are: Being an integral part of poetic form, alliteration gives cohesion to the components of line, strophe, stanza or poem.[20] It may be a vehicle of taunting, sorrow, threat and invective.[21] Alliteration focuses the attention of the audience on the physical details of a person or object etc.[22]

Example: SS 2:8cd: mĕdallēg ʿal-hĕhārîm
mĕgappēṣ ʿal-haggĕbāʿôt

The combination of ĕ - a - ē with *doubled consonants of l,p* (in Piel form) concretizes the jumping action, while *ʿal* gives the sound effect of passing over.

3. *Rhyme*

In general, when two words in proximity or immediate succession, sound the same, they are said to be words in rhyme. The commonest form of rhyme in Hebrew poetry is end-rhyme.[23] The vast majority of the rhymes found in the Old Testament poetry are formed:

(i) by the recurrence of the same pronominal suffixes;
(ii) occasionally on the plural termination, îm or ôt;
(iii) rarely on the plural termination of the verbs.[24]

Rhyme may serve: e.g. to link the components of a poem: SS 2:7ab; to link together two lines: SS 1:9ab; to show a contrast: SS 6:11a, 12a.[25]

4. *Onomatopoeia*

Onomatopoeia is defined as "the imitation of a sound *within the rules of the language*."[26] Onomatopoeia is different from mimicry and

---

[20] Rankin, O. S., "Alliteration in Hebrew Poetry", *JTS* 31 (1930), 285; this type of alliteration is called also "constitutive alliteration", Watson, W. G. E., *Classical*, 226, note 11.
[21] Rankin, O. S., *JTS* 31 (1930), 289.
[22] W. G. E. Watson enumerates three other functions: mnemonic, vocative and endstop, cf. *Classical*, 228.
[23] I. M. Casanowicz, defines rhyme as "the agreement of sound at the end of words", *Paronomasia*, 3.
[24] Smith, G. A., *The Early Poetry*, 25.
[25] Cf. Krinetzki, L., *Das Hohe*, 56.
[26] Watson, W. G. E., *Classical*, 234.

from paronomasia.[27] Onomatopoeia and paronomasia belong to linguistic field and can be lexicalized, though both of them operate with sound and bring out to a certain degree the picturesque and plastic element of language.[28] Sound element in onomatopoeia materializes the sense.[29]

Example: SS 1:2a. The sound effect of the action of kissing is materialized in the pronunciation of *yiššāqēnî minněšîqôt pîhû,* where the root *nšq* means "to kiss."

5. *Pun*

Pun or wordplay is based on *lexical ambiguity,* and exploits the polyvalency of a word. Lexical polyvalency is of two kinds: homonymy (words identical in sound – homophones and homographs – but different in meaning) and polysemy (one and the same word with several meanings).[30] The sound element may be in contrast with the sense.[31] Like in a play or game, there is a constant displacement in word*play* between the phonetic material and the sense.[32] There are various forms of wordplay.[33] What was a wordplay for the original hearers of a literary piece may not appear to be one to later generations or vice versa.[34]

---

[27] Ib. Mimicry is the imitation of sound by a human. Mimicry is achieved through imitation by means of voice-production or of gestures. Onomatopoeia is produced in written language (hence can be lexicalized), comes to effect when pronounced aloud and thus creates association between the expression and the meaning and the ultimate object. For differences between onomatopoeia and paronomasia, cf Casanowicz, I. M., *Paronomasia*, 4-5.

[28] Cf. Casanowicz, I. M., *Paronomasia*, 4. L. P. Wilkinson divides onomatopoeia into seven types: (i) Imitation of sounds; (ii) Sympathetic mouth-gesture; (iii) Expressive mouth-gesture; (iv) Significant euphony and cacophony; (v) Significant rhythm; (vi) Metaphor from verse-technique; (vii) Metaphor from word-form. See, "Onomatopoeia and the Sceptics", *ClasQ* 36 (1942), 121-133, esp. 129-133.

[29] Alonso Schökel, L., "Poésie", *DBS*, VIII, col. 59.

[30] Watson, W. G. E., *Classical*, 237f.

[31] Cf. Alonso Schökel, L., "Poésie", *DBS*, VIII, col. 60.

[32] Peeters, L., "Pour une interprétation du jeu de mots", *Semitics* 2 (1971/72), 127-142, esp. 128 for this statement.

[33] Watson, W. G. E., *Classical*, 238-242.

[34] This seems to be true for ancient languages like Hebrew, Ugaritic etc. In so far as the punning depends strictly on the consonant combinations, the control is easier than in matters where vowels are involved. For discussion on this aspect and some general guidelines, see Holladay, W. L., "Form and Wordplay in David's Lament over Saul and Jonathan", *VT* 20 (1970), 153-189; Eitan, I., "La répétition de la racine en hébreu", *JPOS* 1 (1921), 171-186.

Example: SS 5:4. The word *yād* is used in double meaning, i.e. hand and penis.[35]

6. *Paronomasia*

Paronomasia lies somewhere between homonyms and polysemes.[36] It is also called "annomination."[37] In Hebrew terminology, it is called "*lāšôn mophēl ʿal lāšôn.*"[38] Paronomasia is based on similar sounding words of *different* meaning.[39] L. Peeters defines paronomasia as "un jeu sur une légère altération sonore du mot créant une tension entre les deux sens confrontés par ce changement sonore."[40]

Example: SS 7:14ad: dûdā'îm - dôdî

B. Rhetorical and Poetic Devices

Certain premiminary remarks are in order before the various devices are indicated: The distinction between structural and non-structural devices cannot be exact and so a certain overlapping will occur. So also the distinction between rhetorical and poetic devices cannot be accurately defined to the satisfaction of everyone. The poetic devices do not occur in isolation but within the context of a poem.[41] In the following pages only those rhetorical and poetic devices that have been certainly verified in the Song of Songs are briefly treated.

1. *Refrain*

Refrain is one form of repetition and it may be defined as a block of verse which recurs more than once within a literary piece.[42] Main characteristics of a refrain are:

– Its distinguishing feature is its structuring function.

– Refrain is the repetition of at least one stichos or a complete phrase.[43]

---

[35] Watson, W. G. E., *Classical*, 242.

[36] Ib.

[37] Peeters, L., *Semitics* 2 (1971/72), 139; Krinetzki, L., *Das Hohe*, 61.

[38] Glück, J. J. "Paronomasia in Biblical Literature", *Semitics* 1 (1970), 52.

[39] Cf. Watson, W. G. E., *Classical*, 238.

[40] Peeters, L., *Semitics* 2 (1971/72), 139.

[41] Watson, W. G. E., *Classical*, 273.

[42] Ib., 295 (with a small modification by me).

[43] Watson, W. G. E., *Classical*, 295. He says that a refrain can comprise a single word. When, however, a single word is repeated within a poem, it is usually termed "word-repetition" or "key-word" and the designation "refrain" cannot fit it.

– It is different from inclusion or envelope figure, which occurs only in the beginning and end of a poetic piece.

– Refrain rarely begins a poem.

From the point of view of the function in a poetic unit, the refrain is divided into the following types:[44] (i) Introductory sentence refrain; (ii) Concluding sentence refrain; (iii) Internal refrain; (iv) Suspended refrain.[45]

Examples: a) Strict refrains: SS 2:7; 3:5, 8:4 (with substitution of *'im* with *mah*): conclude a poem or a strophe.[46]

b) Refrains with all elements but in reverse order: SS 2:16; 6:3. Variant of this type: 7:11.

c) Other refrains: (i) SS 2:17; 4:6; cf. 2:9; 8:14 - gazelle resemblance.

(ii) SS 2:6; 8:3 - about embrace.[47]

2. *Allusion*

"Allusion is the reference (usually not explicit) within one body of literature to the culture and letters of another body."[48]

Allusion may be classified as: (i) Inner-biblical allusion: allusion to events, persons etc. within the Bible. (ii) Extra-biblical allusion: allusion to what is found in extrabiblical literature.

Examples: SS 1:5: allusion to Solomon – a biblical personality
SS 8:6: allusion to the mythical god "Mot."[49]

3. *Hyperbole*

Hyperbole is a rhetorical device common to most literatures and it belongs to economy of expression. It is defined as a way of expressing exaggeration of some kind (e.g.size, number, strength etc.) using common language. The main function of hyperbole is to replace overworked

---

[44] W. G. E. Watson, enumerates as sub-types of refrain: (1) strict refrain; (ii) variant refrain; (iii) chorus – all based on structural features. Cf. *Classical*, 295-296.

[45] Crenshaw, J. L., "A Liturgy of Wasted Opportunity", *Semitics*, 1 (1970), 27-37, esp. 27-30.

[46] W. G. E. Watson gives SS 5:8 under strict refrain. *Classical*, 295. It should rather be treated as variant refrain.

[47] For the functions of refrains in the Song of Songs, see Murphy, R. E., *VT* 29 (1979), 436-437; Exum, J. C., *ZAW* 85 (1973), 51ff.

[48] Watson, W. G. E., *Classical*, 299.

[49] Ib., 301.

adjectives with a word or phrase which conveys the same meaning more effectively. The languages which are not rich in adjectives tend to be rich in hyperbolic expressions.[50] Hyperbole is used for a number of purposes.[51]

Example: SS 2:8cd-9ab: speed of the Lover.

4. *Merismus*

Merismus "consists in detailing the individual members, or some of them – usually the first and last, or the more prominent – of a series, and thereby indicating either the genus of which those members are species or the abstract quality which characterises the genus and which the species have in common."[52] In short, merismus is "énumération de quelques membres au lieu de la série complète."[53] Merismus is akin to synecdoche and may be considered as a form of ellipsis.[54] Merismus is different from hendiadys in that "hendiadys describes an object by alluding to its qualities or attributes under two or more different categories, while merismus sets forth its extension on one plane."[55] Merismus is an abbreviated way of expressing a totality.[56] Polar word-pairs help to construct the most abridged and perfect merismus, though every polar word-pair need not be meristic in function. Thus merismus is a functional designation.[57] Merismus can also be expressed by chiastic parallelism and gender-matched parallelism.[58] Merismus is governed by the principle of economy and the unifying nature of merismus counters the polarizing effect of its components.[59]

Example: SS 4:16a: North wind and south wind.[60]

---

[50] Ib., 316-321.

[51] Eybers, I. H., "Some Examples of Hyperbole in Biblical Hebrew", *Semitics* 1 (1970), 38-49.

[52] Honeyman, A. M., "*Merismus* in Biblical Hebrew", *JBL* 71 (1952), 13-14.

[53] Alonso Schökel, L., "Poésie", *DBS*, VIII, col. 57 and col. 70.

[54] Cf. Honeyman, A. M., *JBL* 71 (1952), 13f.

[55] Ib., 17.

[56] Watson, W. G. E., *Classical*, 321.

[57] L. Alonso Schökel says: "Le mérisme embrasserait les binômes polaires, la division en deux parties et les termes corrélatifs. Ses formes fondamentales sont la forme binaire et la forme ternaire; au-delà, on entre dans l'énumération", "Poésie", *DBS*, VIII, col. 70.

[58] Cf. Watson, W. G. E., *Classical*, 323.

[59] Ib., 324.

[60] Berger, P. R., "Zu den Strophen des 10 Psalms", *UF* 2 (1970), 11; Krašovec, J., *Der Merismus im Biblisch-Hebräischen und Nordwestsemitischen*, Biblica et Orientalia - 33, Rome 1977, 138.

5. *Hendiadys*

Hendiadys means literally "one through two," i.e. one idea by means of two words. The words may be collocated, or joined by a copula, or put in apposition. The important aspect of hendiadys is that its components are no longer considered separately but as a single unit in combination. Hendiadys has some affinity with parallel word-pairs.[61] Hendiadys is used for various purposes: e.g. as surrogate for adverb; as hyperbole etc.

Example: SS 2:3c: two verbs in hendiadys used for assonance.[62]

6. *Ballast Variant*

"A ballast variant is simply a *filler,* its function being to fill out a line of poetry that would otherwise be too short."[63] C.H. Gordon, who coined this phrase, says: "If a major word in the first stichos is not paralleled in the second, then one or more of the words in the second stichos tend to be longer than their counterparts in the first stichos."[64] This is a feature of parallelism and is a corollary of the theory of balance.[65] Hence the main function of this device is to maintain the balance of colon-length. Its function may occasionally be also climactic.[66]

Example: SS 6:10: *kĕ* is balanced by *kĕmô* but in reversed order.

7. *List*

The list is a catalogue of nouns set out consecutively. There are three types of lists: (i) simple list; (ii) list with a final total; (iii) list with an initial total. More often than not, rhythm and metre will be present in these lists in poetry.[67]

Example: SS 4:14: list with a final total.

8. *Irony*

Irony is the figure of speech in which the literal meaning becomes subordinate to the derived meaning. Very often the opposite of what is expressed in words is meant.[68]

Example: SS 1:6de. "They put me to guard the vineyards,
My own vineyard I did not guard!"

---

[61] Cf. Watson, W. G. E., *Classical*, 324-328.
[62] Ib., 328.
[63] Ib., 344.
[64] *UT*, 135.
[65] Compare G. B. Gray's "incomplete parallelism with compensation."
[66] Cf. Watson, W. G. E., *Classical*, 346.
[67] Ib., 351f.
[68] W. G. E. Watson defines irony: "Irony is present when the literal meaning is nonsensical and it has to be replaced by a derived meaning, usually in direct opposition to the superficial sense" ib. 307.

9. *Synecdoche and Metonymy*

Metonymy is the use of one word for another. Synecdoche is present when the part stands for the whole, or the species for the genus (and the other way round).[69]

Example: SS 5:16a: Metonymy
SS 7:3a: Synecdoche.

10. *Rhetorical Question*

Rhetorical question is one which is posed not for obtaining an answer or information but for producing a rhetorical effect, e.g. to attract attention; to express emphatically certain sentiment etc.

Example: SS 6:10a: Admiration – calling the attention.

11. *Personification and Apostrophe*

Personification and Apostrophe (Anrede) are somewhat overlapping. Personification consists in considering inanimate things or animals as persons and in attributing personal qualities to them. Apostrophe consists in addressing inanimate things and speaking to them, or addressing persons who are not present. Apostrophe looks more to the technique of the speaker to express his personal feelings through this medium.

Examples: SS 4:16ab - Wind is personified
SS 8:12b - Solomon is addressed.

12. *Repetition*

Repetition is a generic term under which many of the items already seen can be brought:

a) Sound repetition: Assonance, alliteration, rhyme
b) Word repetition: Word-pairs, key-words, etc.
c) Repetition of (i) a phrase: inclusion
(ii) a complete line: refrain
(iii) structural patterns: parallelism etc.

Repetition of verbal roots strengthens or augments the feelings expressed in those words so formed: e.g. intensity, urgency, etc..[70] Such device is used in SS 2:7c; 3:5c; 8:4c, i.e. the verb is repeated in another form, in preference to intensive form.[71]

[69] Ib., 133, note 46.
[70] Muilenburg, J., *VTS* 1 (1953), 97-111, esp. 101-102; Eitan, I., *JPOS* 1 (1921), 171-186.
[71] Eitan, I., *JPOS* 1 (1921), 182.

C. **Imagery**

An image is "a figure of speech expressing some similarity or analogy."[72] Most images are metaphorical, but not all metaphors or comparisons are images. "Imagery ... may be defined as 'words or phrases denoting a sense-perceptible object, used to designate not that object but some other object of thought belonging to a different order or category of being'."[73] In its wider sense imagery means all the formal features of style and composition including the verbal figures. But in the narrower sense it is applied to metaphor and simile.[74] Imagery must be (i) concrete and sense-related, not based on abstract concepts; (ii) should contain an element of surprise. The aim of imagery in poetry is to work on the feelings, in oratory to produce vividness of description. In both cases there is an attempt to stir the feelings.[75]

The whole question of imagery turns around the principle of substitution. S. J. Brown has concisely schematized various images as follows:

Substitution with Comparison	1) Literal comparison		
	2) Explicit Figurative Comparison: Simile	In narrative form	a) Parable b) Fable
	3) Implicit Figurative Comparison: Metaphor	In narrative form	Allegory
	4) Minor Forms of Imagery: Personification, Metonymy, Synecdoche		
Conventional Substitution without Comparison	Symbolism	Literary, artistic, religious, etc. Emblems and Emblem Literature.[76]	

---

[70] Muilenburg, J., *VTS* 1 (1953), 97-111, esp. 101-102; Eitan, I., *JPOS* 1 (1921), 171-186.

[71] Eitan, I., *JPOS* 1 (1921), 182.

[72] Watson, W. G. E., *Classical*, 251. For annotated bibliography, see Alonso Schökel, L., *Estudios*, 269-277: general works on imagery and works on biblical imagery; 278-282: on "language of images"; 282-297: on the image of water; 297-304: on mountains and Zion; 304-307: three other images – all of them particularly in relation to the books of prophets, esp. Isaiah. Brown, S. J., *Image and Truth: Studies in the Imagery of the Bible*, Rome 1955 is very useful. Watson, W. G. E., *Classical*, 251-272 with bibliography. On the Song of Songs: Grill, S., *Die Symbolsprache des Hohenliedes*, Heiligenkreuz 1970²; Müller, H. P., *Vergleich und Metapher im Hohenlied*, Göttingen 1984.

[73] Brown, S. J., *Image*, 11.

[74] Cf. Fisch, H., "The Analogy of Nature. A Note on the Structure of the OT Imagery", *JTS* 6 (1955), 161-173, esp. 163.

[75] Cf. "Longinus", *On the Sublime*, XV.1-2 = 187r, in *Aristotle* XXIII, London 1982, 171.

[76] Brown, S. J., *Image*, 11.

1. *Simile*

Simile and metaphor may be considered together "as different and overlapping aspects of imagery."[77] The peculiar function of the simile is that it deliberately takes two objects (or actions or situations), sets them side by side, and looks at them separately.[78] In simile the resemblance between the object and the imported image is explicitly stated.[79] The element of surprise gives effectiveness to a simile. This aspect of surprise depends somewhat on how basically similar or dissimilar are the objects thrown thus into comparison.[80] Similes are classified in different ways.[81]

The most common particle to introduce simile in Hebrew is *kĕ* and its ballast variant *kĕmô*. The other particles are: *māšal*, "to be like"; *dāmāh*, "to resemble"; *'im*: "like" (specialized meaning) and combinations of *kĕ* ... *kēn* "like...so".[82] Syntactically the simile is analysed as:

a) Comparison-receiver (Vergleichsempfänger)
b) Comparison-giver (Vergleichsspender)
c) The meeting point of the two (tertium comparationis):
e.g. SS 6:4 "You are beautiful like Jerusalem"
You — Vergleichsempfänger
Jerusalem — Vergleichsspender
Beautiful — Tertium comparationis.[83]

In our analysis of the similes in the SS, the following points have been taken into consideration and accordingly presented in the following table:

a) The association, brought out between two things of different categories by the particles *kĕ, kĕmô,* or *kĕ...kēn,* decides the presence of a simile.

b) So also the verb *dāmāh,* used with the preposition *lĕ,* indicates a simile.

c) In the table, come first the comparison-receiver, then the comparison-giver and lastly the aspect or point of resemblance (shown by some qualificative).

d) Reference to the text in SS is useful for locating the similes.

---

[77] Payne, D. F., "A Perspective on the Use of Simile in the Old Testament", *Semitics* 1 (1970), 111-125, the quotation is from pp. 111-112.

[78] Ib., 112.

[79] Brown, S. J., *Image*, 21, note 1.

[80] Cf. Payne, D. F., *Semitics* 1 (1970), 121.

[81] D. F. Payne, classifies the similes as, "inverted simile" (p. 114), "ornamental", "informative" (p. 121). Another way of classifying the similes is: hyperbolical, rhetorical, illustrative, informative, cf. ib. 117. Yet another classification is found in Watson, W. G. E., *Classical*, 258-261. Elliptic simile is what we call in Tamil *eṭuttukkāṭṭuvamai*, i.e. a simile without the particle, but put beside as example.

[82] Watson, W. G. E., *Classical*, 257f.

[83] Müller, H. P., *Vergleich*, 11.

Table of Similes

Person or object	Simile (Imported Image)	Aspect/Reference	Ref. Remark
Beloved			
1) *Self-portrait*			
a) Person:			
I	tents of Kedar	dark (1:5a)	1:5c
I	pavilions of Solomon	beautiful (1:5a)	1:5d
I	"one veiled"		1:7e
me	seal	(on your heart)	8:6a
me	seal	(on your arm)	8:6b
I	evening star		8:10d
b) Parts of the body:			
My breasts	towers		8:10b
2) *By the Lover*			
a) Person:			
You	mare	(Pharaoh's cavalry)	1:9ab
My darling (raʿyātî)	lotus	(among brambles:2:2a)	2:2b
You, my darling	Tirzah	fair (yāpāh)	6:4a
	Jerusalem	beautiful (nā'wāh)	6:4b
	Trophies	awesome	6:4c
b) Parts of the body:			
Hair	flock of goats	streaming down (4:1f)	4:1e
Hair	flock of goats	streaming down (6:5d)	6:5c
Teeth	flock of ewes	coming up washed (4:2b)	4:2a
Teeth	flock of ewes	coming up washed (6:6b)	6:6a
Palate	wine	sweet (ṭôb:7:10a)	7:10a
Lips	scarlet thread	(colour)	4:3a
Temple or Cheeks	slice of pomegranate	(form & colour)	4:3cd
Temple or Cheeks	slice of pomegranate	(form & colour)	6:7ab
Neck	tower of David	(decoration?)	4:4a
Stature	palm tree		7:8a
Breasts	stags or fawns	symmetry & movement (4:5bc)	4:5a
Breasts	clusters	(form?)	7:8b
Breasts	clusters of grapes	(form?)	7:9d
Scent of nipples	apples (scent of)		7:9e
Caresses	wine	sweet(er)	4:10c (comparison)
Fragrance of perfumes	any (kōl) spice	(fragrance)	4:10d
Fragran. of robes	fragrance of Lebanon	fragrance	4:11c

Table of Similes (contd)

Person or object	Simile (Imported Image)	Aspect/Reference	Ref. Remark
3) *Portrait by others*			
a) "Who is this!" 6:10a	Dawn	looking forth	6:10b
	Moon	fair (yāpāh)	6:10c
	Sun	shining	6:10d
	Trophies	awesome	6:10e
Shulamith (Beloved?)	dance(?)		7:1cd
b) Shulamith's body:			
Curves of thighs	ornaments		7:2c
Breasts	stag	symmetry (7:4b)	7:4a
Neck	tower of ivory		7:5a
Nose	tower of Lebanon	(overlooking Damascus) (7:5e)	7:5d
Head	Carmel		7:6a
Locks of head	purple	colour	7:6b
Lover			
Portrait by Beloved			
1) *To him (directly)*			
a) Person:			
My Love (dôdî)	apple tree	(among trees, 2:3a)	2:3b
My Love	gazelle & stag	speed (2:17cf)	2:17d
You	my brother		8:1a
My Love (dôdî)	gazelle & stag	speed (8:14d)	8:14abc
b) Parts of his body:			
Caresses	wine	sweet(er)	1:2b (comparison)
Perfumes	fragrance	sweet(er)	1:3a (comparison)
Name	perfume	(more) diffused	1:3b (comparison)
Caresses	wine	(cherish)	1:4d (comparison)
Love	smooth liquor	(cherish)	1:4e (comparison)

Table of Similes (contd)

Person or object	Simile (Imported Image)	Aspect/Reference	Ref. Remark
2) *About him (to others)*			
a) Person:			
My Love (dôdî)	gazelle & stag	speed (2:8cd)	2:9ab
b) Parts of his body:			
Locks (of hair)	raven	black	5:11bc
Eyes	doves		5:12a
Cheeks	beds of spice		5:13a
Aspect	Lebanon		5:15c
Aspect	cedar	"choice"	5:15d
Other Objects			
"Who is this?"	column of smoke	coming up (3:6b)	3:6c
LOVE	Death	strong	8:6c
PASSION	Sheol	relentless	8:6d

2. *Metaphor*

Metaphor etymologically means "transfer" or "displacement." According to Aristotle, "metaphor is the application of a strange term either transferred from the genus and applied to the species or from the species and applied to the genus, or one species to another or else by analogy."[84] This is the definition taken up by standard dictionaries and improved more or less.[85] Curiously enough, Aristotle classifies under

---

[84] Aristotle, *Aristotle XXIII, Poetics*, XXI.7 = 1457b, 81.

[85] There are specialized studies on metaphor and in great number. To cite a few: Wheelwright, P., *Metaphor and Reality*, University of Indiana Press, Bloomington 1967³, esp. 70-91, studies the epiphoric and diaphoric factors of metaphor. Caminade, P., *Image et Métaphore*: Un problème de poétique contemporaine, Collection Études Supérieures, Bordas 1970: Various opinions of authors are discussed and evaluated; bibliography on pp. 153-156. Teselle, S. M., *Speaking in Parables: A Study in Metaphor and Theology*, Fortress Press, Philadelphia 1975, 43-65 her study of poetic metaphor and radical metaphor is interesting. She examines the role of metaphor in theology. Mac Cormac, E. R., *Metaphor and Myth in Science and Religion*, Duke University Press, Durham NC 1976, 72ff for a philosophical investigation of the language of metaphor. Kurz, G., *Metapher, Allegorie, Symbol*, Vandenhoeck & Ruprecht, Göttingen 1982, examines various theories of metaphor, and his remarks on "Bildspender" and "Bildempfänger"

metaphor what we would call synecdoche (from species to the genus and from genus to the species), and probably also what we call metonymy (from one species to another).[86] In the modern linguistics, the theory of metaphor is still being discussed and there are at least two methods of analysis of metaphor:

a) Theory of metaphor based on the principle of proportion:[87] While Aristotle used the principle of analogy for his fourth type of metaphor, S. J. Brown analyses metaphor on the principle of proportion: "The truth, therefore, of a given metaphor depends upon the truth of an implied equation, an equation not between two objects belonging to different spheres of being (life and a river for instance, or moral degradation and mire), but between two relations, or to use a mathematical term, two *ratios*. The mind perceives an analogy between these two relations, and uses one as an illustration of the other."[88] Metaphor consists not merely, as does all analogy, in a proportion (an equation of simple ratios), but in a proportion between proportions.[89]

b) Theory of metaphor based on "the overlap of two word meanings":[90] Behind this theory lies the definition of metaphor as "an abbreviated simile."[91]

Rhetoricians seem to agree on the following points:

– It is the mark of great natural ability to make correct and balanced use of metaphor. For the ability to use metaphor well implies a perception of resemblances.[92]

---

are analogical with the study of simile by Müller, H. P., *Vergleich*, 11f. For a deeper and multi-disciplinary discussion, see Ricoeur, P., *The Rule of Metaphor* (La Métaphore vive), trans. R. Czerny et alii, University of Toronto Press, Toronto 1984. The study begins with classical rhetoric, passes through semiotics and semantics, and finally reaches hermeneutics; bibliography on pp. 369-380. For a specialized semiotic discussion on metaphor, see Eco, U., *Semiotics and the Philosophy of Language*, Indiana University Press, Bloomington 1984, 87-129 on metaphor.

[86] Eco, U., *Semiotics*, 89ff for discussion.

[87] Brown, S. J., *Image*, 19-21.

[88] Ib., 41.

[89] Ib., 42. E.g. a:b::x:y = Preacher:enlightenment::light:lighting. Cause:effect::cause^1:effect^1 cf. 42-43. Another facet of proportion theory is the "tenor - vehicle - ground" theory. See Good, E. M., "Ezekiel's Ship: Some Extended Metaphors in the Old Testament", *Semitics* 1 (1970), 79-103, esp. 79-81.

[90] Watson, W. G. E., *Classical*, 263.

[91] Cf. Eco, U., *Semiotics*, 90.

[92] Aristotle, *Aristotle XXIII, Poetics*, XXII 16-17 = 1459a. 89-91.

– Metaphor is part and parcel of poetry. So much so that to understand poetry involves coming to grips with metaphor and metaphorical expressions.[93]

– The natural tendency of metaphor "seems to be to darken rather than to clarify thought."[94]

– Since the creation and use of metaphor would seem to be the outcome of an emotional mood reacting on the imagination, to grasp the significance of metaphor there is needed an imagination equal in intensity and vividness to that which first evoked it.[95]

In our study, we follow the second theory on metaphor, i.e. the theory which considers the metaphor as an abbreviated simile. In other words, those cases where the comparative particle is substituted by simple identificaion of the object with the imported image, are taken as metaphors. Following is the table of metaphors used in the SS:

Table of Metaphors

Person or object	Metaphor (Imp. Image)	Aspect	Reference
Beloved			
1) *Self-portrait*			
a) Person:			
My (?)	vineyard	(to be guarded)	1:6e
I	crocus of plain		2:1a
	lotus of valley		2:1b
I	a wall		8:10a

[93] Watson, W. G. E., *Classical*, 263.

[94] Brown, S. J., *Image*, 21-26. U. Eco says: "It is obvious that when someone creates metaphors, he is, literally speaking, *lying* – as everybody knows... he *pretends* to make assertions, and yet wants to assert *seriously* something that is beyond literal truth", *Semiotics*, 89.

[95] Cf. Brown, S. J., *Image*, 26. Compare Varadarajan, M., *Ilakkiyat-Tiṟaṉ*, Pari Nilaiyam, Madras 1965², 80-98, where this ability is termed as "literary transmigration".

Table of Metaphors (contd)

Person or object	Metaphor (Imp. Image)	Aspect	Reference
2) *Portrait by Lover*			
a) Person:			
(Beloved)	my dove		2:14a
	my dove		5:2d
	my dove		6:9a
My sister, bride	a locked garden		4:12a
	a locked pool		4:12b
	a sealed spring		4:12b
	a garden spring		4:15a
	a well	(living water)	4:15b
(Beloved?)	my vineyard	(before me)	8:12a.[96]
(Beloved?)	mountain of myrrh		4:6c?
	hill of frankincense		4:6d?
b) Parts of her body:			
Stature	palm tree		7:9b
Eyes	doves		1:15c
Eyes	doves		4:1c
Breasts	fruit-stalks		7:9c
3) *Portrait by others*			
Onlookers:			
(Beloved?)	Shulamith		7:1ac
Vulva	round bowl		7:3a.[97]
Belly	heap of wheat		7:3c
Eyes	pools in Heshbon		7:5c
Brothers:			
Sister (Beloved?)	a wall		8:9a
	a door		8:9c
Lover			
Portrait by Beloved:			
My Love (dôdî)	a bundle of myrrh		1:13a
My Love	a cluster of henna		1:14a
Head	finest gold		5:11a
Lips	lotuses		5:13c
Arms	rods of gold		5:14a
Loins	plate of ivory		5:14c
Legs	alabaster pillars		5:15a
Other Metaphors			
Its (Love's) darts	darts of fire		8:6e
Its (Love's) fire	divine flame		8:6f

[96] Krinetzki, L., *Das Hohe*, 63.

[97] For *šrr* or *šr* meaning "vulva" see Vogt, E., "Einige hebräische Wortbedeutun-

We may bring here under metaphor, the names of historical persons and of geographical places found in the Song of Songs. Most of them – perhaps even all of them – are there not so much for their proper meanings or designations as for their symbolical or metaphorical significations;[98] e.g. Solomon comes almost always in the Song of Songs as a symbol of grandeur and of love-relationship: SS 1:5; 3:6,9,11. So also the geographical names of En-geddi etc. Even the names of common objects by being brought together intentionally into a context of love-affair-description, take on symbolical meanings.[99]

3. *Landscape: Nature: Images*

The landscape and nature that are encountered in the Song of Songs have affected the creation, invention and use of images. There are two main landscapes that are seen in the Song of Songs:

a) Natural Landscape:

(i) Cultivated country side (vineyard, etc.)

(ii) Wild landscape (mountains, hills, etc.)

b) Civilized ambient:

(i) Exterior (city streets, public squares)

(ii) Interior (house, hall, rooms, etc.)

All the images that occur in the different poems may be classified according to these four landscapes and the Nature that is reflected in them. What is interesting to see is that, as a rule, love-affair is at home in natural landscape, but it is thereatened by the society in the civilized environment, though the interior quarters are favourable for love-making.[100] These different landscapes and images connected with them help us to individuate the various poems which make up the anthology.

The images may be objects or actions: Object-images are the similes, metaphors or symbols. Action-images are expressed by verbs and are connected with the activities of the senses: e.g. seeing, hearing, touching, tasting etc. Both the object-images and action-images may vary according to the theme treated in individual poems: e.g. when the theme of search is

---

gen", *Bib.* 48 (1967), 57-74, esp. 69-72. See discussion in Lys, D., *Le plus beau*, 257-259 with bibliography.

[98] Cf Krinetzki, L., *Das Hohe*, 66-67.

[99] Buzy, D., "Un chef-d'oeuvre de poésie pure: le Cantique des Cantiques", dans *Memorial Lagrange*, Gabalda, Paris, 1940, 155-162.

[100] Falk, M., *Love Lyrics*, 88ff. See also Krauss, S., "Die 'Landschaft' im biblischen Hohenliede", *MGWJ* 78 (1934), 81-97.

treated, the action-images like "going out, searching, calling, asking, finding" will naturally be found.[101] When it is a question of contemplation or possession, the sensuous images are found.[102]

D. Specimen Study of SS 1:2-4

a) *Translation*

v.2 Oh that he might kiss me with the kisses of his mouth!
Indeed, sweeter are your caresses than wine,

v.3 Than any fragrance are your perfumes more pleasing,
Than any perfume is your name more diffused,
That is why the maidens love you.

v.4 Draw me with you, let us run;
May the king take me into his chambers!
Let us rejoice and delight in you,
We will cherish your caresses more than wine,
More than smooth liquor, your love!

b) *Delimitation*

There is a general consent among commentators that SS 1:2-4 makes one poem. That this poem is a complete unit is marked off by the following elements:

(i) The speaker is the Beloved and the addressee is the Lover, while the following poem is addressed to the girls of Jerusalem.

(ii) The context of this poem is the place of encounter.

(iii) There is an envelope figure between v. 2b and 4d while there is a semantic inclusion between 2a and 4e.

(iv) The metre changes in v. 5 – an indication of another unit.

c) *Notes on translation*

The proposed translation needs some justification as it has some quite new elements:

---

[101] Alonso Schökel, L., "Poésie", *DBS*, VIII, cols. 77-82.

[102] Murphy, R. E., "A Biblical Model of Human Intimacy: The Song of Songs", *Concilium*, XIV, 1 (1979), 61-66, esp. 64.

v.2: The word *nĕšîqôt* is a dislegomenon (here and in Prov. 27:6) and the cognate verb in Ugaritic is used of kissing in love-making, e.g. UT 52:49-51.[103] *Min* is partitive. The particle *kî* is asseverative.[104] The adjective *ṭôbîm* should be rendered by "sweet" – here comparative "sweeter".[105] The shift of person from third to second ("your caresses") has provoked many emendations.[106] S. Gevirtz has shown that the alteration of grammatical person within one sentence or unit of thought is a peculiarity of West Semitic rhetoric.[107] *dōdêka* is to be translated by "caresses" which fits more concretely in the context than either "breasts" (excluded by the context – the speaker is the Beloved) or "love" – which is abstract, while the imported image for comparison is "wine" – a concrete object.[108]

v.3: The *lamedh* in 3a is parsed as *lamedh comparativum* balancing the *min* in 2b.[109] The word *tûraq* in 3b is a hapax and a crux. Various suggestions have been made on different grounds.[110] R. Gordis and A. Robert take *tûraq* as Hoph. Imperf. from *ryq* "pour forth diffuse," and consider *šemen* as susceptible of being taken as feminine.[111] Recent studies have well established that in Northwest Semitic *t-* serves as a

---

[103] Pope, M. H., *Song*, 297.

[104] Albright, W. F., "Archaic", *Fs.G.R.Driver*, 2, note 3. On the particle itself see Gordis, R., "The Asseverative *kaph* in Ugaritic and Hebrew", *JAOS* 63 (1943), 176-178: Muilenburg, J., "The Linguistic and Rhetorical Usage of the Particle *kî* in the Old Testament", *HUCA* 32 (1961), 135-160.

[105] Albright, W. F., "Archaic", *Fs.G.R.Driver*, 2; Dahood, M. J., "Hebrew-Ugaritic Lexicography-II", *Bib.* 45 (1964), 410; Id., *Psalms* I, 206; *UT*, Glossary n. 1028; *WuS*, n. 1100.

[106] E.g. Hirschberg, H. H., "Some Additional Arabic Etymologies in Old Testament Lexicography", *VT* 11 (1961), 377 makes four emendations.

[107] Gevirtz, S., "On Canaanite Rhetoric: The Evidence of the Amarna Letters from Tyre", *Or* 42 (1973), 170-171 for examples from Phoenician, Aramaic, Ugaritic and Hebrew; cf. e.g. Ex. 21:2-6; Dt. 32:15; Is. 1:29, etc.

[108] See Robert, A., *Le Cantique*, 63 & 432; Gevirtz, S., *Or* 42 (1973), 170.

[109] Driver, G. R., "Hebrew Notes on 'Song of Songs' and 'Lamentations', in *Fs. Alfred Bertholet*, Tübingen 1950, 134 takes it as lamedh emphaticum. On lamedh comparativum, see Fitzmyer, J. A., "Lᵉ as a Preposition and a Particle in Micah 5,1(5,2)", *CBQ* 18 (1956), 10-13; Albright, W. F., "Archaic", *Fs. G. R. Driver* 2; *UT*, Grammar 10:1; Dahood, M.J., *Bib.* 45 (1964), 410; Id., *Ugaritic-Hebrew Philology*, Rome 1965, 30; Id., "Hebrew - Ugaritic Lexicography - IV", *Bib.* 47 (1966), 406.

[110] Some have recommended consonantal changes: See *BHK*; *BHS*; Hamp, V., "Zur Textkritik im Hohenlied", *BZ.NF.* 1 (1957), 212 to read "*tamrûq*" according to Es. 2:3,9,12. To read *mûraq* on the basis of LXX (Aq) and Vulgate (*BHK*; *BHS*; *NEB*). Others have retained the consonantal *tûraq* and explain: (i) K. N. Schoville translates "thy name is *golden oil*", *The Impact*, 36, 41 and note 15; (ii) M. H. Pope renders it, "Turaq oil is your name", *Song*, 300.

[111] Gordis, R., *The Song*, 78; Robert, A., *Le Cantique*, 64.

preformative for the third masculine sing. imperfect. Hence *tûraq* can have the masc. *šemen* for subject.[112] The above translation is the result of further considerations based on poetic structure, parallelism and syntax. The lack of comparative particle before *šemen* in v.3b can be explained in one of the following ways:

a) The *lamedh comparativum* of v.3a functions as a "double-duty modifier."[113]

b) Another possibility is that the final *mem* in *ṭôbîm* is a shared consonant, functioning as the comparative *mem.*[114]

v.4: Studies on the preposition *'aḥar* show that it has the significance of "with" besides the usual "after."[115] With this rendering, the following "let us run..." is enhanced in significance. *hĕbî'anî* is parsed as precative perfect balancing the imperative in preceding colon.[116] The last colon of v.4 presents some difficulties. T. H. Gaster proposes to read *mimêrāš 'ăhābekā* and translates *mêrāš* by "new wine."[117] Many authors take *mêšārîm* as adverbial accusative.[118] Once again, on the basis of poetic structure and parallelism, a better rendering is proposed:

(i) A gradation from concrete to abstract: in you (*bāk*) – your caresses (*dōdêkā*) – your love (*'ahēbûkā*).

---

[112] For Phoenician, Harris, Z. S., *A Grammar of Phoenician Language*, 65; For Ugaritic, *UT*, Grammar 9:14-15; For Hebrew, Meyer, R., *Grammatik*, Band II, 97f. Sarna, N. M., "The Mythological Background of Job 18", *JBL* 82 (1963), 317-318; W. L. Moran, disagrees with him, see "taqtul – Third Masculine Singular?", *Bib.* 45 (1964), 80-82; Other studies on this question are Van Dijk, H. J., "Does Third Masculine Singular Taqtul exist in Hebrew?", *VT* 19 (1969), 440-447; Dahood, M. J., "Third Masculine Singular with Preformative *t-* in Nortwest Semitic", *Or* 48 (1979), 97-106 – some thirty biblical texts are studied or cited.

[113] On this term and the variety of its occurrences, see Dahood, M. J., *CBQ* 29 (1967) 574-579. It is also called "ellipsis", e.g. *UT*, Grammar 13:105.

[114] On shared consonant which is a poetic device in Northwest Semitic, see Watson, W. G. E., "Shared Consonants in Northwest Semitic", *Bib.* 50 (1969), 525-533; Id., "More on Shared Consonants", *Bib.* 52 (1971), 44-50.

[115] Scott, R. B. Y., "Secondary Meanings of *'aḥar*, after, behind", *JTS* 50 (1949), 178-179; cf. Dahood, M. J., *Greg.* 43 (1962), 69. For Ugaritic confirmation, see UT 77:32-33; Krt. 209; *UT*, Grammar 10:3.

[116] On precative perfect: Dahood, M. J., "The Grammar of the Psalter", in *Psalms. III*, Appendix, 414-417; Schoville, K. N., *The Impact*, 42-43.

[117] Gaster, T. H., "Canticles i.4", *Exp.T* 72 (1960/61), 195: The author's reference to UT 128;17-18 should be read rather UT 124:17-18; see also 2 Aqt. VI:7-8; *UT*, Glossary nn. 1558 & 2613.

[118] E. g. Robert, A., "avec raison", *Le Cantique*, 67; cf. Joüon, P., *Grammaire de l'hébreu biblique*, Rome 1965²: 126d; Pope, M. H., *Song*, 305ff, "rightly".

(ii) *'ahēbûkā* is taken as noun in parallelism with *dōdêkā*.[119]

(iii) If this parallelism is accepted, the parallelism between *miyyayin* and *mêšārîm* can be seen. K. N. Schoville's suggestion, "smooth liquor" seems to fit best.[120]

d) *Notes on metre*

(i) *Segmentation*: The poem consists of two strophes, each with peculiar structure. The structure may be described as follows:

I Strophe: A monocolon: 2a: Exclamation: A wish
A tricolon: 2b-3ab: Comparisons in gradation
A monocolon: 3c Conclusion

II Strophe: A bicolon: 4ab: A wish in two forms
A tricolon: 4cde: Rejoicing together, expressed in gradation.

(ii) *Metre*: This poem consists predominantly of metres of three accents – except the last colon of the second strophe (unless one gives two accents to *mêšārîm* and makes the total into three). We may represent the metre as:

I Strophe: 2a: —— —— ——
2b: —— —— ——
3a: —— —— ——
3b: —— —— ——
3c: —— —— ——

II Strophe: 4a: —— —— ——
4b: —— —— ——
4c: —— —— ——
4d: —— —— ——
4e: —— —— 0.

---

[119] Dahood, M. J., "Ugaritic-Hebrew Parallel Pairs", in *Ras Shamra Parallels*, Vol. I, Roma 1972, 164-165; compare *'nt* III:2-4 and 603 rev. 7-8 for Ugaritic parallels and Prov. 5:19; 7:18 for Hebrew. *NEB* recognizes this parallelism.

[120] In T. H. Gaster's direction, R. Gordis, refers to Prov. 23:31 and suggests "fine wine", *The Song*, 78-79; Fox, M. V., "Scholia to Canticles", *VT* 33 (1983), 200 proposes "smooth wine", but he takes *mīyyên mēšārîm* together.

e) *Parallelisms*

I Strophe: 2b-3: Perfect chiastic structure or mirror symmetry or reflexive congruence: A B C : C B A

3a-3b: Partial proper congruence: A B C : A C B

In all the three cola, there is gender matched parallelism: m + m // m + m // m + m.

There is a gradation in the comparisons:

Your caresses – your perfumes – your name (from concrete to abstract, i.e. name but it stands for the person!) The tricolon is knit by the repetition of *ṭôbîm* – *ṭôbîm* – *šĕmānêkā* – *šemen*.

II Strophe: 4ab: Synonymous parallelism, since both phrases say semantically the same thing.

4cd: Synonymous parallelism

4de: There is a chiastic structure with an ellipsis of the verb: A B C : C B –.

In 4cde, there is another gradation of things pertaining to the Lover: in you – your caresses – your love (from concrete to abstract, i.e. love) The *'ăhēbûkā* of v.4e echoes the end-word of the first strophe and closes the poem.

f) *Sound elements and poetic devices*

Alliteration: Repetition of root consonants *nšq*: 2a

Word repetition: *ṭôbîm*: 2b;3a. *Yayin*: 2b;4d.
dôdîm: 2b;4d
šemen: 3ab.

Repetition of consonant clusters: *šm*: 3ab;4ace. [121]

ʿ alliterates with ʾ in 3c.

In 4cd, anaphoric alliteration of *n* – connects words and sentiments.

In 4d, repetition of *n* – *n*, makes an inclusion.

---

[121] Casanowicz, I. M., *Paronomasia*, 32 makes consonantal changes in order to bring about a comparison which appears to be forced.

Rhyme: *kā* and *k*: II suffix: 8 × altogether and *k* in 4b in *melek*.
î: 4ab – connecting the cola.
îm: 2b;3a.

Anacrusis: *kî*.

Onomatopoeia: Kissing sound and effect in *nāšaq* – *nĕšîqāh*: 2a Especially in pronouncing the word *pîhû*, the mouth comes to the position of readiness to kiss!

Paronomasia: *šĕmānêkā* – *šemen* – *šĕmekā*: 3ab.

Hyperbole: *melek*: 4b

Wordplay: *'ăhēbûkā*(3c) and *'ăhēbûkā*(4e) – slight difference in significance.

g) *Tabulation*

Verbs	*Nouns*	*Adjective/Particles*
nāšaq: to kiss	nĕšîqāh(f): kiss	ṭôb: sweet(2 ×)
rîq: to diffuse (Hop)	peh(m): mouth	kî: indeed
'āhēb: to love	dōđîm(m): caresses(2 ×)	min: from(2 ×)
māšak: to draw	yayin(m): wine(2 ×)	lĕ: from (compar.)
rûṣ: to run	rêaḥ(m): fragrance	ʿal-kēn: therefore
bô': to bring (Hiph)	šemen(m): perfume(2 ×)	'aḥar: with
gîl: to rejoice	šem(m): name	bĕ: in
śāmaḥ: to delight	ʿalmāh(f): maiden	
zākar: to cherish	melek(m): king	
	ḥeder(m): chamber	
	mêšārîm(m): liquor	
	'ahăbāh(f): love	

h) *Comments*

The verbs describe the actions of the Lover and the Beloved together, especially the verbs in the second strophe. Most of them suggest an atmosphere of love-making and enjoyment. The mood of the whole poem is one of intense longing to be together, and it is spoken by the Beloved.

There is only one adjective: *ṭôb* "sweet" and it is used both the times in comparison.

The nouns fall under two categories: The nouns which refer to exotic surroundings: wine, perfumes, fragrance, maidens, "king", chamber, and smooth liquor. The others refer to love-making: mouth, kiss, caresses, and love. It is interesting to note that the name of the Lover is included among the exotic objects such as perfumes and fragrance. The intoxicating or exotic actions of these objects are compared with the love-making actions of the Lover, and the latter are declared to be superior. Even the perfumes acquire superiority because of the Lover (v.3a). The comparison that was established in v.2b is resumed in v.4de and a definitive preferential judgement is passed. Ultimately what matters to the Beloved is "your love." It may be remarked how the poem which started with the concrete action of kissing(2a) culminates in the ecstasy of pure "love"(4e). In the centre stands "your name"(3b) which is the person and presence of the Lover and it is presented again in the "in you" of v.4c!

Part Two

Chapter 4.

HISTORICAL INTRODUCTION TO THE CLASSICAL TAMIL LITERATURE

A. Literary Material Extant

All the literary materials that have come down to us from the Classical Age of the Tamils are in poetry. Under the designation "Classical Tamil Literature,"[1] we include the Eṭṭuttokai and the Pattuppāṭṭu. *Eṭṭuttokai* means Eight Anthologies (eṭṭu = eight; tokai = collection, anthology) and *Pattuppāṭṭu*, Ten Songs (pattu = ten; pāṭṭu = song, lay, idyll). Besides Eṭṭuttokai and Pattuppāṭṭu, we include also the most ancient descriptive Tamil grammar called Tolkāppiyam, because it is a grammar that helps us to define and elucidate our discussions on the Classical Tamil Literature. In point of chronology too, it belongs to the same period (probably even earlier) as the classical works.

The Eṭṭuttokai comprises of the following anthologies:

Works on Akattiṇai:

Aiṅkuṟunūṟu
Kuṟuntokai
Naṟṟiṇai
Akanāṉūṟu
Kalittokai

Works on Puṟattiṇai:

Patiṟṟuppattu
Puṟanāṉūṟu
Paripāṭal.[2]

---

[1] Following K. Zvelebil, *The Smile*, 49-50, we shall use this designation in preference to the traditional "Caṅkam (pronounced Sangam) Literature." The traditional designation "Caṅkam Literature" is usually taken to comprise also many literary works which are from later period.

[2] An old veṇpā, i.e. a poem of four lines, enumerates the eight anthologies as follows:
Naṟṟiṇai nalla kuṟuntokai yaiṅkuṟunū-
ṟotta patiṟṟuppat- tōṅku paripāṭaṟ
kaṟṟaṟintā rēttuṅ kaliyō ṭakampuṟameṉ-
ṟittiṟatta -veṭṭut tokai.

The Ten Songs or Lays are:

Works on Akattiṇai:

Kuṟiñcippāṭṭu
Paṭṭiṉappālai
Mullaippāṭṭu
Neṭunalvāṭai

Works on Puṟattiṇai:

Porunarāṟṟuppaṭai
Perumpāṇāṟṟuppaṭai
Ciṟupāṇāṟṟuppaṭai
Malaipaṭukaṭām
Maturaikkāñci

Work of religious nature:

Tirumurukāṟṟuppaṭai.[3]

B. Classification of the Classical Tamil Literature

The whole block of classical Tamil poetry is divided into two large literary genres, according to the viewpoints the ancient Tamils had on human life. Roughly speaking, every man's life consists of two main aspects – one, the personal and intimate; which the Tamils termed *Akam*, and the other, the social and the exterior; which is called *Puṟam*. "This is a fundamental division in Tamil poetry, and is made on the basis of psychological and psychic experience."[4] The whole of classical Tamil Literature treats, therefore, of human sentiments and of exploits.[5]

The division into Akam and Puṟam is based primarily on "Anthropogeography"[6] and consequently also on the behavioral pattern of the inhabitants of the various regions. The word *Tiṇai*, which is attached to both Akam and Puṟam (as Akattiṇai and Puṟattiṇai) is very rich in meaning. "The word 'Tiṇai' occurs in early Tamil literature in more than one sense. In the first place, 'Tiṇai' denotes the fivefold

---

[3] An old veṇpā again enumerates the names of the Ten Lays:
Muruku porunāṟu pāṇiraṇṭu mullai
peruku vaḷamaturaik kāñci - maruviṉiya
kōlaneṭu nalvāṭai kōṟkuṟiñci paṭṭiṉap-
pālai kaṭāttoṭum pattu.

[4] Thani Nayagam, X. S., *Nature in Ancient Tamil Poetry*, Tuticorin 1952, Introduction, xv.

[5] Zvelebil, K., *The Tamil Literature*, Leiden/Köln 1975, 80.

[6] Thani Nayagam, X. S., *Nature*, 1.

physiographical division of the land,[7] namely the Kuriñci ... the Pālai ... the Mullai ... the Marudam ... and the Neydal ... Secondly, it denotes the distinctive modes of behaviour, social or moral, of the people of each physiographical region. Persons living in different regions developed a certain pattern of conduct which became conventionalized into stereotyped codes.[8] Thirdly, 'Tiṇai' refers to the reflection of the above mentioned geographical and social characteristics in literature."[9]

It must be admitted that the two terms – Akam and Puṟam – of Tamil Poetics do not admit of readily intelligible definitions or description, but they are easily understood by those conversant with the classical Tamil poems.[10] What is surprisingly interesting is that Tolkāppiyar himself has nowhere in his grammar formulated specifically any definition of Akam and Puṟam. As a matter of fact, the sections on Akattiṇai and Puṟattiṇai in the Poruḷatikāram of Tolkāppiyam start straightaway to classify and describe the aspects of Akam and Puṟam without giving definitions of the terms.[11] Therefore the definitions of these two terms, viz. Akattiṇai and Puṟattiṇai, have to be inferred inductively.

1. *Akattiṇai*

Akam means "inside, house, place, agricultural tract, breast, mind."[12] In the cultural and literary spheres, the word Akam also means "inner life", "private life" and more specifically "all aspects of love."[13] Akattiṇai denotes the different behavioral patterns of couples as regards their mutual relationships and their family life in the different regions. The ancient Tamils were, it seems evident, convinced of the incommunicability of the personal experience of the intimate life of a couple, and that is why they called the amatory experience Akam, i.e. the interior. In fact, the commentators of Tolkāppiyam Akattiṇaiyiyal define the term Akam precisely under this aspect of incommunicable, personal, interior amatory experience of a young man and a young girl in their

---

[7] The word Tiṇai seems to denote primarily division or general classification. Cf. for example, in Tamil grammar *Uyartiṇai* and *Akṟiṇai* – division of beings into superior, i.e. rational and irrational, lit. non-superior kind.

[8] In this sense, Tiṇai denotes behaviour, conduct, *oḻukkam*.

[9] Pillay, K. K., *A Social History of the Tamils*, Vol. I, University of Madras, 1975[2], 160.

[10] Cf. Thani Nayagam, X. S., "Tolkāppiyam – The Earliest Record", *JTmS* 1 (1972), 62.

[11] Naccinārkkiṉiyar, *Tolkāppiyam, Poruḷatikāram – Akattiṇaiyiyal*, SISSWPS., 1975, 3; *Puṟattiṇaiyiyal*, 128-129.

[12] *DED*, n. 7.

[13] Zvelebil, K., *Smile*, 91.

love-affair.[14] Thus "under Agam poetry comes what is supposed to be the most internal, personal, and directly incommunicable human experience, and that is love and all its phases."[15]

Various attempts have been made by authors to give some kind of descriptive definition of Akam or Akattiṇai.[16] V. Sp. Manickam proposes to infer inductively the definition of Akam, Akattiṇai etc. "from the description of their situations given in Tolkāppiyam and treated in Sangam literature."[17] He gives the following definition: "Aham, in its strict sense and fulness, deals with those love aspects wherein the physical contact with mental union, is involved."[18] Hence "Akam embraces the area of the emotion of interpersonal love between the two sexes and its related sentiments."[19] In short, Akam describes "the *total erotic experience* and the *total story of love of man as such.*"[20]

2. *Puṟattiṇai*

Puṟam means "outside, exterior, that which is foreign..."[21] In reference to literature it means "outward life, public life, political life" and more specifically "heroism, war."[22] Puṟam is whatever is not Akam. In other words, Puṟam treats of all that is outside family affairs, of all the varied aspects of social life of man. Like all the ancient peoples, the Tamils looked at their social life mainly from the point of view of heroic exploits. Hence the Puṟam poems treat "primarily of war and the martial exploits of the people."[23] They are described under seven puṟam themes: *veṭci* — cattle lifting (Tol. Por. Puṟat. 56ff); *vañci* — invasion (Tol. Por. Puṟat. 61ff); *uḻiñai* — siege (Tol. Por. Puṟat. 64ff); *tumpai* — battle (Tol. Por. Puṟat. 69ff); *vākai* — victory (Tol. Por. Puṟat. 73ff); *kāñci* — endurance (Tol. Por. Puṟat. 77ff); *pāṭāṇ* — elegy (Tol. Por. Puṟat. 80f).

---

[14] Nacciṉārkkiṉiyar, *Tolkāppiyam, Poruḷatikāram – Akattiṇaiyiyal*, 3.

[15] Thani Nayagam, X. S., *Nature*, xv.

[16] To cite a couple of them:

"*Aham* is a practical treatise on Psychology, in all its aspects of love, its various emotions, incidents and accidents. It is about the relations of lovers..." – Somasundaram Pillai, J. M., *A History of Tamil Literature*, Annamalainagar 1968, 59. According to M. Arokiaswami, Akam poems deal with "the unaccountable and the indescribable in human love, sex appeal and sexual life..." – *The Classical Age of the Tamils*, University of Madras, 1972, 25.

[17] Manickam, V.Sp., *The Tamil Concept of Love*, Madras 1962, 129.

[18] Ib., 176.

[19] Thani Nayagam, X. S., *JTmS* 1 (1972), 62.

[20] Zvelebil, K., *Smile*, 91.

[21] *DED*, n. 4333.

[22] Zvelebil, K., *Smile*, 91.

[23] Somasundaram Pillai, J. M., *History*, 60.

C. **Date of the Materials Under Consideration**

It must be acknowledged that the problem of the dating of the classical anthologies and Tolkāppiyam is very intricate.[24] There was a time when the western scholars thought and wrote that the earliest Tamil compositions that are extant were from the ninth or tenth centuries AD.[25] In the present state of scholarship, it is agreed by all scholars that Tolkāppiyam and the Eṭṭuttokai are the most ancient Tamil literary works so far known and extant. But in the history of Tamil Literature, the period allotted to them varies according to the authors. For example, according to S. Vaiyapuri Pillai, the earliest Tamil works extant were produced between the 2nd century AD and the end of the 3rd century AD.[26] S.K. Chatterji thinks that the original Caṅkam literature were gradually changed from 'Ancient Tamil' to the 'Cen-tamiz' of literature c. 350 AD.[27] A. Chidambaranatha Chettiar ascribes the Caṅkam Literature to 200 BC to 200 AD.[28] K. Zvelebil, in his article of 1957, ascribed most of the Eṭṭuttokai and Pattuppāṭṭu texts to the 3rd-4th century AD.[29] In a later article, he says: "The majority of poet creators of the oldest Tamil lyrics lived between 100 and 300 BC."[30] Later again he writes: "Taking into consideration the cumulative evidence of the linguistic, epigraphic, archaeological, numismatic and historical data, both internal and external, it is undoubtedly possible to arrive at the following final conclusion: *the earliest corpus of Tamil literature may be dated between 100 BC and 250 AD.*"[31] In a later work, he assigns the period as: the bardic corpus: ?150 BC – ca. 250 AD.[32]

It would be useful to summarize the results of further studies in this field and bring more precision on the question of the date of Tolkāppiyam and the Anthologies of Love-Poems:

---

[24] For the various problems connected with the dating of the early Tamil classics, see the excellent treatment of K. Zvelebil in *Smile*, 23-44 with a chart on p. 42.

[25] Caldwell, R., *Comparative Grammar of the Dravidian or South-Indian Family of Languages*, New Delhi 1974³, 88.

[26] Vaiyapuri Pillai, S., "History of Tamil Language and Literature", *TC*, III, 3 & 4 (1954), 357.

[27] Chatterji, S. K., "Old Tamil, Ancient Tamil and Primitive Dravidian", *TC*, V, 2 (1956), 173-174.

[28] Chidambaranatha Chettiar, A., "Introduction to Tamil Poetry", *TC*, VII, 1 (1958), 56.

[29] Zvelebil, K., "Tentative Periodization of the Development of Tamil", *TC*, VI, 1 (1957), 50-51. The author ascribes this period as the upper limit, while putting an interrogation mark for the lower limit to show that the origin is not ascertainable.

[30] Zvelebil, K., "Tamil Poetry 2000 Years Ago", *TC*, X, 2 (1963), 23.

[31] Zvelebil, K., *Smile*, 41.

[32] Zvelebil, K., *The Tamil*, 33, cf. also p. 46 & p. 106 and note 122.

1. *Tolkāppiyam*

Many scholars have attempted to fix the date of the composition of Tolkāppiyam.[33] All agree that "the problem of the dating of Tolkāppiyam is an extremely difficult one." [34] K. Zvelebil has given a concise but clear presentation of the whole question in his work.[35] Here are his own conclusions:

1) "The earliest, original version of the *Tolkāppiyam* belongs to the 'pre-Caṅkam' period; the oldest layer of the grammar is somewhat earlier in time than the majority of extant classical Tamil poems." [36]

2) Approximately the 5th century AD is fixed by him "as the earliest possible date of *Poruḷatikāram*, and as *the date of the final redaction of the Tolkāppiyam.*" [37]

3) "Thus, the nuclear portions of *Tolkāppiyam* were probably born sometime in the 2nd or 1st century BC., but hardly before 150 BC... The final redaction of the *Tolkāppiyam* as we know it today did not very probably take place before the 5th century AD., so that the ultimate shape of the *sūtras* as we have them before us is probably not earlier than the middle of the first millenium of our era." [38]

It will be briefly shown from the various studies of different scholars

1) that the criteria on which is based the somewhat late dating of Tolkāppiyam, are not conclusively convincing;

2) and that the main portions of all the three parts of Tolkāppiyam, esp. the third part – Poruḷatikāram – with its main rulings, predate the existing anthologies.

K. Zvelebil fixes the lower limit of Tolkāppiyam basing his argument on "the relation of the language described in *Tolkāppiyam* (specifically in the Eḻuttatikāram) and of Tolkāppiyam's metalanguage, to the graphemic and phonological system of the earliest Tamil inscriptions in

---

[33] See e.g. Vellaivaranan, K., *Tolkāppiyam: Tamiḻ Ilakkiya Varalāṟu*, Annamalai Palkalaik kaḻakam, 1957, esp. 86-126.

[34] Zvelebil, K., *Smile*, 138. V.T. Manickam, in his *Marutam*: Karaikudi 1982, in appendix 229-230 gives reference to thirty authors who have dealt with the date of Tolkāppiyam. In his list the two extremes are M.S. Purnalingam Pillai, who fixes 6000 BC as the age of Tolkāppiyam and K. Kailācapati, who fixes it at 500 AD.

[35] Zvelebil, K., *Smile*, 131-154 on Tolkāppiyam. The question of the date of Tolkāppiyam is treated in 138-147.

[36] Ib., 143.

[37] Ib., 145-146. The author adds: "This is our second, but not our final conclusion."

[38] Ib., 147. See also *The Tamil*, 46, 69.

Brahmi."[39] The earliest Tamil-Brahmi inscriptions were produced between 200-100 BC. Since the language of the Tamil-Brahmi inscriptions and the language of Tolkāppiyam are "two styles, two varieties of one language – Old Tamil", Tolkāppiyam is "contemporaneous or almost contemporaneous" with the inscriptions. Hence the lower limit cannot be beyond 150 BC. For, according to him, "about 250 BC or slightly later, Aśoka's (272-232 BC) Southern Brahmi script was adapted to the Tamil phonological system."[40]

It is an historical fact that at the time of the Aśoka Rock Edicts the three Tamil kingdoms of Chola, Pandiya and Chera were already in existence.[41] The fact that Aśoka used the means of inscription for propagating the Buddhist humanitarianism in the South makes us understand that the people to whom the inscriptions were meant were literate, capable of deciphering written characters.[42] Further researches on Brahmi inscriptions seem to indicate that before the advent of Aśoka-Brahmi writing system into the South, there was already a Tamil-Brahmi system for writing Tamil which used geometrical compound signs and on the basis of which the Aśoka-Brahmi system was designed.[43] K. G. Krishnan has shown at least the probability that "the Tamil script began to take shape in a period prior to Aśoka's time."[44] S. Shankar Raju Naidu even contends that "Tamil alphabet stands as the root of Nagari and all the other indigenous alphabets of India" and that

---

[39] Zvelebil, K., *Smile*, 138.

[40] Ib., 140-141 & 147. The author relies heavily on the article of Mahadevan, I., "Tamil-Brahmi Inscriptions of the Sangam Age", in *PSICSTS*, Vol. I, IATR, 1971, 73-106; and his own articles; "The Brahmi Hybrid Inscriptions", *ArOr* (1964), 545-575; Id., "From Proto-South Dravidian to Old Tamil and Malayalam", in *PSICSTS*, Vol. I, IATR, 1971, 54-72. Ramachandran, K. S., *Archaeology of South India: Tamil Nadu*, Sundeep Prakashan, Delhi 1980, 88 thinks that "a script for Tamil language was adopted from the existing Aśokan Brahmi, the Bhattiprolu inscription forming an intermediary stage, sometime during the early first century AD." I. Mahadevan maintains the same conclusions in a more recent article, "Origin of the Tamil Script", in *Origin, Evolution and Reform of the Tamil Script*, Madras 1983, 7-14.

[41] The Rock Edict No. 2 mentions all the three kingdoms; Rock Edict No. 13 does not mention specifically the Keralaputra, i.e. the Cheras. See Alexander, P. C., "Asoka and the Spread of Buddhism in Cheranadu", *TC*, I, 2 (1952), 125-131, esp. 129.

[42] Sēnāthi Rājā, E. S. W., "The Pre-Sanskrit Element in Ancient Tamil Literature", *JRAS* XIX (1887), 558-582, esp. 567. Narasimhaiah, B., *Neolithic and Megalithic Cultures in Tamil Nadu*, Sundeep Prakashan, Delhi 1980, 191. According to him, the urn-burial system referred to by the Caṅkam poets is spread quite widely in Tamilnadu already ca. 350-200 BC cf. the table of tentative dating in p. 188. See also Krishnan, K. G., "Origin of the Tamil Script", in *Origin, Evolution and Reform*, 15-19.

[43] Siromoney, G., "Origin of the Tamil-Brahmi Script", in *Origin, Evolution and Reform*, 21-29; see p. 27 for this conclusion.

[44] Krishnan, K. G., "Origin", in *Origin, Evolution and Reform*, 16-18; the citation is from p. 18.

Brahmi itself evolved "its elaborate system out of the simpler alphabetical system of Tamil."[45] The presupposition that the languages of these inscriptions are truly representative of the standard of the Tamil language is extremely problematic. According to K.K. Pillay, "the Brahmi inscriptions of South India... cannot be taken to represent the contemporary language and that it is clearly unhistoric to post-date the classics on the basis of these strange records."[46] In a recent article, S.N. Kandaswamy on the date of Tolkāppiyam brings one argument on syntax which is very significant: "Causal verbs are very rare in the language of *Tolkāppiyam*. A solitary occurrence is 'kēṭpikkum'. But the Tamil-Brahmi inscriptions possess the paradigms of the causal verb /koṭuppitta/ occurring about ten times and /aṟuppitta/ and /ceyyvitta/ each occurring twice. It is reasonable to derive from this observation that the causal verb gained currency after the advent of *Tolkāppiyam*."[47]

While considering the arguments to show that Tolkāppiyam predates the existing anthologies, the following points are in order:

1) It is a fact recognized by all critics that there are interpolations in Tolkāppiyam. These insertions were most probably meant to update or complement the grammar and also "enrich" it with the grammatical features from Sanskrit vyākarṇas. Given the historical fact of almost inundating Sanskrit influence on Tamil, this trend seems understandable.[48] Interpolations have been detected in all the three parts of Tolkāppiyam, particularly in the Poruḷatikāram.[49] Hence a critic should be careful not to argue for the date of Tolkāppiyam from

---

[45] Shankar Raju Naidu, S., "A Comparative Study of Tamil and Nagari Alphabets", *TC*, IX, 1 (1961), 33-42, esp. 41 & 42 for the citations.

[46] Pillay, K.K., "The Brahmi Inscriptions of South India and the Sangam Age", *TC*, V, 2 (1956), 175-185; esp. 184-185 for the quotation. See also Subramoniam, V.I., "The Dating of Sangam Literature", in *PTICSTS*, Pondichéry 1973, 76.

[47] Kandaswamy, S.N., "The Age of *Tolkāppiyam*", *JTamS* 20 (1981), 37-71; see p. 42 for the quotation.

[48] Zvelebil, K., *Smile*, 146; Id., *The Tamil*, 69-70.

[49] Subbiah, A., "Is the Tamil Alphabet System an Adaptation?", *JTamS* 3 (1973), 64-74 shows that in the Eḻuttatikāram, cūtram 7 is an attempt at complementing as well as synchronizing by a later interpolator. Sankaran, C.R., "Tolkāppiyar and the Science of Phonemics", *TC*, IX (1961), 117-130, contends that even in one cūtram, there has been interpolation. H.S. David thinks that Tolkāppiyam Collatikāram is also "a composite work (esp. Uriyiyal) which has increased in size by means of accretions round an earlier core..." See "The Place of *Tolkāppiyam* in Ancient Tamil Literature", in *PFICSTS*, Vol. II, IATR, 1969, 19-37; cf. p. 26 for the citation. Poruḷatikāram too contains not a few interpolations. S.S. Bharathi shows that "the 15 sūtrams which purport to speak of the four castes and their birthrights are sandwiched between sūtrams 69 and 86 in Marapiyal." See "The Age of Tholkāppiam", *JAU*, VI, 2 (1937), 121-138; esp. 133 for the quotation.

such cūtrams that appear to be interpolations. These cūtrams are at the most criteria for dating the final edition of the present text of the grammar.

2) The relationships or similarities, esp. in Poruḷatikāram, with Sanskrit traditions need not necessarily mean borrowings. For, (a) they might have been mentioned by the author(s) to show parallels or analogies;[50] (b) or both traditions could well come from a common cultural source.[51]

3) When grammatical rules in Tolkāppiyam are clearly violated by the poets of the anthologies, two conclusions are implied: (a) Those rules definitely predate the anthologies; (b) There had been literary productions prior to Tolkāppiyam, from which those rules were deduced and formulated.

A few arguments to show that the main portions of all the three parts of Tolkāppiyam predate the existing anthologies are given below:

For Eḻuttatikāram: Most of the critics admit that this part of Tolkāppiyam predates the anthologies on the basis of the rules – Nos. 28, 29, 31, 32 in Eḻuttattikāram which are violated by the poets of anthologies.[52]

For Collatikāram:

a) Cūt. 221 on optative mood (viyaṅkōḷ) is violated in the poems of the anthologies.[53]

b) Tolkāppiyam does not lay down the rule for the usage of the numeral crore (kōṭi), as it does for other numbers such as one, ten, hundred, thousand, etc. But Puṟam 18 has the usage of this number, i.e. kōṭi.[54]

c) The plural particle-suffix *kaḷ* is used in the classical poems even for Uyartiṇai.[55]

---

[50] Bharathi, S. S., *JAU* VI, 2 (1937), 135.

[51] Cf. Pillay, K. K., *A Social History*, 113.

[52] See Bharathi, S. S., "The Age of Tholkāppiam", *IAU*, VI, 3 (1937), 224. David, H. S., "The Place of *Tolkāppiyam*", in *PFICSTS*, Vol. II, 27-34; Kandaswamy, S. N., *JTamS* 20 (1981), 40.

[53] Bharathi, S. S., *JAU*, VI, 3 (1937), 225-226. According to Tolkāppiyam the optative mood should be used only for the third person. In the classics it is used for first and second persons.

[54] Pillay, K. K., *A Social History*, 117.

[55] Cf. Adaikalasamy, M. R., *Tamiḻ Ilakkiya Varalāṟu*, Madras 1981, 28.

d) Tolkāppiyam does not prescribe any rules for the usage of the term "yavaṉa" (whereas Naṉṉūl prescribes). But the Yavaṉar were well known at the time of the production of classical poetry.[56]

For Poruḷatikāram:

a) Tolkāppiyam says that *kali* metre and *paripāṭal* are to be used for composing poems on love-themes.[57] Contrary to this rule, most of the Akam poems in the anthologies are composed in *akaval*.[58]

b) Rules formulated by Tolkāppiyam for the usage of comparative particles are not followed in the classical poetry.[59] Besides, fourteen of the comparative particles listed by Tolkāppiyam do not make their appearance at all in the classical anthologies. Further, there are about 28 comparative particles and their ballast variants that newly appear in classical poems and these are not listed or mentioned in Tolkāppiyam.[60]

c) Many rules in Marapu-iyal have been violated by the poets of classical age.[61] Moreover, "this section (i.e. Marapu-iyal) indicates that the language has been so long in use, that already it has evolved distinctive obsolete forms, and words exist which have shifted their meanings or need explanation for Tolkāppiyar's contemporaries."[62]

d) K.P. Aravaanan gives about nine arguments to show that Tolkāppiyam predates the classical anthologies and among them, seven are related to matters dealt with in Poruḷatikāram.[63]

From these and such arguments, X. S. Thani Nayagam concludes:

1) "The *Tolkāppiyam* is a book which has at least three or more strata of evidence concerning the development of the Tamil language as well as the subject matter and the interpretation and criticism of Tamil poetry."[64]

---

[56] Kalidos, R., *History and Culture of the Tamils*, Vijay Publications. Dindigul 1976, 68.

[57] Nacciṉārkkiṉiyar, *Tol. Por. Commentary*, 120, on cūtram 53.

[58] Bharathi, S. S., *JAU* VI, 3 (1937), 227; Pillay, K. K., *A Social History*, 117.

[59] Bharathi, S. S., *JAU*, VI, 3 (1937), 228.

[60] Cīṉivācaṉ, R., *Caṅka Ilakkiyattil Uvamaikaḷ*, Madras 1973, 74-76.

[61] Bharathi, S. S., *JAU* VI, 3 (1937), 227.

[62] Thani Nayagam, X. S., *JTamS* 1 (1972), 67.

[63] Aravaanan, K. P., *Aṟṟaināḷ Kātalum Vīramum*, Madras 1978, 16-33.

[64] Thani Nayagam, X. S., *Tamil Humanism: The Classical Period*, Jaffna College, Jaffna 1972, 9.

2) "Insoluble problems arise when on account of some discrepancy or other the compilation of the major part of the book is dated later than the *Caṅkam* anthologies .../... Most of the *Tolkāppiyam* is very intelligible when considered as pre-*Caṅkam*, but most of it hardly makes sense when considered as post-*Caṅkam*." [65]

2. *Anthologies of Love Poems*

The problem of the chronology of the eight anthologies is no less intricate and only a brief assessment of the results of researches can be attempted here. That the poems contained in the classical anthologies had been composed before the Pallava period is somewhat evident. For absolutely no reference to the Pallavas is found in any of them. The beginning of the Pallava period is fixed in first half of the 3rd century AD.[66] What we are interested in now is the possible lower date of the most ancient love poems contained in the anthologies. Of course the date that will be proposed here can only be tentative and provisory.

To decide upon the date of the poems of the anthologies, the following criteria are proposed:[67]

1) Historical allusions

2) Linguistic criteria:

a) Development of linguistic forms

b) Ratio of Sanskrit words used

c) "Loanwords from Prakrit and Pali are very probably older than Sanskrit loanwords." [68]

3) Linguistic and Poetic criteria:

a) The simpler the metre and the other prosodic properties the older the poem.

b) "Affinity with folk-songs and echoes of colloquial utterances may probably be also regarded as indications of relative antiquity." [69]

---

[65] Thani Nayagam, X. S., *JTamS* 1 (1972), 61-70, see 68-69 for the quotation.

[66] Rajamanickam, M., "Saivism in the Pre-Pallava Period", *TC*, V, 4 (1956), 328-339, esp. 329; Zvelebil, K., *Smile*, 34.

[67] Srinivas Iyengar, P. T., *History of the Tamils*, Madras 1929, 158-162; Zvelebil, K., *Smile*, 117-118; Id., *The Tamil*, 88-89.

[68] Zvelebil, K., *Smile*, 118.

[69] Ib., 117.

c) "Straightforward descriptions of fighting, mating, nature etc. are probably older than poems which bear traces or elements of reflection and philosophy." [70]

4) Poetic and Thematic criteria:

a) The fauna and flora specifically belonging to the same regions (and not mingled) are indications of antiquity.

b) Analysis of the themes, motifs and formulae: e.g. Kaikkiḷai and Peruntiṇai may probably be late themes.

c) Thought-content: "Poems showing traces of Jainism and Buddhism are probably earlier than poems showing Brahminic influence." [71]

5) Cultural criteria:

a) Tamil customs peculiar to the five regions indicate that the poems are ancient.

b) Non-Aryan superstitions are indications of antiquity.

c) Anonymity and "poetic baptism":[72] "Perhaps this anonymity is due to the fact that being very old poems, the names of the authors had been forgotten by the time they were included in the anthologies." [73]

d) Non-Aryan bards: known from their names.

Starting from the anonymity and the consequent "poetic-baptism," H. S. David has studied in particular the Kuṟuntokai anthology and has shown that Kuṟuntokai was "the first of the eight anthologies to be *compiled*, in other words the earliest Tamil literary work extant." [74] In an earlier article, the same author, basing himself mostly on linguistic criteria such as the obsolete diction, the old grammatical pattern of nominal system, the peculiar adverbs, the archaic verbal system, the ancient syntactical features etc., has shown that in the Kuṟuntokai we possess the earliest poems extant in Tamil.[75]

---

[70] Ib., 118.

[71] Ib.

[72] When the authors of poems are not known by name, they have been named from some striking phrase or simile in the poems. This is known as "poetic baptism" among the critics of Tamil Literature. There are at least 20 such cases in the Kuṟuntokai anthology alone.

[73] Srinivas Iyengar, P. T., *History*, 162.

[74] David, H. S., "The Kutunhthokai Anthology", *TC*, VII, 4 (1958), 323-349, see p. 328 for the citation. The writer speaks of literary and not grammatical work. Elsewhere he shows that Tolkāppiyam is earlier than Kuṟuntokai. See Id., "The Place of *Tolkāppiyam*", in *PFICSTS*, Vol. II, 26 et passim.

[75] David, H. S., "The Earliest Tamil Poems Extant", *TC*, IV, 1 (1955), 90-98, see p. 93 for the conclusion.

That historical allusions are a firm criterion for dating the poems which contain them is recognized by all. On this basis H. S. David contends that Akam 251, 265 and Kuṟ. 75 which mention the Nanda kings and their capital Pāṭali, are the most ancient poems – belonging to the decade preceding the fall of the Nandas ca. 324 BC.[76] This conclusion seems to be confirmed on other grounds also; e.g. Mauryan potteries have been found out in Koṟkai. "This shows that a great commercial concourse of the South and the North existed in the 3rd century BC." [77]

V. I. Subramoniam uses the grammatical analysis, esp. Phonology, Morphophonemics and Morphology to fix the dates of the anthologies. He proposes the following tentative dates for the anthologies:

Kuṟuntokai	180 BC.
Aiṅkuṟunūṟu	120 BC.
Akanāṉūṟu	210 AD.
Naṟṟiṇai	230 AD.
Kalittokai	250 AD.

"The time depth of the Sangam anthologies – tokai and pāṭṭu – is between 180 BC and 290 AD. The nine works between themselves show a time difference of 470 years." [78]

---

[76] Ib., 96-98. This argument is not accepted by K. Zvelebil, who says: "The definite dating proposed by him (H. S. David) for Kuṟ. 75 and Ak. 265 based on the allusions to the Nandas and to Pāṭaliputra (ca. 320) is unacceptable. These allusions are to well known facts which are neither contemporary nor recent, but the subject of almost legendary accounts, of a "folklore" of the distant past", *The Tamil*, 85, note 25. The ground on which K. Zvelebil dismisses the allusions to the Nandas and to Pāṭaliputra as legendary accounts does not appear to be sound, for the following reasons:

a) Ak. 251 and 265 both belong to the *Pālaittiṇai* where the wealth to be acquired is compared to the pleasure with the lady-love and the later is preferred. Compare esp. Ak. 251:5-6 with the Paṭṭiṉappālai lines 218-220.

b) The localization of Pāṭali on the bank of River Cōṇai is a detail of almost an eye-witness.

c) It is accepted by the historians that there was an intense trade contact between the South and the North during the reign of the Nandas and the Mauryas. See, Srinivas Iyengar, P. T., *The History*, 141-142.

d) Ak. 251 and 265 seem to reflect a veritable historical context of a *talaivaṉ* who had gone on trade (Poruḷvayiṉ pirivu) to the North.

[77] Sundararaj, T., "Rise and Fall of Koṟkai", *JTamS* 19 (1981), 55-63; see p. 56 for the citation.

[78] Subramoniam, V. I., "The Dating of Sangam", in *PTICSTS*, 83.

Conclusion

Without pretending to have solved the problems involved in the dating of the early classical corpus and the grammar of Tolkāppiyam, the following relative and approximate periods are proposed: The earliest Tamil poems contained in the extant anthologies go back at least to the beginning of the 3rd century BC. The main strata of the three parts of Tolkāppiyam (which as a whole K. Zvelebil calls Ur-Tolkāppiyam) belong at least to the 3rd century BC. The presence of Jainism and the absence of the trace of Buddhistic philosophy or ideas in it bespeak pre-Aśokan, if not pre-Buddhist, period for the composition of Tolkāppiyam.[79] Now, Tolkāppiyar quotes many works of grammar, referring to them either explicitly or implicitly, which served him as models and in whose tradition he places himself.[80] "It is obvious that much literature must have existed before the time of Tolkāppiyam as we have it, and that the author(s) of the grammar made use of earlier grammatical works."[81] These grammars themselves must have been based on preceding literatures. These literatures must have belonged to at least a century or two before Tolkāppiyam itself. Tentatively, then, we may say that the early literary production in Tamil must have commenced at least in the 5th-4th centuries BC.[82]

D. **Short Notes on the Akam Anthologies**

1. *Aiṅkuṟunūṟu*

Literally it means "five-short-hundred" (aiṅ = five; kuṟu = short; nūṟu = hundred). It is a collection of five hundred short poems divided

---

[79] Kandaswamy, S. N., *JTamS* 20 (1981), 67-68.

[80] According to M. R. Adaikalasamy, *Tamiḻ Ilakkiya*, 27, there are about 260 such references. K. P. Aravaanan has counted around 372 places of either explicit or implicit citations: *Aṟṟaiṇāḷ*, 33. See also Arumugha Mudaliar, S., "The Antiquity of Tamil and Tolkappiyam", *TC* 2 (1953), 340-361, esp. 361 for the various methods of giving such references. In fact, this point has been, as a whole, accepted by all critics. One should also grant that among these references there could be and in fact there are quite a few which are from the interpolators. It is recognized by the critics that the characteristic phrases like *eṉmaṉār pulavar*, etc. belong not so much to individual grammarians as to grammatical school(s). See David, H. S., "The Place of *Tolkāppiyam*", in *PFICSTS*, Vol. II, 26. Of course, not all such references could be from the interpolators!

[81] Zvelebil, K., *Smile*, 134, 139. See also Victor, M., *The Tamil-Islamic Cultural Encounter in Cīṟāppurāṇam*, Unpublished Thesis at Univeristas Gregoriana, Rome 1985, Vol. I, 14-16, and corresponding notes.

[82] Thani Nayagam, X. S., *JTamS* 1 (1972), 62; Kandaswamy, S. N., *JTamS* 20 (1981), 68; cf also Manickam, V. T., *Marutam*, 188 note 6; Srinivas Iyengar, P. T., *The History*, 162, 250ff. Balasubramanian, C., "The Age of Kutunthokai", in *An Insight into Tamilology*, Kovai 1972, 121-133, esp. 131.

into five groups of hundred stanzas each. Each group treats about one of the five tiṇais (called aintiṇai = five regions) in the following order: Marutam "riverine" by Ōrampōkiyār; Neytal "littoral" by Ammūvaṉār; Kuṟiñci "montane" by Kapilar; Pālai "arid" by Ōtalāntaiyār; and Mullai "pastoral" by Pēyaṉār. Each hundred is subdivided into tens. The poems have three to six lines each. Two poems in neytal hundred, viz. 129 and 130 are not extant and two other poems in mullai, i.e. 416 and 490 are fragmentary. An invocatory stanza on Siva by Peruntēvaṉār (who sang Pāratam) is prefixed to the whole collection.[83] A colophon at the end of the collections tells us that the whole collection was made by Pulatturai muṟṟiya Kūṭalūr Kiḻār under the direction or patronage of Yāṉaikkaṭ Cēy Māntarañ Cēral Irumpoṟai, a Cēral king. The work was first published in 1903 by U.V. Swaminatha Aiyar, who has printed at the end of the collection six other stanzas that he found in one of the manuscripts of Aiṅkuṟunūṟu.[84]

K. Zvelebil considers that Aiṅkuṟunūṟu comes chronologically first among the anthologies.[85] On the contrary, J.R. Marr thinks that Aiṅkuṟunūṟu is a work of later date.[86] None of the poems of Aiṅkuṟunūṟu, according to P.T. Srinivas Iyengar, could have been composed earlier than the 5th century AD.[87] The reason for the present sequence of the five tiṇais as marutam, neytal, kuṟiñci, pālai and mullai is not clear. One could suggest some plausible explanation why marutam and neytal occupy the present position,[88] but not for others.[89]

2. *Kuṟuntokai*

The name means "the short-collection", i.e. the collection of short poems (kuṟum = short, tokai = collection). It contains 401 stanzas and one invocatory stanza on Murukaṉ by Peruntēvaṉār. It is called "short-collection" because the poems in it (from 4 to 8 lines, though poems 307 and 391 have 9 lines) are the shortest in comparison to those of Naṟṟiṇai and of Akanāṉūṟu. The compiler, according to the colophon at the end, was Pūrikkō. All the 401 stanzas are on the akam themes and

---

[83] The invocatory poems on different gods in the anthologies are all by Peruntēvaṉār, a poet belonging to a much later period – probably 8th or 9th century AD.

[84] See *Aiṅkuṟunūṟu* Mūlamum Paḻaiyavuraiyum, (ed.) U.V. Swaminatha Aiyar, 1980^6, 206-207.

[85] Zvelebil, K., *Smile*, 50; Id., *The Tamil*, 46.

[86] Marr, J.R., *The Eight Tamil Anthologies*, Unpublished Ph.D. Thesis, University of London, 1958, 368-370.

[87] Srinivas Iyengar, P.T., *The History*, 583.

[88] For one such explanation see *Aiṅkuṟunūṟu* Mūlamum Paḻaiyavuraiyum, viii.

[89] It appears that one might speculate that the whole collection could be poems which were composed as exercises in the art of composing poems on Akam themes.

they were composed by 205 poets. There are ten stanzas whose authors are not known by name.[90] The poems have been collected without any order among themselves. The apparent criteria for collecting them and naming them seem to be the subject matter or theme, i.e. akam theme, and the length of the poems.[91] T. S. Arangasami Ayyangar published Kuṟuntokai in 1915 for the first time.

3. *Naṟṟiṇai*

The literal meaning of the name is "good tiṇai" (nal = good; tiṇai = region; behaviour), i.e. the collection of poems on excellent tiṇai or the collection of excellent poems on the tiṇai.[92] The anthology is supposed to contain 400 poems, though in the extant form one poem is missing, i.e. poem 234. In the edition of SISSPWS, of 1976, a poem quoted as an illustration by the scholiast for the cūtram 28 of Iṟaiyaṉār Akapporuḷ has been included in the place of poem 234.[93] Moreover, there is another poem put at the end as an appendix and this poem has been cited as illustration for Tol. Kaḷ. cūtr. 23.[94] The length of the poems ranges from 8 to 13 lines. The compiler's name is not known, but the patron of this collection is the king Paṉṉāṭu tanta Pāṇṭiyaṉ Māṟaṉ Vaḻuti. Naṟṟiṇai was first published by P. A. Narayanaswami Aiyar in 1914, with a commentary by him. Of the poets whose poems are included in this anthology, 174 are known by their names. The invocatory poem on Tirumāl has been contributed by Peruntēvaṉār.

4. *Akanāṉūṟu*

"Akam-four hundred" is the meaning of the name (akam + nāṉūṟu = akam four hundred), i.e. four hundred poems on akam themes. Iṟaiyaṉār Akapporuḷurai mentions another name, viz. Neṭuntokai which means "anthology of long (poems)" – the qualificative "long" referring to the length of the poems ranging from 13 to 31 lines. The collection contains 400 poems on love, plus one invocatory poem on Siva, again by Peruntēvaṉār. The anthology was compiled by certain Uruttiracaṉmaṉ, the son of Uppūri Kuṭi Kiḻāṉ of Maturai, under the direction of the Pāṇṭiya king Ukkiraperuvaḻuti. The first printed edition of Akanāṉūṟu was published in 1920 by V. Rajagopala Iyengar. The number of poets is 143 (+ Peruntēvaṉār); poems 114, 117 and 165 are by anonymous authors.

[90] *Kuṟuntokai*, SISSWPS, Madras 1978, Introduction, 6.
[91] Marr, J. R., *Eight Tamil*, 347.
[92] Zvelebil, K., *Smile*, 51.
[93] *Naṟṟiṇai*, SISSWPS, Madras 1976, 404.
[94] Ib., 674.

The compiler has followed a peculiar scheme for the arrangement of the poems: the poems bearing odd numbers belong to pālai (i.e. 1, 3, 5, 7 ... 399 – the total being 200 poems – half of the collection); poems bearing number 2, 8, 12, 18, 22, 28 etc. belong to kuṟiñci tiṇai (80 in all); poems bearing number 4, 14, 24, 34, 44 etc. are of mullai tiṇai (40 in all); poems with number 6, 16, 26, 36 etc. are marutam (40 in all); all poems having ten or its multiples, i.e. 10, 20, 30 etc. are neytal (40 in all).[95] The anthology Akanāṉūṟu is divided into three parts under the following names: Kaḷiṟṟiyāṉai Nirai (poems 1-120), Maṇimiṭai Pavaḷam (poems 121-300), and Nittilakkōvai (poems 301-400). It seems that these names were given by literary critics who found certain characteristics peculiar to each group.[96]

5. *Kalittokai*

Kalittokai means "the kali-metre anthology" and it is a collection of altogether 150 poems. Of these poems, one is an invocatory song on Siva by Peruntēvaṉār, and the remaining are on love themes. They are divided into five traditional tiṇais, and attributed by a stray veṇpā to five authors as follows: 29 on kuṟiñci to Kapilar; 35 on pālai to Cēramāṉ Peruṅkaṭuṅkō; 17 on mullai to Uruttiraṉ; 35 on marutam to Marutaṉ Iḷanākaṉār; 33 on neytal to Nallantuvaṉār who is said to be also the compiler.[97] Kalittokai was first published by S. V. Damodaram Pillai in 1887.

The problem of authorship and the date of Kalittokai has to be mentioned at least in passing. The traditional theory of fivefold authorship is considered by many critics as unauthentic. Scholars like

---

95 S. Vaiyapuri Pillai sees in this fact an indication that Akanāṉūṟu was collected after Naṟṟiṇai and Kuṟuntokai; cf. Id., *History of Tamil Language and Literature*, Madras 1956, 27. This conclusion is not so evident. According to J. R. Marr, the order of the enumeration of the anthologies in Iṟaiyaṉār Akapporuḷurai, as Neṭuntokai, Kuṟuntokai, Naṟṟiṇai, Puṟanāṉūṟu etc. seems to indicate the chronological order: cf. *Eight Tamil*, 355 & 410. The fact that the number of lines in poems appears to have been the primary criterion for separating, classifying and naming the anthologies, argues in favour of contemporaneity of compiling activity. There could have been, therefore, many stages in the compiling activity. With the scheme of arrangement of Akanāṉūṟu poems, one may compare the arrangements of the poetic units in the Song of Songs; cf. the schemes proposed by J. C. Exum, W. H. Shea, and E. C. Webster in their articles.

96 Venkatachalam Pillai, R., "Presidential Address", in *Akanāṉūṟṟuc Coṟpoḻivukaḷ*: SISSWPS, Madras 1977, 8. But the explanations are, according to the same author, not so evident and satisfying.

97 The veṇpā about the five authors runs as follows:
Peruṅkaṭuṅkōṉ pālai, kapilaṉ kuṟiñci
marutaṉiḷa nākaṉ marutam - aruñcōḻaṉ
nallut tiraṉmullai nallan tuvaṉeytal
kalvivalār kaṇṭa kali.

S. V. Damodaram Pillai and K. N. Sivaraja Pillai regard Kalittokai as the work of one poet.[98] But M. Rajamanickam argues that it is neither the work of one author, as the above mentioned scholars hold, nor the work of five poets, as the veṇpā says, but a veritable anthology of kali-metre songs by many poets, like the other anthologies.[99]

As regards the date, K. Zvelebil holds that Kalittokai should be dated roughly between the 5th-7th century AD.[100] He says that it seems to be separated at least by three centuries from the earlier collections.[101] According to M. Rajamanickam, the poems in Kalittokai belong roughly from 2nd century BC to 6th century AD.[102]

In my study, I shall deal mainly with love poems found in Kuṟuntokai, Naṟṟiṇai, Aiṅkuṟunūṟu and Akanāṉūṟu. Though Kalittokai also belongs to the classical Tamil poetry, I shall not draw main conclusions from it, because it is considered as a whole of later period. However, since it too represents pure Tamil culture – without the mixture of Sanskrit *poetic* tradition – a moderate and cautious use may still be made.

---

[98] Zvelebil, K., *Smile*, 123.

[99] Rajamanickam, M., "Kuṟiñcikkali", in *Kalittokaic Coṟpoḻivukaḷ*: SISSWPS, Madras 1970, 39-46.

[100] Zvelebil, K., *Smile*, 120.

[101] Ib., 124.

[102] Rajamanickam, M., "Kuṟiñcikkali", in *Kalittokaic*, 46-53, esp. 52.

CHAPTER 5.

LITERARY PRESENTATION OF AKAM POEMS

A. Number of Poems and Poets

One cannot pretend to know the exact number of Tamil poems composed at the classical period or coming from that period, and the number of poets who composed them.[1] One can only calculate from the printed editions of the Eṭṭuttokai and Pattuppāṭṭu. According to the calculation of V. Sp. Manickam,[2] the total number of published Tamil poems as coming from the classical period amounts to 2381. Of these, 519 poems belong to Puṟam category. The remaining 1862 poems treat of Akattiṇai or Akapporuḷ.[3] Among these 1862 poems on Akam, 882 speak of Kaḷavu, i.e. pre-marital love and 966 of Kaṟpu, i.e. wedded love, while 4 poems are about Kaikkiḷai, i.e. unrequited love, and 10 poems about Peruntiṇai, i.e. mismatched love.[4]

The total number of poets whose poems form the classical Tamil poetry amounts to 473, of whom 88 poets' names are not known. Of

---

[1] There are many reasons for this uncertainty. As regards the number of poems: The artificial schemes on which the poems have been collected and later edited show that there was certainly a selection in collecting and therefore not all poems have come down to us. There could be poems of the classical period which could not have found their way into the existing anthologies; e.g. certain poems cited by the commentators of Tolkāppiyam may belong to the classical corpus, although they are not found in the anthologies. The possibility of poems of post-classical age finding their way into the anthologies, though cannot be ruled out, is very minimal. As regards the number of poets: The problems involved are many. There are poems whose authors are not known by their names. The authors of some other poems have been named after some striking phrase or simile found in their poems. It is not impossible that the poets known by name could have been the authors of one or many of the poems whose authors are at present either not known or named by "poetic baptism". Even in counting the number of poets known by name, there can be differences. For, poets with the same name, e.g. Nakkīrar, Kapilar (e.g. Tolkapilar, Kapilar – two poets or one only?) could have existed and may be found in the list.

[2] Manickam, V. Sp., *Tamil Concept,* 1, 3, 58-59, 61, & 200-201; Id., *Tamiḻk Kātal,* Pari Nilaiyam, Madras 1980[3], 13, 92, 96, & 354ff.

[3] In this total number, he includes those poems which are entirely missing in the existing editions. The total is based on the number of poems supposed to have been contained in each anthology; cf. Chapter 4, "Short Notes on the Akam Anthologies."

[4] The classification of Akam poems according to Kaḷavu and Kaṟpu is, no doubt, later than the composition of the poems themselves.

these 88 poets, some 35 have been "named after some significant expression in their poems." [5] According to the calculation of V. Sp. Manickam, among the 473 poets, those who composed only Puṟam poems, number 95 (Men: 86; Women: 9) and the remaining 378 (Men: 355; Women: 23) composed poems on Akam. Of these 378, some 71 have contributed for both Puṟam and Akam. In short, the classification of Akam poems and poets is as follows:[6]

Kind of theme		*No. of poems*		*No. of poets*
Kaḷavu	AINTIṆAI	882	1848	238 (anonymous 41)
Kaṟpu		966		233 (anonymous 28)
Kaikkiḷai		4		2
Peruntiṇai		10		1

B. Classification of Akam Aspects

In Tamil poetic tradition, as we have seen earlier, Akam poetry is synonymous with love poetry. "Love in all its variety – love in separation and in union, before and after marriage, in chastity and betrayal – is the theme of *akam*." [7] The love relations that are portrayed in Akam poetry serve as a paradigm of all love relations and they are portrayed as an archetype, through statements by various characters in the relationship, at specific episodic moments in its unfolding.[8] Tolkāppiyar in his grammar enumerates, without defining, the love aspects and goes on to give some of the generalities of conventions on Akam poetry.[9]

---

[5] Zvelebil, K., *Smile*, 48.

[6] Manickam, V. Sp., *Tamil Concept, 200.*

According to the strict criteria we set up for ourselves, only the following are the Akam poems:

Aiṅkuṟunūṟu	500-2: 498
Kuṟuntokai	401
Naṟṟiṇai	399
Akanāṉūṟu	400
Kalittokai	149
Pattuppāṭṭu	4
Total	1851

Of these poems, 1698 will be our primary source of study. The other 153 will be our secondary source.

[7] Ramanujan, A. K., *The Interior Landscape*, Peter Owen, London 1970, 104.

[8] *Kuṟuntokai*, Eng. trans. M. Shanmugam Pillai & David E. Ludden, Koodal Publishers, Madurai 1976, 3.

In general, the love relation of a man and a woman falls under two main divisions, if considered from the chronological aspect of life. They are technically known as Kaḷavu and Kaṟpu in Tamil Akam literature. Kaḷavu roughly refers to pre-marital love relations and Kaṟpu to post-marital state.

1. *Kaḷavu*

The Kaḷavu aspect of Akam-life covers "the period of courtship, finally resulting in happy wedlock."[10] Following are some of the main themes of Kaḷavu, which represent certain stages or situations, logical or chronological, in courtship:

- Union through Destiny: Iyaṟkaippuṇarcci
  - Union of hearts or mental union: Uḷḷappuṇarcci or Kāmappuṇarcci.[11]
  - Physical union: Meyyuṟupuṇarcci
- Meeting at the same place, i.e. tryst or renewed meetings: Iṭantalaippāṭu.
- Meetings arranged by friends:
  - By the male companion of the lover: Pāṅkaṟkūṭṭam
  - By the female companion of the lady love: Tōḻiyiṟpuṇarcci
- Discreet revelation of heroine's love-affair: Aṟattoṭu niṟṟal.
- Elopement: Uṭanpōkku.[12]

Tolkāppiyar speaks of this aspect of love-life in Kaḷaviyal cūtrams 92-141.[13] Kaḷavu is only a preparation and a means to an end which is Kaṟpu, i.e. married life.[14]

---

[9] For convenient English translation of Tolkāppiyam and critical studies, see Ilakkuvaṉār, S., *Tholkāppiyam* (in English), Madurai 1963. Akattiṇaiyiyal, cūtrams: 1-55, on pp. 153-162; critical comments, 393-411. The English translation of Tolkāppiyam rules quoted in our study, are from this work.

[10] Somasundaram Pillai, J. M., *History*, 59. He remarks: "Kaḷaviyal is sometimes mistakenly translated as clandestine or furtive love, thus robbing it of all its charm, beauty and naturalness. It is but a natural union of two hearts bereft of the usual conventions of the society, but not in any way violating the principle of virtue and righteousness."

[11] In this phrase – kāmappuṇarcci – the term *kāmam* does not mean lust. The word comes from the root *kamam* meaning "to fill". Hence it here means "love that fills the heart". Thus kāmappuṇarcci means the intermingling of hearts filled with love; cf. Natarajan, A. D., "An Introduction to the Traditional Doctrine of Love", in *PFICSTS*, Vol. II, IATR, 1969, 81.

[12] Manickam, V. Sp., *Tamil Concept*, 26-59; Id., *Tamiḻk*, 41-92; *Kuṟuntokai*, trans. M. Shanmugam Pillai, 10-11.

[13] Ilakkuvaṉār, S., *Tholkāppiyam*, 175-188 and comments in 412-425. For a summary exposé, see Victor, M., *Tamil-Islamic*, Vol. I, 27-34; Balakrishna Mudaliyar, N. R., *The Golden Anthology of Ancient Tamil Literature*, Vol. II, SISSWPS, Madras 1959, xx-xxi.

[14] Pillay, K. K., *Social History*, 178.

2. *Kaṟpu*

Kaṟpu comprises the life of wedlock and the ideal domestic felicity.[15] Tolkāppiyam treats of wedded love in Kaṟpiyal cūtrams: 142-194.[16] The poems on Kaṟpu in the classical corpus describe not only the love relations of the husband and wife, but also their agonies in separation, quarrels in case of betrayal by man, etc. Some of such situations in married life are the following:

- Separation for wealth: Poruḷvayiṟpirivu
    - Delay in departure: Celavu aḻuṅkal
    - During separation, mutual comfort of the lady love and her companion: Āṟṟutal and āṟṟuvittal
- Advent of the season of Monsoon: Paruva varavu
- Return of the hero: Viṉai muṟṟittirumpal
- Seeking the company of prostitutes: Parattaiyiṟ pirivu.[17]

It must be mentioned that though Kaḷavu is a means to the end that is Kaṟpu, the latter need not always be preceded by Kaḷavu.[18] In other words, there were other ways in which Kaṟpu was undertaken, e.g. marriage arranged by parents.[19] That Kaṟpu was the goal of Kaḷavu seems to be proved also by the fact that poems on Kaṟpu are more numerous than those on Kaḷavu.[20]

These two main divisions of love-life are further subdivided and treated under the seven tiṇai, which we may conveniently call the seven behavioral patterns. Tolkāppiyar speaks of these sevenfold tiṇai division in the very first cūtram on Akattiṇaiyiyal: "From *Kaikkiḷai* to *Peruntiṇai* are the seven conducts described foremost, say the scholars" (Tol. Por. Akat. cūt. 1). The seven conducts are: Kaikkiḷai, Kuṟiñci, Mullai, Pālai, Marutam, Neytal, Peruntiṇai. Of these seven, the first and the last are not considered as belonging to ideal love relation or behaviour, and are therefore not favoured themes in the extant poems. The seven conducts may be represented by a diagram:

---

[15] Somasundaram Pillai, J. M., *History*, 59.

[16] Translation and critical comments in Ilakkuvaṉār, S., *Tholkāppiyam*, 189-202 and 425-450 respectively. Balakrishna Mudaliyar, N. R., *Golden*, xxii-xxiii.

[17] Manickam, V. Sp., *Tamil Concept*, 59-70; Id., *Tamiḻk*, 93-108.

[18] Pillay, K. K., *Social History*, 178; Manickam, V. Sp., *Tamil Concept*, 59.

[19] Manickavasagom, M. E., "Patterns of Early Tamil Marriages", *TC*, XI, 4 (1964), 329-338. The author studies about five patterns of marriages that are found in the classical Tamil poems. The Kaḷavu pattern is one of the five.

[20] Manickam, V. Sp., *Tamil Concept*, 61.

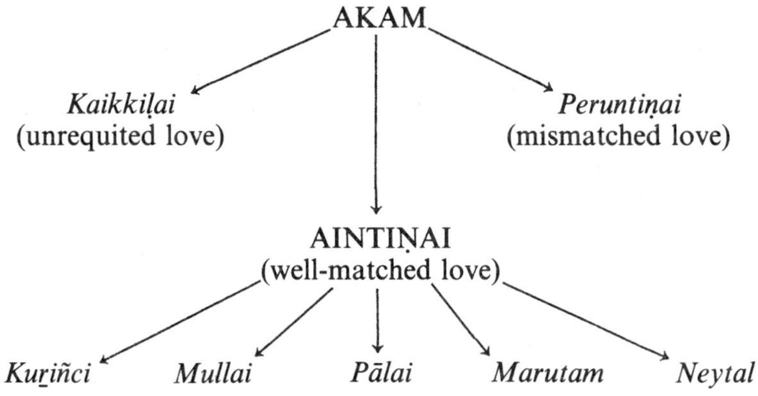

C. The Two Extremes: Kaikkiḷai and Peruntiṇai

In the very first rule in Akattiṇaiyiyal, Tolkāppiyar mentions Kaikkiḷai in the beginning and Peruntiṇai in the end, i.e. "Kaikkiḷai mutalāp peruntiṇai iṟuvāy..." Hence in the order of enumeration, these two occur as extremes. Why are they named at both ends of the enumeration? K. P. Aravaanan sees in this order an historical sequence of people's behaviour and development of love-conducts.[21] Most of the commentators and critics think that Kaikkiḷai and Peruntiṇai belong to non-ideal love relations, but in different ways: namely,

> Kaikkiḷai, *per defectum*, i.e. unrequited, unreciprocated love; some even call it "subnormal love";
>
> Peruntiṇai, *per excessum*, i.e. mismatched, ill-assorted love; some even term it "abnormal love."[22]

Kaikkiḷai: Tolkāppiyar, as usual, only describes, without giving a definition of Kaikkiḷai, the situation in which this love-relation may be found: "Unreciprocated love occurs in the act of having pleasure in addressing a young girl who is not matured for enjoyment, he being possessed of agony of love, having afflictions which cannot be removed and attributing good and evil to himself and to her without having any reply from her" (Tol. Por. Akat. cūt. 50). From the description of the situation, it is clear that the mental attitude of Kaikkiḷai belongs

---

[21] Aravaanan, K. P., *Aṟṟaināḷ*, 90-94.

[22] E.g. Balakrishna Mudaliyar, N. R., *Golden*, 15; Ilakkuvaṉār, S., *Tholkāppiyam*, 394ff; Gnanasambandan, A. S., *Akamum Puṟamum: Akam*, Pari Nilaiyam, Madras 1956, 14.

exclusively to the male sex.[23] "The concept of Kaikkiḷai is to bring into picture a passing mental phenomenon of the masculine sexual character born of confusion of condition or deceptive appearance."[24] The absence of "union of hearts" – in other words, the absence of reciprocation on the part of the girl who appears physically mature but not yet psychologically and sexually mature, is the chief feature to be noted in Kaikkiḷai. In short, "Kaikkiḷai may be said to be an abortive form of Ahattiṇai."[25] In the whole of Akam classics, only four poems on Kaikkiḷai are extant and they are all in the Kalittokai collection: Kali. 56, 57, 58. 109 — three by Kapilar and one by Nalluruttiraṉār.[26]

Peruntiṇai: Tolkāppiyar describes, again, the situation of Peruntiṇai and offers us no definition in Tol. Por. Akat. cūt. 51. More than one interpretation has been given to this cūtram and Peruntiṇai has been defined and explained in different ways by authors.[27] A critical and detailed study of this question by V. Sp. Manickam shows that "the function of Peruntiṇai is to describe four kinds of excessive or intemperate behaviour of the hero and heroine of Aintiṇai." He argues that "the adjective 'perum' connotes the overstepping of certain limits enunciated in Aintiṇai, by the lovers of mutual union."[28] In other words, there is the "union of hearts" and reciprocity between the lovers, but due to certain external circumstances in life the lovers exceed the borders of ideal love conduct. There are four situations in which such excessive behaviours may occur:

On the part of the hero: 1) Actual riding of the *maṭal* horse when he is unable to secure the object of his love.[29]

---

[23] Manickam, V. Sp., *Tamil Concept*, 70-73, esp. 128-138; Id., *Tamiḻk*, 108-112, esp. 228-243, where the author has studied the notion of Kaikkiḷai elaborately and in my opinion convincingly established his interpretation.

[24] Manickam, V. Sp., *Tamil Concept*, 134.

[25] Ib., 136.

[26] Ib., 72. In footnote 2 on p. 73, the author ascribes Kuṟ. 78 to Kaikkiḷai.

[27] See Natarajan, A. D., "Introduction", in *PFICSTS*, Vol. II, 75; Shanmugam Pillai, M., *Kuṟuntokai*, 21; Aravaanan, K. P., *Aṟṟaināḷ*, 94.

[28] Manickam, V. Sp., *Tamil Concept*, 141. See the complete discussion on the cūtram and its interpretation in *Tamil Concept*, 138-150; Id., *Tamiḻk*, 246-276.

[29] Maṭalēṟutal: Maṭal means the palmyra leaf. The figure of a horse would be made by using this palmyra leaf. The young man, who is prevented by the parents or brothers of his lady-love to marry her, would mount this horse and cause it to be drawn through the streets. He would wear garlands of *erukkam* buds (calatropis gigantea), hold aloft a flag with a figure of his beloved painted on it and thus make his love for her publicly known. This is supposed to be meant to draw the attention of the elders of the village, who would eventually mediate for his marriage with his beloved; cf. Ilakkuvaṉār, S., *Tholkāppiyam*, 407-408. See Naṟ. 146,152 for description of maṭalēṟutal.

2) Protracted separation so as to lose the cream of youth without sexual enjoyment.

On the part of the heroine: 1) Pining away beyond consolation.

2) Any venture resorted to by the heroine due to excessive lust.[30]

There are altogether ten poems, only in Kalittokai, 138-147 by Nallantuvaṉār. Of these, four describe masculine Peruntiṇai and six feminine Peruntiṇai.[31]

D. The Ideal Five

Once the two extremes – Kaikkiḷai and Peruntiṇai – are excluded, whatever remains in love-life may be considered as belonging to balanced and ideal aspects of love. This is the way at least the Tamil poetic tradition treats the love-life. Universal experience, age-long observation and a deep analysis of lovers' psychology seem to lie at the origin of the literary execution and grammatical formulation in Tamil of these five ideal aspects of Akam. These five aspects are technically called *Aintiṇai*, i.e. five conducts or five behavioral patterns.

Experience has fixed the age limit within which a balanced enjoyment of sexual life is possible: "Aintiṇai takes notice of the state of the body, mind and heart of both sexes, only from the time when they begin to feel sexual excitement mentally and physically. It continues its treatment as long as the lovers possess physical stamina and sexual hunger."[32] Observation and reflection have reduced the whole of love-life to two basic factors: Union and separation of lovers. Separation may occur in two ways: 1) For just reasons, i.e. for reasons that are intimately connected with the duties of the hero; e.g. to serve in the battle; to earn wealth in order to support the family and relatives. 2) For frivolous reason: the only such reason treated in Tamil Akam poems is the seeking of the harlots by the hero, namely Parattaiyiṟ pirivu. Separation for just reasons may take place either before or after the marriage, for example, to earn wealth for paying the bride price (thus before marriage) or for supporting the family (thus after the marriage). There are two main moods in which the lovers may react when they are separated for just reasons: a) Patient waiting; b) Pining. The actions and

---

[30] Manickam, V. Sp., *Tamil Concept*, 72-73.

[31] Ib., 73. In the footnote 2, he ascribes Ak. 135, Kuṟ. 31,325, to Peruntiṇai.

[32] Ib., 158.

reactions of the lovers when separation occurs due to the infidelity of the hero may be brought under "quarrel and reconciliation." Hence there are altogether five behavioral patterns or tiṇais in the life of balanced love. A great number of life-situations may be possible within these five tiṇais — which in turn are termed *tuṟai*. We may show the five aspects of balanced love-life as:

Love-Life

Union (Puṇartal) Kuṟiñci

Separation (Pirital) Pālai

For just reason

For frivolous reason

Patient waiting (Iruttal) Mullai

Pining (Iraṅkal) Neytal

Quarrel & Reconciliation (Ūṭal) Marutam

Thus it appears that "the intrinsic stratum of all tiṇai in Akam except *kuṟiñji* is separation in one form or the other."[33]

E. **Landscape – Nature – Love Aspects**

None would deny the intimate – almost causal relation between environment and culture. Landscape, climate and the natural surroundings of the habitat exercise a considerable influence on human behaviour and consequently also on the behaviour of the lovers. Literature reflects culture. If so, the Akam poems veritably reflect the behaviour of lovers in the natural surroundings of Tamilnadu. "The physical texture of the South Indian landscape with its mountains and rivers and its clearly defined contours, gave the South of India not only an excuse for its small kingdoms and smaller chieftaincies, but also formed the basis for the division of poetry on geographical regions as for example 'mountain poetry', 'pasture-land poetry' and 'seaside poetry'."[34] The physiographical divisions of the landscape, the behavioral patterns of lovers in the respective regions, the poetry that originated and reflected those behavioral patterns and the imagery used in those poems are all intimately connected and reciprocally influential.[35]

---

[33] Mahadevan, K., "Refractions in Akam Poetry", in PFifICSTS, Vol. I, sec. 7, IATR, Madras 1981, 17-20, the citation is from p. 18.

[34] Thani Nayagam, X. S., *Nature*, 2-3.

[35] Ib., 4ff. The whole thesis is about the interplay of Nature and Poetry in Classical Tamil Literature. Chapters II, III, IV & VII are particularly related to our study.

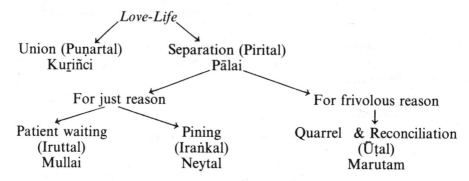

In Tamil poetry, the five ideal love aspects bear the conventional names of the geographical regions in which such behaviours were peculiar or prevalent. Usually, fact gives birth to fashion. So too, culture gives birth to conventions. In Tamil poetry, the literary conventions reflect in fact the culture of the people. "The Tamil literary conventions are not rules unconsciously followed by poets and codified by critics of a later age, like Aristotle's canons of epic poetry and those described by Horace. Ancient Tamil literary conventions were petrifications of old customs developed by the action of the environment on human life. Literary conventions, especially of the early, unsophisticated stages of literature... were based on the actual customs and manners of the people."[36] In the words of X.S. Thani Nayagam, "what later became the fashion was then the fact."[37]

The five aspects of ideal love are associated with five tracts of land. It is certain that four of these tracts of land are actually found in Tamilnadu and their names come from the flowers which grow in those regions. About the origin of the name of one region called Pālai, there is no consensus among scholars. The five symbolic names of love aspects are: Kuṟiñci, Mullai, Pālai, Marutam, and Neytal.[38] Tolkāppiyar has classified and described these literary conventions under the headings: Mutaṟporuḷ, Karupporuḷ, and Uripporuḷ.

1. *Mutaṟporuḷ*

The spatio-temporal substratum of the drama of love is called the Mutaṟporuḷ. The temporal aspect in the cūtram about spatio-temporal setting is not the time which is the basis of chronology and in which an historian is interested, but the temporal aspect or the time in which a geographer and even more a psychologist are interested.[39] Space and time are important for history which belongs to exterior world. But they are even more important for the interior world – which is love-life.

The spatial substratum is called Nilam, i.e. geographical region. The temporal substratum is designated by the word Poḻutu which means time. The time is divided into Perumpoḻutu, i.e. the season of the year, like

[36] Srinivas Iyengar, P.T., *The History*, 63. See also 69-70.

[37] Thani Nayagam, X.S., *Nature*, 108. That literary conventions in Tamil poetry had their origin in real life is accepted by the majority of critics; e.g. K. Zvelebil, *TC*, X, 2 (1963), 26-27. A.A. Manavalan, however, maintains that the fivefold division of Akaṉaintiṇai is a purely poetic convention; see "Caṅka Ilakkiyam", in *Tamiḻ Ilakkiyak Koḷkai*, IITS, Madras 1975, 25-64, esp. 33.

[38] J.R. Marr writes: "It would seem reasonable to suggest that the words were the names of plants first of all, and were then applied to the regions in which these plants grow... The words then came to denote the aspects of love with which each region was associated", *Eight Tamil*, 20-21; cf. also 22.

[39] Cf. Rasanayagama, Y., "Physico and Poetic Tradition in Tamil Literature of the Tholkāppiyam and Sangam Periods", in *PFifICSTS*, Vol. I, sec. 7, 37.

summer or winter etc. and Cirupolutu, i.e. the time of the day, like morning or midday or evening. Tolkāppiyar speaks about these temporal aspects in Tol. Por. Akat. cūts. 4,6-11. "The season ascribed to each aspect of conjugal behaviour is not only the one that is conducive to it but also the pre-eminent one in the land."[40]

The physiographical division of the (Tamil) world is hinted at Tol. Por. Akat. cūt. 2 and formulated in cūt. 5. According to cūt. 5, forest- region (lit. forest-world) occupied by Māyōṉ (Tirumāl), mountainous- region occupied by Cēyōṉ (Murukaṉ), water-logged region occupied by Vēntaṉ (Indra), sea-shore region occupied by Varuṇaṉ — these are said to be Mullai, Kuṟiñci, Marutam and Neytal respectively. It is noteworthy that each class is defined in this cūtram both by reference to the god of choice and also by its physical features or vegetation. Thus it is clear that cultural-sphere and physiography have been the basis of classification adopted in this cūtram.[41] The god of choice belongs actually to the Karupporuḷ.

2. *Karupporuḷ*

Karu lit. means 'nucleus, embryo'. Hence Karupporuḷ means the embryonic elements or the native elements of each region. According to Tol. Por. Akat. cūt. 18, "God, food, animal, tree, bird, drum, profession, lute and such others" are said to form the Karupporuḷ.

3. *Uripporuḷ*

This is the proper or specific matter of poetry. Tol. Por. Akat. cūt. 14, enumenrates: Union – Puṇartal, Separation – Pirital, Patient waiting – Iruttal, Pining – Iraṅkal, Love quarrel – Ūṭal and their causes are the specific aspects of the five tiṇai.

---

[40] Ib., 41.

[41] Ib., 38. The cūtrams of Tol. Por. Akat. are in themselves not very clear and precise as regards the division of the landscapes and allotment of uripporuḷ. Notice that cūt. 2 mentions "the middle five tiṇais", i.e. excepting Kaikkiḷai and Peruntiṇai, (cf. cūt. 1) and states that the world is apportioned to them, except to the tiṇai which is in the middle (of the five tiṇais). What is the name of that middle of the five tiṇais? Cūtram 5 gives only four regions by name – but what is the name of the fifth region? Even in cūt. 9, where the seasons and the time of the day are allotted, the name of the tiṇai is not given; it is referred only as "the middle placed tiṇai". Nor is the assignment of uripporuḷ clear from the cūtram 14. For, there is merely the enumeration, but how to correspond them to the four named and the one unnamed tiṇai? Cūtram 5 gives the order, mullai, kuṟiñci, marutam, and neytal, while cūt. 14 gives the order, puṇartal, pirital, iruttal, iraṅkal and ūṭal, but which fits where? Only by way of an inference from cūtrams 9-10 through cūt. 11, one *might* conclude that separation may be the uripporuḷ of the unnamed middle tiṇai! Even then the name *Pālai* for that tiṇai appears nowhere! The first one to give the name Pālai to that middle tiṇai is the commentator of the grammar called Kaḷaviyal or Iṟaiyaṉār Akapporuḷ and that too in this order: kuṟiñci, neytal, pālai, mullai, marutam. Pālai is in the middle, of course, but the others have been displaced! See *Kaḷaviyal*, SISSWPS, Madras 1953, 17.

The following table gives the essentials of the mutal, karu and uripporuḷ of the four named and one unnamed regions as they are found in the cūtrams of Tolkāppiyam:

	Mullai	Kuṟiñci	"the middle" (Pālai)	Marutam	Neytal
Mutaṟporuḷ					
1) Nilam	Forest region	Mountainous region	——	Water-logged region	Sea-shore region
2) Poḻutu					
a) Perum:	Rainy season	Cold season Dewy season	Summer Later part of snow season	——	——
b) Ciṟu:	Evening	Midnight	Midday	Last hours of night & the dawn	Sunset
Karupporuḷ					
God, etc.	Māyōṉ	Cēyōṉ	——	Vēntaṉ	Varuṇaṉ
Uripporuḷ					
Love-aspect	Iruttal (Patient waiting)	Puṇartal (Union)	Pirital (Separation)	Ūṭal (Love-quarrel)	Iraṅkal (Pining)

The detailed table at the end of this chapter tries to bring together all those items which belong to karupporuḷ. This and similar tables of karupporuḷ, etc. are inspired by Iṟaiyaṉār Akapporuḷurai.[42] Most of these items found in the commentary of Iṟaiyaṉār Akapporuḷ have been integrated into the grammar by the author of Nampiyakapporuḷ.[43]

Observations: The following observations, critical and literary, may help to appreciate the regional concepts of love life and the poetic conventions associated with them.

---

[42] *Kaḷaviyal*, 19-23, where the commentator elaborates the list of karupporuḷ found in Tol. Por. Akat. cūt. 18. The detailed table in pp. 120-123 is from Singaravelu, S., *Social Life of the Tamils: The Classical Period*, Kuala Lumpur 1966, 19ff.

[43] Nāṟkavirāca Nampi *Nampiyakapporuḷ*, SISSWPS, Madras 1943, Cūtrams 19-24.

1) It is to be emphasized that Tolkāppiyar is following the previous tradition in his classification of the regions and love aspects. In cūtrams 1, 4, 7, 10, 11 and 12, he explicitly refers to scholars or poets. One vital element of the karupporuḷ, namely God, is deliberately brought in for classifying the land. Thus it is made clear that the classification is not only based on the physiography but also influenced by the cultural-biosphere. It is gratifying to discern the close connection between geography, culture and literature.[44]

2) Bio-geography is the basis for the nomenclature of the regions. In other words, "each region got its name by the flower of the most typical of it."[45] Thus kuṟiñci, mullai, marutam, and neytal got their names from Strobilanthes (conehead), Jasminum sambac (Arabian jasmine), Terminalia tomentosa, and Nymphaea lotus alba (white Indian water-lily or blue nelumbo) respectively. Pālai, which has no proper region or tract, has also been ascribed a flower that is called Mimusops kauki (silvery-leaved ape-flower).[46] K. P. Aravaanan thinks that in the initial stage, these flowers of the four regions might have served as totemic symbols.[47] Whatever it is, naming a town or a village after the name of the flower or tree that grows predominantly in that locality is not unknown in Tamilnadu.[48] It seems probable that kuṟiñci, mullai and neytal got their names from flowers and marutam and pālai from the trees which are typical.[49]

3) How the unnamed middle tiṇai got its present name of Pālai is a matter of discussion, since Tolkāppiyam has allotted to it neither nilam, i.e. region nor god. In other words, only Poḻutu from Mutaṟporuḷ and the Uripporuḷ, i.e. Pirital are mentioned. The commentator of Iṟaiyaṉār Akapporuḷ refers to "others" (piṟar) who hold Bakhavati and Ātittaṉ as gods of Pālai.[50] A later grammar on Akam, called Nampiyakapporuḷ, is the first Akam-grammar which gives the name Pālai to this tiṇai along with others in this order: Kuṟiñci, Pālai, Mullai, Marutam and Neytal.[51]

---

[44] Rasanayagama, Y., "Physico", in *PFifICSTS*, Vol. I, sec. 7, 39.

[45] Ib., 41. Flowers played and still continue to play a predominant role in Tamil culture. See Baskaran, K., "Plants and Tamil Culture", *JTamS* 12 (1979), 58-62; Thani Nayagam, X. S., "The Tamils said it all with Flowers", *TC* 2 (1953), 164-175.

[46] Zvelebil, K., *Smile*, 100. The commentary on Iṟaiyaṉār Akapporuḷ allotts marāmpū, kurāmpū and pātirippū to Pālai, cf. *Kaḷaviyal*, 21. Nampiyakapporuḷ cūt. 21 enumerates only marāam and kurāam flowers. But it enumerates pālai tree among the trees that belong to Pālai.

[47] Cf. Aravaanan, K. P., "Mara Vaḻipāṭu", *JTamS* 20 (1981), 113.

[48] One of the typical cases is the name of the town called Chingleput near Madras. The town was originally named after the flower Ceṅkaḻunīr, thus *Ceṅkaḻunīr paṭṭu* (i.e. the village of Ceṅkaḻunīr flower. This name in course of time became Chingleput! Compare also such names as Puṉṉaikkāyal, Kāñciyūr, Kāñcīpuram, etc.

[49] Marutam tree has, no doubt, flowers. But the tree is more significant and characteristic than the flower as such. So also for pālai, the tree is more typical than the flower; e.g. Veṭpālai tree has got flowers but the tree is more important in dry areas.

[50] *Kaḷaviyal*, 21.

[51] See cūtram 6. Notice the order: Pālai is not in the middle as Tolkāppiyam maintains.

There are two opinions about the history of the name Pālai for this tiṇai or region:

a) Tolkāppiyar did not assign a permanent region and a god to Pālai simply because "desert land" does not exist in Tamilnadu. It is a temporary situation of one or more of the four regions, due to lack of rain for a long time, esp. the kuṟiñci and mullai tracts. This opinion has in its favour Cilappatikāram, XI, 64-66: "The mullai and kuṟiñci regions, being dried and become waste, take the form of pālai."[52]

b) Another view is represented by Y. Rasanayagama: "Pālai is from Pāl or Paku meaning to divide or separate...[53] ... Originally the region which came in between the four categories of land was called Pālai Nilam. Generally such land was marginal land uninhabited or very sparsely inhabited. The extent of such marginal land was swelled by spells of drought in the other four categories. The marginal strips in these four categories themselves became Pālai land when parched up by drought."[54] The Uripporuḷ of Pālai is symbolically connected with the geographically dividing strip of land which *de facto* cannot be fixed. Tol. Por. Akat. cūt. 9 seems to use the expression "the middle placed tiṇai" in double-entendre. The dictum of Cilappatikāram fits well in this explanation also! An interesting botanical observation is that the trees which grow in such dry waste lands have in most cases a milky sap (pāl) and bear names which have the ending *pālai*, e.g. Veṭpālai (Hollarhena-Antidysentrica), Nila pālai (Wrightia tinctoria).[55]

---

[52] E.g. Thani Nayagam, X. S., *Nature*, 93 & 111.

[53] Compare in grammar *āṇpāl, peṇpāl, pālpakā* akṟiṇai etc. where *pāl* seems to denote division or separation.

[54] Rasanayagama, Y., "Physico", *PFifICSTS*, Vol. I, sec. 7, 39-40 & 44.

[55] Samy, P. L., "Common Names and Myths of the Flora and Fauna in Dravidian and Indo-Aryan Languages", *PFifICSTS*, Vol. II, sec. 8, IATR, Madras 1981, 43-53, esp. 43-44. The author has made various studies on this point at different times. See esp. his study, *Caṅka Ilakkiyattil Ceṭikoṭi Viḷakkam*, Madras 1967.

Both the explanations can be combined. It is true that there is no desert land as such to be found anywhere in Tamilnadu. But there are tracts of land which, due to lack of rain and water for a considerable period of time, can and do in fact become tracts of land which conform very well – almost literally with the description of pālai poems. Such tracts were the border lands between regions. The existence of villages with such names as Vadapālai (i.e. north-wasteland) in South Arcot district is a proof of it. Besides, there were such arid tracts or even a long stretch of such a tract between the Tamil country and the country of different language (moḻipeyar tēyam). Historically, this was the "region between the river Krishna in the north and a little south of Tungabadra and North Pennar, studded with hills and mountain ranges" – namely the traditional northern boundary of ancient Tamilnadu. This region is "still the hottest part (ca. 120° to 125°F) in South India." The graphic description of pālai tract as found in poems like Ak. 27,85,141,177,209,253,393; cf. also 31,127,211,213,265; and Naṟ. 48; Kuṟ. 174, reflect the geographical situation of this region. The name of the region Vēṅkaṭam (kaṭam – arid

4) As regards the priority within the three poruḷ, i.e. mutaṟporuḷ, karupporuḷ and uripporuḷ, – there are two main opinions among the commentators of Tolkāppiyam. The cūtram itself (Tol. Por. Akat. 3) is capable of being understood in both ways. Authors use comparisons to explain the cūtram and defend their respective interpretations. For example, the mutaṟporuḷ is compared to the maternal womb, the karupporuḷ to embryo and the uripporuḷ to the child.[56] Another author compares the mutal to "frame and skeleton", the karu to "members, flesh and blood" and the uripporuḷ to "life principle."[57] The controversy seems to gain importance in relation to classification of poems according to the Aintiṇai. Among the ancient commentators, Iḷampūraṇar holds that the mutaṟporuḷ is the most important.[58] The compilers of Akanāṉūṟu seem to have adopted Iḷampūraṇar's system to classify the poems in it.[59] Nacciṉārkkiṉiyar holds that uripporuḷ is the most important one.[60] This position is defended by some authors.[61] The fact that there are many poems which lack either mutal or karu or both, but have only the uripporuḷ, seems to argue in favour of this position.

Both the positions are right, but from two viewpoints: classifier and composer viewpoints. When the classifier is at work, for him the mutaṟporuḷ is the most important, and then come the karupporuḷ and uripporuḷ. He has to base his classification on mutaṟporuḷ, for want of which, he has to rely on karupporuḷ and if that also is lacking, then on the uripporuḷ. The rule that mutaṟporuḷ, i.e. region cannot intermingle, but karupporuḷ and uripporuḷ may be mingled in other regions, seems to support this approach.[62] From the composer's viewpoint, uripporuḷ is the most important. In practical terms, when a poet has to compose, say a

---

waste; vēm – contraction of vēkum – meaning "burning") testifies to its historicity. Cf. Kothandapani Pillai, K., "Vada Venkatam", *TC*, IX, 1 (1961), 65-92, esp. 79 for the quotations. Even today when one travels in summer by train from Madras to Bombay, one comes across part of this arid tract and there realizes how realistic the descriptions of this region are in pālai poems referred to above. The phrase *moḻipeyar tēyam* is another indication of the border nature, besides the testimony of the preface of Tolkāppiyam.

[56] Manikkam, N., "Mutal, karu, uri – Ōr Āyvu", *Tamiḻkkalai*, I, 2 (1983), 22-29.

[57] Manavalan, A. A., "Caṅka Ilakkiyam", in *Tamiḻ Ilakkiyak*, 25-64, esp. 32.

[58] Figuratively the mother is more important than the child. N. Manikkam agrees with Iḷampūraṇar, cf. "Mutal", *Tamiḻkkalai*, I, 2 (1983), 23ff.

[59] Cf. Rasanayagama, Y., "Physico", *PFifICSTS*, Vol. I, sec. 7, 42. The author herself is in agreement with Iḷampūraṇar's system.

[60] See Nacciṉārkkiṉiyar, *Tol. Por. Akat.* Commentary, 6ff.

[61] E.g. Manavalan, A. A., "Caṅka Ilakkiyam", *Tamiḻ Ilakkiyak*, 32; Varadarajan, M., "Literary Theories in Early Tamil - Eṭṭuttokai", in *PFICSTS*, Vol. II, IATR, Madras 1969, 45-54, esp. 47.

[62] See below on "Intermingling". The fact that poems which lack either mutal or both mutal and karupporuḷ have been classified on the basis of uripporuḷ alone, and not the other way about, is a strong proof; e.g. see the poem Kuṟ. 40 in specimen analysis.

short poem, he may leave out the mutaṟporuḷ, and include karu and urripporuḷ, or even he may overlook both mutal and karu and treat only the uripporuḷ, but never the other way about, i.e. he cannot omit the uripporuḷ.[63]

5) Intermingling: Tol. Por. Akat. cūts. 12-13 speak about the so-called *Tiṇaimayakkam*, i.e. the intermingling of one tiṇai or oḻukkam with another. The rules are explained according to the position taken with regard to the priority of the elements discussed above. The plain interpretation of the two rules on interchange seems to be the following: Intermingling of regions, i.e. the nilam, is not allowed. The interchange of behaviour is not prevented. Those other than uripporuḷ may overlap.[64] In other words, karupporuḷ may be intermingled. In cūt. 19, the grammarian explicitly mentions "the flower and the bird" as causing the tiṇaimayakkam.[65] There can be no interchange of gods. They are exclusive to one region.[66] In short, the regions, i.e. the landscapes and their respective gods do not move or mingle with others. The other elements may, to some extent, be intermingled.

---

[63] The typical and classical examples are the Kuṟaḷ veṇpās on love themes. Practically all of them have only uripporuḷ. So too many of the Aiṅkuṟunūṟu poems and some of the Kuṟuntokai poems. "For poetry the hierarchy of components is inverted; the Human Elements (uri), the Native Elements (karu), and the First Elements (mutal) are in a descending order of importance for a poet." Ramanujan, A. K., *Interior*, 108.

[64] Ilakkuvaṉār, S., *Tholkāppiyam*, 154 & 401. Nacciṉārkkiṉiyar and the followers of his opinion seem to think otherwise, see Thani Nayagam, X. S., *Nature*, 113.

[65] See also Subramanian, N., "The Avifauna of the Tamil Country", *TC* 12 (1966) 259-268, esp. 259-260.

[66] Thani Nayagam, X. S., *Nature*, 107. Tol. Por. Akat. has no cūtram forbidding explicitly the intermingling of gods. Could it be an inference from the cūtram that speaks about the division of fourfold regions and their respective gods?

CLASSIFICATION OF *KARUPPORUḶ* ('OBJECTS')

REGIONS	(1) PHRATRIES (Inhabitants)	(2) FAUNA (Animals)	(3) AVIFAUNA (Birds)	(4) FLORA (Flowers)
MONTANE (*Kuṟiñci*)	*Kuṟavar* (m), *Kuṟattiyar* (f), *Kāṉavar* (m).	Tiger. Bear, Elephant, Lion, Ram.	Peacock, Parrot.	*Kuṟiñci* (*Strobilanthus*), *Vēṅkai* (flower of *Kino tree*), *Gloriosa superba*. *Kaṭampu* (*Eugenia racemosa*).
ARID (*Pālai*)	*Eyiṉar* (m), *Eyiṟṟiyar* (f), *Maṟavar* (m), *Maṟattiyar* (f).	Jackal, Ass.	Eagle, Vulture, Pigeon.	*Pālai* (*Mimuscops Hexandrus*). *Kurāmpū* (*Webera corymbosa*).
PASTORAL (*Mullai*)	*Āyar* (m), *Āycciyar* (f), *Iṭaiyar* (m), Iṭaicciyar (f).	Gazelle, Wild hare, Cow, Bull, Sheep, Goat.	Wild fowl	*Jasmine* (*Mullai*), *Koṉṟai* (*Cassia*), *Kullai* (*Cannabis*), *Piṭavam*, *Tōṉṟi*.
AGRICULTURAL (*Marutam*)	*Uḻavar* (m), *Uḻattiyar* (f), *Kaṭaiyar* (m), *Kaṭaicciyar* (f).	Buffalo, Otter, Freshwater fish. Carp.	Heron, Swan, Water-fowl, Duck.	Aquatic plants, Lotus, Water-lily.
LITTORAL (*Neytal*)	*Nuḷayar* (m), *Nuḷaicciyar* (f), *Aḷavar* (m), *Aḷattiyar* (f), *Paratar* (m), *Parattiyar* (f).	Shark, Fish.	Sea-gull.	*Neytal* (*Nymphae alba*), *Tāḻampū* (*Pandanus*), *Muṇṭakam*, *Aṭampam*, Water-lily, Water-hyacinth.

CLASSIFICATION OF *KARUPPORUḶ* ('OBJECTS') (contd)

REGIONS	(5) TREES	(6) OCCUPATION AND	PASTIMES/ FESTIVITIES
MONTANE *(Kuṟiñci)*	Bamboo, Sandal wood. Teak, Aquila, *Acoka (Uvaria longifolia)*, *Nākam,* Margosa.	Hunting, Digging roots, Gathering honey, Seasonal cultivation of hill-paddy and millet.	*Veṟi-ātal* (Frenzied dancing), Bathing in hill stream, Bird-driving.
ARID *(Pālai)*	*Pālai, Ōmai (Salvadara persica), Iruppai (Bassia longifolia), Uḻiñai (Oerva lanater).*	Soldiering, Marauding, Highway robbery.	
PASTORAL *(Mullai)*	*Koṉṟai (Cassia). Kāyā, Kuruntam.*	Minor cultivation of crops like *vāraku, cāmai* etc., Shepherding, Cowherding.	*Kuravai* dance, Bull-fighting, River-bathing.
AGRICULTURAL *(Marutam)*	*Marutam (Terminalia alata), Kāñci, Vañci.*	Farming, Harvesting, Threshing.	River-bathing, Festivals, (agricultural).
LITTORAL *(Neytal)*	Alexandrine laurel, Mangrove.	Coastal and inland fishing, Deep-sea fishing, Drying the fish, Making salt, Pearl-diving, Selling fish.	Sailing, Bird-driving, Sea-bathing, Playing on sea-shore, Worshipping of skeleton of shark.

CLASSIFICATION OF *KARUPPORUḶ* ('OBJECTS') (contd)

REGIONS	(7) FOODSTUFFS	(8) WATER-RESOURCES	(9) DRUM	(10) MUSICAL INSTRUMENT
MONTANE *(Kuṟiñci)*	Meat, Hill paddy-rice, Bamboo rice, Millet, Honey, Roots.	Hill streams, and pools.	*Toṇṭakam*	*Kuṟiñci* lyre
ARID *(Pālai)*	Meat, Grass-rice, Roots.	Stagnant water in pits. Liquor.	*Tuṭi*	*Pālai* lyre
PASTORAL *(Mullai)*	*Varaku, Cāmai, Mutirai,* Milk and milk products.	Rivers, Tanks.	*Ēṟaṅkōl*	*Mullai* lyre
AGRICULTURAL *(Marutam)*	Paddy-rice, Sugar-cane.	River, Pond, Lake, Well.	*Kiṇai (For harvesting), Muḻavu (For wedding etc.)*	*Marutam* lyre
LITTORAL *(Neytal)*	Fish, and products obtained from other regions through barter.	Sea, Salt lakes, Sea-side canals.	*Mīn-kōl (For fishing), Nāvāy (For sailing).*	*Viḷari*

CLASSIFICATION OF *KARUPPORUḶ* ('OBJECTS') (contd)

	(11)	(12)	(13)	(14)
REGIONS	MUSICAL TUNE	SETTLEMENT	TITLES OF CHIEFTAIN AND HIS SPOUSE	DEITY
MONTANE (*Kuṟiñci*)	*Kuṟiñci*	*Ciṟukuṭi*	*Poruppaṉ* (m), *Verpaṉ* (m), or *Cilampaṉ* (m), *Kuṟatti* or *Koṭicci* (f).	Murukaṉ or Cēy.
ARID (*Pālai*)	*Pañcuram*	*Kuṟumpu*	*Viṭalai* (m), *Kāḷai* (m), or *Mīḷi* (m), *Eyiṟṟi* (f).	Turkkai, Kaṉṉi, or Koṟṟavai.
PASTORAL (*Mullai*)	*Cātāri*	*Pāṭi*	*Kuṟumpoṟai-nātaṉ* (m), or *Tōṉṟal* (m), *Maṉaivi* (f), or *Kiḻatti* (f).	Neṭumāl, or Tirumāl.
AGRICULTURAL (*Marutam*)	*Marutam*	*Pērūr*	*Ūraṉ* (m), or Makiḻnaṉ (m), Kiḻatti (f), or Maṉaivi (f).	Intiraṉ, or Vēntaṉ.
LITTORAL (*Neytal*)	*Sevvaḻi*	*Pākkam, Paṭṭiṉam.*	*Cērppaṉ* (m), or *Pulampaṉ* (m). *Paratti* (f), or *Nuḷaicci* (f).	Varuṇaṉ.

CHAPTER 6.

POETRY AND SYMBOLISM

A. **Poetry: The Akaval Metre**

The entire corpus of early classical Tamil poetry, namely the Anthologies (considering Kalittokai as belonging to the later classics) is composed in the akaval metre. Hence only the metrics of akaval or āciriyappā will be explained in a somewhat summary treatment.[1]

Tolkāppiyam Poruḷatikāram Ceyyuḷiyal deals with Tamil prosody. The first cūtram of Ceyyuḷiyal enumerates thirty-four component parts of poetry.[2] This enumeration includes "the elaborations of our phonetic experiences" such as the letter, duration, etc. and "the prosodic elaborations of such an experience."[3] This cūtram seems to give a comprehensive view of how to analyze and appreciate poetry. The metrics proper is expounded from cūtram 315 onwards.

Tamil prosody has four basic constituents: a) Acai or the basic metrical unit;[4] b) Cīr or a foot which is composed of one or more acais; c) Taḷai, i.e. the manner in which different feet are connected; d) Aṭi or the line.

a) *Acai*: The acai is the most basic component of Tamil metrics and it is either nēr or nirai (called nēracai or niraiyacai respectively). These

---

[1] Our primary source for this study is naturally Tolkāppiyam Poruḷatikāram Ceyyuḷiyal cūtrams: 313-555, and Pērāciriyar's Commentary, SISSWPS, 1975[5]. For English translation Ilakkuvaṉār, S., *Tholkāppiyam,* 223-248 & 460-466. For a more critical and elaborate study of Tamil Prosody, one may conveniently refer to the following works: Chidambaranatha Chettiar, A., *Advanced Studies in Tamil Prosody*, Annamalai University, Annamalainagar 1943, Repr. 1955, 1957. References in our study are to the edition of 1943. Zvelebil, K., *An Introduction to Tamil Classical Prosody*, Hoe & Co., Madras 1972; Marr, J. R., *Eight Tamil*, chapter on Prosody.

[2] They are: 1) Māttirai, 2) Eḻuttu, 3) Acai, 4) Cīr, 5) Aṭi, 6) Yāppu, 7) Marapu, 8) Tūkku, 9) Toṭai, 10) Nōkku, 11) Pā, 12) Aḷavu, 13) Tiṇai, 14) Kaikōḷ, 15) Kūṟṟu, 16) Kēṭpōr, 17) Kaḷaṉ, 18) Kālam, 19) Payaṉ, 20) Meyppāṭu, 21) Eccam, 22) Muṉṉam, 23) Poruḷ, 24) Tuṟai, 25) Māṭṭu, 26) Vaṇṇam, 27) Ammai, 28) Aḻaku, 29) Toṉmai, 30) Tōl, 31) Viruntu, 32) Iyaipu, 33) Pulaṉ, 34) Iḻaipu.

[3] Meenakshisundaram, T. P., "The Theory of Poetry in Tolkappiyar", *TC*, I, 2 (1952), 106.

[4] Ilakkuvaṉār, S., *Tholkāppiyam*, 223, 460, et passim, Meenakshisundaram, T. P., *TC* I, 2 (1952), 105, and Chidambaranatha Chettiar, A., *Advanced*, 21, all translate acai by syllable. But K. Zvelebil prefers "metrical unit" for rendering acai, see *Smile*, 65 and note 2. After explaining what it is, we shall use the very word *acai.*

two acais – nēr and nirai – have besides two other modified forms, and thus there are altogether four acais or basic metrical units. They are formed and recognized as follows:

Nēr acai: Simple metrical unit, long or short, which may or may not be followed by a consonant: (C)V(C).[5] In other words,

– One short letter (i.e. short vowel or short vowelled consonant) alone or followed by a vowelless consonant (which stops the movement, i.e. acai, lit. move, stir.).

– One long letter (i.e. long vowel or long vowelled consonant) alone or followed by a vowelless consonant (Tol. Por. Cey. 315).

Nirai acai: Compound metrical unit, made up of two short syllables or a short, followed by a long syllable, with or without a consonant following: (C)VCV(C). In other words,

– Two short letters with or without a pure consonant, i.e. a vowelless consonant, following.

– One short *and* one long letter with or without a pure consonant following. The initial syllable (i.e. vowel or vowelled consonant) is always short. If long, it would make by itself a nēr acai (Tol. Por. Cey. 315).

Nērpu acai: This is the modified nēr acai. If a nēr is followed by -u or by the shortened -u, it is called nērpu, i.e. nēr modified by -u (Tol. Por. Cey. 316). If, however, the -u follows a single short letter (i.e. syllable), e.g. cuṭu, kuḻu, it will be a nirai acai and not a nērpu acai. Both nēr acai and nērpu acai may be symbolized by —.

Niraipu acai: If a nirai is followed by -u or by the shortened -u it is called niraipu, i.e. nirai modified by -u (Tol. Por. Cey. 316). The symbol for nirai and niraipu acai is ═.

b) *Cīr*: A cīr or foot is composed of one or more acais. The smallest foot consists of one acai and is called ōracaiccīr (i.e. a foot of one metrical unit or acai). The next smallest and most commonplace foot consists of two acais and is called by a general term, akavaṟcīr (namely,

---

[5] These symbols are from Zvelebil, K., *Smile*, 65-66. We follow his method of symbolization.

the foot which pertains to akaval) or āciriyaccīr (namely, the foot which belongs to āciriyappā). Now, there are sixteen possible combinations of the above mentioned four basic metrical units (nēr, nērpu, nirai and niraipu) and theoretically all the sixteen combinations are allowed in akaval or āciriyappā.[6]

The formation of a cīr by the combination of nēr and nirai is called iyaṟcīr, i.e. the foot which is *natural* (iyal, iyalpu – nature) to akaval. The formation of a cīr by the combination of nērpu and niraipu is called āciriya-vuriccīr, i.e. the foot which *belongs* to āciriyappā (Tol. Por. Cey. 325 and Comm.). The formation of a cīr by other combinations is called either iyaṟcīr or āciriya-vuriccīr by extension (Tol. Por. Cey. 326-328 and Comm. by Pērāciriyar).[7]

c) *Taḷai*: The next term to be explained is taḷai, which means tying or binding. It is called also *yāppu* which means also tying or connection. Here connection between the successive feet is designated by taḷai. In akaval or āciriyappā, the taḷai is, as a rule, "antipastic, that is, if one foot (cīr) ends in a nirai, the next begins with a nirai." [8] The feet which are natural to the akaval are, as has been seen, called iyaṟcīr or akavaṟcīr or

---

[6] Zvelebil, K., *Smile*, 65. The sixteen possible combinations are: Nērnēr, Nērnērpu, Nērnirai, Nērniraipu, Nirainēr, Nirainērpu, Nirainirai, Nirainiraipu, Nērpunēr, Nērpunērpu, Nērpunirai, Nērpuniraipu, Niraipunēr, Niraipunērpu, Niraipunirai, Niraipuniraipu.

[7] The distribution is as follows:

nēr nēr nēr nirai nirai nēr nirai nirai	Iyaṟcīr
nērpu nērpu nērpu niraipu niraipu nērpu niraipu niraipu	Āciriya-vuriccīr (Tol. Por. Cey. 325 Comm.)
nērpu nirai niraipu nirai	Āciriya-vuriccīr by extension (Tol. Cey. 326 Comm.)
nērpu nēr niraipu nēr nēr nērpu nēr niraipu nirai nērpu nirai niraipu	Iyaṟcīr by extension (Tol. Cey. 327-328 Comm.)

[8] Hart, G. I. III, *The Poems of Ancient Tamil*, University of California Press, 1975, 199.

āciriyaccīr (this last name coming from āciriyam – another name for akaval, see Tol. Por. Cey. 393).

d) *Aṭi*: The combination of feet constitutes a line in the poetry – in Tamil called aṭi. The ideal line is constituted by four feet, which is termed aḷavaṭi, i.e. measured line. In the akaval metre the standard line has four feet or eight acais except the penultimate line which consists of three feet (Tol. Por. Cey. 380). Elsewhere, a three feet line is exceptional.

Two other constituents of poetry which are useful to know are Toṭai and Nōkku:

e) *Toṭai*: Toṭai means fastening. It is translated usually by "rhyme".[9] Toṭai is in fact *the art of stringing* together lines into a poem, like flowers into a garland (toṭu – knit, string; hence, toṭai means garland of flowers). In Cey. cūt. 400, Tolkāppiyar mentions four major types of rhyme or toṭai:

1) Mōṉai: A rhyme where initial letters agree
2) Etukai: A rhyme where the second letters agree (cf. alliteration and assonance)
3) Muraṇ: The contrary either in mere word or in its meaning (compare, word antithesis and semantic antithesis)
4) Iyaipu: A rhyme where the last letters or syllables or feet agree.[10] This is similar to end-rhyme.

Rhyme may be between successive lines (in that case they are called aṭittoṭai) or between the four or three feet making up a line (in an akavaṟpā). Tolkāppiyar mentions in Cey. cūt. 402 three main types of toṭai between feet, i.e. poḻippu, orūu and centoṭai.[11]

f) *Nōkku*: The last constituent for our purpose is nōkku. Tol. Por. Cey. 416 states: "The *nōkku* is said to be the way of viewing the composition from the unit of time to the perfection of line." In other

---

[9] Ilakkuvaṉār, S., *Tholkāppiyam*, 223 & 460; Chidambaranatha Chettiar, A., *Advanced*, 49-50; Hart, G. L. III, *The Poems, 208*.

[10] Chidambaranatha Chettiar, A., *Advanced*, 49.

[11] Poḻippu: Rhyme between 1st and 3rd feet
Orūu: Rhyme between the 1st and 4th feet
Centoṭai: the other types
Cūtram 413 says that "there are thirteen thousand seven hundred and eight rhymes in accordance with the traditional grammar", Pērāciriyar, *Tol. Por. Cey. Commentary*, 273ff; Ilakkuvaṉār, S., *Tholkāppiyam*, 233.

words, nōkku is that which gives orientation, cohesion and unity to the various constituents to make one single whole.[12] The cūtram implies that each line in a poem is, as a rule, a meaningful whole.

Observations

1) Tamil metre "is based on length, like Latin and Greek metres; however, unlike most metres in those languages, it is quantitative, not syllabic."[13]

2) There is a great difference between the Sanskrit prosody and that of Tamil. "Whereas Sanskrit prosody is based on a number of syllables (*akṣara*) or prosodic units (*morae*, *mātrā*), classical Tamil metrics is based on an entirely different principle of basic metrical units (*acai*), eight of which constitute a line with four accents (*ictus*)."[14]

3) The name akavaṟpā for āciriyam comes from the verb *akavu* which means "to utter a sound as a peacock, sing, dance as a peacock, call, summon."[15] See, Kuṟ. 151:3; 249:1; 264:3 etc.

4) The Tamil akaval has no analogy in Sanskrit poetry. The nearest comparison from Western prosody is perhaps the English blank verse.[16]

5) The initial rhyme, esp. the mōṉai and etukai are characteristic of Tamil poetry. As X. S. Thani Nayagam remarks, "initial rhyme imposes metrical functions which end-rhyme does not. The one initiates new lines of thought while the other completes thought."[17]

B. Symbolism in Tamil Literary Theory

There are some important factors that lie as foundations of symbolism in Tamil Akam poetry and they will briefly be discussed here below:

---

[12] Marutanayakam, P., "Tolkāppiyamum mēlaināṭṭuk kavitaiyiyalum", *Tamiḻkkalai*, I, 4 (1983), 7.

[13] Hart, G. L. III, *Poets of the Tamil Anthologies*, Princeton University Press, Princeton 1979, 13. Tolkāppiyam even speaks of the number of letters that are allowed in a metrical foot (Cey. cūt. 353), and of the number of letters in different lines, i.e. aṭi (Cey. cūts. 348-352).

[14] Zvelebil, K., *Tamil*, 99.

[15] *DED*, n. 10.

[16] Zvelebil, K., *TC*, X, 2 (1963), 23.

[17] Thani Nayagam, X. S., "Apperception in Tamil Literary Studies", in *PFICSTS*, Vol. II, IATR, Madras 1969, 124.

1. *Linguistic Factors*

Some features which are peculiar to Tamil language seem almost to compel the speaker or the poet to have recourse to indirect ways of communicating his ideas:

a) Tamil has no relative pronoun and so it is difficult to construct two or more long adjectival subordinate clauses and make them modify the same noun. Relative descriptive clauses must be turned into phrases ending in adjectival participles. Similarly to modify a verb of action one has to use either continuatives (adverbial participles) which have retrospective or prospective function, or infinitives which signify simultaneity or causality. Hence the possibility of different combinations and multiple significance.[18]

b) Loose connection of adjectives: Economy of words being at the base of Tamil classical poetry, each noun is furnished with one or more adjectives, or adjectival phrases. In the adjectival phrase itself, the noun may be qualified by an adjective or epithet and so on. Thus the poem would be a literary piece studded with adjectives and adjectival phrases.[19]

c) The ease with which many vaguely related things can be included in the same sentence gives rise to more than one combination or coordination and thus more meanings and connotations.[20]

d) The use of large sentences with conventional formulas and phrases is another basis for strict coherence of the poem and for different combinations of utterances.[21]

2. *Metric Factors*

Some of the metric factors that contribute towards symbolism are the following:

a) The akaval metre is so precise and defined that it does not admit of artificiality and toying with form. It is so to say a rhythmic lyric prose, associated with numerous alliterations and assonances.[22] Besides, akaval sustains an atmosphere of suspense.[23]

---

[18] Cf. Hart, G. L. III, *Poems*, 182.

[19] Srinivas Iyengar, P. T., *The History*, 300, writes: "In poetry every noun is furnished with an adjective, and if the adjective happens to be a phrase, the noun within that phrase is provided with an epithet, till the whole poem looks like the entrance-tower (gopuram) of our temples studded with decorations, which to a mind trained in the principles of Greek art is maddening, and which renders translation into English very difficult."

[20] Hart, G. L. III, *Poems*, 186.

[21] Ib.

[22] Cf. Zvelebil, K., *TC*, X, 2 (1963), 29.

[23] Cf. Thani Nayagam, X. S., "Apperception", in *PFICSTS*, Vol. II, 125.

b) The size of the poems is another ground for the need of symbolism: Though Tolkāppiyam speaks of the possibility of an akaval of 1000 lines, *de facto* in the anthologies (excluding the Kalittokai) the longest poem has only 31 lines (i.e. Akam 86 has 31 lines; Ak. 98 has 30). Even the Kuṟiñcippāṭṭu of Kapilar, the longest akam poem among the Pattuppāṭṭu[24] in akaval metre has only 261 lines. Because the poets composed short poems, they supercharged them so as "to produce suggestive effects whose permutations are virtually unlimited."[25]

c) Sonority: Under toṭai, something on this aspect was already said, i.e. mōṉai, etukai, muraṇ, and iyaipu. Tolkāppiyar adds in Cey. 401 also aḷapeṭai (reduplication of consonants or vowels in a word) as one of the features of rhyme. These rhymes, more than mere ornamentations, contribute through their sonority towards the meaning of the poem. We may call it the symbolism of sonority. For example, the combinations or repetitions of soft consonants (melliṉam) or medial consonants (iṭaiyiṉam) or aḷapeṭai, esp. uyiraḷapeṭai would signify softness and gentleness. The recurrence of long vowels would indicate an atmosphere of joy or sorrow or sobriety. The repetition of hard consonants (valliṉam) is a sign of quickness and toughness. The sound symbolism, however, seems to have been only a secondary feature in the classical Tamil poetry of akaval metre, while in Kalippā and Paripāṭal sonority plays a greater rôle.

3. *Literary Factors or Poetic Conventions*

Poetry is an art and any art should follow rules and principles which are agreed upon by those who produce the art. These principles are termed conventions. Tamil classical poetry has followed a system of conventions which constitute a kind of meta-language. The conventions form, so to say, an inventory well organized into a system of inter-references so much so that every poem presupposes the existence of the entire system. Any situation described in the poem has sense only in reference to all other situations contained in the whole system. Thus each symbol or each image derives its significance from the thematic whole. The conventions function as a collective style.[26]

There is no doubt that "poetry that uses conventions, instead of giving an exact imitation of Nature, gives us 'Nature methodized'."[27] But this does not mean that the poetic or literary conventions are pure productions of mere imagination. In the case of poetic conventions of

---

[24] Paṭṭiṉappālai is longer than Kuṟiñcippāṭṭu, with 301 lines. but it is composed of ca. 153 lines in vañci metre and only the rest is in akaval.

[25] Hart, G. L. III, *Poems*, 180.

[26] Zvelebil, K., *The Tamil*, 98.

[27] Manuel, M., "The Use of Literary Conventions in Tamil Classical Poetry", in *PFICSTS*, Vol. II, IATR, Madras 1969, 63-69, esp. 65 for the citation.

Tamil Akam literature, these conventions are the results of observation, abstraction and organisation. The dramatis personae for akam are idealized types.[28] Aesthetic or artistic purpose need not be contradictory or even contrary to realistic presentation.[29] These conventions thus provide a live vocabulary of symbols.[30] In a sense, they entirely depersonalize the akam poetry and on account of this system, the poetry itself becomes a kind of second language.[31] In other words, the poetic conventions serve as the objective correlatives for the poets to be used.[32]

4. *Imagery*

Imagery is the life principle of poetry and it is imagery that distinguishes poetry from prose.[33] Imagery consists in the way in which the poet successfully communicates his emotions to the listener or reader as if the poem were a picture. Tol. Por. Cey. cūt. 516 states it very clearly. Tolkāppiyar uses the term *meyppāṭu* and says that meyppāṭu is to compose a poem in such a way as to make the reader feel and exhibit his emotions by physical changes on reading or hearing the poem. It is in the level of what in philosophy we would describe as "action-passion" correlative.[34] Imagery may appeal especially to two senses: eyes and ears. In poetry sonority and allied poetic devices appeal to ears. Similes and metaphors appeal to the eyes through the word-pictures that are created. The most important items of imagery used in Tamil poetry esp. in akam poetry are the following:

---

[28] Cf. Ramanujan A. K., *Interior*, 104.

[29] Manuel, M., "The Use of Literary", in *PFICSTS*, Vol. II, 66.

[30] Cf. Ramanujan, A. K., *Interior*, 108.

[31] Ib., 114.

[32] Cf. Marutanayakam, P., *Tamiḻkkalai*, I, 4 (1983), 6.

[33] Periyakaruppan, I., "Oppiyal nōkkil meyppāṭu", in *PFifICSTS*, Vol. III, IATR, Madras 1981, 127-133, esp. 131. See Aravaanan, K. P., *Kavitaiyiṉ uyir, uḷḷam, uṭal*, Pari Nilaiyam, 1976 on this aspect. The question of imagery has been treated esp. in pp. 24-50 where he compares a poem to a human being. The metre of the poem is the frame or skeleton, the words and phrases are flesh and blood, the content is mind, and the way in which it is communicated is the life principle of the poem.

[34] This word *meyppāṭu* is so rich in significance that it cannot be easily translated into English. There is one full chapter in Tolkāppiyam, called *Meyppāṭṭiyal* which treats about the exhibition of feelings. The same term is used in Ceyyuḷiyal cūt. 516 to denote the successful use of words, phrases and figures of speech to communicate and even to cause such feelings in the audience. This is a literary technique – in other words, imagery in poetry. For an excellent exposé of these points and a comparative study with Sanskrit treatise on poetics and dramaturgy of Bharata, see Sundaramoorthy, G., *Early Literary Theories in Tamil in Comparison with Sanskrit Theories*, Madurai 1974. See also, Thirugnanasambandhan, P., "A Study of Rasa – Tholkāppiyar and Bharata", in *PFICSTS*, Vol. II, IATR, Madras 1969, 10-18; Periyakaruppan, I., "Oppiyal", in *PFifICSTS*, Vol. III, 127-133; Kurucāmi, M. R. P., *Tamiḻ Nūlkaḷil Kuṟippup Poruḷ*, Tamiḻp Puttakālayam, Cennai 1980, esp. 110-161.

a) *Simile*

Simile "is a form of expression which intentionally deviates from the ordinary mode of speech for the sake of a more powerful, pleasing and distinctive effect."[35] Tolkāppiyam has one full chapter on simile – called Uvamaviyal.[36] The grammarian seems to have thought that uvamai, i.e. simile is an essential and integral part of the poem which contributes to the realization of the poetic truth. It is noteworthy that Tolkāppiyar has never used the word aṇi or alaṅkāram in any place to denote uvamai.[37] According to Tolkāppiyam (Por. Uvam. cūt. 276), there are four principles or foundations on which a comparison may be based: action (viṉai), result (payaṉ), body (mey) and colour (uru).[38] These four principles are the common grounds between the two objects to be compared. In Tamil that which is to be described is called *poruḷ*, i.e. object and the thing with which the poruḷ is compared is called *uvamam* or *uvamai*. Tol. Por. Uvam. cūt. 279-280 tell us that a simile is born out of five causes, namely a) superiority or excellence (ciṟappu), b) goodness or beauty (nalaṉ), c) love or affection (kātal), d) heroism or strength (vali) and e) inferiority (kiḻakkiṭu poruḷ).[39] Among these causes we may distinguish two types, namely objective and subjective causes: superiority, goodness and strength are found in the poruḷ which induce the poet to establish a comparison; hence we may call them objective causes. On the other hand, love which appreciates and *kiḻakkiṭu poruḷ* lit. "to depreciate a thing" are the motives why the poet uses simile; hence we may term them subjective causes. The following diagram may be useful to illustrate the process:

---

[35] Manickam, V. T., *Marutam*, 53.

[36] See Pērāciriyar, *Tol. Por. Uvamaviyal Commentary*, 57-111; Gnanasambandan, A. S., *Ilakkiyak Kalai*, SISSWPS, Madras 1964⁴ esp. 169-184; Id., "Tolkāppiyar's Concept of Uvamai", *JTamS* 4 (1973), 1-12; Cīṉivācaṉ, R., *Caṅka Ilakkiyattil*, 1-80, 163-218.

[37] This is very significant when we compare Sanskrit Grammars which treat simile – upamā – as an alankāra, i.e. as an ornament to poetry; Gnanasambandan, A. S., *JTamS* 4 (1973), 2.

[38] Ilakkuvaṉār, S., *Tholkāppiyam*, 218, translates *mey* by body while Sundaramoorthy, G., *Early Literary*, 100, translates by quality. Both translate *uru* by colour.

[39] Cf. Gnanasambandan, A. S., *JTamS* 4 (1973), 3-4.

Four Principles

Action Viṉai	Result Payaṉ	Body Mey	Colour Uru

↓

SIMILE

↑

Objective Causes

Superiority Ciṟappu	Goodness Nalaṉ	Strength Vali

↑

Subjective Causes

Appreciation Kātal	Depreciation Kiḻakkiṭu poruḷ

As a rule, the uvamam should be superior to the poruḷ (cf. cūt. 278), except, of course, in the case of depreciation. Uvamam is twofold:

1) Uḷḷuṟai uvamam — ambient allegory used only in Akam poems (see below)

2) Ēṉai uvamam[40] — Other similes used in both Puṟam and Akam poems.

In cūtrams 286-291, Tolkāppiyar gives a list of ca. 36 comparative particles and the aspects of comparison for which they are employed; e.g. *pōla*, *oppa* are comparative particles which serve to denote colour-comparison, cf. cūt. 291.[41] R. Cīṉivācaṉ has classified, explained and illustrated some twenty types of similes that occur in Classical Tamil poetry.[42]

---

[40] This *ēṉai uvamam* is called velippaṭai uvamam by the author of Nampiyakapporuḷ: see *Nampiyakapporuḷ*, cūt. 237,239.

[41] For a detailed study, see Cīṉivācaṉ, R., *Caṅka Ilakkiyattil*, 62-80 on comparative particles; for lists, see 266-303.

[42] Cīṉivācaṉ, R., *Caṅka Ilakkiyattil*, 8-55. He considers both the Akam and Puṟam literature of both Classical and Late Classical Tamil Poetry.

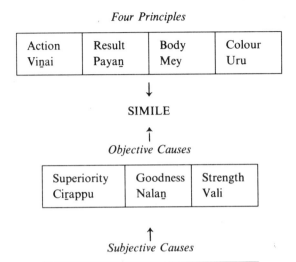

b) *Metaphor*

It is worth noting here that Tolkāppiyar does not treat separately about metaphor but speaks about it briefly in the same chapter as that on simile.[43] Tamil rhetoric speaks about what is called *uvamaittokai*, i.e. a comparative phrase in which the comparative particle is understood. According to Tamil rhetoric, the origin of metaphor is explained as follows: "It may be said that the effectiveness of an *uvamai* is inversely proportionate to the number of words and the breaks between them. Hence, a transference was tried and so *pavaḷa vāy*, for example, became, *vāyp pavaḷam*. When this reduction is effected, the suggestion made by the *uvamai* is more spontaneous than in the original version. The ambiguity which may occur here is disposed of by the conventional understanding of what is subject and what is standard."[44] Thus e.g. pavaḷam pōṉṟa vāy: uvamai — three words and two breaks; pavaḷa vāy: uvamaittokai — two words and one break; vāyppavaḷam: metaphor — one word and no break. Tolkāppiyar in Uvam.cūtram 284 indicates this process: "If the compared object is used as the object of comparison, it becomes an object of comparison without fault."[45]

c) *Uḷḷuṟai Uvamam*

We may approximately translate it by "Ambient Allegory." In Tamil rhetoric, uḷḷuṟai uvamam means more than what the English word "allegory" says. Hence the adjective "ambient" has been used here.[46]

---

[43] Modern linguistics has not yet succeeded in deciding whether metaphor is really different from simile, and all critics agree that simile and metaphor in some way overlap. Tolkāppiyar had the insight to include metaphor in simile! For discussions on metaphor, see Cīṉivācaṉ, R., *Caṅka Ilakkiyattil*, 81-94 and for lists 266-328. According to him, there are some four types of metaphor used in the Classical Tamil Poetry. See also Gnanasambandan, A. S., *Ilakkiyak Kalai*, 185-200.

[44] Gnanasambandan, A. S., *JTamS* 4 (1973), 7.

[45] According to Iḷampūraṇar, this cūtram explains how simile is transferred into a metaphor. Pērāciriyar disagrees with him. A. S. Gnanasambandan agrees with Iḷampūraṇar. For discussion, see *Ilakkiyak Kalai*, 187-189; Id., *JTamS* 4 (1973), 7.

[46] Tolkāppiyar speaks of this imagery-technique in Akattiṇaiyiyal cūts. 46-48 and again mentions it in Poruḷiyal cūts. 242-243. See Ilakkuvaṉār, S., *Tholkāppiyam*, 160 & 211 for translation and 409-410 for comments. Quite a few studies have been published on this point both in Tamil and in English. To cite some of them: Commentaries on these cūtrams of Tol. Por. Akat. and Por. by Iḷampūraṇar and Pērāciriyar. Bharathi, S. S., "Tholkappiya Araichi – Ullurai", *JAU*, VIII, (1938), 35-41. Gnanasambandan, A. S., *Ilakkiyak Kalai*, 107-113; Id., *JTamS* 4 (1973), 1-12; Manickam, V. Sp., *Tamil Concept*, 124-125; Id., *Tamiḻk*, 220-221; Cīṉivācaṉ, R., *Caṅka Ilakkiyattil*, 223-241 and the list of occurrences in 242-265; Kurucāmi, M. R. P., *Tamiḻ Nūlkaḷil*, 110-161; Id., "Uḷḷuṟaiyum Iṟaicciyum", *Aintām Ulakat Tamiḻ Mānāṭu, Maturai 1981, Viḻa Malar*, 168-172.

Uḷḷuṟai uvamam has been rendered in English in different ways by various authors.[47]

Authors are at variance in interpreting what Tolkāppiyam says on Uḷḷuṟai uvamam. The issue becomes more complicated when it is considered together with Iṟaicci and others that are mentioned in Tol. Por. Poruḷiyal cūt. 242. The following exposition is an attempt to present the theory in a somewhat less complicated way:

Uḷḷuṟai uvamam is one type of uvamam or simile, but it is employed only in the composition of Akam poems (Tol. Por. Akat. cūt. 46). It is also called Uvamappōli (Tol. Por. Uvam. 299) or pseudosimile or sham simile.[48] Uḷḷuṟai uvamam is constructed with the karupporuḷ of the respective regions, except the god of the region. In other words, the god of the region cannot be employed in uḷḷuṟai uvamam (Tol. Por. Akat. 47). It is almost like the figure of speech called *piṟitumoḻital aṇi*, which is used in order to describe one set of ideas with a different one obtained from other objects or things.[49] Uḷḷuṟai uvamam is conceived and construed in such a way that what is described with the karupporuḷ becomes as such a simile and conveys a message, by being applied correspondingly to the characters in love themes. The behaviour of the karupporuḷs described in the poem becomes the allegory to the behaviour of the characters (Tol. Por. Akat. 48). It is built with words which are pregnant with double meanings. No extra words except those found in the poem are required for understanding the suggested message. Like allegory, even word for word application is possible.[50] Uḷḷuṟai uvamam, like the other similes, may be construed on the basis of action, result, form, colour and birth (Tol. Por. Uvam. 300).[51]

The uḷḷuṟai uvamam is built on the principle of possibility and congruity of the combinations of karupporuḷ. In other words, the

---

[47] Zvelebil, K. *Smile*, 102 translates it by 'implied simile' or 'implied metaphor', and in 109 by 'allegory'. Manickam, V. Sp., *Tamil Concept*, 124, 'a kind of implied simile'; Varadarajan, M., *The Treatment of Nature in Sangam Literature*, SISSWPS, Madras 1957, 63 uses 'suppressed simile'; Id., "Literary Theories", in *PFICSTS*, Vol. II, 49 translates by 'implied simile', 'simile incognito' and 'allegory'. Thani Nayagam, X. S., *Nature*, 144 favours 'allegory'; Gnanasambandan, A. S., *JTamS* 4 (1973), 2, has 'antimetaphor'; Manickam. V. T. calls it 'implied or suggestive simile', *Marutam*, 54. Allegory fits better.

[48] Cīṉivācaṉ, R., *Caṅka Ilakkiyattil*, 5; Manickam, V. T., *Marutam*, 54; Thiyagarajan, D., "Symbolism in Tamil Literature", in *An Insight into Tamilology*, Kovai 1972, 140-149, esp. 141.

[49] See Manickam, V. T., *Marutam*, 54.

[50] Cf. Gnanasambandan, A. S., *JTamS* 4 (1973), 10-11; Bharathi, S. S., *JAU*, VIII (1938), 38, 40-41; Kurucāmi, M. R. P., *Tamiḻ Nūlkaḷil*, 129-130; Id., "Uḷḷuṟaiyum", *Viḻā Malar*, 170.

[51] Thiyagarajan, D., "Symbolism", in *An Insight*, 141-142.

behaviour of the karupporuḷ which serves as the uḷḷuṟai is not intrinsically impossible. In fact, many of the details and combinations in uḷḷuṟai are results of separate observations and various experiences. What are described are based on facts and results of observations but their combination for one occasion or in one poem may well be due to the constructive and cumulative imagination of the poet.[52] That is why the poets would sometimes allow themselves the liberty of arranging and adjusting the course of the things in describing nature, so as to convey the implied meanings. Psychological attitude gives meaning to the descriptions of the karupporuḷ in uḷḷuṟai uvamam, e.g. Akam. 46.[53]

If the lady love uses uḷḷuṟai uvamam, she has to use only the symbols based on the karupporuḷ she knows, i.e. what surrounds her house or locality or what pertains to general notions and hearsay (Tol. Por. Uvam. 301). The maid companion can use symbols on all things in her land (Tol. Por. Uvam. 301). For, her world of experience is supposed to be wider than that of the lady love.[54] There are no limits to the hero's experience and therefore to his imagery. Hence he can use similes drawn from other tracts of land also. But he is supposed to use symbols to express love or kindness while others may use symbols on all situations.[55]

d) *Iṟaicci*

We may conveniently call this technique "Suggestion". Tolkāppiyar speaks of iṟaicci in Tol. Por. Poruḷiyal cūt. 229-230 and in cūt. 242, it is called by another name *uṭaṉuṟai.*[56] Iṟaicci is a meaning that is obtained beyond and besides the plain meaning of the words in the poem (Tol. Por. Por. 229). That meaning, however, is suggested by the words of the poem. Iṟaicci contains in it subtle messages or meanings and they may appear "to those who are capable of understanding the true nature of

---

[52] A typical example is found in Ak. 8. There are three uḷḷuṟai uvamams: 1) The bear that looked for food and hurt unknowingly the snake in the ant-hill; 2) The tiger while hunting its game spoiled the fragrant smell of jack fruit and 3) The male elephant that fell in a pit while looking for plantain fruits and that had to be saved by the female elephant. Each one separately might happen — for observations have proved them to happen. But all the three may not happen at one and the same time or place. In Ak. 72 there are two uḷḷuṟai uvamams, see Manavalan, A. A., "Caṅka Ilakkiyam", in *Tamiḻ Ilakkiyak*, 36-37.

[53] Cf. Manickam, V. Sp., *Tamil Concept*, 125.

[54] The commentators add also the foster-mother to the maid companion.

[55] See Thiyagarajan, D., "Symbolism", in *An Insight*, 142; Ramanujan, A. K., *Interior*, 114; Manickam, V. T., *Marutam*, 55.

[56] Different terminologies are attempted by authors to bring out the meaning of iṟaicci which is a technique of suggestion. A. S. Gnanasambandan, describes iṟaicci as 'To read between lines', *JTamS* 4 (1973), 9; K. Zvelebil, tries to bring out the meaning by 'suggestion', 'implication', *Smile*, 102; M. Varadarajan, "Literary Theories", in *PFICSTS*, Vol. II, 48-49 favours 'suggestion'.

them" (Tol. Por. Por. 230). Iṟaicci may or may not be built on the karupporuḷ of respective regions. It is often compared to the Sanskrit "vyañjanā", "vyaṅgya".[57] or to "dhvāni".[58]

e) *Other Techniques*

Besides uḷḷuṟai uvamam and iṟaicci, three more techniques of suggestion are mentioned in Tol. Por. Por. cūt. 242:

(i) Cuṭṭu: One thing is said but another is aimed at.

(ii) Nakai: A situation is described which provokes laughter but implies something serious.[59]

(iii) Ciṟappu: "The way of applying epithet by means of simile to the object of 'iṟaicci' is termed 'ciṟappu'."[60]

The following diagram tries to show the place of these elements of poetry and of suggestion in a poem:

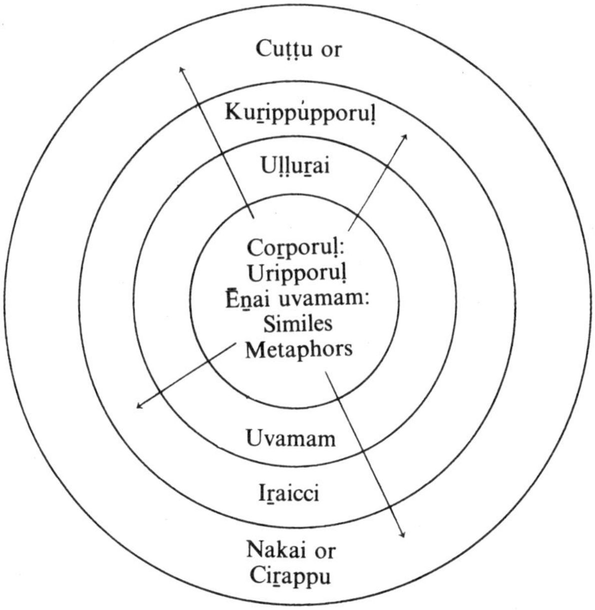

[57] Zvelebil, K., *Smile*, 109.
[58] Sundaramoorthy, G., *Early Literary*, 121, note 8.
[59] Cf. Thiyagarajan, D., "Symbolism", *An Insight*, 142-144.
[60] Ilakkuvaṉār, S., *Tholkāppiyam*, 211, note 1.

C. Symbolism in Function

In this section, a brief exposition will be given to indicate how symbolism may function in the love aspects of the five regions.

Tamil poetic tradition has formalized the whole universe into a symbolism and uses the exterior world to express the interior world of human love.[61] Thus the very names of the five tracts are symbolical because "the actual objective landscapes of Tamil country become the interior landscape of Tamil poetry",[62] and consequently each phase of love gets its characteristic type of imagery from a particular landscape. This is clear from the fact that the actual exterior world is classified into mutaṟporuḷ and karupporuḷ and that they are employed to reveal the interior nature of human love which is the uripporuḷ. In fact the uripporuḷ (the inner world) is the one which bestows symbolism on the exterior world which serves as the locus of revelation of the former. There is essential reciprocity between the mutal – karupporuḷ and the uripporuḷ.

1. *Kuṟiñci*

Mountainous region with its hills and slopes, valleys and swift streams form the landscape. The aspect of love – the uripporuḷ of kuṟiñci is the union of lovers, i.e. puṇartal. In the union of lovers, there is the feeling of mystery and the consequent sense of wonder.[63] The inner peace and sense of fulfilment which the lovers enjoy when they are in each other's embrace are beyond comparison, and the whole nature around them cooperates with them for their happiness. That is why, it seems, the surroundings are described in paradisiacal terms. The same nature will be described as dangerous to them when they are separated.

In poems on this theme, the mutaṟporuḷ forms the fundamental symbol, namely the hill tract (Nilam) and night time (Ciṟupoḻutu). For they "are the ideal time and place for union of lovers."[64] In general, tiṉaippuṉam, i.e. the millet-field is the locus of union during the day (almost always the midday) and the garden of the lady love's house, during the night (almost always the midnight). Thus the millet-field and the house garden become symbols of union of lovers.

The animals of the mountainous regions and their behaviour are mentioned or described only in so far as they can highlight the theme of union or the mutual longing of the lovers. Birds in general serve as symbols to express the craving of the lovers for freedom and union.[65] Uḷḷuṟai uvamam plays an important rôle in such descriptions of karupporuḷ.

---

[61] Cf. Ramanujan, A. K., *Interior*, 115.

[62] Ib., 108.

[63] Cf. Hart, G. L. III, *Poets*, 6.

[64] Thiyagarajan, D., "Symbolism", in *An Insight,* 141.

[65] Varadàrajan, M., "A Type of Apostrophes in Sangam Literature", in *PTICSTS*, Pondichéry 1973, 91-96, esp. 94.

The typical flower of the region which is the kuriñci flower (Strobilanthes) gave its name and symbolism to the region.[66] Two other flowers of this region which are symbols of union of lovers are Vēṅkai, i.e. flower of Kino tree and Kāntaḷ, i.e. Gloriosa superba. The blossoming of the vēṅkai tree will invariably coincide with the ripening of the millet grain and the harvest of the millet grain will take place immediately after. The blossoming of the vēṅkai, so to say, predicts the harvest of millet grain. This seasonal connection between the blossoming of vēṅkai and the ripening of millet grain gave rise to a subtle symbolism, i.e. the ripening of the millet grain symbolizes the ripening of the courtship that started at the same time when the millet grain started to ripen and the girl came to drive away the parrots![67] Besides, "there is room to believe that, at first, marriages were celebrated under the flowering *vengai*, because it was the shadiest and loveliest tree of the region. Hence its flowering was understood to introduce auspicious days for lovers."[68] Hence it was natural that betrothed couples waited eagerly for vēṅkai to burst into flower; cf. Akam. 2,12,378; Naṟ. 206; Kuṟiñcikkali. 8. Moreover, this flower or garland made of this flower was among those things which the lovers preferred to give their beloveds, esp. during courtship and was used by the bride to adorn her hair during the marriage ceremony; cf. Naṟ. 313. The other flower kāntaḷ i.e. gloriosa superba, also symbolizes the union of lovers. For it is the flower preferred

---

[66] Interesting and scientific studies have been made on Strobilanthes. Samy, P. L., "Kurinjci", *TC*, IV, 2 (1955), 132-139; Varadaraja Iyer, E. S., "The Kuriñji Girl", *JAU*, XVII (1952), 144-152. The Gazetteer of the Nilgiris mentions that Strobilanthes flowers every twelfth year. The Todas of Nilgiris even now calculate the age of their children by reckoning the flowering of this plant. According to botanists, the Strobilanthes flowers after about nine years and continues flowering till the twelfth year and then dies. For instance, it was seen to flower in 1910, 1922, 1934, 1946. According to the Cilappatikāram, *Kaṇṇaki* was married at the age of twelve. Is there a possible connection between the Strobilanthes flowering every twelfth year and the marriageable age of a girl and consequently the theme of union of lovers symbolized by this flower? It is significant that in Tamil when a girl comes to puberty, it is called *pūppeytal* (literally, to reach the state of flowering) – a symbolic expression, no doubt!

[67] Varadaraja Iyer, E. S., *JAU*, XVII, (1952), 145-146. That is why this detail about the blossoming of Vēṅkai buds and the ripening and imminent harvest of millet grain is given by the maid companion whenever she urges the hero to hasten to marry the lady love. Besides, the reference to the harvest indicates that the family of the heroine is economically ready to celebrate the marriage festivals. A similar connection of harvest and marriage celebrations is implied in the proverb "Tai piṟantāl vaḻi piṟakkum" used in agricultural regions where paddy is harvested in the month of Tai, i.e. Mid-January to mid-February.

[68] Thani Nayagam, X. S., *TC*, II, (1953), 164-175, citation is from p. 167. Parents carried out deliberations regarding their children's espousals and dances on the marriage day took place under a flowering vēṅkai; cf. Naṟ. 313; Kuṟ. 241; Kalit. 42. See Thani Nayagam, X. S., *Nature*, 28-30.

by Murukan, the god of kuṟiñci landscape, and Murukan is the divine type for the lover. That is why this flower used to be offered by the lover to his lady love during the courtship; see Kuṟ. 1.[69]

2. *Mullai*

The landscape for mullai tiṇai is the forest region. The typical flower of this region, called mullai, i.e. jasmine, not only gave its name to the landscape, but also conferred the fundamental symbolism for the poems of one love aspect. Jasmine flower is one of the karupporuḷ of the forest region. Now it is said that mullai flower would keep fresh for two or three days even after it is plucked from the creeper. Thus this flower came to symbolize the patient waiting and sustained hope of the heroine during separation.[70] The poems of mullai tiṇai can refer to any period of waiting, in either phase of love – namely either in Kaḷavu, or in Kaṟpu. In Kaḷavu, the lady love waits for the hero to come with his people and make arrangements for marriage. In Kaṟpu, she waits for the hero to return from his journey that he undertook either to earn wealth or to serve in the army etc. This separation for earning wealth may also take place before marriage, for example, in order to pay the bride price; cf. Ak. 90, 280, 390; Naṟ. 300; Aiṅ. 147; Kalit. 103. So unless explicitly indicated in the poem, the patient waiting of the heroine can be understood in either way.[71]

Because of their natural connection with the mullai flower, which is the fundamental symbol, and because of their psychological connection with a lonely love partner, the rainy season (perumpoḻutu), and the evening (ciṟupoḻutu) which belong to mutaṟporuḷ, become symbolical of patient waiting. Consequently all the karupporuḷ connected with winter and evening, e.g. clouds, rain, north-wind; the return of the shepherds in the evening with their herds, the flute music; the changes in vegetation etc., take on symbolical meaning. The coming of the rainy season is intimately connected with the hero's return, and thus also with the heroine's hope, and therefore that season becomes the forerunner of the hero's return. "As the land is refreshed and enlivened by the coming of the rainy season, after the dryness of summer, so she will be refreshed by his return, and by the raining of his love on her."[72] There is an interaction between Nature (renewing itself through rain after dryness) and the physical, psychical and psychological conditions of the heroine.

---

[69] Nadarajah, D., "The Gloriosa Superba in Classical Poetry", *TC*, XI, 3 (1964), 280-290, esp. 283. The Gloriosa Superba is red in colour and Murukaṉ is called Cēyōṉ (the Red One)! See Hart, G. L. III, *Poems*, 255 for another basis for the connection of Murukaṉ with kuṟiñci poems.

[70] Cf. Thiyagarajan, D., "Symbolism", *An Insight*, 141.

[71] Cf. Shanmugam Pillai, M.-Ludden, D. E., *Kuṟuntokai*, 17.

[72] Ib., 18.

Consequently the descriptions of Nature in mullai poems become symbolical of the heroine's conditions on any one of these grounds.[73]

Eventually the mullai flower became symbolic of chastity and conjugal felicity; cf. Naṟ. 142:10-11; Ak. 274:13-14; Aiṅ. 408:2. This connection of mullai with chastity might be at the origin of the custom of married women tending the mullai creeper at home near nocci trees that were planted as the fence.[74] One bird which is usually found in this region, called Kuyil (the Indian cuckoo – a kind of lark resembling the nightingale) is a symbol of the love-god.[75]

There are various aspects or situations that have been described in poems of mullai tiṇai.[76]

3. *Pālai*

As has been seen, pālai has no landscape proper. But the season, namely summer (perumpoḻutu) and the time of the day (ciṟupoḻutu), i.e. midday which are the temporal stratum of mutaṟporuḷ are the fundamental symbols for the poems on separation. "The extreme heat of the land and season stand symbolically to denote the great suffering of the separated hero, heroine, mother or foster-mother."[77] The descriptions of the ematiated vegetation and suffering avifauna during the high summer season and midday indicate the condition of the "landscape". It is mostly the psychological consequences of separation on those separated, that transform the karupporuḷ and even part of mutaṟporuḷ into symbol of separation. The sufferings of the separated are

---

[73] Dubianski, A. M., "A Motif of Messenger in the *Mullaittiṇai*", *JTamS* 19 (1981), 15-18; Id., "An Analysis of the *Mullai-Pālai* Fragment of Ancient Tamil Poetry", *JTamS* 17 (1979), 88-103. The author sees behind these two tiṇais (separation and patient waiting culminating in union) and their descriptions in poems a mythical ground, i.e. Myth of barrenness and "chaos" and the Myth of fertility and welfare.

[74] Nadarajah, D., "The Mullai and the Tuḷaci as Symbols of Chastity", in *PFICSTS*, Vol. I, IATR, Madras 1969, 314-319, esp. 314-315. While little girls or nubile maidens are depicted as tending the Gloriosa Superba or the Vayalai and the Puṉṉai (see, Naṟ. 117:1; 172:1-5; 179:1-3), only married women tend the mullai (see, Naṟ. 115:5-6; 142:10-11; Ak. 17:1). There is also a symbolic connection between mullai creeper (which represents the heroine) and the nocci tree support (which represents the hero). This symbolism of chastity has been partly robbed off mullai by tuḷaci (basil plant) which is tended also at home by women. While the symbolism of chastity comes to mullai from nature, the symbolism is conferred on tuḷaci (which word is only an adaptation of the Tamil *tuḷai*) by its religious connection to Vishnu. See on this, Samy, P. L., "Common Names", in *PFifICSTS*, Vol. II, sec. 8, 43-53, esp. 45; Nadarajah, D., *TC*, XI, 3 (1964), 283. In fact even now tuḷaci has replaced mullai, as far as I know, only in Vaishnava families. In other homes mullai (or mallikai its species) is still tended and its flowers adorn the hair of married women.

[75] Subramanian, N., "The Avifauna of the Tamil Country", *Supplement to TC*, XII, 4 (1966), 2-3.

[76] Hart, G. L. III, *Poems*, 229ff.

[77] Thiyagarajan, D., "Symbolism", *An Insight*, 141.

seen as reflected on the things of Nature.[78] The temporarily parched land, the extremely hot temperature, the scarcity of water, the heat waves of the summer wind, the deceptive mirage, the withered and wilted nature of vegetation, the struggle of the birds and animals for survival, etc. become symbols of the psychological state of the heroine and hero. The behaviour of the animals and birds, however, remind the hero and heroine of each other's love and longing and thus ultimately give hope and courage to remain faithful and patiently waiting.[79]

Pālai (pirital) is the opposite of kuṟiñci (puṇartal). It is at the same time a polarization in relation to mullai (patient waiting and eventual reunion).[80] There is an inner and intimate connection between these three tiṇais, which may be schematized as: kuṟiñci – the ideal: union; pālai – temporary separation; mullai – eventual reunion. Pālai (pirital) is not and should not be a permanent factor. For separation is only a temporary situation and does not belong to the original order of Nature. Many themes (tuṟai) are treated under pālai tiṇai, but they are all orientated towards increasing the mutual longing of the hero and heroine so that the reunion may be more happy.[81]

4. *Neytal*

The bewailing waves which form part of the mutaṟporuḷ of seashore region is the fundamental symbol denoting the restlessly and anxiously pining heroine.[82] Sea-shore "is especially associated with the sadness of loneliness; and in fact, the word used most often for miserable loneliness (pulampu) is synonymous with this region."[83] Though the uripporuḷ of neytal is iraṅkal (pining), not all the poems classified as neytal express

---

[78] E.g. Midday in itself does not signify separation. Midday is, for instance, the time of union in kuṟiñci at the millet field.

[79] See Sambamoorthy, L., "The Psychological Symbolism of *Paalai* in *Kutunhthokai*", in *PSICSTS*, Vol. II, IATR, Madras 1971, 25-33.

[80] Dubianski, A. M., *JTamS* 17 (1979), 88-103. The author studies pālai tiṇai exclusively in relation to and in contrast with mullai. He has failed to consider the relation of pālai with kuṟiñci tiṇai. But even when one looks for explanation for Tamil akam poems on the 'mytho-poetical" background, as does Dubianski one should start with kuṟiñci (union) as the ideal, pālai (separation), as an intervening temporary loss of that union, ending finally in mullai (restored union) as the normal goal. Pālai is not a permanent tiṇai nor has it a landscape. This is a significant and strong argument to show that pālai (pirital) is only a temporary situation. Symbolically it is only a transitory love aspect that is, however, necessary for intensifying the mutual love of the couples. The beauty of kuṟiñci and mullai is made prominent because of the intervention of pālai.

[81] The only theme or tuṟai that does not touch directly the love or longing of the lovers, is the kūṟṟu of the foster-mother, i.e. her lament, after the elopement of the heroine. Even there the poems end with a note of the foster-mother's ultimate satisfaction and admiration of the love and attachment of the lovers; cf. Naṟ. 66. See Hart, G. L. III, *Poems*, 223ff.

[82] Cf. Thiyagarajan, D., "Symbolism", *An Insight*, 141.

[83] Shanmugam Pillai, M.-Ludden, D. E., *Kuṟuntokai*, 18. The hero who causes this situation is designated by *pulampaṉ*.

this mood. There are some poems of neytal tiṇai which speak of union of the lovers during the day in a grove along the seashore or at night along the beach or even in the house of the heroine. One can notice a parallel theme here to that of kuṟiñci. Actually, the mood of pining and lamenting may be considered as an extreme point in mullai, and the meeting as part of kuṟiñci but for the natural geographical setting of the seashore.[84]

There is, however, one important difference between mullai and neytal as regards the season (perumpoḻutu). Ciṟupoḻutu is the same evening or sunset. But, while the patient waiting in mullai is attributed to the rainy season, the pining has no particular season; which means, it may take place in any part of the year, but in the evening.[85] Again, there seems to be a subtle difference also between the themes of kuṟiñci and similar themes found in neytal. In the neytal poems speaking on meeting of the lovers, there is almost always a note of pining and lamenting of the heroine at least hinted at by the speaker.[86]

Among the karupporuḷ of neytal, about twenty-two water-birds are named in the anthologies.[87] Of these, the aṉṟil and the makaṉṟil are said to be famous for the constancy of their conjugal love.[88] Consequently they became symbols of conjugal fidelity. The conjugal fidelity of these birds seems to be founded on a legend.[89]

---

[84] Cf. Parthasarathi, J., "The Love Poetry of Old Tamil: A Literary Appreciation", *AUJRL*, XIX, (1971), 29 on the intimate connection between mullai and neytal tiṇais. Critics have expressed extreme views on this tiṇai; e.g. G. L. Hart says: "It appears that neytal is the least specific tiṇai in the akam poems ...", *Poems*, 243. M. Shanmugam Pillai, on the contrary, says: "The seashore is the only region that has as its central aspect a specific mood", *Kuṟuntokai*, 18. The question should be viewed differently: Mullai, neytal and marutam were logically and psychologically based on pālai - separation, but branched off from and developed *in reference to* kuṟiñci - union. The present conventional uripporuḷ of neytal was originally the predominant or typical behavioral pattern of the region, but later overlapped with the uripporuḷ of kuṟiñci, and thus appears as a kind of uripporuḷ-mayakkam in respect to kuṟiñci.

[85] See the Table of karupporuḷ etc., cf. Thani Nayagam, X. S., *Nature*, 100-101. The explanation is to be found in the actual situation of the people living in the respective regions: men of forest region go away from their region to other regions in search of pasture land till their own region becomes fertile by rain during rainy season; or they go in search of wealth even beyond Tamil country. The men of seashore region go on fishing or for trade purposes at any time of the year! "Between these regions there is a progressive length of separation, a progressive element of danger, and consequently a progressive sorrow", Thani Nayagam, X. S., *Nature*, 102-103; the citation is from p. 102.

[86] Cf. Puvarakam Pillai, A., "Neytal", in *Naṟṟiṇaic Coṟpoḻivukaḷ*, SISSWPS, Madras 1975[4], 72-112, esp. 84.

[87] Samy, P. L., *Caṅka Ilakkiyattil Puḷḷiṉa Viḷakkam*, SISSWPS, Madras 1976, 4.

[88] Subramanian, N., *TC*, XII, (1966), 259-268, esp. 261.

[89] Cf. Samy, P.L., "Common Names", in *PFifICSTS*, Vol. II, sec. 8, 48. For a very detailed background study of Neytal nilam, see Muttuk Kaṇṇappaṉ, T., *Caṅka Ilakkiyattil Neytal Nilam*, Atipattar Patippakam, Cennai 1978.

5. *Marutam*

The region watered by river is the landscape for marutam. The region is fertile and has a lot of opportunities for amusements and enjoyments. Hence also the possible chance of the husband being unfaithful to his wife on account of the harlots.

The poems of marutat-tiṇai obtain their fundamental symbolism from the uripporuḷ, i.e. the love quarrel.[90] The cause for the quarrel between the lady love and her husband is his frequenting the harlots, and neglecting his wife.[91] The predominant theme in marutam is reproaching the husband for his philandering. What is very remarkable in such reproaches is the polished and cultured way of bringing the man to his senses by using the uḷḷuṟai uvamam in speaking to him. One animal that has become more or less the exclusive symbol of such conduct is the buffalo; see e.g. Ak. 46. It is to be noted that this is the tiṇai among the Aintiṇai, which has got the least number of poems.[92]

D. **Specimen Study of Kuṟ. 40**

Here below Kuṟuntokai 40 will be analysed according to the basic prosodic and rhetoric features of Tamil classical poetic tradition. It serves as a specimen for the method to be used for analysing Tamil poems.

Transliteration

Yāyum ñāyum yārā kiyarō
ventaiyu nuntaiyu memmuṟaik kēḷir
yāṉu nīyu mevvaḻi yaṟituñ
cempulap peyaṉīr pōla
vaṉpuṭai neñcan tāṅkalan taṉavē.

Literal translation

My mother and thy mother who-they-are?
My father and thy father by-which-relation-they-are-relatives?
I and thou, in-which-way-we-know?
Red-terrain-rain-water-like
Love-having-heart they are mingled.

---

[90] Cf. Thiyagarajan, D., "Symbolism", *An Insight*, 141.

[91] For a specialized study on this aspect of Akam, see Manickam, V.T., *Marutam*, Karaikudi 1982.

[92] Cf. Gnanasambandan, A.S., *Akamum Puṟamum: Akam*, 199.

Translation (by me)

My mother and your mother,
 who are they to each other?

My father and your father,
 how are they relatives?

You and I
 how do we know each other?

Like red earth and rain water
Loving hearts are mingled as one!

Prosodic pattern or metre

— — / — — / — — / ═ —
— ═ / — ═ / — ═ / — —
— — / — — / — ═ / ═ —
— ═ / ═ — / — — — —
— ═ / — — / — ═ / ═ —.

This is a poem of five lines. Each line consists of four feet except the penultimate line which has three feet. The metre contains only feet of two metrical units or acai, i.e. all of them are īr-acai-cīr – "two-unit-feet". The metre is thus akaval, and except in five cases, all the taḷai (link) are antipastic, i.e. nēr followed by nēr or nirai followed by nirai.[93]

As for the toṭai, there is no etukai or mōn̲ai between the respective lines. But there are cases of etukai and mōn̲ai within the lines. Here are the indications:

ME	oE	Mo	oE		
ME	oE	Mo	oo	M:	Mōn̲ai
Mo	oo	oo	Mo	E:	Etukai
oo	Mo	Mo		o:	absence of any of them.
oE	oo	Mo	ME		

[93] The first two feet of the second line, i.e. *ventaiyu nuntaiyu* are to be scanned as nērnirai, nērnirai. For the 'ai' in both places is not long but short. See Tol. El̲utt. cūt. 57 on shortening of 'ai' and 'au'. See Iḷampūraṇar, *Tolkāppiyam: El̲uttatikāram Commentary*, SISSWPS, Madras 1974, 36.

Phonaesthetic Analysis

Lines: 1. ȲY̆M N̿Y̆M ȲR̄ K̆Y̆R̄
2. V̆NT̆Y̆ N̆NT̆Y̆ M̆MM̆Ṟ̄K K̄Ḷ̆R
3. ȲṈ̆ N̄Y̆ M̆VV̆Ḻ̆ Y̆Ṟ̆T̆Ñ
4. ČMP̆L̆P P̆Y̆Ṉ̄R P̄L̆
5. V̆ṈP̆Ṭ̄ N̆ÑČN T̄NK̆L̆N T̆Ṉ̆V̄.

Consonant distribution

Lines:	1	2	3	4	5	Total
Hard:	1	5	2	5	6	19
Soft:	3	6	4	2	7	22
Medial:	7	5	6	4	3	25

Vowel distribution

Lines:	1	2	3	4	5	Total
Long:	5	2	2	2	3	14
Short:	4	9	8	6	8	35

Observe that soft (nasal) and medial (liquid) consonants are more widely distributed than the hard (occlusive) ones. Even though numerically there are 19 hard consonants, nine of them have been reduced in their "hardness" by being preceded by soft consonants! Two others (in lines 2 and 4) are connecting consonants. One is indicative of past tense (in line 1). Hence only 6 hard consonants. Short vowel distribution is two and half times more than the long vowels. But it is interesting to note that long vowels initiate and close the whole poem.

Each one of the first three lines is a finished and self-contained unit and they are all questions building up the tension and suspense. Notice the way the questions are formulated: my mother – your mother: question on identity; my father – your father: question on blood relation; I – you: question on acquaintance. Observe also the perfect symmetry of the terms, and the order of enumeration: Mother – Father – Self. The answer is given only at the end. But it is prepared by a simile which releases already the tension and solves the suspense. The identification of the terms of relationship should be taken in the same order, i.e. the red terrain denotes the hero and the rain water, the heroine.[94] The comparative particle *pōla* denotes similarity on the basis of colour (Tol. Por. Uvam. 291). In Tamil, the phrase "loving heart(s)" – literally, love-having-heart – is singular, and semantically the poem has ended, i.e. the union of the two hearts into one is achieved. What follows is the verbal explication of this union. Hence the poet has to bring in a plural subject (tām) and end the poem with a verb in plural (kalantaṉavē). The movement of the poem and its articulation are perfect: It starts with "my" and "your", progresses to "I" and "you" and ends up with "One"! The hard terrain and the soft and softening rain water are apt similes for the male and female sexes respectively. The simile brings out also the inseparable nature of the union of the two hearts.

There is no indication of mutaṟporuḷ or karupporuḷ in this poem. The uripporuḷ of the poem, however, cannot be mistaken. Since the whole poem culminates in union (puṇartal), it is a poem belonging to kuṟiñci tiṇai. There might be a love symbolism in the colour of the terrain, because red is the colour of Murukan (Cēyōn) who is the god of the hills (kuṟiñci). And the red terrain here indicates and stands for the hero, who is in the place of Murukan in this love scene.[95]

Let us try to contextualize the poem: There is no indication in the poem itself to tell us who spoke these words, to whom and in which situation. These details of context have to be inferred not from any mutaṟporuḷ or karupporuḷ – which are lacking here – but from the uripporuḷ – the only one that is available and clear from the words and esp. from the simile of the poem. It is in this juncture that the system of poetic conventions in Akam literature comes to our help. We shall use the conventions in order to discover the details of the context.

Who is the speaker and who is the addressee? Theoretically either the young man or the young maid could be the speaker or the listener. But the poetic convention (and the cultural background on which the conventions are based and which cannot be ignored) tells us that between the lovers, only the young man may explicitly speak out his love for the beloved and that especially at the first meeting (Compare Tol. Por. Kaḷ. cūts. 98, 99, 102, 108, esp. 118). If so, since it is clear from the poem that the meeting is the first one (this is surely the implication of the three questions), the speaker is naturally the hero and the listener the heroine.

---

[94] Hart, G. L. III, *Poets*, 9 identifies rain with hero and earth with heroine: "male rain" "female earth". His preoccupation to see fertility myth wherever possible leads him to miss the order of identification.

[95] Shanmugam Pillai, M. suspects the presence of an Advaita aspect in the image used here; cf. *Kuṟunrokai*, 37.

Why does he speak these words which appear to be an assurance of the union of hearts – a union that cannot be broken? The answer to this question is the kuṟippupporuḷ, i.e. the iṟaicci or suggestion. The young man and the young girl meet through Destiny (Iyaṟkaippuṇarcci) and their hearts have become united (Uḷḷappuṇarcci). Now the young man has to part with the girl and he cannot be with her always unless and until they are married and live together in a family. This the girl knows and since this is the first meeting, she is not sure whether he will come back to meet her and then ultimately marry her. These doubts in her mind are reflected in her face and so the hero, knowing what goes on in her mind, assures her that their love and union of hearts are like the union of red terrain and rain water, so much so that nothing can possibly separate their hearts. This is the iṟaicci or suggestion implied in the words of the poem.

The poet's name has not come down to us. But the simile he has used in his poem has earned him the 'poetic baptism' and so he is known as *Cempulappeyaṉīrār*.

E. **Purpose of Akam Poems**

It is true that the purpose of the Akam poems has not been explicitly formulated by anyone in any of the extant poems. But that does not necessarily mean that there was no ultimate purpose for this Akam literature. It seems to me that these poems had an ultimate purpose and that purpose may legitimately be inferred from the following factors:

1. *Conventions on the Subject Matter*: There are three levels of conventions that are seen in the classical Tamil poetry and all of them point towards a purposefulness: a) There is the fundamental and generic convention of classical Tamil poetry into Puṟam and Akam genres. The whole human situation has been brought under two categories of "exterior" behavioral patterns and "interior" behavioral patterns. Two emotions were at the very basis: heroism for Puṟam and love for Akam. This is the first step of abstraction that is at the origin of literary conventions and productions in Tamil.[96] b) Next come the specific conventions in the level of the tiṇais, esp. with regard to Akam literature. The conventions of tiṇai, kaikōḷ, and kūṟṟu belong to this specification of Akam literary genre. These conventions are, needless to say, closely connected with the fundamental convention[97] and they point already to purposefulness. That is the reason why the two extreme tiṇais, namely

---

[96] See Mīṉāṭcicuntaram, K., "Caṅka Ilakkiyam – Kaṟpaṉai Marapu", in *PFifICSTS*, Vol. III, IATR, Madras 1981, 520-527, esp. 522-523.

[97] Ib., 527. For details on Kaikōḷ and Kūṟṟu, see Tol. Por. Akat. cūtrams 36-45.

Kaikkiḷai and Peruntiṇai, were relegated to secondary positions. c) Finally, the convention on the specific subject-matter centres on the uripporuḷ of each tiṇai which is supposed to be the typical emotion (not the exclusive or only emotion) of a given region. Convention in all these three levels was motivated by a purpose for idealization.[98]

2. *Conventions for Composition*: There are certain conventions that have been imposed on the composers of Akam poems. Some of them are implied or revealed in the poems themselves: a) Tol. Por. Akat. cūt. 54 says that "the name of any particular person finds no place" in the Akaṉaintiṇai (the five aspects of love). Proper names are replaced by 'universals based on landscapes' such as *nāṭaṉ* (the man in whose country or the man to whom the country belongs in which etc.), *poṟpaṉ, ūraṉ, cērppaṉ* etc.[99] b) The love aspects are to be formulated by way of kūṟṟu, i.e. as the speech of someone involved in the love affair, namely in the literary form of dramatic monologues.[100] These two conventions for composition control and direct the imagination of the poets. c) Besides, there were also some rules on propriety that the poets must follow: e.g. it is not proper to describe the heroine as riding on the horse made of palmyra stem or even threatening to ride such horse (Tol. Por. Akat. 35); uncultured description of the heroine is not allowed in akam poems.[101]

3. *Consequences of these Conventions*: A few of the main consequences of these conventions are the following: a) The poet has to conceal his identity and speak through the mouth of one of the characters. However, the value of the emotions expressed in the poems may carry indirectly the imprimatur of the poet's personal experience.[102] b) The hero and the heroine, so to say, have to be 'universalized' or 'typologized'.[103] c) This resulted in the creation of a poetic meta-language. Therefore "the classical poets aimed not at expressing their

---

[98] Mīṉāṭcicuntaram, K., "Caṅka Ilakkiyam", in *PFifICSTS*, Vol. III, 524 & 527. The author concludes that already at the level of subject matter, a body of literary men were responsible for these conventions.

[99] Such universals based on landscapes are not found for pālai tiṇai. The same seems to be true also for mullai tiṇai. The fact that the inhabitants of the pālai tract found no place in the akattiṇai as heros and heroines, and that no part of the pālai nilam was set as the background for the meeting of lovers, confirms it. A deeper study of this question will prove useful for knowing the historical origin of the five-fold-region convention!

[100] Shanmugam, R., "The Background Myth in Sangam Poetry", in *PFifICSTS*, Vol. I, sec. 7, IATR, Madras 1981, 11-15, esp. 13; Meenakshisundaram, T. P., *TC*, I, 2 (1952), 110-111; Ramanujan, A. K., *Interior*, 112.

[101] Sundaramoorthy, G., *Early Literary*, 146-147.

[102] Meenakshisundaram, T. P., *TC*, I, 2 (1952), 108; Thani Nayagam, X. S., *Nature*, 44-45; Varadarajan, M., "Literary Theories", in *PFICSTS*, Vol. II, 46.

[103] Sundaramoorthy, G., *Early Literary*, 171-172; Natarajan, A. D., "An Introduction", in *PFICSTS*, Vol. II, 78.

personality, but to create a pattern of meaning which should be timeless or significant to all times..."[104] These conventions in fact purged the imagination of falseness and taught it to select all familiar images — every object of daily observation, provided it is true.[105]

4. *Facts attested in the Literary Materials Extant*: Here are some of them: a) The akam poets have given expression or literary articulation to the inner feelings not of the individual but of the ideal man and woman.[106] They have chosen the best of the types they described. Thus, "the heros and heroines are depicted as ideal persons; for Tolkāppiyar and the poets believed in another principle enunciated also by Aristotle that a class is represented by the best of its type."[107] b) In the poems themselves, one comes across a delicate refinement of the characteristic sentiments of the respective tiṇais. The sentiments are purified and deepened and "the reader also achieves an inner equilibrium in participating in this inner core."[108] c) Even where correction is needed, e.g. in marutattiṇai poems, it is done in an exquisitely delicate and polished way by means of uḷḷuṟai uvamam. The unity, dignity and peace of the family are safeguarded by all means.[109] d) Of course no direct advice is given in the poems for ideal family life. However ideals are suggested or hinted at by the main characters, esp. the maid companion and the heroine. There is at least an indirect call for emulation when ideals are suggested. In a sense, the whole akam literature is a kind of uḷḷuṟai uvamam in relation to the hearer or reader. c) Within the poems, there are didactic statements which aim at ideal family life; see Kuṟ. 290,302; Naṟ. 289,397; Ak. 71,289, esp. Ak. 155,375.[110]

An indirect confirmation seems to come from the fact of the paucity of poems on the two extremes, i.e. Kaikkiḷai and Peruntiṇai. There are two possible explanations for this fact: Either, not many poems were composed on these themes or many poems were composed but were not included by the compilers in the extant anthologies.[111] The fact that there are some poems on these two tiṇais included and have

---

[104] Cf. Manuel, M., "The Use of Literary", in *PFICSTS*, Vol. II, 67.

[105] Cf. Jesudason, C., "A Study of Kabilar, the Sangam Poet", *TC*, III, (1954), 18-35, esp. 34; Mīṉāṭcicuntaram, K., "Caṅka Ilakkiyam", in *PFifICSTS*, Vol. III, 524.

[106] Varadarajan, M., "Literary Theories", in *PFICSTS*, Vol. II, 48.

[107] Thani Nayagam, X. S., "The Ethical Interpretation of Nature in Ancient Tamil Poetry", *TC*, I, (1952), 186-196, esp. 192 for the quotation.

[108] Chellappan, K., "Towards a Theory of Tamil Aesthetics with Special Reference to Sangam Poetry and Cilappatikāram", in *PFifICSTS*, Vol. I, sec. 3, IATR, Madras 1981, 1-5, the quotation is from p. 1. In this sense, "the Sangam Poetry is presentational rather than representational", ib.

[109] Cf. Manickam, V. Sp., *Tamil Concept*, 172f.

[110] See Varadarajan, M., *Ōvac Ceyti*, Madras 1963[4], passim.

[111] J. R. Marr, favours the second explanation: See *Eight Tamil*, 30. The fact is undeniable that among the existing poems only about a decade of them speak of the two extreme cases of love relations.

been "justified" within the range of the five ideal aspects, seems to suggest the first alternative, namely already in the compositional level, these two aspects were not favoured by poets and the few that were composed needed to be included somewhere.

Conclusion

The overall impression one gets from the nature, structure and content of akam poems is that they were meant, at least in the secondary place, to give the sense of refinement of sexual tendencies and to prepare for a happy family life.[112] Certainly the poems testify to the nobility and dignity of human love between the sexes, experienced and expressed, in the ultimate union between man and woman, and thus serve at least remotely as some sort of sex education. This is confirmed also from the fact that the Tamil akam poems treat not only about the romantic aspect of pre-marital love but also about the married life – the poems on Kaṟpu being even numerically more than the Kaḷavu poems!

---

[112] Cf. Manickam, V.Sp., *Tamil Concept*, 189-193 & 321-323; Varadarajan, M., *Ovac Ceyti*, 163ff; Manuel, M., "The Use of Literary", in *PFICSTS*, Vol. II, 65.

Part Three

Chapter 7.

SIMILARITIES BETWEEN THE SONG OF SONGS AND THE ANCIENT TAMIL LOVE POEMS

As one reads the Song of Songs and the Tamil akam poetry of the Classical Age, with sufficient acquaintance of both cultures and literatures, one cannot fail to be "impressed with the sense of familiarity and similarity." [1] Similarity between the SS and Tamil akam poetry is not only on the level of the theme: they both speak of human love; nor merely under the aspect of the general literary form: both belong to the literary genre of anthology; nor are the similarities simply sporadic and random so as to merit some esoteric footnotes but the similarities between them are in different levels and under different aspects.

A. **From the Literary Point of View**

We have already seen that the Song of Songs is a collection of love poems, probably coming from different regions and periods and possibly from different poets.[2] The poet-authors of the individual poems in this collection are not known by names; nor are the delimitations of the different poems unanimously agreed upon among the critics.[3]

The love poems contained in the Tamil classical anthologies too come from different regions, periods and poets. Most of the poets are known by name, but there are some sixty-nine poems whose authors are not known[4]–excluding those who have been named after certain striking simile or phrase from their poems.[5] More important for us here is the fact that the speakers of the individual poems were not indicated by the poet-authors themselves. The indications of the speakers in the poems come from the time of the compilation, classification and edition.[6] The

---

[1] Craigie, P. C., *SR* 8 (1979), 170.
[2] See Part One, Chapter 1, pp. 35-37.
[3] See Part One, Chapter 1, pp. 44-45.
[4] See Part Two, Chapter 5, p. 106.
[5] See Part Two, Chapter 4, note 72.
[6] Cf. Zvelebil, K., *Smile*, 24.

fact that a certain number of poems have been assigned to more than one speaker as alternatives is a proof that the original composer did not indicate the speaker; e.g. Ak. 98; 308 which can pass in the mouth of the Lady-Love or in that of her companion.

1. *Literary Form of the Individual Poems*

All the individual poems in the SS may be classified under two basic categories: dialogues or monologues. Dialogues in our study refer to poems in which conversation takes place between speakers or groups of speakers. These dialogues are of three types:

a) Love dialogue between individual lovers in I–Thou conversation: SS 1:7-8; 1:9-14; 1:15-17; 2:1-3; 4:12-5:1; 8:13-14.

b) Dialogue between one lover and a definite group: SS 8:8-10.

c) A group of unidentifiable persons addressing one of the lovers: SS 7:1-6.

Monologues are poems having no change of speaker within them. These may be classified as:

a) Love monologues spoken by an I-speaker who is one of the love partners (L – Lover, male partner; **B** – Beloved, female partner):

(i) Simple narrative monologues: SS 6:8-10; 6:11-12(L)

(ii) Spoken directly to the other partner: SS 1:2-4(B); 2:14(L); 2:16-17(B); 4:1-7(L); 4:8-11(L); 6:4-7(L); 7:7-10(L); 7:11-14(B); 8:1-5a(B); 8:5b-7(B).

(iii) Monologue by one of the love partners addressed to a definite group outside the love relationship: SS 1:5-6(B).

(iv) Monologues by one of the love partners, closing with an apostrophe (Anrede) to a definite person or persons: SS 2:4-7(B); 3:1-5(B); 8:11-12(L).

(v) Monologues by one of the love partners in which the other partner or outsiders come in conversation: SS 2:8-13(B); 5:2-6:3(B).

b) A monologue spoken by an unidentifiable speaker or speakers to an unidentifiable audience: SS 2:15; 3:6-11.

The speakers in the poems have to be identified by way of inference from the gender of the verbs or of the nouns. More complicated is the question of the concrete situation (Sitz im Leben) of the individual poems. Nothing is indicated in the text itself where and when a given dialogue takes place. The place and time have also to be inferred from the clues available in the text. This problem of concrete situation touches also the monologues. Besides there is the question of the listener to the monologues. One may even ask whether the love partner is speaking in phantasy! Even if a monologue is spoken in a concrete situation, one may suppose a double audience: an apparent or explicit audience such as a group of outsiders and the real or implicit hearer, who is always the other partner. In the SS, double audience is likely to be found more for the love monologues spoken by females than for those by males: e.g. 2:4-7. Such poems as referring to the love partner in the third person imply a second audience besides the partner. In all the monologues, the focus of feeling remains the other partner, who is the implicit audience.[7] One thing may be affirmed with certainty: each monologue, "is the intensely personal speech of a single I-speaker, whose real audience is a single hearer, the beloved Thou."[8]

In so far as these poems in SS, whether dialogues or monologues, are literary pieces, the ultimate audience is the reader of the poems. "The reader is eavesdropping, hearing the public and private words of lovers."[9]

The case of the Tamil love poems is very similar to that of the individual poems in SS. No poet speaks indeed through them in his own voice, and no poem is really addressed to a particular hearer. "The reader only overhears what the characters say to each other, to themselves..."[10] In fact, all poems in akam anthologies are monologues. There is hardly any dialogue in the strict sense of the term. The literary critics are agreed that they are "in the form of dramatic monologues."[11] One author has called these poems "pen-pictures."[12] Here too the speakers of the poems have to be identified from the nouns, verbs or appellations within the poem: e.g. Ikuḷai — female companion addressed by the Lady-Love, etc. In the case of Tamil poems, the poetic conventions that have been "canonized" in grammar help to identify the speakers – but not always!

As in the case of the poems in SS, the Tamil love poems also have a double audience: an explicit audience, addressed and spoken to in the poem itself, and an implicit audience to whom the speaker in fact wants to speak, i.e. the love partner. This double audience is certainly clear in the monologues of the beloved to her companion or vice versa, and in

---

[7] Cf. Falk, M., *Love Lyrics*, 72-74.

[8] Ib., 75.

[9] Craigie, P.C., *SR* 8 (1979), 170.

[10] Ramanujan, A.K., *The Interior*, 112.

[11] Varadarajan, M., "A Type of Apostrophes", in *PTICSTS*, 91; Shanmugaṁ, R., "The Background Myth", *PFifICSTS*, Vol. I, sec. 7, 13.

[12] Jesudason, C., *TC*, III, (1954), 29.

those of the lover to his friend or to the female companion of the beloved: e.g. Kuṟ. 13 by the beloved to her companion.

Each poem, then, in the akam anthologies is a Kūṟṟu, namely a speech and is "expected to be spoken by one, addressed to some other, at a particular place and time, inspired by an urge or purpose."[13] It gives "expression to the one unique poetic moment revealing the depth, value and significance of the suggested inner reality of love... What goes before it and what follows after it are left to the imagination of the reader."[14] These love poems "take one small event, one image that seems trivial, and with that material describe an intense human experience in a sudden and wonderful way, creating in a few words a richness of suggestion and feeling that resonates in the reader's mind long afterward."[15] Thus the ultimate audience for these Tamil love poems, in so far as they are literary pieces, is the reader.

2. *Relation between the Poets and the Poems*

The identity and the personality of the poets who composed the individual poems in the SS are not revealed in and through the poems. What they have expressed in their poems could be, but need not necessarily be, representative of their own personal love experience. The aspects of the love experience that are put as burden in the poems are at the same time universal and paradigmatical so that they are applicable to every lover. The love experiences revealed in these poems remain in the direction of universalized ideal. No wonder, then, that the identity or the individuality of the composers of the particular poems in the SS has not come down to us. For that matter, even the compiler's name is not known.

As for the Tamil akam poems, though the names of most of the poets are known, "the poet's individuality, however, seldom comes into the foreground. The majority of poems, though naturally varying in quality, are anonymous in content and style and altogether homogeneous."[16] The poet aimed at revealing a particular moment and pattern in love experience. At the same time, "he gives something which is already familiar to the readers, something which assures them of a continuity of the past art, but he gives it with his colourings distinguished by his own rich experience and imagination. And thus instead of monotony we feel a surprise that so many variations of the same theme should be possible."[17]

---

[13] Meenakshisundaram, T. P., *TC*, I, 2 (1952), 109.
[14] Shanmugam, R., "The Background", *PFifICSTS*, Vol. I, sec. 7, 13.
[15] Hart, G. L. III, *Poets of the Tamil*, 16.
[16] Zvelebil, K., *TC*, X, 2 (1963), 29-30.
[17] Varadarajan, M., "Literary Theories", in *PFICSTS*, Vol. II, 46.

That variations of the same theme are found also in the poems of the SS is evident and needs no demonstration. When we analyse the process of the literary conception of these poems in the SS and in the Tamil akam anthologies, we may discover two stages: first, the poet conceals his personality and secondly he identifies himself with the character or speaker of the poem and *becomes* the character itself.[18]

3. *On the Compositional Level*

From the point of view of literary composition, one similarity that comes to the forefront between the poems in the SS and the ancient Tamil poems is the use of fixed expressions or formulas, fixed similes and metaphors.

Leaving out the refrains in the SS,[19] we can note the repeated occurrence of the following compositional elements:

a) Love epithets: These are used for the love partners:

(i) Love epithets for the male:

dôdî: 32x: 26 by the love partner
5 by daughters of Jerusalem
1 by himself (SS 7:10).

še 'āhăbāh napšî: 5x – all by the beloved in two poems (1:7; 3:1-4).

(ii) Love epithets for the female:

hayyāpāh bannāšîm: 3x: once (1:8) by lover; twice (5:9; 6:1) by the daughters of Jerusalem.

raʿyātî: 9x – all by the lover (1:9; 1:15; 2:2; 2:10,13; 4:1,7; 5:2; 6:4).

'ăḥōtî: 5x – all by the lover (4:9,10; 4:12; 5:1; 5:2)

kallāh: 6x – all by the lover (4:8,9,10,11; 4:12; 5:1)

tammātî: 2x – by the lover (once vocative: 5:2; and once in nominative: 6:9).

---

[18] Cf. Mīṉāṭcicuntaram, K., "Caṅka Ilakkiyam", in *PFifICSTS*, Vol. III, 525. The author, of course, speaks of Tamil akam poems in his article. But one can easily see the applicability of what he says, also to the poems of the SS.

[19] On this point, see Part One, Chapter 1, p. 37 and corresponding note with bibliography.

b) Fixed expressions or formulas:

(i) hinnāk yāpāh: 1:15 (2x); 4:1 (2x) – by male.
hinnĕkā yāpeh: 1:16 once only – by female.

(ii) ḥôlat 'ahăbāh 'ānî: 2:5; 5:8 – both by female.

(iii) śĕmō'lô taḥat lĕrō'šî / wîmînô tĕḥabbĕqēnî:
2:6; 8:3 – both by female – but notice the omission of the preposition *lĕ* before *rō'šî* in 8:3 – a slight variation in the formula!

(iv) qôl dôdî: 2:8; 5:2 – both by female – but notice the variation of the usage of the formula.

(v) dôdî lî wa'ănî lô / hārō'eh baššôšannîm: 2:16; 6:3; 7:11a – all by female – but notice that the order of the first part of the formula is changed in 6:3, while 7:11a contains only half of the first part of the formula and that too with a combination of another phrase!

(vi) 'ad šeyyāpûaḥ hayyôm / wĕnāsû haṣṣĕlālîm: 2:17; 4:6 – identical formula but in the mouth of the female and male partners and in different contexts.

(vii) līr'ôt hăpārḥāh haggepen / hēnēṣû hārīmmonîm: 6:11; 7:13 – formula in varied form and in the mouth of the male and female respectively.

c) Fixed similes: the male – like gazelle and stag: 2:9; 2:17; 8:14.
the female – like trophies: 6:4; 6:10.
female's hair – like flock of goats: 4:1; 6:5.
female's teeth – like flock of ewes: 4:2; 6:6.
female's cheeks – like slice of pomegranates: 4:3; 6:7.
female's neck – like tower: 4:4; 7:5a (with variation of qualificatives).
female's breasts – like fawns: 4:5; 7:4.
caresses of both – sweeter than wine: 1:2,4; 7:10.

d) Fixed metaphors: female – dove: 2:14; 5:2; 6:9 – by lover; her eyes – doves: 1:15; 4:1 (compare 5:12 where the eyes of the male partner are *like doves*, according to the female partner).

It is to be noted that these fixed epithets, expressions or formulas, similes and metaphors are spread out in different poems. To these lists may be added the list of the parallel pairs or word-pairs that have been verified in the SS.[20] The most reasonable explanation is to think that the poems were composed and transmitted orally; for oral composition depends on fixed expressions since improvisation is an essential part in oral poetry. This explains also the variations of these fixed expressions and formulas.[21]

With regard to the ancient Tamil anthologies, the structural elements of fixed expressions and formulas have been studied by a couple of scholars.[22] Here are adduced some examples of such fixed elements of different categories for the sake of comparison:[23]

a) Love epithets:

(i) For the male:

Neṭuntakai (noble person/great person): Naṟ. 361:7; Aiṅ. 244:2; 408:3; Ak. 49:10; 310:2; 324:14; 384:13.

Kātalar (lover): Naṟ. 79:10; 174:5; 186:10; Kuṟ. 4:3; 75:5; 152:5; Aiṅ. 221:1; 311:3; Ak. 22:20; 68:10; 135:10.

Iṉiyaṉ or Iṉiyar (sweet person): Naṟ. 1:1; Kuṟ. 172:4; 288:3; Ak. 241:2; 352:17.

Aṉpiṉaṉ or Aṉpiṉar (loving person): Naṟ. 115:9; 208:8; Kuṟ. 85:1; Aiṅ. 475:5; Ak. 91:9; 255:19.

Eṉṉai (my lord or husband): Kuṟ. 24:2; 203:5; 223:7.

(ii) For the female:

Kātali (beloved): Naṟ. 356:8; Kuṟ. 120:2; 151:5; Aiṅ. 291:4; 325:4; Ak. 19:18; 54:21; 142:7.

Iṉiyōḷ (sweet girl): Naṟ. 3:8; Kuṟ. 206:2.

---

[20] M. J. Dahood has collected some 23 word-pairs occurring in the SS. Although a few may be unconvincing, most of them are valid cases of word-pairs. See his "Ugaritic - Hebrew", in *Ras Shamra Parallels*, Vol. I, 71-382. See additional word-pairs – some seven of them in his "Ugaritic - Hebrew Parallel Pairs", in *Ras Shamra Parallels*, Vol. III, (ed.) S. Rummel, AnOr-51, PIB, 1981, 1-206.

[21] On this point of "parallel word-pairs and oral poetry" see esp. Watson, W. G. E., *Classical*, 136-144. Cf. also 66-83.

[22] For Puṟam poetry, see esp. Kailasapathy, K., *Tamil Heroic Poetry*, Oxford University Press, London 1968, 147-170. For Akam Poetry, see the short treatment by Zvelebil, K., *Smile*, 111-114; esp. Ramanujan, A. K., *Poems of Love and War*, Columbia University Press, New York 1985, 269-286.

[23] It is not necessary for our purpose to collocate all the fixed expressions or formulas and fixed similes found in Tamil akam poems.

Māayōḷ (girl of dark complexion): Naṟ. 139:7; 157:10; Kuṟ. 9:1; 132:6; Aiṅ. 306:4; 324:5; Ak. 62:5; 208:24.

Aṇaṅkiyōḷ (causing pain): Kuṟ. 119:4; Aiṅ. 250:5; 259:6; Ak. 322:14; 372:16.

Nallōḷ (good girl): Naṟ. 137:2; 323:6; Kuṟ. 14:5; 62:4; Aiṅ. 166:4; Ak. 392:7.

b) Fixed expressions and formulas:

amma vāḻi tōḻi (lit. listen, may you prosper, 0 friend): Naṟ. 79:9; 194:1; Kuṟ. 77:1; 134:1; Aiṅ. 40:1; 111:1; Ak. 101:1; 141:1.

aravu nuṅku mati (moon eaten by snake): Ak. 114:5; 313:7.

pāṉāṭ-kaṅkul (lit. half-day-night; in the middle of the night): Kuṟ. 301:4; 355:4; Ak. 57:18; 58:2; 92:2.

karuṅkāl vēṅkai (lit. black-legged vēṅkai. Here black-stemmed vēṅkai tree): Kuṟ. 26:1; 47:1; Naṟ. 168:1; 257:5; Aiṅ. 219:1.

araiyiruḷ naṭunāḷ (thick dark midday, i.e. midnight): Naṟ. 68:8; Kuṟ. 190:5; – the same phrase with slight variations in Naṟ. 228:3; Ak. 126:7; 141:8.

c) Fixed similes:

(i) For the lover: like a male elephant: Naṟ. 182:9; Ak. 32:16; 55:5; 308:9; 368:11.

(ii) For the beloved: like heavenly maid: Ak. 32:7; 162:25.
like a statue of masterpiece: Ak. 62:15; 212:1; Naṟ. 185:11; 362:1.
like a peacock: Naṟ. 264:4; Ak. 198:7.

her body: like gold: Naṟ. 10:2; 166:2; Kuṟ. 101:4; 319:6.

forehead: like the moon: Naṟ. 128:3; 167:11; Kuṟ. 129:5; 226:3; Aiṅ. 443:3.

hair: like the feather of a peacock: Naṟ. 264:4-5; 265:8-9.

eyes: like water-lily (Neytal): Kuṟ. 101:4; 226:1; Ak. 42:3.

look: like that of a doe: Naṟ. 101:9; 179:4; Ak. 261:9.

teeth: like pearls: Aiṅ. 185:1-2; 380:2; Ak. 27:9-10.

upper arms: like the bamboo: Naṟ. 82:2; 166:4; Kuṟ. 226:9.

walk: like that of a peacock: Aiṅ. 258:2; Ak. 158:5.

d) Fixed metaphors:

(i) For the lover: Kāḷai (bull): Naṟ. 179:8; 184:2; Ak. 263:9; 321:12; 388:15.

(ii) For the beloved: Antīṅkiḷavi (lit. pretty-sweet-word; sweet speech): Ak. 262:18; 288:17.

These fixed epithets and expressions, similes and metaphors are evidences that the Tamil classical poems were also composed and transmitted orally and later put into writing. Thus the two love literatures – the SS and the Tamil love poems – are similar on the level of composition too.[24]

B. **From the Spatio-Temporal Aspect**

The spatio-temporal categories have close relation to human love in both these literatures. Some of the stirking points are indicated here below:

1. *Landscape and Love*

In the SS, almost all the love dialogues and many of the love monologues take place at least in part in the country side. In so far as this country side is cultivated landscape and thus represents the harmonious blending of human effort and Nature's productive capacity, it serves as a conducive site and inviting ambient for love-making and reunion.[25] Such ambient is reflected in the following poems in the SS:

1:7-8: reference to pasture land.
1:15-17: a watch-hut.[26]
2:1-3: valley and grove.
2:8-13: the land with flowers and fruits.
4:12-5:1: reference to the garden.
6:11-12: in the garden.
7:11-14: vineyard and garden.
8:5d-7: shade of the apple tree.
8:13-14: garden.

---

[24] There are even lines that have been repeated: e.g. Kuṟ. 54:1 in 97:1; Naṟ. 68:8 in Kuṟ. 190:5; Kuṟ. 105:1 in 133:1; three lines with small variations in Ak. 14:2-4 and Ak. 304:13-15. Hart, G. L. III, *Poems*, 152ff seems to overlook these instances. However, he too admits the fact of oral composition of poems in Tamil anthologies, although he would like to modify the conclusions of both K. Kailasapathy and K. Zvelebil.

[25] Cf. Falk, M., *Love Lyrics*, 88-89.

[26] Stuiber, A., "Die Wachhütte im Weingarten (Vgl. Ct. 1,5. Vg)", *JbAC* 2 (1959), 86-89, fig. 10-12; Fox, M. V., *VT* 33 (1983), 202-203.

That the love encounter took place in the cultivated country side is implied or hinted at in SS 1:5-6. The cultivated piece of land, namely the vineyard seems to serve as a symbol of love affair in SS 2:15, and as a metaphor of the beloved in SS 8:11-12.

Hill and mountains, peaks and caverns generally represent remoteness and circumstances which are either dangers on the way or hindrances for the meeting of the lovers. The poems in which these elements occur, contain invitation to leave such surroundings and come over to the love partner, or contain the sentiments of anxiety, longing and urgency:

2:8-13: the mountains and hills – remoteness.

4:8-11: mountains and animals – remoteness, hindrance and danger.

In SS 2:14, the mention of rocks and ravines seems to indicate simply the place where the lover asks his partner to show her face and raise her voice. Those elements do not represent, strictly speaking, either remoteness or danger. For no verb of movement, such as "come", "leave", "leap" etc. has been used along with these rocks and ravines.

The animals, birds and plants which are mentioned in these poems serve as natural background "against which the emotional life of the lovers move."[27] The symbolism and significance of these animals, etc. have to be inferred from the human sentiments expressed in the poems.

That different landscapes and love-aspects are intimately connected in the Tamil akam poetry, has been already sufficiently explained and documented. The significance of the mountains and hills in kuṟiñci poems correspond almost exactly to that of the mountains and hills in the SS. They correspond to the cultivated country side of the SS, where the lovers encounter – hence favourable for the union of lovers: Compare for example, the watch-hut in millet fields or the field itself in kuṟiñci poems, where the encounter takes place: Naṟ. 194, 213, 351; Kuṟ. 141, 142, 198; Ak. 28, 32, 38, 308 etc. The mountains, hills and swift torrents in this region become elements of danger and hindrances to the meeting of the lovers, esp. at night-tryst: e.g. Naṟ. 36,51,85,104; Kuṟ. 268,355; Ak. 18,122 etc. In Tamil kuṟiñci poems, the descriptions of the landscape prepare the hearer or reader, and explain the emotional content of the poems. They often "serve to place the poem in its narrative context, by symbolizing the episodic context from which the expressed emotion

---

[27] Rabin, C., *SR* 3:3 (1973/4), 210. See also Emily Sr., "Akattiṇaiyum Ati-uṉṉata Caṅkītamum", *Thozhan* 24 (1983), 170-178.

arises."[28] The gardens and groves in the SS, where the meetings of the lovers take place, may be compared to the groves and forest-areas in Tamil poems where similar unions between the lover and the beloved take place: See Naṟ. 96,172,187,227; Kuṟ. 266,299,303; Ak. 30,80,240, etc.

The civilized ambient, namely the city streets and public squares, and as a rule the society as such, are less sympathetic to the lovers in the SS.[29] Poems in the SS, which contain this motif are:

1:5-6: the daughters of Jerusalem – cynical attitude.
2:5; 3:5; 8:4: the same girls are considered as disturbers.
3:1-5: watchmen of the city – indifferent and apparently uncooperative.
5:2-6:3: watchmen of the city – harmful to the beloved.
8:1-5ac: the society is likely to despise the sincere sign of love of the woman, i.e. kissing her lover.

This unsympathetic and even cynical attitude of the women of the city in the SS, has a parallel in the gossipping women of the village in Tamil akam poems: See Naṟ. 36,76,149; Kuṟ. 51,262,311; Aiṅ. 236,279; Ak. 98,218,282,368, etc. In Tamil, the gossip of the women about the love-affair of other girls is called *ampal* and *alar – ampal* being the initial stage of the gossip while *alar* signifying the gossip well known.[30] The motif of the watchmen being a hindrance as well as danger to the meeting of the lovers is well known in kuṟiñci poems: See, Naṟ. 98,132,255; Kuṟ. 375; Ak. 122 162, etc.

The third spatial category that has to do with the meeting of the lovers is the interior quarters of residences: the mother's house, wine-halls and chambers. These appear to be secure environments for love-making. The poems in SS, which seem to refer to such interior places where the lovers may be alone, are:

1:2-4, esp. v. 4: a wish expressed.[31]
1:9-14, esp. v. 12 (?): an intimate dialogue.
2:4-7, esp. v. 4: narrating the experience.
3:1-5, esp. v. 4: probably in dream.
8:1-5ac, esp. v. 2: a wishful thinking!

---

[28] Shanmugam Pillai, M.-Ludden, D. E., *Kuṟuntokai*, 23.

[29] Falk, M., *Love Lyrics*, 90.

[30] Cf. Pillay, K. K., *The Social History*, 353. These two words – *ampal* and *alar* – are significantly related to flower language: *Ampal*, originally from *Arumpal* (to bud or sprout), and *alar* from *alartal* (to blossom), are verbs denoting the stages of flowering. Compare with this expression, the word *pūppeytal*, meaning "coming to puberty" of a girl. See Part Two, Chapter 6, note 66. The gossip of the women leads to the revelation of the secret-love-affair to the parents and eventually to marriage.

[31] Fox, M. V., *VT* 33(1983), 199-206. He understands "the chambers" here and "the wine house" in 2:4 as referring to the booth in 1:16-17.

As a rule, the interior chambers are rarely mentioned in Tamil akam poems as places of meeting, although such unions are recalled as having happened: for instance, in Kuṟ. 244; Ak. 102,311, the night visits of the lover and meeting inside the house of the girl are mentioned. There are also poems in which the lady companion suggests to the young man to stay for the night in the house of the beloved *as a guest*, i.e. in the eyes of the parents and relatives of the girl: See, Naṟ. 215,254,276,331,392; Ak. 340,350. But the majority of the night visits of the hero to the heroine takes place in the garden near the house of the girl: See, Kuṟ. 141,266,312,321,335,360; Ak. 2,22,58,68,122, etc.

2. *Season and Love*

There is at least one poem in the SS, which explicitly speaks of a season of the year as having influence on the love-life of the lovers, i.e. SS 2:8-13. Winter is past and the rain is over, namely the Spring has arrived. Vegetation has been revived in nature: blossoms appear, turtle-dove sings, figs ripen and vines in blossom give out fragrance. Nature is inviting the lovers to come together and that is expressed in words by the lover to his beloved: "Come". The same seasonal significance or symbolism appears to be present also in the following poems of SS:

2:15: the vineyard is in blossom – but vulnerable!
6:11-12: to see whether the vines are in blossom – the place of tryst is the garden and the season is implied in the blossoming of the vines.
7:11-14: a blossoming season is implied.

The intimate connection and interaction between seasons and different love-aspects are evident in Tamil akam poems. According to the mentality of the Tamil poets, the human love is so to say the display and perfect revelation of the primeval energy of which nature is the reservoir. Love is seen as part of a cosmic process of regeneration through death and decay in nature. The fertility of the land (the forest or *mullai*) has a dimension of sexual symbolism.[32] The Tamil poems relating to mullaittiṇai are the nearest parallels to these poems in SS. At the coming of the season, the woman (sometimes, also the man) relates her feelings through descriptions of her relation to the season itself. She compares her own condition to the colours and occurrences of the season.[33] The arrival of the season makes the lovers long for each other's company: See, Naṟ. 69,224,242,243,246; Kuṟ. 220,221,254; Aiṅ.

[32] Chellappan, K., "Towards a Theory", in *PFifICSTS*, Vol. I, sec. 3, 2.
[33] Cf. Shanmugam Pillai, M.-Ludden, D. E., *Kuṟuntokai*, 17.

420,484,494, etc. In kuṟiñci poems, the blossoming of vēṅkai flowers indicates the season for the union, i.e. *puṇartal.*[34]

When we come to consider the time of the day which is conducive to the union of lovers, the following may be said with regard to the SS. The love relationship in the SS appears to be a secret affair – see SS 2:9 – and it can be consummated only at night, when the lovers are not exposed to scrutiny. "Sometimes even in the domesticated country side, where both male and female speakers express the desire to meet, the lovers seem to feel that their rendezvous must be kept secret, confined to night-time."[35] If we examine still more closely, we see that the rendezvous, always secret, takes place in the cultivated country-side during the day, and in the house or in its interior chambers at night: See for instance SS 1:7-8; 6:11-12; 7:11-14, esp. v. 13 (while verse 12 refers to the night) for the rendezvous during the day; and SS 2:16-17, esp. v. 17; 5:2-6:1 where it is explicitly, though in dream, described that the rendezvous are at night. SS 4:6 also seems to imply the rendezvous at night. The dewy season and night-time implied in SS 5:2 corrresponds exactly to the Poḻutu of the kuṟiñci poems in Tamil.[36]

In the majority of the kuṟiñci poems in Tamil, the secret meeting takes place at night, more precisely in the middle of the night, when the whole world is silent and sleeping. The love-affair is certainly secret according to the Tamil poems – hence the name kaḷavu — secret love-affair.[37] But there are also poems which speak of meeting of the lovers – always in secret intimacy – during the day: e.g. in the vicinity of the millet field in kuṟiñci, or in the groves near the sea-shore, i.e. in neytal.[38] In short, according to Tamil akam poetry, the day-rendezvous takes place in the cultivated countryside and the night tryst either in the house or in the house-garden of the beloved – very similar to the SS.[39]

Similar to the girl in the SS, the maiden of the Tamil akam poems, keeps awake at night and waits for the lover who will come to the vicinity of the house-garden. For the rendezvous during the day, see Naṟ. 156,285; Kuṟ. 198,303; Ak. 18,92,182,240; for the night-tryst, see Naṟ. 49,323,331; Kuṟ. 244, 345; Ak. 80,148,308. In Kuṟ. 312, the hero recalls how his girl spent the night with him, and how she concealed the next day any sign of the meeting from her parents and relatives.

---

[34] See Part Two, Chapter 6 "Symbolism in Function", pp. 138f.
[35] Falk, M., *Love Lyrics*, 93-94.
[36] See Part Two, Chapter 5, p. 115.
[37] See Part Two, Chapter 5, p. 107.
[38] See Part Two, Chapter 6, p. 142-3.
[39] See Part Two, Chapter 6, p. 138.

The evening time is very painful to endure, when the lovers are separated from each other. They think of each other and often spend the night without sleep, all the time longing for the other. Hence evening is a time which increases the longing of the love-partners. In SS 3:1-5 and 5:2-6:3, this intense longing of the girl is clear. It is not, however, explicit from the SS, that the boy also suffers the loneliness of the evening and spends sleepless nights.

In Tamil poems, evening for the separated lovers is the time of longing for the other partner, and they spend sleepless nights. This is true not only during the time of courtship but also during the long separation for the sake of earning wealth, i.e. both in kuṟiñci (and neytal) and mullai poems. Spending sleepless nights because of the longing for the other during courtship belongs to both the boy – see Naṟ. 319; Aiṅ. 172,195, etc. – and the girl – see Naṟ. 303,348; Kuṟ. 28,243,261; Aiṅ. 142, etc. Evening is especially painful for the girl: see Kuṟ. 118,122,243,261,301.[40] We have already seen that evening is the specific *Ciṟupoḻutu* for mullai and neytal.

3. *Occupation and Love-affair*

The occupation or profession of either of the lovers serves as an occasion for their first meeting or further meetings. In the SS, there are some poems which imply such occupations, in a given landscape, as chances of meeting for the lovers. For example,

- 1:5-6: The girl says that she was asked to guard the vineyard where she did not guard "hers".
- 1:7-8: A shepherd boy and a shepherd girl are using their occupation of tending the sheep to fix a tryst.
- 1:15-17: The watch-hut, where the encounter takes place, seems to be one meant for guarding the vineyards.
- 2:15: It appears to be the saying of the girl, and to refer to her occupation of guarding the vineyard, cf. 1:5-6.
- 6:11-12: The boy goes to the garden to see the blossoms.
- 7:11-14: The girl invites the lover to go to the garden to see the blossoming vines.
- 8:13-14: Both of them are already there.

Of these last three poems, the first two might refer to such occupational context. The last one is not so clear, but the possibility cannot be excluded.

[40] See Part Two, Chapter 6, p. 140.

In Tamil akam poems too there are references to similar occupations of mostly the girl which serve as occasions either for the first meeting or for further meetings of the lovers: See, for instance, Ak. 82 where the maiden tells her lady companion how she became love-sick at the sight of the young man who came to the millet field where she was guarding the ripe millet;[41] see also Naṟ. 128; Ak. 32. In Ak. 308, the occupation helps for further encounters; see Kuṟ. 141 too. A girl from the neytal nilam, i.e. sea-shore-side goes about selling salt and in course of her selling, a young man becomes enarmoured of her: Ak. 140,390, etc. Naṟ. 101 and Ak. 80 tell us about girls who chase away birds from dry fish and this occupation gives a chance for the lovers to meet.

C. **Presentation of the Characters**

1. *The Lovers*

It is evident that the lovers in the SS, do not carry any personal proper names of their own. That means, they are types or ideal figures. According to some exponents "the lovers are only images of the poet, his fictions, his reflections of experience. They have no existence outside the poem, and its impression on the world."[42] In their relationship with society, the lovers may represent any boy and girl from any social milieu. "It is altogether likely that the trajectory of this poetry has moved through more than one social-class location, from the generation of idioms and scenes, and possibly whole surviving specimens."[43] They could represent peasant-couples as well as couples from royal court or oppulent society. Thus the lovers in the SS reflect the society, while at the same time they remain unknown. We can see in fact that the poems have survived the poets, that the lovers emerge from the poems to speak out their love-experience and then disappear or go to the background, leaving only the impression of love-sentiments in the real world of the readers!

In Tamil akam poems, not only the names of the lovers are not *de facto* known to us, but according to the poetic convention, the characters in the love-affair must not be indicated by their proper names.[44] Hence Tamil akam poetry is no personal love-poetry in the strict sense of the word. For, "the personnel is anonymous – they are types, typified common people or rather people in general."[45] The male and female of the Tamil akam poetry serve at once as types of humanity

---

[41] See the poem in the appendix.

[42] Landy, F., *Paradoxes*, 62.

[43] Gottwald, N. K., *The Hebrew Bible – A Socio-Literary Introduction*, Philadelphia 1985, 551.

[44] See Part Two, Chapter 6, p. 149.

[45] Zvelebil, K., *Smile*, 15.

and individuals.[46] The lovers are idealized types.[47] Here too, the authors of the poems, though known by names, have disappeared, the characters emerge to the foreground, express their sentiments and recede to the rear. The love-sentiments expressed in the poems live long after the poet or even the characters. For, this love relation has been by now made a paradigm for all love-relations into which anyone sees himself or herself reflected and thus feels at home.[48]

2. *Designation of Lovers*

How are the lovers in the SS designated without revealing their personal proper identity? An analysis of all the names by which they are spoken of or spoken to, will give us the answer (See above also the list of love-epithets under fixed expressions):

a) Designations used for the male:

(i) By the female partner:

Indirectly – as third person:

. "He": Never by the pronoun *hû'*, but always implied in the verb.

. zeh: Twice in 5:16 to the daughters of Jerusalem.

. dôdî: "my beloved one": 1:13,14; 2:3,8,9,10,16; 4:16; 5:2,4,5,6 (twice), 8,10,16; 6:2,3 (twice); 7:11.

. rēʿî: "my companion": 5:16.

. še 'āhăbāh napšî: "whom my soul loves": 3:1,2,3,4.

Directly, i.e. in direct speech as vocative:

. dôdî: 1:16; 2:17; 7:12,14; 8:14.

. še 'āhăbāh napšî: 1:7.

(ii) By others: dôdēk: 5:9 (twice); 6:1 (twice)
dôdāhh: 8:5. — All by the daughters of Jerusalem.

(iii) By himself: lĕdôdî: "for its beloved":[49] 7:10 – in third person to his beloved.

---

[46] Natarajan, A. D., "An Intoduction", in *PFICSTS*, Vol. II, 78.
[47] Cf. Ramanujan, A. K., *The Interior*, 104.
[48] Cf. Sundaramoorthy, G., *Early Literary*, 171-172.
[49] For the parsing of *yod* in *lĕdôdî* as third person mas.sing.suffix referring to wine, see Dahood, M. J., *Psalms I*, 300; Schoville, K. N., *The Impact*, 96-99.

Comments

1) The designations "your beloved" "her beloved" by the daughters of Jerusalem about the male partner and "its beloved" by the man about himself are only repetitions of what the female partner said, and so they are not particularly significant.

2) Among the other designations used by the maid for her lover, the demonstrative pronoun *zeh* (this), has no particular significance in this context of description, and it can simply mean "such is my lover, etc."

3) There remain three other designations which are worth studying: *dôdî* (my beloved one) is the most frequently used both in the third person and in the second (as vocative). This designation is closely connected with the *dôdēkā* in 1:2,4, etc. referring to caressing or love-making. Thus she seems to imply by *dôdî* a lover who has manifested his love in concrete actions. The designation "my companion" used only once implies the joy of being together, and now absent or far removed. The context in 5:16 confirms this significance. The reference by "whom my soul loves" (used four times in indirect speech and once in direct to the lover) is more interiorized and permanent, although the desire or longing is not completely excluded.[50] The most interesting designation of the male by the maid is the pronominal one, i.e. "he, him, his ..." always implied in the verb. Because the lover fills her heart and thought so much that it is enough for the maid to say "he", and she knows whom she refers to and still more, she presumes that everybody else must know whom she refers to. This is in fact the climax of love relation! See SS 1:2a; 2:4,6; 8:10 where this pronominal designation is clear.[51]

b) Designations used for the female:

(i) By the male partner:

Indirectly, i.e. in the third person:

. "She" – *hî'*: thrice in 6:9.
. raʿyātî: "my companion": 2:2.
. yônātî: "my dove": 6:9.
. tammātî: "my perfect one": 6:9.

---

[50] Compare the nuance of the word *nepeš* which means also sexual desire in SS 5:6 – the context is similar. For the significance of *nepeš*, see *BDB*, ad vocem-6; Dahood, M. J., *Greg* 43 (1962), 71 and note 37. That *npš* has this meaning is confirmed from UT, 49:II:17-19; Glossary, n. 1681; cf. also Prov. 19:2.

[51] A similar case seems to be present in the Gospel of St. John in the post-resurrection narrative: Jn. 20:14-15.

Directly, i.e. in the vocative.

. "You" – *'at*: 6:4.
. yāpāh bannāšîm: "fairest among women": 1:8.
. yāpātî: "my fair one": 2:10,13.
. tammātî: 5:2.
. yônātî: 2:14; 5:2.
. 'ăḥōtî: "my sister": 4:9,10,12; 5:1,2.
. raʿyātî: 1:9,15; 2:10,13; 4:1,7; 5:2; 6:4.
. kallāh: "bride": 4:8,9,10,11,12; 5:1.
. 'ahăbāh: "love": 7:7.
. bāt ʿănûgîm: "daughter of delights": 7:7.

(ii) By others: "fairest among women": 5:9; 6:1 – both vocatives by the daughters of Jerusalem. "Shulamite": 7:1; "Daughter of a prince": 7:2b – both vocative by onlookers. "Sister": 8:8ac – twice nominative; "She" *hî'*: 8:9ac – twice by the brothers.

(iii) By herself: "Shulamite": 7:1c – in the third person.

Comments

1) The designation "Shulamite" by the girl about herself is a mere repetition of what the onlookers said, and hence it has no particular significance.

2) The designations "sister" "our sister" and "she" are by the brothers of the maid. In regard to love-relation, these designations have no significant connotations.

3) The designation "fairest among women" by the maids of Jerusalem is an echo of what the lover said in 1:8, and represents the appreciation of the beauty of the girl by them. By "daughter of a prince" and "Shulamite" the onlookers express their appreciation of her beauty and possibly her noble birth — and these latter two are probably poetic fiction (for which see below).

4) The designations by the male partner are many and interesting. The epithets in vocative case (addressed directly to the girl) are far more numerous than the ones in indirect speech. The epithets in indirect speech and the pronoun"she" (thrice) are all meant to show more the uniqueness of the beloved among others than the place she occupies in his thought or heart. The pronoun "she" is not used in an absolute sense, since it comes always in combination with a complementary designation. The epithets in direct speech may be grouped according to their emphasis on particular aspects:

–epithets of endearment: "my companion" (8x), "bride" (6x), "my sister" (5x), "love" and perhaps also "my dove" (2x).

–epithets of beauty: "fairest among women", "my fair one", "my perfect one" and "my dove".

–epithet referring to pleasure: "daughter of delights".

It is to be noted that the designations of the girl with terms of endearment take the pride of place, then follow the epithets of beauty and finally that of pleasure.

5) If we compare the use of love epithets in direct and indirect speeches by the male and female characters, we notice: (a) The girl is using love-epithets about her lover to others more than to the lover himself. She is proud of her love-relationship with him and seems to enjoy telling it to others. In his presence and face to face with him, she seems to be in ecstacy and so speechless! Moreover, all the epithets in her mouth refer directly to love-relationship, though they are not many. (b) The boy uses numerically more epithets about his girl to herself than about her to others. In her presence and face to face with her, he seems to be in ecstacy and therefore more eloquent than otherwise! Moreover, he uses also epithets of beauty and pleasure, besides epithets which refer to love-relationship. On the whole the girl is more meditative and mystical, and the boy is more concrete and forthright!

When we come to Tamil akam poetry, the designations of the hero and the heroine are too many to collocate all of them here and analyze their significance. We shall therefore consider only the most important ones:

1) Designations from landscape: The designations of the hero and the heroine of the different regions take their origin from their respective regions: e.g. the hero of kuṟiñci tract is called poruppaṉ, veṟpaṉ (Ak. 38:5), cilampaṉ (Ak. 22:9), nāṭaṉ (Kuṟ. 3:4) or malaināṭaṉ (Ak. 138:14); the heroine of that region is called kuṟatti (Ak. 52:3), koṭicci (Naṟ. 22:1). Similarly for the hero and the heroine of the other regions too.[52] When these designations occur in the poems, we may often, if not always, expect a description of his land or village etc. in such a way that his quality or behavioral pattern will be revealed through the uḷḷuṟai uvamam or through the iṟaicci.

2) Other designations: These are the various epithets which are used by the speakers to designate the hero or the heroine of the

[52] For other details and designations, see the Table of the Classification of karupporuḷ on pages 120-123. See also Zvelebil, *Smile*, 100.

love-affair. For a strict comparison with the SS, we shall adduce only the epithets from poems that refer to the premarital meetings of the hero and the heroine.[53] Even among the epithets used for the love-partners, we shall deal specially with those used by the heroine and her companion for the hero, and those used by the hero and the lady companion for the heroine. The reason is simply because only designations used by these people refer directly to the love-relationship between the hero and the heroine.[54]

a) Designations used for the hero:

(i) By the heroine:

Indirectly, i.e. as third person:

. Avar (he): 28 times: Naṟ. 65,72,255,338; Kuṟ. 112, 153, 219, 249,299 (2x), 305,340,361,395 (2x); Aiṅ. 201,203,209 (2x), 213,215,224,262; Ak. 8,98, 128,252,398.

. Kātalar (lover): 12 times: Naṟ. 64; Kuṟ. 60,118,130, 152,157,160,290,340,399; Aiṅ. 221; Ak. 22.

. Iṉiyar (sweet person): Naṟ. 1; Kuṟ. 288; Ak. 352.

. Eṉṉai (my lord or my husband): Kuṟ. 223; Aiṅ. 201,312.

. Naṇpiṉar: Kuṟ. 302; Naṭpiṉaṉ: Kuṟ. 385 – both mean "friend".

. Kaḷvaṉ (thief): Kuṟ. 25,318 – referring to Kaḷavu.[55]

. Kāḷai (young man like a bull): Aiṅ. 385; Ak. 388.

---

[53] For the principles on which poems have been classified as referring to courtship or premarital meetings, see note 74 below.

[54] It would be interesting to collocate all the epithets of all akam poems of the five regions, analyse them and study the sentimental values expressed by them. For the epithets vary according to the regions and their corresponding aspects of love-sentiments. For example, the epithets used by the hero for the heroine in pālaittiṇai are different from those of kuṟiñci or mullai, etc.

[55] There is a variant reading in Kuṟ. 25, which reads kaḷavaṉ instead of kaḷvaṉ. The word kaḷavaṉ means both "the one who was on the spot" and "the one who is a witness and therefore the judge of the situation", from kaḷam – place or spot. Some authors prefer the first reading, i.e. kaḷvaṉ, see Zvelebil, K., *Smile*, 83; Ramanujan, A.K., *Poems of Love*, 17. Others defend the reading kaḷavaṉ: see, *Kuṟuntokai*, SISSWPS, Madras 1978, 38; Irākavaiyaṅkār, R., *Kuṟuntokai Viḷakkam*, Annamalai Palkalaik-Kaḻakam, 1956², ix & 52 where the second reading is defended. Both meanings fit the context well.

The following designations are used once each:

Māṇtakkōṉ (noble man): Kuṟ. 31; Pīṭukeḻu kuricil (man of singular greatness): Kuṟ. 31; Em-nāṭar (my landsman): Kuṟ. 87; Kaṭavaṉ and Puṇaivaṉ (duty-bound man and help-mate like a boat): Kuṟ. 318; Puraiyōr (great man): Naṟ. 1; Viṟalōṉ (hero): Naṟ. 304; Cāṉṟōr (man of perfection): Naṟ. 327; Pēṇalaṉ (protector): Naṟ. 332. (pēṇal = to protect).

Directly, i.e. in direct address: The Tamil heroine very rarely addresses the hero directly [56] and speaks to him. She refers to him almost always in the third person, even when she knows that he is listening to her words. This is what is technically called in Tamil poetics or grammar *muṉṉilaippuṟamoḻi* (lit. direct-indirect speech).

(ii) By the lady companion:

Indirectly:

. Avar: 25 times: Naṟ. 11,68,88,154,191,222,251,263,311; Kuṟ. 23,177,262,297,366,367,375,392; Aiṅ. 102,106,207,208, 210,227; Ak. 28,392.

. Kātalar: 14 times: Naṟ. 5,83,129,134,282,339,392,393; Kuṟ. 48; Aiṅ. 223,225,235,270; Ak. 68.

. Naṉṉarāḷaṉ: Ak. 88,362; Naṉṉar neñcattaṉ: Kuṟ. 265 – Both expressions mean "a man of good will".

. Aṟavaṉ (righteous man): Kuṟ. 284; Aiṅ. 212.

. Aṇaṅkiyōr (he who caused pain): Aiṅ. 245,250.

. Tuṇai (life-partner): Kuṟ. 321; Ak. 178.

The following epithets are used once each:

Ācāku entai (lit. my father who is my support: ācu + āku + entai. ācu = support DED 342. Hence supporting "father"). Kuṟ. 176; Namar (our man): Kuṟ. 369; Neṭuntakai (noble man): Aiṅ. 244; Puraiyōṉ (great man): Aiṅ. 252; Aṟampuri ceṅkōl maṉṉaṉ (king of good and just rule): Aiṅ. 290; Kiḻavaṉ (the man who has the right for the girl, i.e. husband): Kuṟ. 34; Kātalmakaṉ (loving young man): Naṟ. 45; Niṉ-nacaiyiṉaṉ (the one who desires you): Naṟ. 85; Tōṉṟal (man of great appearance): Naṟ. 267; Koṇkaṉ (husband): Naṟ. 278; Celvaṉ (lit. wealthy man – hence man of worth): Naṟ. 344; Kāḷai: Ak. 221; Eṉṉai (my lord): Aiṅ. 110.

---

[56] We take into consideration only poems referring to courtship. The present writer knows only one case Ak. 58 where the heroine, during courtship, addresses the hero directly and speaks. See the poem in the appendix. In fact, in marutam poems, the heroine does address the hero directly and speak.

Directly: The lady companion has used in direct speech to the hero the following epithets in vocative case:

. Cāṉṟōy (0 man of perfection): Naṟ. 353

. Peruma (0 great man): Kuṟ. 324

. Tōṉṟal (0 man of great appearance or 0 chief): Ak. 394.[57]

Comments

1) The most numerous designation used by the heroine for the hero is the demonstrative pronoun – *avar* (he). In her speech to her companion or to anyone or even in the *muṉṉilaippuṟamoḻi* the heroine uses this demonstrative pronoun which in the grammar of akam poetry is called *Neñcaṟi cuṭṭu*, i.e. the demonstrative which the heart understands. There is only one man she knows, and it is he – her lover. She talks about only one man and it is he – her lover. This demonstrative pronoun by the heroine is the best and perfect way of expressing her immense love for her lover. Interesting also to note is that the lady companion uses this same demonstrative for the lover in her conversation with the heroine. Enough to say "he", the heroine understands whom the companion is referring to. These two girls use a love-code demonstrative which others may not understand!

2) The second designation in order, Kātalar (lover) comes as if to clarify the demonstrative "he". Naturally, this epithet is formed from the root-word *kātal* which means "love". The same order is to be found in the speeches of the lady companion. She uses this epithet twice more than the heroine, while the *avar* is found more often in the mouth of the heroine!

3) The heroine calls her lover *Iṉiyar* three times. This term refers in her mouth not only to the ordinary meaning of pleasant qualities, but also to the pleasure she has experienced with him.

4) Thrice the heroine refers to the hero as *Eṉṉai*, i.e. my lord or my husband, even during the time of courtship. Even before their love relationship is recognized and sealed in the society by marriage, they are wedded in their heart and soul one to the other as husband and wife. This designation then is of particular significance.

5) Twice she expresses her relation with the hero in terms of friendship, and twice she calls him *kaḷvaṉ* (or once kaḷavaṉ and once kaḷvaṉ) referring to his first secret meeting with her, but now apparently indifferent or disinterested in her.

[57] Outside this "love-triad" of the hero, heroine and the lady companion, those who have used epithets for the hero, are: the mother of the heroine: kātalaṉ: Naṟ. 66; kāḷai: Naṟ. 271,293; the foster-mother of the heroine: kātalōṉ: Kuṟ. 356; kāḷai: Kuṟ. 378; avaṉ: Kuṟ. 396; the wayfarers: villōṉ (a man with a bow): Kuṟ. 7; tuṇai: Kuṟ. 390.

6) All the other epithets used by her, and most of the epithets used by her companion for the hero, refer to his manliness and nobility. It is to be noted that no epithet of beauty is used for him. Some of them signify also the duty or rôle of a husband in regard to his life-partner, e.g. Puṇaivaṉ: one who is a help-mate; Pēṇalaṉ: one who protects.

The similarity between the beloved of the SS and the Tamil maid is worth noting. Both of them enjoy thinking and contemplating of the lover without much talk directly to him. In this aspect, the heroine in Tamil akam poetry very rarely talks directly to him. There is a certain delicacy and respect in talking to the lover in the third person – and that when he is listening without being noticed by others! In particular, one may compare the following epithets:

dôdî // Kātalar, Iṉiyar.
rēʿî // Naṇpiṉar and Naṭpiṉaṉ, Puṇaivaṉ.
He (implied in verbs) // Avar (explicitly told).[58]

b) Designations used for the heroine:

(i) By the hero:

Indirectly, i.e. in the third person:

. Kuṟumakaḷ (young girl): Naṟ. 6,77,80,190,209,319; Kuṟ. 70,95,101,280; Aiṅ. 185; Ak. 99,126, 230,258,280.

. Maṭamakaḷ (young girl): Naṟ. 101,201; Kuṟ. 184,337; Aiṅ. 255,256,259; Ak. 140.

. Maṭavōḷ (young girl): Naṟ. 8.

. Maṭantai (young girl): Naṟ. 264; Kuṟ. 147; Aiṅ. 293.

. Māayōḷ (maid of dark complexion): Naṟ. 146; Kuṟ. 132,199; Ak. 62 (2x), 208,338.

. Pētai ("simple" girl): Kuṟ. 142; Ak. 390.

. Arivai (lady): Naṟ. 377; Kuṟ. 2,14; Aiṅ. 171,172; Ak. 198,212.

. Nallaḷ (good girl): Kuṟ. 120; Aiṅ. 204 (2x).

. Nallōḷ (good girl): Kuṟ. 14,62.

---

[58] The expression "whom my soul loves" has, strictly speaking, no parallel single epithet in Tamil. But such ideas are expressed more often through verbal expressions; see under "Words and phrases on love relationships".

. Em-aṇaṅkiyōḷ: Kuṟ. 119; Aiṅ. 259; Nam-aṇaṅkiyōḷ: Ak. 322,372 — Both expressions mean "the one who caused us pain."

. Kātali (beloved): Naṟ. 356; Kuṟ. 120,151,312; Aiṅ. 291; Ak. 142.

. Kātalmakaḷ (beloved girl): Naṟ. 44.

. Ariyōḷ (precious, difficult to be obtained): Kuṟ. 120,128; Ak. 162,212.

. Ivaḷ (this one here): Naṟ. 160,265; Kuṟ. 165.

The following epithets are used once each: Yāṉayantuṟaivōḷ (the one who lives in me because of my desire for her): Kuṟ. 116; Iḷaiyaḷ (young maid): Kuṟ. 119; Iṉiyōḷ (sweet girl): Kuṟ. 206; Taḷiraṉṉōḷ (tender like a shoot): Kuṟ. 222; Avaḷ (that one – she): Kuṟ. 291; Maṉaiyōḷ (wife): Naṟ. 77 (?); Kaḷvi (thief): Kuṟ. 312; Nam-vayiṉōḷ (belonging to us): Naṟ. 265; Eṉ-neñcamarntōr (the one who is seated on my heart): Aiṅ. 293; Pāyal koṇṭoḷittōḷ (the one who robbed me of my sleep): Aiṅ. 195; Antīṅkiḷavi (girl with sweet speech): Ak. 262; Cuṭar nutal (girl with bright forehead): Aiṅ. 94.

Directly, i.e. in vocative case to the heroine:

. Arivai: Naṟ. 192; Kuṟ. 137.

. Maṭantai: Naṟ. 155,204; Aiṅ. 92,175,396.

. Māayōyē (0 woman of dark complexion): Kuṟ. 300.

. Māayōḷē (0 woman of dark complexion): Naṟ. 362.

. Vāleyiṟṟōyē (0 you with shining teeth): Naṟ. 9.

. Kuṟumakaḷ: Aiṅ. 395.

In Aiṅ. 255,256; Kuṟ. 101,132,168,286, etc. the hero piles up descriptive epithets that refer to female beauty and pleasure.[59]

(ii) By the lady companion:

Indirectly:

. Ivaḷ (this one here): 48 times: Naṟ. 10,19,53,55,223 (2x), 270,301,326,339; Kuṟ. 18,225,263,345,362; Aiṅ. 28,29, 30, 91,93, 103,106,180,208, 220,234,238,243,245, 248, 250, 277, 285, 294; Ak. 2,10, 78,92, 112,120,148,156, 158,182,270, 300,340,350.

---

[59] This aspect will be studied in detail below under "Portrait of the Beloved".

. Avaḷ (that one – she): Naṟ. 159; Aiṅ. 210.

. Kuṟumakaḷ (young girl): Naṟ. 134,147,207,306; Kuṟ. 89; Aiṅ. 254,257; Ak. 172.

. Nī-nayantōḷ (the one whom you like or love): Naṟ. 195,317; Kuṟ. 365; Aiṅ. 264,266.

. Niṉ-nayantuṟaivi (the one who lives for love of you): Naṟ. 168; Aiṅ. 273.

. Niṉṉalatu-ilaḷ and Niṉ-aḷi-ilatu-ilaḷ (the one who cannot live without you): Kuṟ. 115; Ak. 118.

. Melliyal (soft girl): Naṟ. 398; Ak. 12.

. Nallōḷ (good girl): Naṟ. 323; Aiṅ. 166.

. Maṭantai: Naṟ. 60; Aiṅ. 297.

. Arivai: Ak. 90; Aiṅ. 168.

The following epithets are used once each: Nāṇuṭaiyaḷ (modest girl): Aiṅ. 205; Pētai: Kuṟ. 113; Maṭamakaḷ: Naṟ. 353; Tuṇai (life-partner): Ak. 38; Antīṅkiḷavi (girl – with sweet – pretty words): Ak. 288; Māyōḷ (girl of dark complexion): Aiṅ. 145; Maṭavaral (young girl): Aiṅ. 196; Maṉaiyōḷ (wife): Ak. 394.

Directly in the vocative:

. Antīṅkiḷavi (0 girl with sweet pretty words): Aiṅ. 300.

. Miṉṉir ōti (0 girl with shining hair): Ak. 356.[60]

Comments

1) The designations which are used more than once by the hero about his beloved may be grouped according to their emphasis on particular aspects:

–epithets about the physical state or age: Kuṟumakaḷ, Maṭamakaḷ, Maṭavōḷ, Maṭantai, Pētai and Arivai.

–epithet of complexion: Māayōḷ.

–epithets of general goodness: Nallaḷ and Nallōḷ.

–epithets that denote the effect on him: Em-aṇaṅkiyōḷ and Nam-aṇaṅkiyōḷ.

---

[60] Among the outsiders, the mother refers to her daughter as *ivaḷ*: Naṟ. 234; the foster-mother as taḷiraṉṉōḷ (tender like s shoot): Kuṟ. 356; arivai: Kuṟ. 378; the wayfarers, as toṭiyōḷ (a girl with anklets): Kuṟ 7; ciṟupiṭi (a small female elephant): Kuṟ. 390.

- epithets of love relationship: Kātali and Kātalmakaḷ.
- epithet about her availability: Ariyōḷ.
- demonstrative pronoun: Ivaḷ (and Avaḷ).

Among the epithets used only once each, almost all of them refer to the physical attractiveness of the heroine. Thus we see that the physical beauty and attractiveness of the girl occupies a greater place in the attributes used by the boy.

2) Nouns of love relationship, i.e. Kātali and kātalmakaḷ are very much enhanced by three expressions: Yāṉayantuṟaivōḷ, Nam-vayiṉōḷ and Eṉ-neñcamarntōr.

3) Like the girls, but unlike the lover of the SS, the hero uses numerically more epithets in indirect speech than in the direct. Again this shows that the young man enjoys contemplating his beloved and speaking of her to his friend or to the companion of the beloved.

4) Among the nouns in vocative, three refer to her youthfulness, i.e. Arivai, Kuṟumakaḷ and Maṭantai, one (in two morphemes) to colour, i.e. Māayōyē and Māayōḷē, and one to her shining teeth.

5) The demonstrative "she" (Ivaḷ: this one) is not particularly significant in Kuṟ. 165 and Naṟ. 265, because these poems are spoken by him to his own heart – to himself. The other one in Naṟ. 160 is spoken to his friend and so is more significant, but not so significant as the "avar" by the heroine. For the *ivaḷ* of Naṟ. 160 is the summing up and identification of the five parts of the body which are being described. The one *avaḷ* in Kuṟ. 291, spoken to his friend, is the most meaningful and is parallel to the *avar* by the heroine!

A short comment on the nouns used by her companion: The two demonstratives *ivaḷ* (48x) and *avaḷ* (2x) are pronounced in a context where the heroine is near her companion. Hence they are mostly mere demonstratives. Kuṟumakaḷ is almost an echo of the hero's usage – notice the proportion. The other phrases emphasize the intimate and strong attachment and love between the hero and the heroine – hence they are very significant. The nouns *melliyal* and those used once only, refer mainly to the physical attraction or beauty, and are mostly repetitions of the ones employed by the hero.

3. *Poetic-Fiction*

The male and female lovers in the SS, take on a fictional rôle in the poems, and this fictional rôle may conveniently be termed "poetic fiction". There seem to be two types of such poetic fictions in the SS.

a) *"Royal" Fiction*: The male lover is mentioned twice clearly as "king" by the female partner (1:4,12) and once there is a mention by the onlookers of "a king" in 7:6 who is held prisoner in the locks of hair of the Shulamite. This king need not necessarily be identified with King Solomon. On the contrary, it is more in the line of love-language to consider this noun as referring to the lover who is "king" *for the beloved.*[61] Whatever may be the young man *in reality*, in the eyes of the lady-love he is a king! In SS 7:6 the reference to the king may be interpreted in two ways:

(i) as a hyperbole, referring to any king who will be captured by the hair of the Shulamite.
(ii) as a generic reference to King Solomon who has become a type for any admirer and captive of female beauty (see below).

There is only one such "royal fiction" referring to Shulamite, i.e. daughter of a prince in 7:2, and it is by the onlookers and not by the lover. It could just be a term of praise of her nobility or more probably a continuation in generic term of the designation "Shulamite" in 7:1 (which appears as a proper name) to make it correspond to the "king" in 7:6.[62]

b) *"Solomonic" Fiction*: The occurrence of the proper names of Solomon and a certain Shulamite has provoked a lot of discussions among the exponents of the SS as regards the historical character of these figures and their rôle in the SS. It seems to be clear that by the time of compilation and edition of the poems in the SS, the historical Solomon has become a type or archetype of any lover and the Shulamite, the archetype of any beloved.[63] In my opinion, it is more likely that Solomon

---

[61] M. Falk, says: "As in poem 5 (i.e. SS 1:12), 'the king' should be read as a metaphor for the beloved (i.e. the male partner)"; *Love Lyrics*, 109. M. V. Fox, is clear in stating that the king is not king Solomon but the designation is a term of affection. See *VT* 33 (1983) 202-203.

[62] In fact, there is an inclusion of royal designations in this waṣf. The "O daughter of the prince" in 7:2 balances and closes the poem with "the king" in 7:6 at the end. In 7:1a the "prince's daughter" is named as Shulamite while Solomon may be hinted at and understood in 7:6.

[63] Without indulging into long discussion, the main arguments may be given in summary here: The name Solomon occurs in the following places:

1:5d – in a phrase with a simile.
3:7,9,11: three times in this poem (3:6-11) spoken by onlookers.
There are three possible life-contexts for this poem:

a) The royal wedding procession of the historical Solomon and his bride: e.g. cf. Gordis, R., *Song*, 20.
b) It could be any royal wedding procession in which the palanquin of Solomon's make was used. In that case, the occurrences of the name Solomon in vv. 7 and 9 would refer to the historical Solomon in the

and Shulamite serve in the SS, as poetic fictions for the lover and the beloved, but having an historical background for this process.[64]

This technique of "poetic-fiction" is present in Tamil akam poems, esp. in the poems of kuṟiñci tiṇai. Such "poetic-fictions" are used mostly by the lady companion and by the heroine about the hero, but not, as far as the present writer is aware, by the hero about the heroine. The heroines of the SS, and of Tamil akam poetry are similar also in this respect. The following may be cited as examples of "poetic fictions" in Tamil akam poetry:

a) *"Royal" Fiction*: Designations or names like, "Malaināṭaṉ" (Naṟ. 365:8), "Malaikeḻu-nāṭaṉ" (Naṟ. 116:6), "Kuṉṟanāṭaṉ" (Kuṟ. 36:2), etc. might imply that the hero is the chief of the mountains or of the hills. But the designation, "Malaikiḻavōṉ" (Naṟ. 51:11; 102:7; Kuṟ. 239:6; Aiṅ. 204:5) does certainly refer to the hero as chieftain or small king — hence as a royal personality.[65] More often the descriptions of the hero or the similes used for the description of the hero suggest that the maid considers him to be a royal figure; e.g. in Ak. 32:3 the heroine tells her companion that the hero looked like a king.

There is one poem in Aiṅkuṟunūṟu, i.e. Aiṅ. 290 where the royal fiction is very clear. The lady companion says that the parrots of the field, which merit the look of the kuṟiñci girl, are much better than the righteous - good king (aṟampuri-ceṅkōl-maṉṉaṉ), namely the lover.[66]

---

past, while the occurrence in v. 11 would refer to the royal prince in the present. In this verse, then, the name Solomon would have already become a type for royal bridegroom.

c) It could simply be any wedding procession of any bridegroom and bride, but described with words and phrases referring to Solomon, who has become a type of any lover at all.

8:11,12: The first occurrence is a reference in the third person in the past. The second one is an apostrophe, in which the lover addresses Solomon – the archetype of lovers – and declares the superiority of his vineyard over that of Solomon's.

As for the Shulamite, the case seems to be more conclusive in favour of the name Shulamite being an archetype of the beloved. See Rowley, H. H., "The Meaning of 'the Shulamite'", *AJSL* 56 (1939), 84-91. Robinson, T. H., *The Poetry of the Old Testament*, London 1969⁴, 202; Shea, W. H., *ZAW* 92 (1980), 392. These authors are of opinion that the name Shulamite is the feminine form of the consonants of the name Solomon and it is to be rendered as "Solomoness". McCown, C. C., "Solomon and the Shunamite", *JPOS* 1 (1920), 116-121, uses *The Testament of Solomon*, an apocryphal book, to explain the history of the development of the legend according to which the Shunamite of 1 Kg. and the Shulamite of the SS came to be identified and eventually stand for "the most beautiful woman" — thus an archetype.

[64] Falk, M., *Love Lyrics*, 108, writes: "the references to Solomon and to 'the king' seem to be part of a literary motif, used to create poetic contrasts. It is unlikely that the historical person king Solomon is a persona in any of the poems."

[65] Thani Nayagam, X. S., *Nature*, 51 & 118.

[66] See the poem in appendix.

The descriptions of the hero by the heroine in Kuṟ. 31 imply royal status for the lover who is in fact only a dancer like the girl.[67]

b) *Archetypes from History*: Similar to the archetypes of Solomon and Solomoness (i.e. Shulamite in the SS), there are two historical personages who, by the time of the composition of some of the poems in akam anthologies, have become types of lover and beloved. They are used as similes for love-situations, esp. for separation and pining (pirital and iraṅkal). It should be said, however, that the lovers in Tamil poems are not called by the names of these personages, as the lovers in the SS are called, but they are only given as historical similes: See Ak. 222,236 (both poems are by Paraṇar) where Āṭṭaṉatti and Ātimanti serve as historical similes. In Ak. 45 (by Veḷḷivītiyār), 76,135 (by Paraṇar), Ātimanti is used as simile for a woman who is separated from her lover and pines after him.[68]

c) *"Guest" Fiction*: The lady companion refers to the hero as a guest because he visited the heroine as a traveller or a guest, i.e. viruntu: See Kuṟ. 292; Ak. 110. This strategy is often proposed by the lady companion to the hero for further visits in the house: Kuṟ. 179,345; Naṟ. 215,254,276; Ak. 300,340,350.

4. *The Central Character: the Beloved*

One of the three features that set the SS apart from ancient oriental love poetry, according to C. Rabin, is the fact that "the woman expresses her feelings of love, and appears in fact as the chief person in the Song."[69] Even from the statistical point of view, her speeches are far more numerous than those of the man, and it is evident that she is the main character and central figure in the SS.[70] The woman in the SS is psychologically deeper and more serious than the man. For, "while most of what he says are descriptions of her beauty, she expresses deep and complicated emotions."[71] The lover speaks in a proper masculine and aggressive manner but the dominant note of the woman's utterances is

---

[67] See the poem in appendix.

[68] It is to be noted that this historical simile is used only by two poets, namely by Paraṇar (4 times) and by Veḷḷivītiyār (once). It is interesting further that this Veḷḷivītiyār herself has become later an historical simile in Ak. 147:9 — a poem by Avvaiyār — another poetess.

[69] Rabin, C., *SR* 3:3 (1973/4), 210.

[70] Rabin, C. says that fifty-six verses are clearly put into the woman's mouth as against thirty-six into the man's (omitting all cases where the attribution is debatable), *SR* 3:3 (1973/4), 210. The present writer would attribute 64 verses to the woman as against 39 to the man, and 15 to outsiders. See Pope, M. H., *Song*, 134 for the opinion of Pusin that "the central, pivotal figure ... is a woman."

[71] Rabin, C., *SR* 3:3 (1973/4), 210.

longing and reaching out for a lover who is far away.[72] The self-assertion of the maid throughout the SS is very striking. The first person pronoun *'ănî* occurs in the SS altogether eleven times, and all of them are pronounced by the girl (SS 1:5,6; 2:1,5,16; 5:2,5,8; 6:3; 7:11; 8:10). The formula of declaration of belonging is uttered by the maid three times (all the three times with the first person pronoun *'ănî*) and never once by the man (see SS 2:16; 6:3; 7:11). She emerges as the central point around which everything turns in love-affair![73]

In Tamil akam poetry too the central and pivotal figure is the heroine, i.e. the beloved. Among the poems that refer to premarital courtship which are extant in the akam collections, the distribution of poems spoken by the lover, the beloved, the lady companion and the others, is in the following proportion:[74]

The attribution of poems to different speakers are given below according to the anthologies:

Anthology	Hero	Heroine	Companion	Mother	F. Mother	Friend
Aiṅkuṟunūṟu	25	40	131	—	—	1
Kuṟuntokai	39	80	90	—	7	2
Naṟṟiṇai	30	45	145	11	1	—
Akanāṉūṟu	21	30	77	12	12	—
Kalittokai (kuṟiñci)	5	5	19	—	—	—
Total	120	200	462	23	20	3

[72] Ib., 211.

[73] The prominence of the woman's wishing, imagining and fantasizing may be explained in two ways: (a) Mostly it is the men who were permitted the social initiatives in love and marriage in ancient Hebrew society, while women must wait on men's actions; Falk, M., *Love Lyrics*, 74-75, quotes from a personal correspondence of a scholar. (b) "One might on the other hand speculate that women in ancient Hebrew society were more self-reflective and socially more communicative than men, and thus they more often verbalized their emotions to themselves and to others", Falk, M., *Love Lyrics*, 75. A third and psychological explanation is proposed and applied to the SS, by F. Landy following and using the study of L. Krinetzki. See Landy, F., *Paradoxes*, 63-68. There are even scholars who think that the real author of the SS is a poetess; cf. Landy, F., "Beauty and the Enigma", *JSOT* 17 (1980), 99 note 54; Id., *Paradoxes*, 68 and note 5 on p. 299. It is not impossible that the whole theme of SS is romantic love versus marriages arranged by considerations of money (8:7) or by power of the king (8:11-12) as seen from a woman's standpoint.

[74] For the sake of rigorous comparison, the writer has collocated all the poems and only the poems which refer to the courtship. For classifying the poems and attributing them to the respective speaker, the following methodological principles have been followed:

This comparative table shows the following facts:

1) As a rule, women are the prominent characters and speak of love relationship more than men: 705 poems spoken by women, as against 123 by men. As one exponent on the SS puts it so well "women are the principal creators of the poetry of eroticism",[75] also in Tamil, in the sense that women are the main *speakers*, in both literatures.

2) The lady companion is the one who has spoken the most numerous poems. All of them have the heroine as the object of concern in one of the following circumstances. She speaks:

a) to the hero to fix up the rendezvous with the heroine, i.e. kuṟiyiṭam peyarttal.

b) to the hero to hurry up the marriage with the heroine, i.e. varaivu kaṭāvutal.

c) to the heroine to console her or to assure her of the sincere love of the hero, etc.

d) to the mother or foster-mother to reveal discreetly the love relationship of the girl with the hero so that they may arrange for marriage, i.e. aṟattoṭu niṟṟal.

3) The heroine expresses often her intense love for the hero, her longing for him, her suffering during his absence, her anxieties on account of the dangers on his way when he comes at night to meet her, etc. The listener to her words is mostly the lady companion, even when

---

a) For deciding the regional aspect, i.e. kuṟiñci, the colophons in the commentaries have been followed, esp. for Naṟṟiṇai, Aiṅkuṟunūṟu and Akanāṉūṟu. But when there are cases of *tiṇaimayakkam*, those poems, even though indicated in colophons as kuṟiñci, are left out: e.g. if there is a marutam poem in kuṟiñci nilam, as Naṟ. 176,217; Aiṅ. 240. Similarly among poems that are classified as marutam there are some which really refer to courtship: e.g. Naṟ. 60; Aiṅ. 92; Ak. 126, etc.

b) Since neytal tiṇai poems too speak often of courtship, they have been individually examined and distributed.

c) Poems which refer to elopement, even though classified in colophons under pālaittiṇai, have been included here because they refer actually to puṇartal, i.e. union of lovers, which is the uripporuḷ of kuṟiñci.

d) Since colophons on tiṇai classification for Kuṟuntokai are not given in the commentary, they were examined individually and classified.

e) When more than one possibility is indicated by the colophons or commentaries with regard to the speakers, the attribution in favour of the heroine is preferred to that of the lady companion.

f) The poems spoken by wayfarers are not included here since it is not clear whether they are exclusively men or women.

[75] Trible, P., *God and the Rhetoric*, 145.

she means to speak to her lover. All the poems spoken by the heroine are testimonies of her deep love and earnest longing to be permanently in union with her lover.

4) In all the poems spoken by the mother or the foster-mother, the heroine is the central or pivotal figure. There is sorrow mixed with admiration and even joy in the words of these mothers that the girl has gone with the lover to whom she should belong!

5) The poems spoken by the hero refer to one of the points:

a) Some poems are directly addressed to the beloved, esp. in the first meeting to express his "union of heart" with her: e.g. Kuṟ. 40.

b) Many are spoken either to his own friend (Pāṅkaṉ) or to the lady companion to express how much he is suffering because of the fascinating beauty of the heroine. More often these poems describe the physical beauty of the beloved.

c) A few poems, addressed to the companion, are meant to request her to arrange for a rendezvous with the heroine.

d) Some others are spoken to his own heart — but in fact they are meant to be overheard by the heroine and/or by the companion. It is mostly in these poems that the boy makes explicit his sincere love and longing for his beloved.

6) The two poems by the hero's friend (Kuṟ. 78,204) are a friendly reproach to the hero that he should not be thinking too much of the girl whom he saw, and that it would be below his dignity. Often such words create an occasion for the hero to express his love for the heroine.[76]

---

[76] The prominence of the woman's longing for recognized and permanent union through marriage is well explained by the social initiatives on the part of men in ancient Tamil society. Man can openly speak of his love for a girl and make arrangements for the marriage: See Naṟ. 94:1-2. The woman can only indirectly and discreetly reveal her love for a particular man and thus try to prevent a marriage with another young man — may be even a relative — but referred to in akam poems as *notumalar varaivu*, i.e. marriage with stranger. Even a blood relative is a stranger when he does not happen to be the lover! The social situation was favourable for the Tamil women to become more self-reflective and more communicative than men and so they verbalized more often their emotions to themselves and to others. The reaction against arranged marriage is then not absent from Tamil akam poems. It would be interesting to study also the psychological explanation of L. Krinetzki and F. Landy in relation to Tamil love poems which are not only by poetesses like Veḷḷivītiyar and Avvaiyār, but also by many poets like Kapilar, etc.

5. *The Other Characters*

Under this section, we shall consider the rôle of all the other personages that are mentioned in the SS. For the sake of convenience, we may bring those people under three groups:

a) Members of the family circle
b) Persons of acquaintance
c) The onlookers

a) *Members of the Family Circle*

First of all, we note that there is no mention of the father of the maid or of the boy in the SS. The mothers of both are mentioned in the poems:

(i) Mother of the maid:

SS 3:1-5: In verse 4, the maid simply states that she brought her lover to the house of her mother and to the room of her who bore her.

SS 6:8-10: In verse 9, the lad praises his beloved inasmuch as the girl is unique to her mother.

SS 8:1-5c: In verses 1-2, the girl mentions her mother in a wishful thinking that if the lover were to be her brother or one who sucked the breasts of her mother, she would lead him to her mother's house, etc.

(ii) Mother of the lad:

SS 8:5d-7: The maid refers, in verse 5e-f, to the event that the mother of the lad conceived him under the apple tree.

Commentators are inclined to conclude from these references to the mother of the girl that "in the Song, the mother is a friend of the couple." [77] But it seems to me that such a conclusion on the friendly attitude of the mother of the maid towards the couple is not guaranteed by the text itself. For the text has nothing to say explicitly on the attitude of the mother. At the most, these words of the girl show her intense desire to be with her lover and give him a treat. These are wishful phantasizings

---

[77] White, J. B., *A Study*, 140.

of the girl.[78] On the other hand, SS 2:8-13, esp. vv. 9-10, and in the two poems, SS 3:1-5 and 5:2-6:3, esp. v. 5:2, the time-factor (it is night time) argue to the contrary that even in the house or in the vicinity of the house the lover and the beloved are meeting in secrecy!

Next to the mother, the brothers of the maid are mentioned once explicitly in SS 1:6 (the sons of my mother) and once they seem to be the implied speakers in SS 8:8-9.[79] In the first poem, the brothers are angry with their sister. The reason seems to be implied in the sentence "My own vineyard I did not guard" (1:6), which *could refer* to her love-affair. In SS 8:8-10, the "paternalistic" protectiveness of the brothers may be seen in a context of arranged marriage.[80] In both cases, therefore, the brothers of the girl might be said to be at least hindrances, if not antagonists, to her love-affair!

b) *Persons of Acquaintance*

Under this category come the city-watchmen and the daughters of Jerusalem. The watchmen do not speak but act. They are a real danger and harm to the love-affair of the girl. They attack her and rob her of her mantle (SS 5:7 – all in her dream!). The daughters of Jerusalem merit a detailed consideration:

(i) In the three adjuration formulas, 2:4-7, esp. v. 7; 3:1-5, esp. v. 5; and 8:1-5c, esp. v. 4, the Jerusalem girls are considered as hindrances to the intimacy of the maid with her lover. Whether the Jerusalem girls in these three contexts are face to face with the maid in reality or only in phantasy, there is no way of ascertaining.[81] In SS 1:5-6, they seem to be in reality face to face with the maid and their staring at the beloved gives an occasion for the maid to assert herself.

(ii) The only occasion in which these girls are sympathetic and even friendly is in the dream narrative SS 5:2-6:3 and hence in phantasy. In 5:8 the maid asks them to bring a message to her lover if they find him. Their question in 5:9 creates an opportunity for the maid to give them a

[78] For, the poem SS 3:1-5 is generally interpreted "as a dream sequence", as J. B. White himself notes in p. 157, note 32. Lys, D., *Le plus beau*, 139ff treats it as "rêve d'amour". Even if she had in reality brought him to her mother's house, it does not follow necessarily that the mother was favouring the action. That the mother is favourable to the love affair is easily presupposed by the mere fact of the mention of the word "mother".

[79] For different opinions on the speakers of the verses 8:8-9, see Falk, M., *Love Lyrics*, 132 on Poem 29; Landy, F., *Paradoxes*, 160 and note 27 on p. 324 with references.

[80] White, J. B., *A Study*, 143; Falk, M., *Love Lyrics*, 96 & 132.

[81] It seems probable that their presence in 8:4 is fantasized. If 3:1-5 is a dream narrative, then their appearance in 3:5 is certainly in phantasy. In 2:4-7, they *could* be really present at least in the vicinity of the wine-hall, if and since they are the ones to whom the maid speaks in 2:5.

portrait of her lover (5:10-16). In 6:1, they show their good will to look for him with her. Hence we can say that at least once the Jerusalem girls present themselves as companions of the maid and favourable to her love affair. They are addressed by unknown speakers in 3:6-11 to look at king "Solomon" and his crown — a context in which they have nothing to do with the maid and her lover.

The lad mentions twice (5:1 companions and lovers, and 8:13 friends) some others who keep company with him. Their identity and function are not very clear from the texts.[82]

c) *The Onlookers*

There are two poems in SS, which are spoken by people who remain unidentifiable, but who speak out their appreciation:

SS 3:6-11: Description of probably a wedding procession.

SS 7:1-6: Some people (the verb in plural) ask the Shulamite to dance so that they may look at her, and later they describe her from foot to head.

From their words, these two groups appear to be friendly towards the lovers.[83]

In Tamil akam literature too we have many other characters besides the hero and the heroine. We shall say a few words about them, grouping them also under these three categories:

a) *Members of the Family Circle*

In kuṟiñci poems, among the members of the maid's family, the father, the mother and brothers are mentioned. No mention of her sisters is made. The father and the brothers of the girl have no kūṟṟu, i.e. they do not say anything (contrast the brothers of the maid in SS, who speak). All the members of the maid's family are at least hindrances for her meeting with the lover. The lover has to come in secret to meet her.[84] The

---

[82] Cf. Pope, M. H., *Song*, 507-509, on this text, i.e. 5:1, which involves problems of translation, identification of the addressees and interpretation.

[83] This statement is valid only on the position taken here that the Shulamite is a poetic-fiction for the beloved, see above on "Solomonic fiction".

[84] Rabin, C., *SR* 3:3 (1973/4), 213, writes, "As in the Tamil poems the lovelorn maiden speaks to her 'confidante' and her problems are discussed with her mother or foster-mother, so the maiden of the Song of Songs appeals to 'the maidens of Jerusalem' and her mother and her lover's mother are mentioned; but in neither is there a mention of the maiden's father." These statements need more precision: It is true that the father of the maiden of the SS is not mentioned; but the father of the Tamil maiden in akam poems is mentioned, but he is never one of the speakers. So also the brothers are mentioned, but they don't speak like those in SS 8:8-9. The problems of the maiden in Tamil akam poems are discussed with the mother or foster-mother *not* by the maiden herself, but by the companion of the maiden.

girl on her part tries to dodge and escape the protective surveillance of her mother and her foster-mother: See Kuṟ. 312; Ak. 158,198. This situation is called *iṟceṟippu*, i.e. being kept at home. For the father and brothers being hindrances, see Naṟ. 98; Kuṟ. 123,269,335; Ak. 12; for the protective watch of the mother, see Kuṟ. 244,246,262,294; Ak. 252, etc. The only poems in kuṟiñci tiṇai in which the mother seems to have a favourable attitude towards the girl's love-affair are Aiṅ. 272 and Ak. 248!

b) *Persons of Acquaintance*

In this category come the lady companion, the foster-mother of the girl, and the friend of the lover. The foster-mother takes a protective attitude towards the maid and thus she is a hindrance to the girl's love-affair. The two others are always helpful to the lover and the beloved:

(i) The lady companion is so to say the second-self of the heroine: See Ak. 12: the heroine and her companion are like the bird with two heads but one life-principle. The companion is like the brain, to arrange for their meetings (cf. Kuṟ. 113,198 ...), to listen to the laments of both the hero (cf. Naṟ. 75; Kuṟ. 276,298,337) and the heroine (cf. Kuṟ. 185,269,296), to counsel the hero to hurry up for the marriage (cf. Kuṟ. 244,292; Ak. 2,12, etc.), to report in an extremely discreet way to the parents of the maid either directly or through the mediation of the foster-mother the love relation (cf. Kuṟ. 214,259; Ak. 48) and see that the marriage is happily concluded. In case of necessity, she even encourages for their elopement (see Naṟ. 10; Kuṟ. 115,217,262,297,343,388; Ak. 221,259). Often she creates an occasion in which the heroine speaks out clearly her love and admiration for the lover (cf. Kuṟ. 288,313; Ak. 328,348, etc.). Sometimes she operates as messenger between the girl and her lover (cf. Kuṟ. 141,392). In these two aspects, the lady companion may be compared to the daughters of Jerusalem in SS 5:8-9. Otherwise, the rôle of the lady companion has no parallel in the SS.

(ii) The friend of the hero plays a similar rôle for fostering the love-meetings, but in a lesser way. To him the hero expresses how hopelessly he is in love with the maid, and gives the description of her. He is more a listener than a speaker.

c) *The Onlookers*

Sometimes the hero takes the heroine and elopes with her. Both of them pass through arid land and in their journey meet some wayfarers. These strangers get an occasion either to speak to the couple or comment on them. Either the mother or the foster-mother of the maid may go in search of the couple after the elopement, and meet on the way some travellers who may give the description of the young couple. Such reports fall under the category of *kaṇṭōrkkūṟṟu*, i.e. report of those who saw.

Though these poems may be classified in pālai because of the mutaṟporul (i.e. landscape), they belong to kuṟiñci by uripporuḷ (i.e. union). These onlookers may, to some extent, be compared to the speakers of SS 3:6-11 and 7:1-6, inasmuch as they comment on the lover and the beloved: see Naṟ. 324; Kuṟ. 229; esp. Kuṟ. 7 which is a comment by the wayfarers.[85]

D. Aesthetic and Descriptive Language

The SS and the Tamil love poems have many things in common as regards their sense of beauty of the lover and esp. of the girl, and the way in which they describe beauty. We shall study this point under two sections:

1. The portrait of the lover and the beloved
2. Selection and use of imagery.

1. *Portrait of the Lover and the Beloved*

As is to be expected, in both the collections of love poems – in SS and Tamil akam poems – only the main characters are described in their physical features. We shall compare the portrait of the main figures one by one.

a) *Portrait of the Lover*

The portrait of the lover in the SS, can be gathered only from the words of the beloved. Nobody else gives any description of him. Even the beloved does not generally describe the physical beauty of the man. The beauty of the man seems to be a subject almost neglected in oriental love poems.[86] The only description, somewhat in detail, of the lover and his beauty (?) by the beloved is given in SS 5:10-16 and that in dream! Many have tried to "represent" the lover through the words of the beloved – but practically with no success.[87] As regards poetic imagination, it is apparent that SS 5:10-16 is "less sensuous and imaginative" than SS 4:1-7 and 7:2-6.[88] The hermeneutical direction suggested by R. N. Soulen is that the imagery of the *waṣf* is "a means of arousing emotions consonant with those experienced" by the speaker.[89] The similes and metaphors

---

[85] Pāṇaṉ (bard), parattai (prostitute), etc. do not come in strictly kuṟiñci poems.

[86] Stephan, S. H., *JPOS* 2 (1922), 199.

[87] Angénieux, J., *ETL* 42 (1966), 582-596. He shows that the description of the lover is an imitational composition based on the description of the beloved in SS 4:1-7. The scholars who adhere to allegorical interpretation, seek to identify the members of the lover to places, things, etc., pertaining to the Temple or something connected with Yahweh; see Robert, A., "La description de l'Époux et de l'Épouse dans Cant., V,11-15 et VII,2-6", in *Mélanges E. Podechard*, Facultés Catholiques, Lyon 1945, 211-223.

[88] Cf. Soulen, R. N., "The *Waṣfs* of the Song of Songs and Hermeneutic", *JBL* 86 (1967), 184, note 6.

[89] Ib., 189.

used by the speakers – esp. by the beloved are more presentational than representational. They are based on value judgements of the beloved about her lover. We shall collocate all the statements of the beloved about how her lover looks like:

SS 1:13 – sachet of myrrh: precious and dear – fragrance

SS 1:14 – cluster of henna: precious and dear – fragrance

SS 2:3 – apple tree: uniqueness, protective power

SS 2:9 – gazelle and stag: speed, perhaps also nobility

SS 2:17 – gazelle and stag: speed.

SS 5:10-16: The whole waṣf begins and ends with value statements. The lover is unique among myriads (cf. 2:3). The adjectives of colour, *ṣaḥ wĕ 'ādôm* do not mean extraordinary beauty but simply "the colour of healthy complexion which is pleasing to the eye", i.e. brown or pink,[90] and its shining character. The closing statement, "all of him is desirable" is again a value statement. Hence the whole waṣf needs to be seen as made of value statements. It is remarkable that all the metaphors used by the girl to describe the lover's head (finest gold), lips (lotuses), arms (rods of gold), loins (plate of ivory) and legs (alabaster pillars) are qualified by expressions or epithets which are value statements, like "dripping myrrh, etc ...". There are partial representational elements in the metaphors used for his arms and legs. The similes used for his locks of hair (black like raven), eyes (like doves), cheeks (like beds of spice) contain some elements of description. Perhaps the metaphor for his lips (lotuses) may partially be descriptive. Elsewhere she says that in his look she sees his love for her: SS 2:4. But what is interesting to note is that the maid has either borrowed from the lover's words (e.g. doves for eyes from 4:1) or modified the images used by him (cf. on hair, cheeks and lips). At the end, the statements fall back to value statements of nobility or majesty (e.g. his aspect). As *descriptive* remarks, the words of the beloved about her lover are not very imaginative. But *as value statements*, her words are supreme! The lover is incomparably precious and delightful in the beloved's eyes!

In Tamil akam poetry, the heroine does not describe the beauty of the hero, or of his limbs. There is not one single instance in which the heroine attempts to speak about or describe the various parts of the lover's body as in SS 5:10-16. But the heroine of the Tamil poems is very

---

[90] Ullendorff, E., "The Contribution of South Semitic to Hebrew Lexicography", *VT* 6 (1956), 191-192; esp. Brenner, A., *Colour Terms in the Old Testament*, JSOT - Supplement Series-21, Sheffield 1982, 73-74.

similar to the girl of SS, in that she too makes value statements about her lover. She speaks about his majestic appearance, valour, courage, etc. which are naturally value statements. They are not descriptive in the sense that they are representational.

The following are the descriptive elements in the portrait of the hero by the heroine:[91]

Appearance: like an elephant: Kuṟ. 161; Ak. 32
like a strong tiger: Ak. 22
a young man like a bull (lit. a bull)
and with a look of excellence: Ak. 388
like the sun (in his effect on the heroine): Kuṟ. 315
a man with shining ornaments like a king: Ak. 32.

Parts of his body:

Head: One with flowers on his head: Naṟ. 128; Ak. 102

Chest: fragrant and cool chest: Aiṅ. 222.[92]
chest with sandal-paste: Kuṟ. 150; Ak. 388
One whose chest smells sandal-fragrance: Kuṟ. 161
chest that causes love-pain: Naṟ. 17; cf. Naṟ. 94
One who has garland on his chest: Naṟ. 128; Ak. 102
chest with fragrant garland: Naṟ. 304
fragrant and broad chest: Ak. 22
One on whose chest was a garland of flowers: Ak. 82.

Legs: One whose legs have anklets (kaḻal): Naṟ. 128

Hands: holding arrows and bow: Ak. 82,388
holding a spear in his right hand: Ak. 102
holding a shining spear in hand: Ak. 298.

It is clear that the heroine is not describing the parts of her lover's body for themselves, but always to bring out his excellence, courage and majestic appearance. The only part of his body that is described

---

[91] We do not include here the descriptive remarks by the lady companion, the mother of the girl, the foster-mother and the wayfaring onlookers.

[92] This is according to a variant reading. In the text, it is "one who has fragrant-cool desire or love", i.e. *naṟuntaṇ- mārvaṉ*. The variant reading *naruntaṇmārpaṉ* is to be preferred.

somewhat for its sake is his broad chest on which she has reposed her head during their meetings. The broad chest with garlands and sandal paste gives the hero his majestic look. All the similes that are used for describing his appearance refer to his manliness and fortitude rather than to his physical beauty.[93]

b) *Portrait of the Beloved*

The portrait of the beloved in the SS, is given in three aspects: a) the self-portrait of the beloved; b) the portrait by the lover; and c) the portrait by the onlookers or outsiders.[94] Here we are concerned with the aesthetical point of view of these portraits.

There is no doubt that the lover and the onlookers are particularly interested in praising the physical beauty of the maid. The maid, however, in her self-portrait is discreet about her physical beauty. In order to have a complete picture, we shall collocate all the aesthetical elements that occur in the portraits, according to the parts of the beloved's body, so that we may see how the female beauty is conceived among the Hebrews. In our collocation of the aesthetical elements, the speakers are indicated by abbreviations: SP – Self-portrait; L – Lover; O – Others:

Appearance of the beloved:

dark but beautiful (1:5 SP)
rustic, strong and fair like wildflowers (2:1 SP).[95]
attractive (7:1cd SP)
attractive and enticing like a mare (1:9 L)
unique among women (2:2b L)
shining and pleasing to the eyes (8:10d SP)
fair, beautiful and awesome (6:4 L)
rising, fair, shining and awesome (6:10 O)
timid and fair (2:14; 5:2; 6:9 L)
desirable and enjoyable (4:6cd L)
noble appearance (7:2 O).

---

[93] The description of the hero by others is also in the same direction: by lady companion: Naṟ. 25,168,276; Kuṟ. 182,198,321; Aiṅ. 206; Ak. 18,38,48,221,308; by the mother of the heroine: Naṟ. 179,184; Ak. 55,203; by the foster-mother: Kuṟ. 356; Ak. 117,263,321,397; by the wayfaring onlookers: Kuṟ. 390.

[94] See Part One, Chapter 3. pp. 72ff. for the similes and metaphors used in the three types of portraits.

[95] Cf. Falk, M., *Love Lyrics*, 115.

Parts of her body:

Stature:	tall and majestic like a palm tree (7:8,9 L)	
Head:	majestic like Carmel (7:6 O)	
Hair:	colourful – purple (7:6 O) flowing and waving (4:1; 6:5 L)	
Face:	beautiful (2:14 L)	
Eyes:	shining and pretty (7:5 O) movement in blinking (1:15c; 4:1 L) ravishing the heart (4:9; 6:5 L)	
Nose:	projecting (7:5 O)	
Mouth:	Lips:	red (4:3; 7:10d L) drip nectar, i.e. sweet (4:11 L)
	Palate:	sweet (7:10a L)
	Tongue:	honey and milk, i.e. sweet (4:11 L)
	Teeth:	white (4:2; 6:6 L)
Voice:	sweet (2:14 L)	
Cheeks:	semi-round and red (4:3; 6:7 L)	
Neck:	long (4:4 L; 7:5 O)	
Breasts:	bulging like towers (8:10b SP) symmetrical and moving (4:5 L; 7:4 O) round and dilectable (7:8b,9c,9d L)	
Nipples:	fragrant (7:9e L)	
Belly:	golden colour (7:3 O)	
Vulva:	well-shaped (7:3 O)	
Curves of thighs:	extremely beautiful (7:2 O)	
Feet:	sandaled and beautiful (7:2 O).	

From the aesthetic point of view, the Hebrew idea of female beauty is perfect when the complexion is dark with sheen. Dark complexion means, not black, but "the colour of sunburnt skin, that is, 'brown' in our mode of speech." For, "psychologically speaking, 'black' is a specification of the concept of 'dark' or 'darkness'."[96] The sheen that emanates from the dark skin of the maid is the element which makes her attractive, fair, shining, enticing, etc. There is always something specially attractive in a rustic girl that is not to be found in a girl from city side!

[96] Brenner, A., *Colour Terms*, 97-98.

When a maid is timid, she is particularly attractive and desirable. The beauty of the girl is at the same time awe-inspiring and hence unapproachable. The awesomeness of the girl is mentioned twice in the SS, – once by the lover and once by the onlookers.[97]

Among the parts of the beloved's body, her breasts occupy the pride of place in description – mentioned in all the portraits, altogether six times. The symmetry and round-shaped projection of the breasts and a fragrance from the nipples are part of the ideal female beauty.

Purple hair in locks, flowing from the head down on the shoulders adds to a woman's beauty. The eyes are mentioned five times and so they comme next to the breasts as regards the attractiveness and beauty of a woman. The white eyes, when they move here and there as they blink, are specially beautiful. The doves are an excellent metaphor for the eyes in SS. Tall stature, raised head and half-rounded cheeks are attractive features of the beauty of a girl. Massive neck and prominent nose are signs of special female beauty.[98]

The mouth and its parts receive a rather detailed description and that exclusively from the lover. There is no doubt that the white teeth and red lips enhance the beauty of the visage, esp. when the girl laughs. The sweetness of her mouth is much appreciated by the lover, for he has "tasted" it. The lower parts of her body are not described by the lover but by the onlookers. The belly, vulva and the curves of thighs are pretty because of their colour and shape, and attractive esp. because of their sexual function.[99] Sandaled feet are considered more beautiful than bare feet!

In Tamil love poems, the beauty of the heroine is portrayed by various speakers with very sober and dignified poetic touches:[100]

(i) There are poems in which the heroine gives self-portrait — but mostly in a context where she speaks about the absence of her lover due to which her physical beauty is being ruined by sallowness (pacalai) from love-sickness: e.g. Naṟ. 177,244; Kuṟ. 159,195,205, esp. 27,266,371; Ak. 290,398. Such self-portrait is often found in poems of pālai and mullai tiṇai: Ak. 75,183,247, etc.

---

[97] Cf. Landy, F., *Paradoxes*, 137-139.

[98] "A large neck, like a prominent nose (cf. 7:5), was a mark of beauty to the ancients" — Gordis, R., *Song*, 86 on 4:4. M. Jastrow says that in aesthetic taste, a massive neck, huge breasts, and a prominent nose were regarded as marks of special beauty: See *Song of Songs*, Philadelphia 1921, 133.

[99] Cf. Gordis, R., *Song*, 40.

[100] Cf. Varadarajan, M., "Literary Theories", in *PFICSTS*, Vol. II, 53.

(ii) The heroine's beauty is described by the lady companion in two contexts: a) To discourage the hero to undertake a long journey to a distant country: Ak. 179,307,319,387. b) To sympathize and console the beloved during the long separation of the lover: Ak. 74,177,197, 223,253,295, etc.

(iii) The outsiders, namely the mother (Ak. 35,275,315), the foster-mother (Ak. 7,117,153,189,385,397) or the wayfarers (Naṟ. 324) describe the beauty of the girl in relation to her elopement and difficult journey in the arid land.

(iv) The most important and pertinent is the portrait of the beloved by the lover. The hero may describe the physical beauty of the girl:

—To his friend to tell him how desperately he is in love with the girl he saw: e.g. Naṟ. 160,201; Kuṟ. 72,95,100,119,129,132,184,206,272,280, 286,291; Aiṅ. 255; Ak. 130,390.

—To his heart, (a) during the courtship: Naṟ. 6,8,77,146,190, 209,265,319,356; Kuṟ. 62,70,116,128,165,199,222; Aiṅ. 259,299; Ak. 62,126, 142,152,162,198,208,212,230,258,262,280,322,338,342,372; (b) while hesitating to undertake a long journey: Naṟ. 16,62,366; Kuṟ. 71,168; Ak. 3,43, 51,193,335; (c) while on journey: Kuṟ. 147; Ak. 21,83,109,169,279, 343,361; (d) while in far away country: Aiṅ. 443; Ak. 174.

—To his beloved herself, (a) during the courtship: Naṟ. 39,76, 82,155,192,213,245 (his words are cited); Aiṅ. 293; (b) while hesitating to undertake the long journey: Naṟ. 166,256; Kuṟ. 300; Ak. 75; (c) during the journey in case of elopement: Naṟ. 9,264,362; Ak. 99,257; (d) after the return from his journey: Ak. 29,39.

—To the lady companion, (a) during the courtship: Naṟ. 75,101, 185,204,377; Kuṟ. 14,101,337; Aiṅ. 185,256; (b) after the return from his journey: Ak. 261.

—To his charioteer while returning from his journey: Naṟ. 221; Kuṟ. 250,323; Ak. 9,44,54,204,334,374.

—To some irrational being: Kuṟ. 2.

It would be beyond our scope to collocate every description of the heroine and every part of her body in all the poems, and then to evaluate the aesthetics of ideal female beauty according to the Tamil mind. We shall take an objective approach to this question, i.e. we shall enumerate all the parts of the heroine's body which are described *only by the hero*, and draw conclusions. Even here the collocation of the descriptive elements is not exhaustive. The listeners are indicated by abbreviations: B – Beloved; H – Heart; F – Friend; C – Companion of the beloved; CH – Charioteer.

Appearance of the beloved:

- awesome and pain-causing (Naṟ. 39 B; Aiṅ. 259 H)
- awesome and pain-causing like heavenly maid (Ak-32 B – his words are cited by the beloved)
- like a sea-dwelling heavenly maid (Naṟ. 155 B)
- brilliant like the statue that shines in the rising sun (Naṟ. 192 B)
- lady with jewels (Naṟ. 76 B)
- more beautiful (cāyal) than a peacock (Aiṅ. 299 H)
- like the morning star (Naṟ. 356 H)
- Moon (used as metaphor, cf. Naṟ. 62 H).

Her body in general:

- dark complexion with beauty spots (Naṟ. 362 B; Kuṟ. 300 B)
- dark pretty complexion (Naṟ. 192 B)
- dark complexion like a tender leaf (Ak. 75 B)
- beauty that never satiates the lookers (Naṟ. 155 B)
- body like gold (Kuṟ. 101 C)
- delicate like a tender shoot (Kuṟ. 222 H)
- cool and fragrant (Kuṟ. 70 H)
- fragrant like kāntaḷ flower (Aiṅ. 259 H)
- fragrant like a garland of kāntaḷ-mullai-kuvaḷai flowers, tender like a shoot and delightful to embrace (Kuṟ. 62 H).

Parts of her body:

Face: beautiful face (Naṟ. 39 B)
brilliant fair face (Ak. 130 F)
lightful face like a (kuvaḷai) flower (Ak. 162 H)
like a lotus (Ak. 361 H)
face with vermilion like the moon (Naṟ. 62 H).

Hair: fragrant and copious (Ak. 39 B; Ak. 257 B)
thick dark hair with the fragrance of kuvaḷai flower (Kuṟ. 300 B)
long curly hairs flowing freely (Ak. 390 B – cited to F)
hair in five locks (Naṟ. 160 F)
like the trunk of a female elephant (Ak. 9 CH)
black like sapphire and fragrant (Naṟ. 166 B)
dark like thick cloud (Ak. 126 H)
curly like the black layer of sand along the rivers (Kuṟ. 286 C)

cool, fragrant and copious like the black layer of sand in the ford of Uṟantai (Kuṟ. 116 H)
swaying like the blue dark feathers of peacock (Naṟ. 264 B; Naṟ. 265 H).

Forehead: thin and shining (Ak. 39 B; Ak. 325 B – cited by B)
beautiful like pure gold (Naṟ. 160 F)
like an eighth day crescent moon rising in the dark sea (Kuṟ. 129 F; Aiṅ. 443 H)
fragrant like a kāntaḷ flower (Ak. 338 H)
fragrant with the fragrance of mullai flower (Kuṟ. 323 CH; Ak. 43 H).

Eye-brows: eye-brows with raised sides or cusps (Ak. 39 B).

Eyes: red at the extremes (Naṟ. 39 B)
long-dark-painted eyes (Naṟ. 155 B; Ak. 390 B – cited to F)
large blinking eyes (Naṟ. 256 B)
like the two halves of a mango split with a knife (Ak. 29 B)
beautiful and cool like a blossoming neytal-flower (Ak. 83 H)
more blossomed than a kuvaḷai flower (Aiṅ. 299 H)
beautiful and cool like kuvaḷai flower (Naṟ. 6,77; Ak. 62,162 all to H)
like two fighting fishes (Kuṟ. 250 CH; Ak. 140 F; Ak. 126,169 H)
red like blood-stained arrow-points (Naṟ. 75 C; Kuṟ. 272 F)
blinking like the eyes of a deer caught in a net (Naṟ. 190 H).

Look: a look that gives ever increasing joy (Ak. 29 B)
majestic look (Kuṟ. 286 F; Ak. 130 F)
joyful and youthful look (Naṟ. 77 H)
sweet look (Naṟ. 16 H)
a blinking look with moving eyes (Ak. 3 H)
like that of a deer (Naṟ. 101 C; Ak. 261 C).

Mouth: red (Naṟ. 190 H)
red like coral (Ak. 29,39 B)
red like a blossoming (murukkam) petals (Ak. 3 H)
red-sweet-honeyed mouth (Kuṟ. 300 B)
red mouth with nectar (Kuṟ. 14 C; Kuṟ. 286 F; Ak. 335 H).

Teeth: white teeth (Naṟ. 9 B)
shining teeth (Kuṟ. 119 F; Ak. 29 B)
sharp like thorns (Naṟ. 155 B; Kuṟ. 286 F; Ak. 39 B; Ak. 325 B – cited by B)
like the white roots of peacock feathers (Ak. 193 H)
white like the mullai buds in two lines (Ak. 21,162 H)
like the pearls of Koṟkai (Aiṅ. 185 C).

Smile: broad smile (Naṟ. 155 B)
sweet smile (Ak. 29 B)
blossoming smile (Ak. 390 B – cited to F; Kuṟ. 286 F)
smile of a red mouth (Naṟ. 190 H).

Speech: sweet words (Ak. 3 H; Kuṟ. 250 CH)
beautiful sweet words (Naṟ. 221 CH)
sweet words like nectar (Kuṟ. 206 F)
sweet melodious words (Ak. 54 CH; Ak. 212 H)
words melodious like a harp (Ak. 109,142 H)

Upper arms: (tōḷ) large (Kuṟ. 71 H; Kuṟ. 280 F)
long upper arms (Naṟ. 213 B)
like bamboo (Naṟ. 9 B; Aiṅ. 293 B; Ak. 390 B – cited to F)
beautiful like bamboo (Naṟ. 82 B)
soft like bamboo (Ak. 257 B)
upper arms like that part of the bamboo between two nodes (Ak. 152 H)
with sugar-cane figure painted with *toyyil* (Naṟ. 39 B).

Chest (ākam): beautiful-sweet chest (Ak. 43,343 H)
broad chest (Ak. 279 H)
broad chest like a courtyard (Ak. 51 H)
thin-pleasant-soft chest (Kuṟ. 280 F; Ak. 44 CH)
chest on which jewels are hanging (Naṟ. 81 CH).

Breasts: pretty breasts with beauty spots (Naṟ. 9 B; Naṟ. 319 H)
budding breasts (Ak. 62 H)
prominent, bulging, tender breasts with beauty spots (Kuṟ. 71 H)

soft-bulging breasts with plenty of beauty spots (Ak. 279 H)
bulging-youthful-pretty breasts with beauty spots (Naṟ. 160 F)
like the buds of kōṅku (Ak. 99 but in inverse order to B; cf. Ak. 240 by the Companion – the same simile).

Belly: beautiful belly (Ak. 21 H *avvayiṟu*)
beautiful curved belly – *avvāṅku unti* (Ak. 390 B to F).

Waist (nucuppu): thin waist (Naṟ. 101 C; Kuṟ. 71 H; Ak. 75 B).

Vulva (alkul): broad (Naṟ. 101 C)
soft-large (Ak. 390 B cited to F)
vulva with beauty spots (Naṟ. 77 H)
vulva with beauty stripes (Kuṟ. 101 C; Ak. 33,342 H)
vulva with raised sides or cusps (Naṟ. 213 B; Ak. 75 B)
vulva that appears like a spread-out-hood of a cobra (Naṟ. 366 H).

Arms and Fingers: with tinkling bangles (Ak. 257 B; Kuṟ. 119 F; Ak. 142 H)
with a few shining bangles (Ak. 390 B to F)
with plenty of bracelets (Naṟ. 77 H)
like kāntaḷ flower (Aiṅ. 293 B).

Feet: red-soft feet (Naṟ. 76 B)
tiny feet with anklets full of tinkling pearls (Ak. 257 B)
tiny feet worthy of being sung by poets (Naṟ. 256 B).

Walk or gait: pretty walk (Naṟ. 82 B)
swinging walk (Ak. 390 B cited to F)
like a female swan (Ak. 279 H)
like a peacock (Naṟ. 264 B)
walking like a statue of masterpiece (Naṟ. 362 B; Ak. 142 H).

In Tamil, the term that denotes the total attractiveness of the female physical features is *cāyal* and the manly passion of a young man, subdued or calmed by this *cāyal* is termed *uraṉ*. They are compared to water and fire respectively in Kuṟ. 95. Cāyal is that which pleases all five senses.[101]

---

[101] Cf. Balasubramanian, C., *The Status of Women in Tamilnadu during the Sangam Age*, Madras 1976, 4.

From the collocation of the descriptive elements of female physical features by the young man, one may see the aesthetics of the ancient Tamils about female beauty: The appearance of a beautiful woman is at the same time attractive and awesome: because attractive, her beauty causes pain, *aṇaṅku*,[102] and because awesome, she is difficult to reach. Dark brown complexion of the woman was largely admired. The colour is called *māmai*, the woman of that colour is called *māyōḷ*. Māmai is the colour of the mango shoot.[103] Even when one speaks of "body like gold" (poṉpōl mēṉi), e.g. Kuṟ. 101, what is really meant is the pink colour.[104] The ideal face of a woman is cool like moon, round like lotus, cool like blue water-lily (kuvaḷai) and shining. Thick, dark, copiously wavy and curly hair forms an excellent background for the shining face. Tamil women made their hair into five locks.[105]

According to mullaikkali 8, a woman's forehead (nutal), waist (nucuppu or iṭai) and feet are to be thin and small, while her upper arms (tōḷ), eyes and vulva (alkul) should be large. This ideal seems to be a conclusion of the descriptions of these female organs in the early classical akam poems. The forehead of a woman with the background of thick black hair is very fittingly likened to the crescent moon rising up from the dark sea. The eyes socketed, so to say, below the eyebrows with raised cusps (kōṭu ēntu puruvam) resemble a water lily. Women painted their eye-lids with some dark paint (maiyuṇ-kaṇ) and made them attractive. For eyes "are supposed to be the windows of heart and the gateways of erotic desire."[106] In this connection, the simile "the two halves of a tender mango split with a knife" is incomparably beautiful in Ak. 29:5-8! The outward corners of the eyes were considered very attractive when they looked red like the tips of blood stained arrows or spears. The look of these eyes betrays the attitude of the woman towards the young man. The classical simile to a woman's look is the look of a deer, e.g. Ak. 261.

---

[102] Venkatarajulu Reddiar, V., *Kapilar*, Madras Unversity Tamil Series No. 5, Madras 1936, 129, note 1. The first meaning of the word *aṇaṅku* is desire, and then it means, pain caused by the thing that is desired.

[103] In fact, the word, *māmai* comes from the word *mā*, i.e. mango-leaf. Thus the mango shoot has become a frequent simile for woman's complexion. Cf. Nadarajah, D., *Women in Tamil Society: The Classical Period*, University of Malaya, 1969, 28.

[104] Cf. Nadarajah, D., "The Tamil Ideals of Female Beauty", in *PSICSTS*, Vol. II, IATR, Madras 1971, 37.

[105] Kanakasabhai, V., *The Tamils Eighteen Hundred Years Ago*, SISSWPS, Madras 1966, 118. The women used certain paste to decorate or to dye their hair and it was called *takaram:* see Naṟ. 170; Ak. 117,141,385,393. "According to one interpretation a woman's tresses were called *aimpāl* or five kind because of five qualities they are supposed to posses – darkness, waves and curls, length, coolness and beauty", Nadarajah, D., *Women in Tamil*, 41. See also Vasuki, M., "Variety of Hair-Dos in Ancient Tamil Nadu", *JTamS* 9 (1976), 50-58, esp. 54 for aimpāl.

[106] Nadarajah, D., *Women in Tamil*, 33.

That a woman's mouth is pretty when the lips are red is universally accepted. There is nectar in the mouth of a woman! The beauty of teeth consists of course in whiteness and sharpness. Excellent similes have been used for the teeth: Naṟ. 155; Kuṟ. 286; Ak. 21,39,193. The smile of a woman is enticing and it is described as "blossoming smile" (mūral muṟuval): Kuṟ. 286; Ak. 390. A woman's voice is sweet and her words are melodious like that of a harp: Ak. 142.

The term tōḷ, though used nowadays to denote shoulders, is in akam poems used actually to denote the upper arms, i.e. the part between the shoulder joint and the elbows. This is clear from the precision of the simile in Ak. 152; cf. also Ak. 18,271. The ideal was a long, tender and well formed arm. The women painted on their upper arms often with *t-oyyil* – unguents – the figures of sugar-cane etc. cf. Naṟ. 39.[107]

Broad chest with bulging or budding breasts is admired by the young man. The breasts are made lovelier by the white beauty spots called cuṇaṅku: Naṟ. 9. The young man does not use similes for the breasts of his beloved, but he uses numerous epithets, adjectives and participles which enhance the description of her breasts.[108] The belly of a woman does not get much of description except that a curved belly is considered beautiful: Ak. 390.

The waist should be thin. The vulva (alkul) is to be large or broad with raised cusps (kōṭēntu alkul), and sprinkled with beauty spots or beauty stripes. In one poem, the hero compares the appearance of his beloved's vulva to the spreading hood of a cobra: Naṟ. 366.[109] The arms are described as having many bracelets or bangles. The fingers of the beloved are compared to the petals of kāntaḷ flower: Aiṅ. 293; cf. also Kuṟ. 167; Naṟ. 379. The feet of a woman are said to be soft and tiny with anklets on them. One lover says that the tiny feet of his beloved

---

[107] There seems to have been a medical reason for painting with *toyyil*: see Kumaraswamy, R.-Meenakshinathan, E., "Ethno-medical Studies on Thoyyil Painting in Sangam Period", in *PFifICSTS*, Vol. II, sec. 13, IATR, Madras 1981, 33-38. Different materials must have been used for painting it at different occasions, namely for beautifying or medical reason.

[108] It is interesting to see that while the hero does not use similes to describe the female breasts, he uses in one poem, Ak. 99 the female breasts as simile to describe the buds of kōṅku flower. The poem treats about the elopement of the boy and the girl together through an arid tract, where he describes the flower-buds. The blossoming breasts of his beloved are so vivid in his mind and present before his eyes that they supply a ready simile to something in nature – a flower-bud! Note that the same kōṅku buds are used as similes by the lady companion to describe the breasts of the lady-love in Ak. 240.

[109] D. Nadarajah, translates *alkul* by hips: *Women in Tamil*, 30; Ead., "The Tamil Ideals", in *PSICSTS*, Vol. II, 37. In Tamil akam poems, it denotes that space between the hips and loins, where *mons veneris* is situated. See Winslow, M., *A Comprehensive Tamil and English Dictionary*, New Delhi 1984, ad vocem. Hence I translate alkul by vulva. The *DED*, n. 253 renders alkul by pudendum muliebre.

merit the praise of poets! Naṟ. 256. The walk and gait of the beloved are much admired by the lover. She walks like a peacock: Naṟ. 264, or like a female swan: Ak. 279 or even like a statue of extreme workmanship: Ak. 142. The hero would even ask sometimes his beloved to walk in front and would admire her beauty from behind! See Ak. 261.

There are quite a number of similarities in the aesthetics of female beauty in the portraits of the beloved in the SS and in Tamil poems: e.g. the colour of complexion, hair, eyes (esp. their movement), mouth, teeth, breasts, belly, vulva and feet. It is somewhat curious to note that no description of the nose or neck is found in Tamil poems!

2. *Selection and Use of Imagery*

Between the SS and the Tamil love poems interesting similarities are found in the selection and use of imagery. By imagery we understand not only the similes and metaphors but also other symbols developed from both of them.

a) *Imagery drawn from Geographical Places*

The most important of imageries drawn from geographical places and used for the beloved in the SS, are the similes of Tirzah and Jerusalem, the capital cities of North and South kingdoms.[110] The use of two cities as similes for a girl has puzzled and "has long vexed translators and commentators."[111] In that poem (SS 6:4-7), the phrase "awesome like trophies" plays a connecting rôle between verse 6:4ab and 6:5ab. The images in the rest of that poem refer to pastoral (e.g. flock of goats, flock of ewes) and/or agricultural (e.g. slice of pomegranates) ambient. We may surmise that the speaker of the poem is from rural side and in him, the capital cities excite a sense of wonderment. In comparison with his rural village, Tirzah and Jerusalem are symbols of beauty and majesty. In addition, the roots of these two city-names have exotic connotations.[112] In Jewish literary tradition, cities – surely Jerusalem – are considered as mother-symbols (cf. Pss. 87,147; Is. 49:19-21, etc.).

In Tamil akam poems, the maid is many times compared to cities, towns and hills: at least seven times by the hero (Naṟ. 39,190; Aiṅ. 171,174,175; Ak. 44,322). Of these four are cities:[113] Kūṭal, i.e. Maturai,

---

[110] It is noteworthy that Tirzah takes the first place and then comes Jerusalem — may be a sign that this poem SS 6:4-7 is of northern origin?

[111] Pope, M.H., *Song*, 558-560 for detailed discussion. Cf. also Landy, F., *Paradoxes*, 283, note 28.

[112] Driver., G.R., "Hebrew Notes", in *Fs. A. Bertholet*, 144; Buzy, D., "Un chef-d'oeuvre", in *Memorial Lagrange*, 152-153.

[113] In Naṟ. 265 – by the hero – the identification is not sure to me. The commentary takes the two towns Pāram and Ārēru as referring to the beloved. In Aiṅ.

the capital city of the Pāṇṭiyaṉ (Naṟ. 39), Ārkkāṭu – a town (Naṟ. 190), Kuṭavāyil – another town (Ak. 44), Toṇṭi – a sea port in the Cēra kingdom (Aiṅ. 171,174,175) and one hill – Potiyil (Ak. 322); nine times by the heroine (Naṟ. 73,260,340,350,358; Ak. 6,113,115,249 — all cities, towns or regions, referring to herself or to parts of her body; twenty-eight times by the lady companion (Naṟ. 35,131,253,258,367,395; Kuṟ. 34,238,258; Aiṅ. 54,55,56,57,58,177,179,180; Ak. 10,46,60, 61, 81,97,-231,270,340,356,359) – of these, thrice to hills: Potiṉi (Ak. 61), Pāri's hill (Naṟ. 253), Naṉṉaṉ's Paṟampu (Ak. 356) and the other twenty-five to towns – all referring to the heroine or to her body.[114] Almost always the particular aspect of comparison is indicated in the poems themselves. In general, those aspects refer to wonderment, abundance, rejoicing, beauty and grandeur, especially of the royal cities and sea-ports.[115] These aspects of the cities are easily transferred to the beloved as regards her beauty and grandeur, etc.

There are place names that occur in the SS, because of certain products or objects or aspects for which they were known and which serve as similes or metaphors for the lover or the beloved. Such are: En-gedi – gardens or vineyards (1:14); Sharon – flowers (2:1); Lebanon – cedars (3:9); Gilead – slope (4:1; 6:5); Lebanon, Amana, Shenir and Hermon – unapproachability (4:8); Lebanon – fragrant objects (4:11); Lebanon – cascade (4:15); Lebanon – majestic appearance (5:15); Heshbon – pools (7:5); Bat-Rabbim – gates (7:5); Lebanon – prominence (7:5); Carmel – prominence (7:6); Baal-Hamon – vineyard of Solomon (8:11). *Historically*, these places *need not de facto* be famous for these items, but *in the value statements* of the lover or beloved, *they are!*

In Tamil poems too we find place names that occur because of products, etc. for which they were known and which serve as similes or metaphors: e.g. Ārkkāṭu – its fields – unapproachable to enemies (Naṟ. 190); Potiyil hill – unapproachable and hence unobtainable (Ak. 322); Koṟkai – for neytal flowers (Naṟ. 23; Ak. 130; cf. Aiṅ. 188), for pearls (Aiṅ. 185; cf. Ak. 27); Kolli hill – for kāntaḷ flowers (Naṟ. 185), for the statue (Naṟ. 192,201; Kuṟ. 100; cf. 89; Ak. 62; cf. 209), for peacocks (Naṟ. 265), for flowers (Naṟ. 346; Ak. 208), for fine bamboos (Ak. 33; cf. 213),

---

178, the hero *seems* to use the city of Toṇṭi as simile to himself. This would be the only case where a man is compared to a city — but the aspect of comparison is not evident in the poem.

[114] It may be remarked that all the city-similes used by the lover refer to the beauty of the beloved during courtship; those used by the companion to the beauty of the beloved during the period of courtship and separation; those by the heroine, mostly to separation or marutam.

[115] Cf. Nadarajah, D., *Women in Tamil*, 26.

for stability (Ak. 338); Potiyil hill – for kāntaḷ flowers (cf. Naṟ. 379; cf. Kuṟ. 84), for sandal wood (Kuṟ. 376). These names are used as similes for the beloved.[116]

b) *Imagery drawn from Animals*

Many names of animals appear in the SS, "in foregrounds and backgrounds, as real, metaphorical, and symbolical."[117] Animals appear:

(i) as real: Animals are real in the depiction of the natural landscape. In the SS, only in 1:7-8 the sheep and kids occur as real to denote the occupation of the boy and the girl.

(ii) as imagery: Animals appear as imageries in three levels:

as similes: for the lover: 2:8,17; 8:14 – gazelle and stag: speed and fugitive nature.[118]

for the beloved: 1:9 – mare.

for parts of her body:

. hair: 4:1; 6:5 – flock of goats
. teeth: 4:2; 6:6 – flock of ewes
. breasts: 4:5; 7:4 – fawns or stags.[119]

as metaphor: No animal is used as metaphor.

as symbolic: 2:7; 3:5 – gazelles and hinds
2:15 – foxes
4:8 – lions and panthers.

In 2:7 and 3:5, the gazelles and hinds are mentioned in the formula of adjuration not to disturb the union of love. They are used in adjuration formula, because these two animals are symbols for love-affair in the Canaanite and the Mesopotamian mythologies.[120] In 2:15, foxes are mentioned as dangerous for "our vineyard" which is in blossom. The

---

[116] Those references which are prefixed with "cf" are not the words of the hero himself. The others are his words.

[117] Falk, M., *Love Lyrics*, 97.

[118] Marcus, D., "Animal Similes in Assyrian Royal Inscriptions", *Or* 46 (1977), 89; Dahood, M. J., "UT, 128 IV 6-7,17-18 and Isaiah 23:8-9", *Or* 44 (1975), 440.

[119] All these similes are taken from country side animals: cf. White, J. B., *A Study*, 147f.

[120] Cf. Pope, M. H., *Song*, 385-386; Gray, J., *The Legacy of Canaan*, *VTS. V*, Leiden 1957, 96 and note 2 and p. 164 with bibliography, where he shows that there may be a possible allusion to the Canaanite god Rešef who is depicted with gazelle-horns.

reputation of the foxes as being wily and cunning especially in avoiding detection and capture is known in the oriental literatures.[121] In this poem the little but harmful foxes appear to be used as symbol of those who might destroy the love-relationship ("our vineyard in blossom") — probably young men other than the lover, seeking the beloved's hand.[122] In fact, this small poem (2:15) seems to have two levels of meaning: real and concrete – referring to the vineyard in blossom and the foxes, and the symbolic – referring to the love-relationship and the rival suitors. The lions and panthers in 4:8 are used in relation to the abode of the beloved which is both unapproachable and dangerous for the lover. In other words, the lions and panthers live with the beloved but are obstacles for their union. Hence his insistent invitation to his beloved to come away and join him. Thus those animals seem to be symbols of persons who are living in the same place as the beloved and are a hindrance to the meeting of the lover and the beloved. Lions and panthers are known for their ferociousness. If so, these animals could be the symbols of the brothers (and the father?) of the beloved who are obstacles to the love-meeting (Compare SS 1:6 and 8:8-9 for the attitude of the brothers).

In classical Tamil poems, altogether 35 animals are named[123] and almost all of them occur in akam poetry. They appear often in their natural ambient to serve as foregrounds or backgrounds. Sometimes they serve as similes and metaphors for the hero and the heroine, or other persons, and also as symbols. A few examples may suffice here:

(i) as real: Animals appear as real in the depiction of the natural landscape: crocodiles: Kuṟ. 324; Ak. 80; tiger: Naṟ. 104; Ak. 238,318; snake: Ak. 138,318; elephant: Ak. 318; bear: Ak. 112; lion: Naṟ. 112. These animals are described in their natural habitat and they indicate the danger on the way which the hero has to take to meet his beloved.

(ii) as imagery: Animals serve as imageries in three levels:

as similes: for the lover: wild boar: Ak. 18
tiger: Ak. 22
male elephant: Ak. 308
bull: Ak. 140 etc.

---

[121] Cf. Marcus, D., *Or* 46 (1977), 88.
[122] Cf. Gordis, R., *Song*, 83; Falk, M., *Love Lyrics*, 118.
[123] Samy, P. L., *Caṅka Ilakkiyattil Puḷḷiṉa*, 3.

for the beloved: female deer: Ak. 32,363, etc.
for parts of her body:
. eyes: fishes: Ak. 313, etc.
. vulva: hood of a cobra: Naṟ. 366

as metaphors:

for the lover: bull: Ak. 388
male elephant: Kuṟ. 390

for the beloved: female deer: Ak. 195
female elephant: Kuṟ. 390.

as symbols: Strictly speaking, animals as such do not seem to occur as symbols in Tamil akam poems, but the behaviours of animals serve as symbols. This is what is called in akam grammar uḷḷuṟai uvamam and iṟaicci. Almost every case, where the behaviour of an animal is described in the poem, there will be a second parallel behaviour of the lover or the beloved which is symbolized and is evident from the context. Such animal behavioral symbols occur, for example, in Naṟ. 322,332: the male tiger goes in search of prey to feed the female tiger :: the hero goes in search of wealth in order to marry the heroine. In Ak. 102 an elephant sleeps in the music of a hill-country woman :: the hero forgets himself and his duty in his love for the beloved. There are three such animal behaviours mentioned in Ak. 8: bear, male-tiger and a female elephant — in which the first two refer to the hero's behaviour, and the third to that of the beloved. The behaviour of even monkeys (e.g. Naṟ. 22,57,151,334; Kuṟ. 69; Ak. 2,352,378), crabs (Naṟ. 123; Ak. 380) and tortoises (Ak. 160) serves as symbol for the behaviour of the hero and the heroine.

c) *Imagery drawn from Birds*

Birds too are mentioned in the SS, in different connotations, i.e. as real and as imagery. There are only three birds named in the SS:

(i) as real: turtle-dove (or songbird): 2:12 – it is described in its natural ambient and its song indicates that the spring-time has arrived. The bird is associated with the season in which the lover invites his beloved to come and join him.

(ii) as imagery:

as similes: raven: 5:11 – serves as a simile for the blackness of the lover's hair.
dove: 5:12 – as simile for the lover's eyes.

as metaphor: The name of dove occurs altogether six times, of which once it is used as simile (5:12 above) and the rest as a metaphor:

for the beloved: 2:14; 5:2; 6:9.
for her eyes: 1:15; 4:1.

We have already noted that the timid nature and beauty of the dove are the tertium comparationis on account of which it became a metaphor for the beloved.[124] The white colour of the dove seems to have served as a point of comparison, and eventually as metaphor for the eyes,[125] though there is no indication in the text itself.

Many more birds are named in Tamil love poems.[126] They are mentioned as in SS, in different functions:

(i) as real: birds are mentioned in their natural habitat as backgrounds for the various landscapes:

for kuṟiñci: parrots Kuṟ. 141; peacocks Naṟ. 288; bees or insects Ak. 132.

for mullai: cuckoo: kuyil Kuṟ. 192,201; wild cock Naṟ. 21; dove Ak. 254; bat (vāval): Kuṟ. 172,352.

for pālai: yellow wattle[127]: Kuṟ. 350; Naṟ. 212; vulture: Ak. 31,215; eagles: Ak. 117; spotted doves: Ak. 167.

for neytal: aṉṟil and makaṉṟil: Kuṟ. 160,177,301, etc.; crane: Kuṟ. 117; marine crow: Naṟ. 272; sea-gull: Naṟ. 231, etc.

The one bird which has exactly the same rôle as the turtle dove of SS 2:12 is the Indian cuckoo or kuyil (resembling nightingale), whose singing announces the spring – the season of the return of the hero and hence the season for reunion of lovers: See Naṟ. 224; Ak. 279, etc.

(ii) as imagery: Birds serve as similes for the beloved:

peacock: Naṟ. 264; Ak. 198,358,385
swan: Ak. 279.

---

[124] Marcus, D., *Or* 46 (1977), 96.

[125] Krinetzki, L., *Das Hohe*, 63 & 65.

[126] According to P. L. Samy, in Caṅkam Classics there are 58 birds mentioned and among them 22 are water-birds: cf. *Caṅka Ilakkiyattil Puḷḷiṉa*, 3.

[127] Cf. Samy, P. L., *Ilakkiya Āyvu: Aṟiviyal*, Cennai 1982, 22,36ff on this bird in detail.

"It is commonly said that the aṉṉam (i.e. swan) is timid and modest and mayil (i.e. peacock) is aggressive and coquettish in its ways."[128] Both are used as similes for women till today: the peacock for feminine beauty and pretty look, the swan for a woman's walk.

As far as the present writer is aware, there is no bird which has been used as metaphor for the beloved. But numerous are the cases of birds, in particular, birds in pairs which are used as uḷḷuṟai uvamam for the love-relation of the hero and the heroine: e.g. pair of peacocks: Naṟ. 288; doves: Ak. 254; Kuṟ. 285; cuckoos: Naṟ. 157; kites: Ak. 33; even insects: Naṟ. 277; aṉṟils: Naṟ. 152; cranes: Ak. 290; marine crows: Naṟ. 272; etc.

It may be noted in passing that doves appear in both SS and Tamil poems in somewhat analogous rôle.

Aṉṟil seems to be the only bird which has become a symbol of conjugal fidelity already at the time of the classical akam poetry.[129]

d) *Imagery drawn from Vegetation*

Imagery drawn from vegetation seems to be the most extensive in the SS. Plants mentioned in the SS, are more numerous than the animals and birds. It appears that "over twenty-five varieties of trees, shrubs, flowers, herbs, fruits, nuts, spices and nectars" are found in the SS.[130] All the references to vegetation in the SS, including the gardens, vineyards, etc. may be grouped as follows:

(i) as real, i.e. in their plain meaning to denote the vegetation of the landscapes:

vineyard: 1:6d; 7:13a; 8:11ac
fields: 7:12
gardens: 1:14b (lit. vineyards); 8:13
walnut grove: 6:11
my garden: 4:16c(?)
his garden: 4:16e(?)
my garden: 5:1a(?)
trees and plants: cedars and cypresses: 1:16c-17
vines in blossom: 2:13b; 6:11c; 7:13bc
wood from Lebanon: 3:9b
pomegranates: 6:11d; 7:13d.
apple tree or quince tree[131]: 8:5c.

---

[128] Subramanian, N., *Suppl. to TC*, 12, 4 (1966), 13.
[129] See Part Two, Chapter 6, under neytal and notes 88 & 89.
[130] Cf. Falk, M., *Love Lyrics*, 97.
[131] M. Falk, prefers to translate by "quince tree" and she says that apple was not growing in Palestine at that time, *Love Lyrics*, 115.

flowers: blossoms: 2:12a

fruits: raisin-cakes: 2:5a
apples: 2:5b
figs: 2:13a
mandrakes: 7:14a
its fruits: 8:11,12e.

(ii) as imagery:

vineyard: my own vineyard: 1:6e – metaphor (?)
our vineyard: 2:15cd – metaphor (?)
my own vineyard: 8:12a – metaphor (?)

gardens: locked garden: 4:12a – metaphor
beds of spice: 5:13a – simile
gardens: 6:2ac – metaphor (?)

trees: apple tree: 2:3ab – simile
pomegranate grove: 4:13a – metaphor (?)
fragrant woods: 4:14 – metaphor (?)
cedars: 5:15d – simile
palm tree: 7:8a – simile; 7:9b – metaphor.

flowers: crocus: 2:1a – metaphor
lotus: 2:1b – metaphor.[132]
lotus: 2:2b – simile
lotus: 2:16c – metaphor (?)
lotuses: 4:5c – metaphor (?)
lotuses: 5:13c – metaphor.[133]
lotuses: 6:2d and 3c – metaphors (?)
lotuses: 7:3d – metaphor (?).[134]

fruits: his fruits: 2:3d – metaphor (?)
slice of pomegranate: 4:3c; 6:7a – simile
fruits: 4:13a and 16f – metaphors (?)
clusters: 7:8b and 9d – simile; 7:9c – metaphor
apple-fruit's scent: 7:9e – simile.

---

[132] M. Falk, identifies these two flowers as "Tulipa sharonensis" (for ḥăbaṣṣelet haššārôn) and "Narcissus tazetta" (for šôšannat hā ʿămāqîm) in 2:1ab. They are wild flowers designating the rustic girl, *Love Lyrics*, 114-115.

[133] Falk, M., *Love Lyrics*, 37, translates the lotus in 5:13c by lilies.

[134] In 7:3d Falk, M., *Love Lyrics*, 44, prefers to render by daffodils.

In their plain meaning, the vineyards and gardens are localities. Sometimes they stand for the place of the rendezvous of the lovers or the place of their first encounter: e.g. 1:6d – vineyard: first encounter (?); 7:12-13: further rendezvous; 4:16ce; 5:1a; 6:11; 8:13 – garden or grove: places of meeting. The apple tree in 8:5c is also a place of tryst. All the other cases are indications of the season of spring or simply references to places.

Those references that come under imagery are more complicated and therefore more disputed. Those which are certain from the text have been classified as similes and metaphors. Those which *can* be taken as metaphorical or plain usages, are taken as metaphors but with an interrogation mark, because the identification or precision of the metaphor is not evident from the text itself. Hence the possibility of different interpretations. According to the present writer, they may be both — namely, in the foreground the plain meaning and a metaphorical or symbolical meaning in the background.

Among the flowers, the lotus occupies the place of pride because of its softness and fragrance; and among fruits, vine-grapes, because of sweetness and intoxication.

In Tamil akam poetry, "over two hundred plants of all the five Tamil regions are named, described, used in insets and comparisons. Root, stem, bark, bud, petal, inflorescence, seasons, special kinds of pollination, etc., are observed and alluded to. And their properties are aptly used to evoke human relationships."[135] Here are some of the examples for real and symbolical use of vegetations:

(i) as real: Fields and groves in their natural condition, serve as places of first or further encounters of the lovers: See Naṟ. 213,351 – millet-field; Naṟ. 156,285 – for further trysts; Naṟ. 323; Ak. 240 – groves for rendezvous. Trees and their shades serve too as places of encounter, as in SS: e.g. vēṅkai tree: Kuṟ. 266; puṉṉai tree: Kuṟ. 299. Trees, flowers and fruits are mentioned in the respective landscapes as signs of the arrival of the seasons: e.g. vēṅkai blossom for kuṟiñci: Naṟ. 259; mullai for spring in forest land: Kuṟ. 82,126,220; condition of trees and plants for summer and heat: Naṟ. 296; neytal flower in the sea-shore: Naṟ. 275, etc.[136]

(ii) as imagery: There seems to be no case, in Tamil akam poetry, in which the field or grove is used as simile or metaphor for the beloved, like in SS 4:12a. Nor are there cases where trees are used as similes or metaphors as in SS 2:3ab for the lover, and in SS 7:8,9 for the beloved.

---

[135] Ramanujan, A. K., *Poems of Love*, 249.
[136] See Part Two, Chapter 6 in detail.

But there are flowers which come as similes and metaphors for the beloved or for the parts of her body: e.g. a creeper with flowers, *Pūṅkoṭi,* a metaphor for the beloved in Ak. 54; a bunch of flowers, *Pūntuṇar* as a simile for her in Ak. 41; cf. Ak. 269, by the lady companion, ceṅkaḻunīr-flower as a simile for the maid's eye. We have already spoken on the symbolism of kuṟiñci and mullai flowers.[137]

More than the mere trees, plants, etc., their conditions are used as uḷḷuṟai uvamam for the conditions of the love-relationship or for those of the beloved – as in the case of animals and birds (see above). Such symbolic usages of vegetation are extremely numerous: e.g. Kuṟ. 315: Neruñci flower which turns wherever the sun goes:: for the beloved and the lover; Naṟ. 122,257,309; Kuṟ. 327; Ak. 202, where the vēṅkai flower in the uḷḷuṟai uvamam refers to the lover. Similar examples are found in all the landscapes: e.g. Naṟ. 259 – kuṟiñci; Kuṟ. 336 – neytal; Kuṟ. 36 – pālai; Kuṟ. 94 – mullai. More interesting are the cases in which the insect or the bee represents the lover who visits the beloved who in turn is represented by a flower: e.g. Naṟ. 17,399; Kuṟ. 239 for kuṟiñci; Ak. 130 for neytal. Because pālai stands for separation and mullai for patient waiting during separation, this combination of the insect and flower does not appear in both of them. The faded flower or dried leaf represents the condition of the beloved in these cases: e.g. Naṟ. 296; Ak. 143 for pālai; Kuṟ. 98, esp. 122 for mullai. A creeper clinging to a tree or plant is used as suggestive simile for the clinging of the beloved to her lover: e.g. Aiṅ. 400,456; cf. Aiṅ. 11,14.

As in SS, fruits appear as simile: e.g. Ak. 29, but not as metaphor in Tamil akam poems. The passionate love of the girl for the boy is well represented by a fruit simile in Kuṟ. 18: big fruit (jack fruit) hanging from a thin branch:: immense passionate love depends on a very small life – principle!

The association of trees and flowers further developed into symbolism: e.g. presenting a kāntaḷ flower (Kuṟ. 1), a skirt made of acōku-leaves (Kuṟ. 214), any leaf-skirt (Naṟ. 359), a garland of kuvaḷai flowers (Kuṟ. 346), or of neytal flowers (Naṟ. 138), etc., symbolizes courtship. From the colour of the kāntaḷ-flower, the red colour itself acquired a symbolism: e.g. Kuṟ. 1,40; Ak. 195,394. So also the change of colour would indicate the change of situation in love-relationship: e.g. Ak. 242: change of the colour of peacock's feathers:: change of beloved's skin colour which betrays the love-affair; cf. also Naṟ. 302; Kuṟ. 98; Ak. 210.

---

[137] See Part Two, Chapter 6. See further on Kuṟiñci flower in Ramanujan, A.K., *Poems of Love*, 249-250.

There are also other objects whose conditions or associations become symbolical for the love-relationships or for the lovers: e.g. fire and water in Kuṟ. 95 as simile; small millet grain and heavy rain: Kuṟ. 133; a stone shot by a sling: Ak. 292; streams: Kuṟ. 42; Ak. 172; abandoned toddy pot: Naṟ. 295; moon and sea: Naṟ. 375; rain and earth: Kuṟ. 40,174; unsteady clouds: Ak. 139, etc.

It must be emphasized that in Tamil akam poetry, the symbolism is revealed by the adjectives, adverbs and verbs which are used with these objects, etc. Almost all of them have double application: one to the objects and the other to the love-relationship. Such helps are not often available in the SS to see clearly the symbolism.

e) *Imagery drawn from Sidereal Beings*

Sidereal beings are used as similes in both collections of love poems. In the SS, only the beloved is compared to sidereal beings:

6:10b: looking forth like the Dawn
6:10c: fair like the moon
6:10d: shining like the sun
8:10d: like the evening star.

In the first instance (6:10), the onlookers compare the beloved to the emerging Dawn, fair moon, and the shining sun, while in the second case, the beloved defines herself in relation to the lover "in his eyes I have become like the evening star!" The lover does not use such similes.

In Tamil akam poems too sidereal beings are used a few times as similes (the speakers are shown by abbreviations: L – lover; B – beloved; C – companion):

Sun for the lover: Kuṟ. 315 B.
for the truthfulness of his word: Naṟ. 283 C.

Moon for the beloved: Naṟ. 62 L; cf. also Kali (kuṟiñcikkali): 20 L; negatively in Ak. 299 L.
for her forehead: Kuṟ. 129 L; Aiṅ. 443 L.

Morning star, i.e. the Venus – for the beloved: Naṟ. 356 L.

Aruntati (a star in the Great Bear) – for the beloved's chastity: Aiṅ. 442 L.

The sun is used as a simile for the lover, while the moon and the stars for the beloved (Compare and contrast the similes in the SS).

f) *Imagery drawn from Mythology*

In the SS, there are certain similes which are originally drawn from mythological figures. Mention has already been made to the gazelles and hinds which might have been taken from the Canaanite and the Mesopotamian mythologies, as symbols.[138] In SS 6:10, Shahar appears as a symbol of beauty with which the beloved is compared as we have just now seen. According to J.W. McKay, the Shahar was originally a Dawngoddess, who, in course of time, was taken as referring either to a point of time or to a natural phenomenon.[139] In SS 8:10d, the beloved refers to herself as evening star. This imagery again is drawn from the Ugaritic myth of *šḥr w šlm*, i.e. "Dawn and Dusk."[140] We may note that both these mythological beings are used as similes for the beloved: *šḥr* in 6:10 and *šlm* in 8:10d.[141] The lover receives no such simile. All commentators agree that Death and Sheol in 8:6 are mythological figures used as similes for Love and Passion respectively. The figure of Mot is drawn from Ugaritic mythology.[142]

In Tamil, Murukaṉ, the god of the hill country, stands as a symbol for the lover in Ak. 388:26 where he is referred to "your king or your god": *nummiṟai*. In Naṟ. 82, the same god Murukaṉ and his consort Vaḷḷi serve as similes for the hero and his beloved. The heavenly maid is used as a metaphor in Ak. 198 for the beloved. In Ak. 158, the god Murukaṉ comes as a simile for the angry father of the girl. These are the only mythological figures who come as imageries in kuṟiñci poems.

g) *Imagery drawn from Artifacts*

In the SS, artifacts have supplied similes and metaphors for the parts of the body of either the lover or the beloved: The following is the list of similes and metaphors drawn from artifacts:

Of the lover: head – finest gold: 5:11a
arms – rods of gold: 5:14a
loins – plate of ivory: 5:14c
legs – alabaster pillars: 5:15a

---

138 See "Imagery drawn from animals" above.

139 McKay, J.W., "Helel and the Dawn-Goddess", A re-examination of the Myth in Isaiah XIV 12-15, *VT* 20 (1970), 451-464.

140 Schoville, K.N., *The Impact*, 109.

141 Pope, M.H., *Song*, 572 notes that "the Venus star as the Morning and Evening star is male in the morning and female in the evening."

142 Pope, M.H., *Song*, 668. It is more than probable that the phrase *'azzāh kammāwet* as such is from the common heritage of North-west Semitic languages. Especially worth mentioning are the two occurrences in the Ras Shamra texts: UT, 49:VI:17-20 and more relevantly in UT, 54:11-13. H.G. May sees also in SS 8:7 — the wisdom comment — a mythological imagery. See his "Some Cosmic Connotations of Mayim Rabbîm, Many Waters", *JBL* 74 (1955), 9-21.

Of the beloved: neck – tower of David (simile): 4:4a
– tower of ivory (simile): 7:5a
nose – tower of Lebanon (simile): 7:5d
curves of thighs – ornaments (simile): 7:2c
vulva – round bowl (metaphor): 7:3a
breasts – towers (simile): 8:10b.

It is interesting to note: (a) All the metaphors drawn from artifacts and used for the parts of the lover's body are by the beloved. She uses no simile. (b) The lover has used only one simile (4:4a – tower of David) for the neck of the beloved. He has used no metaphor. (c) Three similes and one metaphor are used by the onlookers for the parts of the beloved's body. (d) One simile is by herself for her breasts.

In Tamil akam poetry, the present writer knows no case of simile or metaphor drawn from artifacts and used for the lover or his members. But for the beloved, such imagery has been used.

like a statue shaped by god: Ak. 62 L [143]; Ak. 209 C.
like a statue of pure gold in the sunshine: Ak. 212 L.
like a statue fully made of gold: Ak. 392 L cited by C.
like a statue of masterpiece shaped by a divine being: Naṟ. 185 L.
like a statue newly made by a superhuman being: Naṟ. 192 L.
like a statue that has not lost its beauty and shape: Naṟ. 201 L.
like a statue of workmanship: Naṟ. 362 L.
my beauty like that of a statue: Aiṅ. 221 Herself.

Of the nine references given here, seven are said by the lover and one by the companion, and these eight cases are similes for the beloved. The only occurrence by the beloved herself is a comparison of the beauty of the statue to her own beauty.

There are other similes drawn from: carefully protected gold (Ak. 258 L), rare treasure (Ak. 372 L), heavenly maidens (Ak. 32,162 L), mountain maids (Aiṅ. 191; Ak. 342 L), sea-maid (Ak. 170 C). These have no analogies in the SS.

E. **The Language and the Idea of Love**

To have an idea of what love is according to SS and the Tamil akam poetry, it is useful to study the love language, the way in which the sentiment has been expressed etc.

---

[143] The commentator understands the phrase *kaṭavuḷ eḻutiya pāvaiyiṉ* as "like the female statue that was set up as god." But this interpretation does not impose itself.

1. *Words and Phrases on Love-Relationship*

The words and phrases which express the sentiment of love between the lovers in the SS are:

'ăhēbûkā: your love: 1:4e
še 'āhăbāh napšî: he whom my soul loves: 1:7b; 3:1b,2c,3c,4b (5 times)
wĕdiglô ʿālay 'ahăbāh: his look on me – love: 2:4b
ḥôlat 'ahăbāh 'ānî: I am sick with love: 2:5c; 5:8e
'et – hā'ahăbāh ...: the love: 2:7d; 3:5d; 8:4d (3 times)
wĕʿālay tĕšûqātô: and on me – his desire: 7:11b
'ahăbāh: love: 8:6c
qin'āh: passion: 8:6d
hā-'ahăbāh: the love: 8:7a
bā-'ahăbāh: for love: 8:7c

It is to be remarked that the relation between the girl and the boy is verbally formulated as love-relation by the girl alone. All the occurrences of the word "love" and its derivatives are from the mouth of the girl. It is the girl who interprets the look of the young man on her as a look of love (2:4b) or as a look of desire (7:11b). She alone declares that she is sick with love (2:5c; 5:8e), and it is she who adjures the outsiders not to disturb the love (2:7d; 3:5d; 8:4d). The occurrences of the words "love" and "passion" in 8:6-7 need not necessarily refer to the love relation between the girl and the boy. It appears to be a wisdom saying adopted and applied, at least in the present context and text, by the girl to her relation with the young man.

The young man has not used any verbal formulation to indicate his relationship with the girl. Only once he has used the word *'ahăbāh* as a vocative to his beloved in 7:7b. One wonders how and why he has not interpreted and formulated his "rapport" with the girl as a love- relation.

In Tamil akam poems, there is no lack of words and phrases on love-relationships. The list would run too long and so only very important ones will be mentioned here:

Words:

Naṭpu: friendship: Kuṟ. 2 L; Kuṟ. 3 B
Avā: desire: Kuṟ. 29 L (only he has used)
Kēṇmai: relationship (from: kēḷ – kēḷir: relative): Aiṅ. 419 L; Naṟ. 1 B

Toṭarpu: connection: Naṟ. 282; Kuṟ. 42 (all by companion)
Kāmam: passion: Kuṟ. 136 L; Kuṟ. 57 B.[144]
Viruppu: desire: Kuṟ. 132 L; Aiṅ. 262 B
Nacai: fondness: Ak. 162 L; Ak. 22 B
Nayappu: affection, desire: Ak. 344 L; Kuṟ. 219 B
Kātal: love: Naṟ. 44 L; Naṟ. 64 B
Aṉpu: love: Kuṟ. 40 L; Kuṟ. 395 B
Namputal: to desire[145]: Ak. 198 L; Naṟ. 327 B; verbal forms, cf. also Naṟ. 208,378; Ak. 275
Kiḻamai: "belongingness" or right: Ak. 32 B
Naṇpu: friendship: Naṟ. 160 L; Naṟ. 378 B
Kaḷavu: secret connection: Ak. 122 B (only she or companion).

Phrases:

Friendship without stain and a friendship like two lives mingled into one: Aiṅ. 419; Ak. 205 – L
Friendship without stain: Naṟ. 214 – B
Friendship mutually essential: Naṟ. 1 – B
Friendship that cannot be dissolved: Kuṟ. 313 – B
A heart full of love: Kuṟ. 40 – L
A heart that is thirsty and desirous for the beloved: Ak. 338 L
Love without diminishing: Ak. 332 – B
Passion that knows no separation or diminishing: Kuṟ. 57 – B
Inalienable (is she) from (my) heart: Naṟ. 201 – L
Inalienable (is he) from (my) small heart: Naṟ. 388 – B
He is the life of my life: Kuṟ. 218 – B.

The mutuality of love-relationship is more evident in Tamil akam poetry than in SS. It must however be remarked:

(i) The word *avā*, i.e. desire is used only by the lover to denote his heart's longing for the beloved, whereas *viruppu* (which means also desire) is used by both.

---

[144] The word *kāman* has two connotations according to its etymology. It means "lust" when it translates the Sanskrit *Kāma*. But it means "passion" in the right sense of the word (very similar to, if not exactly the same as, the Hebrew *qin'āh*), i.e. the kātal sentiment when manifested by means of sensuous signs is called *kāmam*. The word is Tamil *kāmam* and comes from the root *kamam* – to be full. See Tol. Uri-iyal, cūt. 59 on *kamam*. Cf. also Ch. 5, note 11.

[145] Tol. Uri-iyal, cūt. 33 on *nampu*.

(ii) The word *kaḷavu* is used only by the beloved (or her companion) to denote the secret love-relationship. He does not use it.

(iii) *Kiḻamai* in the meaning of "belongingness" is used for the love-relation only by the beloved. The usage of the word by the lover in Ak. 230 has a slightly different nuance.

(iv) The term *toṭarpu* to denote the love-relation is used exclusively by the lady companion.

The similarity and connotation of certain parallel terms in SS and in Tamil akam poetry may be indicated:

'ahăbāh // an̲pu and kātal
tĕšûqāh // avā and viruppu
qin'āh // kāmam (according to Tamil etymology)
še 'āhăbāh napšî // uyirkku uyiran̲n̲ar (the life of my life).

2. *Experience and Expression of Love*

We shall point out only the most important aspects of similarity between SS and Tamil poetry in the experiences and expressions of love between the lover and the beloved.

a) *Sick with Love*

The beloved of the SS, affirms in explicit terms that she is sick with love: once she simply says it (2:5c) and at another time she gives it as a message to her lover through the girls of Jerusalem (5:8e). The lover of SS *seems* to imply such love sickness in 4:9-10, esp. 9ab, and 6:4c ('ăyummāh), 5ab. He has not explicitly formulated his love sickness at any time.

In Tamil love poems, the affirmation of love-sickness is quite frequent from the part of both parties. The lover usually tells about his love-sickness to his friend (Naṟ. 140,185,377; Kuṟ. 58,72,95,156,206; Ak. 152, etc.) or to his own heart (Kuṟ. 128,199, etc.). The beloved too tells it out in various ways: either to her companion (Naṟ. 64,236; Kuṟ. 13,28,97,371; Ak. 52,82, etc.) or to some non-humans (Naṟ. 54,70,196; Kuṟ. 163,327; Ak. 170, esp. 398) or to her own heart (Naṟ. 187, etc.).

In SS 2:4-7, the beloved is in the company of the lover (v. 4), his look upon her excites love in her, she is sick with love (v. 5c) and the lover embraces her (v. 6). His embrace is certainly the medicine for her love-sickness. And this embrace should not be disturbed (v. 7). In the dream experience, too, she finds the medicine for her love-sickness (5:8) in the company and caressing of her lover in phantasy (6:2-3).

In Tamil the lover and the beloved are clear that the medicine for love-sickness is the other partner, and the embrace and pleasure (Naṟ. 304; Ak. 22,102,292 – B; Naṟ. 384; Ak. 162 – L). When the lovers are united, their love-sickness is healed; as soon as they part, they suffer. One girl says that the pallor (*pacalai*) leaves her whenever the lover embraces her but comes back whenever he does not embrace, just like the alga or moss floating on the water in a well leaves when people draw water, and comes back when they take their hands away (Kuṟ. 399). Like the beloved in SS, the girl in Naṟ. 357, seeks her lover's company in phantasy by remembering the first encounter!

b) *Formula of Belonging*

The formula of belonging, "my beloved (dôdî) to me and I to him" occurs three times, and that always from the mouth of the girl: In 2:16, the girl is apparently in the embrace of the lover, for in v. 17 she tells her lover to go away before it is dawn; the identical formula, seemingly in an identical context occurs in 6:3 but in a dream. The formula is only partial in 7:11, but with a compensating phrase "his desire upon me." The context appears to be a musing within her heart, since in the next verse she suggests to her lover to go to the fields to spend the night together. The girl openly acknowledges that she belongs to him and he to her.

Such a clear avowal is not found in the mouth of the lover. In 4:9ab, he says *libbabtînî*. Taking the verb as piel privative, it is to be translated as "you have ravished my heart." [146] That means, the lover accepts that he has lost his heart to his beloved – that she attracts him. The phrase is not quite equivalent to the formula of belonging. In all the love epithets he uses for his beloved, her belonging to him can be inferred from the insistance of the first person possessive pronoun, as in "my sister", "my bride", etc. But his belonging to the girl is never made explicit. In one case, the girl even asks the lover: "Set me as a seal upon your heart, as a seal upon your arm" (8:6ab). In any case, the girl has given herself to him completely and has accepted him completely!

The Tamil beloved does not use such strong and explicit formula of belonging, but only equivalent expressions to say that she belongs to her lover. We have already noted the word *kiḻamai* – belongingness, which she used for her exclusive relation with the lover (Ak. 32). In Kuṟ. 313, the girl says, "We have bound ourselves with him with a friendship that cannot be dissolved by anyone, since it is once and for all perfected." [147]

---

[146] Dahood, M. J., "Comparative Philology Yesterday and Today", *Bib.* 50 (1969), 73.

[147] See Kuṟ. 397 where the lady companion tells the lover that the beloved belongs to none but him, *niṉ varaippiṉaḷ*, and Kuṟ. 373 where she says now to the beloved that the love relation between her and her lover cannot be shaken by anything whatever.

Namar – our man (Kuṟ. 281) expresses his belongingness to her. In many poems (e.g. Naṟ. 1,226, cf. 286; Kuṟ. 103,218,334; Aiṅ. 111,213), the girl says that she cannot live without him.

The boy in Tamil poems is similar to that of SS, in that he too does not make use of formula of belonging. He acknowledges her belonging to him by the use of first person possessive pronoun, as in "our beloved" "the one who lives by thinking of us," etc. (Naṟ. 157; Kuṟ. 151; Ak. 19). However, he too uses certain expressions which amount to the avowal of exclusive belonging to her: e.g. she who has possessed my heart (Aiṅ. 171:4); she has possessed the heart (Aiṅ. 172:1); she who hid herself, after having ravished my heart which I could not keep back (Aiṅ. 191:4-5). These phrases are exactly the same as *libbabtînî* in SS 4:9ab. Stronger and nobler are the following expressions: "O woman, is there anyone else except you who are seated on my heart?" (Aiṅ. 293; cf. Kuṟ. 56); "Does she know that my heart has stayed back with her while I am here sleepless?" (Kuṟ. 142); "she has bound my heart day and night" (Kuṟ. 280); "even if I am offered the whole world surrounded by the sea, I will not think of giving up your friendship" (Kuṟ. 300; cf. Naṟ. 95). Once he openly says that he cannot live if he is separated from her (Kuṟ. 168).

The self-giving out of love from the part of the girls is something strikingly similar in both literatures! Among the lovers, the lover in Tamil poems is clearly more pronounced than the one in the SS in his avowal that he cannot live without his beloved.

c) *Searching and Finding*

The theme of seeking and finding is seen in SS 3:1-5, while that of searching and *not* finding is narrated in 5:2-6:3. Strictly speaking, SS 3:1-5 presents itself as an event taking place at night, although many authors [148] consider it as a dream experience just like 5:2-6:3. In other words, those two poems would be simply doublet, but one with positive ending, i.e. finding the lover, while the other with a negative result. Discussions have been carried on whether oriental women would go out at night in search of their lovers.[149] At least on one thing all are agreed: the intensity of love is well brought out in the language of search for the other. In actuality, it may be a true event or it may simply be a literary fiction to express the intense love. Without excluding the possibility of the first alternative, the present writer takes it as a literary fiction.

What is to be noted, however, in the SS is that it is the girl who goes out searching for the lover. The lover knows where the beloved is,

---

[148] Robinson, T. H., *The Poetry*, 200; White, J. B., *A Study*, 157, note 32 with bibliography.

[149] Murphy, R. E., *CBQ* 15 (1953), 504.

although the place is difficult to reach. But the beloved does not know where her lover is. Hence she asks others (3:3 – watchmen), or invites others to seek him and tell him her condition (5:8 – the girls of Jerusalem). The girl is desperately pining and feverishly searching when the lover is not with her. The results of both the searches, one of finding (3:4) and the other of not finding (5:5-8), although she seems to know where he has gone (6:2), may well be fantasized reunions.[150]

Similar theme of search for the lover is found also in Tamil akam poetry. Here too it is the beloved — the girl who takes the trouble to search for the lover. As in the SS, the lover knows where the beloved is, though there are obstacles to go to her. When separated, the girl is desperate to know where he is! The poems describe only the sentiments. Whether they refer to actual events of search or belong only to literary fiction can be discussed, as in the case of SS. The theme of search is present in Kuṟ. 305, esp. 31.[151] In Kuṟ. 130, the girl is determined to search her lover from country to country, from village to village and from house to house, and is sure to find him. She too enquires from others whether they have seen him: see Kuṟ. 75.[152] Sometimes the girl expresses her determination to leave her house and relatives, and join definitively the lover: Kuṟ. 322. She too in her longing fantisizes that her lover arrives on his chariot: see Naṟ. 287; Kuṟ. 301.

d) *Presence/Absence*

The theme of presence – absence of the lover is another context in which the love sentiment is expressed. The presence of one to the other is a source of joy and delight, while the absence is a source of pain and sorrow.

The joy of the presence of the lovers is experienced in the SS, esp. in the outdoor world: SS 1:15-17; 2:1-3; 4:12-5:1; 6:11-12; 7:11-14; 8:5-7; 8:13-14. Inner chambers serve as place of intimacy and presence in 1:9-14; 2:4-7. No indication of place is found in the text itself for SS 2:16-17. The vegetation symbolism in 7:7-10 suggests an outdoor rendezvous.

But the absence is perhaps even more significant than presence in love songs, for it gives expression to the meaning of presence, and provides opportunity to express yearning and craving for the presence of the loved one. Psychologically, the loss of a thing increases the value of the thing that has been lost. In a sense, the presence and actual possession rob something of the thrill and delight of expectation and search!

The theme of absence is fundamental for the theme of search and find, which we have considered above, in the case of the beloved. Absence

---

[150] Cf. Falk, M., *Love Lyrics*, 94-95.

[151] See the poem in the appendix.

[152] See the poem in the appendix.

is certainly the context for the theme of invitation to the beloved from the part of the lover in SS 2:14; 8:13; esp. 2:10,13; 4:8.

In Tamil akam poetry, the theme of presence as such occurs very rarely in the speeches of the lover or the beloved. But the joy and delight enjoyed by both during their company and presence are narrated later as an experience of the past. There are quite a number of poems with such themes: e.g. Kuṟ. 299; Ak. 11,22,102,332 – by B; Ak. 51,142,162 – by L. In Kuṟ. 274 the lover says that his hard journey through the arid land will be made pleasant if he thinks of his beloved: joy of presence (through thought) implied! The delight of the lover's presence is mentioned by the lady companion: e.g. Kuṟ. 388; Ak. 107.

The theme of absence pervades almost all the poems of pālai and mullai, quite a number of neytal and some of kuṟiñci poems.[153] In Tamil poems, it is the separation of the hero from the heroine that figures most prominently. This is but natural, because pathos evokes intense emotion, and the agony undergone by both the parties, esp. of the beloved, is effectively depicted by the poets.[154] The agony of separation is told by the girl to her companion: Naṟ. 69,79; Kuṟ. 172,186; Ak. 11,31,293, etc; or to some non-humans: e.g. Naṟ. 193; Ak. 163 – addressing the cold north wind; Naṟ. 238 – addressing the cloud; Naṟ. 277 – the insect. Or she may speak to herself, i.e. to her heart: Naṟ. 187; Kuṟ. 11; Ak. 273,303.

Separation affects also the lover very much. Often he parts with his sweet heart to earn wealth in order to support his relatives and other dependents. During the period of absence, he speaks out his agony rarely to non-humans: e.g. Kuṟ. 147 – to dream; Kuṟ. 162 – to mullai flower; but almost always to himself, i.e. to his heart:[155] e.g. Kuṟ. 168 – agony while planning the journey; Ak. 33 – on the way; Ak. 169 – in the distant land. It is to be remarked that he undergoes agony not so much because of the difficulties on the way or in distant land, as because of the loneliness and sufferings of his sweet heart! In other words, he suffers because of his beloved's sufferings: e.g. Ak. 169,297,299, esp. 339.

e) *Mutuality*

"Mutuality means the reciprocity of feelings between the lover and the beloved."[156] In the SS, this mutuality is mainly expressed by both

---

[153] Maṟutam poems too imply the absence, but there the absence serves as a context for love-quarrel and correction of the man by the beloved and the lady companion.

[154] Cf. Pillay, K.K., *A Social History*, 183.

[155] Interestingly, the lover who, during the courtship, used to speak out his love-sickness and yearning for the beloved to his friend - pāṅkaṉ has no friend to speak out his agony of separation.

[156] Murphy, R.E., *Concilium*, XIV, 1 (1979), 63.

parties through mutual admiration and appreciation: SS 1:2-4, spoken by the beloved is responded by the lover in almost the same words in SS 4:10-11; 7:7-10; see also 1:9-14; 1:15-17; 2:1-3; 4:12-5:1. Mutual admiration founds the reciprocity of love and strong attachment to each other.[157]

In Tamil poems, this aspect is evident in all contexts of love-life, except in marutam poems. Mutual longing for union in kuṟiñci, sorrow when separated in pālai, eagerness to be re-united in mullai, and longing and pining in neytal, have been illustrated above under various topics.

One of the ways in which mutuality is declared in SS, is the claim by both parties that their partner is unique and incomparable: SS 2:2 // 2:3; 5:10 // 6:9. In Tamil poetry, the uniqueness of the beloved is clearly claimed by the lover in Kuṟ. 337, *oru maṭamakaḷ* (the one young maid). In Naṟ. 8, the lover blesses the parents of the girl for having begotten her. The lover claims that the beloved is the only one who can give him delight: Ak. 109; cf. 239. The lady companion says in Aiṅ. 257 that the beloved is a special gift of god. The uniqueness of the lover, as we have seen, is well acknowledged by the beloved in the designation *avar* – the neñcaṟi-cuṭṭu (the demonstrative which the heart understands!). It is implied in poems where she speaks of him as her life-principle: Naṟ. 226,364; Kuṟ. 218. The uniqueness of the boy is once clearly expressed by the foster-mother of the girl: Ak. 117.

f) *Sensuousness*

The experience of love is obtained through the different senses and expressed in terms of sensations. In other words, the rôle of the senses and the language of sensuousness both in the SS, and the Tamil akam poems, are very interesting to compare.

(i) *Sight and Love*: All commentators agree that the most prevalent sensory material in the SS is visual and the sight of one's love-partner is an appealing experience.[158] Here are the references pertaining to the sight in love-experience:

Lover to the beloved:

1:15; 4:1: reference to her eyes
2:14: "Let me see your face" (literally "form")
"Your face (lit. "form") is beautiful"
4:9: "You have ravished my heart with one of your eyes"

---

[157] See also what has been said on "Formula of belonging", "Love epithets" and "Designations of the Lover and the Beloved".

[158] Falk, M., *Love Lyrics*, 106; White, J. B., *A Study, 134.*

6:4: "You are awesome like trophies"
6:5: "Turn your eyes from me,
For they torment me"
6:10: Description of the beloved by women
7:5: reference to her eyes
The portraits of the beloved belong to the sense of sight: 4:1-7; 6:4-7; 7:1-6.

Beloved to or about the lover:

2:4: "His look on me – love"
2:9: reference to his looking and gazing through windows and lattices
5:12: reference to his eyes
7:11: "Upon me – his desire" — probably reference to his amorous look (cf. 2:4).

In Tamil poetry, it is through the sense of seeing that the lovers occupy each other's heart, so much so that the love-sickness is said to have been caused by the sight or through the eyes:

In the words of the lover:

Kuṟ. 184: "my heart is caught in the net of her eyes"
Naṟ. 155: "beauty that does not fade away by looking at"
Naṟ. 160: "the eyes of the maid have disturbed me drastically"
Ak. 130: the power of the girl's look
Ak. 390: to the power of the maid's look, he lost his heart; cf. also Naṟ. 8,16,75,77,82, etc.

In the words of the beloved:

Kuṟ. 305: "passion given by the eyes"
Kuṟ. 299: "my eyes saw him"
Ak. 82: "Many looked at him, but I alone am sleepless because of love, why is it?"[159]
Ak. 290: "When I see him, my eyes blossom like neytal flower, but when he leaves me, they become pale."

Once the passion is enkindled, the love partners would like to look at each other. If the lover is far away, then the beloved consoles herself by looking at the hill of her lover: e.g. Kuṟ. 228,240,249; Aiṅ. 209; Ak. 378 – by B. The same wish is expressed by the companion on behalf of the girl: See Naṟ. 222; cf. Aiṅ. 207,208,210.

---

[159] See the poem in the appendix.

(ii) *Hearing and Love*: The voice of the beloved is one of the objects of desire for the lover in SS. In 2:14 and 8:13, the lover requests the beloved to raise her voice, because her voice is sweet. In 2:8, the beloved hears the voice of her lover, and in 2:10,13 he invites her to come. In 5:6, she calls him but he does not answer.

In Tamil poems, the lover enjoys to hear the voice of the beloved.[160] In Naṟ. 209, the man says: "In the millet field, the parrots recognize the tender words of the girl and musical-sweet-voice. Her voice heals my love-sickness if I hear it. But if I don't hear her voice, everything of me — even my life — will be lost!." Her voice and words can melt even the marrow in the bones: Ak. 225; see also Ak. 3,9,54,109; Aiṅ. 185, etc.

The voice of the lover has no particular rôle to play in love-admiration. But his words and the truthfulness of his words are very important for the beloved: See Kuṟ. 299: "my ears heard him speak." In Naṟ. 1 she defines her lover as *niṉṟa collar*, i.e. he who speaks truthful words (lit. words that stand).[161]

(iii) *Smell and Love*: The olfactory sense is extremely dominant in the SS. Perfumes, spices and flowers are mentioned in abundance: SS 1:2-4; 1:12-14; 5:13 — where the beloved speaks about the lover's perfumes and oils. In 4:6; 4:8-11; 4:12-5:1; 5:5; 7:9, there are references to the perfumes and oils or fragrance of the beloved. These exotic perfumes and oils are not only symbolical for erotic experiences, but they are also meant to excite erotic sensations.

In Tamil poetry, both the lover and the beloved are fragrant on account of the use of perfumes and flowers. The lover is described as wearing garlands of flowers on his head (Naṟ. 128; Ak. 102) called *kaṇṇi* as well as on his chest (Naṟ. 304; Ak. 82) called *tār*; hence he is often called *kaṇṇiyaṉ* and *tāraṉ*, i.e. one wearing garland on head or on chest. He is known to smear sandal-paste on his body, esp. on chest: Kuṟ. 161,198,etc.

Fragrance is prominent in the beloved — in her body and in many parts of her body. Her body is cool and fragrant: Kuṟ. 70,84, etc; Aiṅ. 259; her hair: Kuṟ. 2,52, etc.; her forehead: Kuṟ. 22,205; her upper arms painted with *toyyil* (unguents): Naṟ. 39 – are all fragrant. She too uses sandal paste mixed with various materials to give fragrance to her body: Naṟ. 140.

(iv) *Eating and Drinking*: The language of eating and drinking is used in SS, quite extensively to denote symbolically sexuality and sexual

160 See section on the "Portrait of the Beloved", esp. under "Speech".

161 The beloved is delighted to hear songs about her lover's mountain and such song heals her love-sickness: Kuṟ. 23; Aiṅ. 244 – both by the lady companion.

experience. The beloved says that the lover's fruit is sweet to her palate (SS 2:3). She requests to be sustained and excited with raisin cakes and apples (2:5). In 4:16, she invites her lover to enter his garden and eat its delectable fruits. As an answer to the invitation the lover arrives in his garden, gathers spices, eats honey-comb with honey and drinks wine with milk (5:1). One cannot fail to notice the gradation of the language in this verse: arrival, spices (smell), eating and drinking (taste).

Among the drinks, wine plays a prominent rôle and serves not only as intoxicating and exciting object, but also as symbolic element to denote sexual experience. In 1:2-4, the beloved praises that his caresses are sweeter than wine, and his love will be cherished more than smooth liquor. In 8:2, she wishes to offer him spiced wine and the juice of her pomegranate in intimacy within her mother's house. The lover reciprocates to the beloved the same compliment about her caresses in 4:10, and says that her lips drip honey and her mouth contains honey and milk (4:11). He refers again to wine and sweet palate in 7:10.

The language of eating and drinking is used to symbolize sexual experience and enjoyment also in Tamil poems. To be more precise, the symbolic language of eating is more extensively used than that of drinking. In Kuṟ. 27 the beloved, during the absence of her lover, laments that her dark beauty on the beauty-spotted vulva is being eaten by sallowness (pacalai) without use either for her or for her lover, just like the milk, split while milking, which neither goes into the milk pot nor is being eaten by the calf. The verb "eating" (uṇṇutal) is used in this symbolical sense of sexual experience in Naṟ. 204 and Ak. 32 by the lover, whose words are recalled and cited in the latter case. In Kuṟ. 112, this symbolism is expressed when the girl says that the lover has eaten her *nalaṉ* – which denotes the totality of her female beauty.[162] In one poem, i.e. Ak. 390, the boy asks the girl "the price of the salt that resides in her body" – and the symbolic language of eating is unmistakable here. In Ak. 320, the companion uses the expression *tōḷ uṇṇal* (lit. eating the upper arms) for the sexual enjoyment of the lovers.

The language of drinking for love-making appears in two poems: Ak. 305 by the beloved; Ak. 399 by the companion. The phrase comes in a context of love-making and "he made love with a love that is similar to drinking (of a thirsty man)." See also Naṟ. 332 where thirst and drinking denote sexual enjoyment. In Naṟ. 295, the companion compares the beloved to a toddy pot and her beauty or sexuality (nalam) to toddy.

---

[162] Cf. Dubianski, A.M., *JTamS* 17 (June 1979), 91. According to H.S. David, *Nalaṉ* denotes, in these poems with the verb of "eating", the virginal chastity that is sometimes lost at the hands of her lover: See *TC*, VII, 4 (1958), 338-339.

(v) *Sense of Touch and Love*: The sense of touch occurs in three stages in the SS: caressing, kissing and embracing.

In 1:2,4 the caresses of the lover are praised and cherished by the beloved.[163] The lover too appreciates the caresses of the beloved and in fact he uses almost identical words to praise her caresses in 4:10. The maid invites her lover to the fields where she will give him her caresses (7:13). There are three more references in SS which seem to me to imply caressing: 1:13; 2:16 and 6:3. In 1:13, the lover is indicated by a metaphor – a sachet of myrrh – and he lodges between her breasts – the caressing of the sachet denotes the caressing of the lover. The other two texts are identical phrases (2:16; 6:3) "my beloved to me and I to him, browsing on the lotus" (lit. pasturing on or amidst or in lotuses). What does "browsing on the lotus" mean?[164] The same phrase is used in SS 4:5 as qualificative to the two fawns and gazelles which are similes for the beloved's breasts. The two breasts are like two gazelles who browse – the aspect of comparison between the breasts and gazelles is not only the number but also the action. The action of browsing when applied to the breasts would indicate the delicate movement of the breasts on her chest. Thus it would appear that in 2:16 and 6:3, when seen along with 1:13, the caressing of the lover is meant. SS 7:7-10 is an excellent example of gradation of sensuousness in love-making: admiration (v. 7), sight (v. 8), touch (v. 9a-d), smell (v. 9e) and taste (v. 10) – all implying sexual enjoyment.[165]

Kissing is explicitly mentioned in two places in SS. In 1:2 the beloved wishes to get her lover's kisses, and in 8:1 she wishes that if he were her brother, she would kiss him even on the street. Both are apparently wishful thinking!

Again two texts 2:6 and 8:3 – identical formula refer to the embrace of the lover: "His left hand under my head, his right hand clasps me" – describes the loving embrace by the lover.

In Tamil poetry too, caressing is part of love-making: e.g. Kuṟ. 399 (see above "sick with love"). Mutual caressing of the lovers is expressed in Tamil by phrases like: *tōḷiṭai tuyilal*, i.e. to sleep between the upper arms (Kuṟ. 323 L), *mārpil tuyilal* – to sleep on the chest (Ak. 40 B; Ak. 44 L), *kūntaliṭai tuyilal* – to sleep on the hair of the beloved (Naṟ. 141; Kuṟ. 254) etc. Such phrases are used more in relation to the lover's action than to that of the beloved. Caressing is more from the lover, cf. also Aiṅ. 205; Ak. 240,308, etc.

---

[163] See Part One, Chapter 3, p. 80 for the translation of *dôdêkā* by caresses.

[164] For the survey of interpretations and biblical texts, see Pope, M. H., *Song*, 405-407.

[165] See Young, D. W., "The Ugaritic Myth of the God ḤŌRĀN and Mare", *ÚF* 11 (1979), 839-848.

Kissing is explicit in Naṟ. 204 where the lover wants, lit. "to eat the sharp teeth of the beloved." In all the poems in which the lover praises the mouth of the girl which "oozes out nectar" (amiḻtam ūṟum), kissing is certainly implied: Kuṟ. 286, esp. 267; Ak. 335. It is interesting to note that these expressions are the appreciations by the lover. The beloved does not speak of her kissing him (unlike SS 8:1).

Tamil has many phrases for the action of embracing. Tolkāppiyam mentions especially *kavavu* (Tol. Uriyiyal, cūt. 61) used in Aiṅ. 360. The word means embracing. Other expressions include: to embrace the upper arms (Ak. 87), to join breasts (Kuṟ. 280), to embrace (Naṟ. 319; Kuṟ. 368), to hold together tightly (Kuṟ. 399). In Kuṟ. 299, the beloved describes a gradation analogical but not identical to that of SS 7:7-10: "my eyes saw him, my ears heard his words, my upper arms became beautiful when he surrounded me with his arms, but became thin when he left me" — sight, hearing and touch — all implying sexual enjoyment. The embracing is recalled in detail and appreciated or lamented according to the situation more by the beloved than by the lover: Ak. 1,11,305, 328,367,389,391 – B; Ak. 289,361,379 – L.

When the lover is absent, the beloved wishes to satisfy her desire for caresses of the lover, by allowing herself to be caressed by the wind that comes from his mountain (Naṟ. 236). One girl finds pleasure in embracing a kāntaḷ plant which was swept down from the lover's hill by a stream, and in fostering it in her garden! Kuṟ. 361.[166]

g) *Undisturbed Union in Love*

The participation of all the sensitive faculties leads ultimately to complete union in love.[167] Lovers desire that their union in love is left undisturbed by anyone or anything. In the SS, the formula of adjuration is a testimony that the beloved does not want to be disturbed: 2:7 and 3:5 which occur precisely in the context of the intimacy of the lovers with each other.

Tamil love poems are in agreement that the union in love finds its consummation in physical union.[168] What is interesting, however, is that

---

[166] See Naṟ. 53,68 — by the lady companion who suggests to bathe in the stream coming from the hill of the lover and thus get cured from pallor.

[167] There are a few authors who think that actual physical union comes as consummation of the union of love in the SS: e.g. according to J.C. Exum, SS 4:10-5:1 and 5:2-6:3 are cases of coition: see *ZAW* 85 (1973), 47-79, esp. p. 50 on 5:2-6:3 and p. 60 on 4:10-5:1. But this does not seem to be evident from the text itself. It may be implied.

[168] Authors are at variance about the question whether the lovers in Tamil poems had sexual intercourse before marriage took place. Some scholars answer in the affirmative: e.g. Pillay, K.K., *Social History*, 347; David, H.S., *TC*, VII, 4 (1958), 338-339. Some others deny it saying such descriptions may be called just love-making: e.g.

the beloved in Tamil poems is explicit, just like the beloved of the SS, in wishing the union to be left undisturbed. There are two poems which are very similar to SS 2:7. In Kuṟ. 107, the beloved curses the cock that it be eaten by wild cat because it disturbed and awoke her from "the very sweet sleep with the lover." Another girl says: "The cock crowed and my innocent heart was shocked. For like a sword that divides, came the dawn that separated me from my lover's union!" (Kuṟ. 157).

h) *The Heart in Love*

According to the Hebrew mentality, the heart is the centre of thoughts, decisions and esp. of emotions, in particular, of love. In the SS, the cognitive and emotive aspects are normally indicated by *leb* and *mēʿîm*[169] and the *nepeš* refers to the strong sexual desire.[170] It is somewhat strange that the heart is not mentioned in the SS, more than a couple of times. Once in 4:9, the lover exclaims to his beloved "you have ravished my heart, my sister, my bride." The beloved would like to be set as a seal on the heart of the lover (8:6a). The heart of the beloved plays a rôle which is more positive. Even when she is asleep, her heart keeps awake waiting for her lover: 5:2. This sleepless awaiting of the heart is very expressive of the immense love of the beloved for her lover, her *mēʿîm* thrills at the meeting and her *nepeš* goes out in search of him when he departs (5:6).

In Tamil, heart is designated by two words: Neñcam and Uḷḷam. The heart in Tamil love poems is almost the incarnation of the intense longing and desire for the other. On the part of the lover, the heart is the one who visits the beloved when he is physically far away — both during the courtship and during the separation for earning wealth. Often it is also the sense of duty which impels the lover to go and earn wealth in order to support others. Hence it is quite often personified, addressed and spoken to: e.g. Kuṟ. 120. Indeed whatever belongs to musing to oneself is spoken to the neñcam. According to the calculation of the present writer, there are altogether 115 poems spoken to the neñcam in love poetry in the following ratio:[171]

the lover to his heart explicitly: 69
the lover to his heart implicitly: 40
the beloved to her heart explicitly: 4
the beloved to her heart implicitly: 2

Aravaanan, K. P., "Marriage – A Dravido-African Cultural Comparative Study", in *PFifCSTS* Vol. II, sec. 8, IATR, Madras 1981 1-10. The numerous euphemistic expressions used in Tamil poems seem to argue for an affirmative answer to the question: see Naṟ. 15,135,172; Kuṟ. 36,54,97,101,125,133,226,320,379,381,401.

[169] Cf. Exum, J. C., *ZAW* 85 (1973), 50.

[170] See *BDB*, ad vocem *npš* - 6; Dahood, M. J., *Greg.* 43 (1962), 71 and note 37; UT, 49:II 17-19; *UT*, Glossary n. 1681 for this meaning.

[171] In this calculation, marutam poems are not included.

It is interesting to note: (a) Only the lover and the beloved indulge in musing to oneself and expressing the feelings – and not the others. (b) The lover is addressing his neñcam far more often than the beloved – the reason is that she has her companion to talk to, whereas he has not.

Much more noteworthy in Tamil akam poems is the service the heart or neñcam of one party renders out of love for the other. It is simply fascinating to read such poems. Just a couple of examples: The lover tells his charioteer on his way back home: "Our neñcam (heart) desirous to embrace the sweet-soft upper arms of the youthful beloved, has perhaps reached home, after having hurried up faster than ourselves, and having arrived, stands in a corner in our house, slowly approaches, from behind, our beloved, blindfolds her eyes with hands, touches delicately her locks of hair and embraces her very passionately!" (Ak. 9). The beloved tells her companion what her neñcam does to her lover (Ak. 128): "Dear friend, my passion for my lover is greater than the sea, and I am in this night sick with love. Precisely at this moment of need, my heart which used to stand by me in time of need, has, tonight, without even consulting me or remaining with you to console me, taken a decision and left me to meet our lover on the small mountainous path in which he is coming to us to the night rendezvous, in order to keep watch on his steps and bear his feet when they stumble into the small pits on the way, and thus bring him safe to us!"

i) *Power of Love*

The climactic statement on love comes from the mouth of the beloved in the SS 8:6:

"For, strong as Death is love,
Relentless as Sheol passion;
A divine spark is its spark,
Its fire a divine flame." [172]

Verse 7 is a prosaic comment on the sense of this wisdom saying.[173] Most probably, verse 6 is a *māšāl*, and verse 7, a remark of some sage, and

---

[172] Dahood, M. J., *Bib.* 45 (1964), 407; Id., "Hebrew – Ugaritic Lexicography – V", *Bib.* 48 (1967), 436; Id., "The Phoenician Contribution to Biblical Wisdom Literature", in *The Role of the Phoenicians in the Interaction of Mediterranean Civilizations*, (ed.) W. A. Ward, Beirut 1968, 134; Id., *Psalms III*, (1970), 319 & 383 — His suggestions have inspired this translation. The latter part of verse 6 is a crux for the translators. W. G. E. Watson would render 8:6a "Truly Love is stronger than Death", *Classical*, 301. note 88.

[173] For a form-critical study of v. 6, see Tromp, N. J., "Wisdom and the Canticle", in *La Sagesse*, BETL 51, 1979, 88-95; Sadgrove, M., "The Song of Songs as Wisdom Literature", in *Studia Biblica 1978*, JSOT Supp. Series - 11, Sheffield 1979, 245-248.

both of them have been taken over by the beloved. The beloved attempts to express her I-Thou relationship to her lover by adopting the *māšāl* and the wisdom comment of a sage: "Mighty waters cannot quench the love, no torrents can sweep it away. If a man gave all the wealth of his house for love, they would be despised." (8:7). Both the *māšāl* and the comment concern any I-Thou love relationship and here they are personalized by the beloved. Only she – and not the lover – attempts to speculate through these sayings, on the power of love and passion. The aspect in which love and death, passion and sheol are compared, is their power.

In Tamil love poems, both the lover and the beloved have given expression to the power of their love and passion, and have attempted to reflect on the power of love in general. In other words, the reflection is personal and personalized in Tamil poems: See Naṟ. 166 – L; Aiṅ. 184; Naṟ. 397; Kuṟ. 3; Ak. 128 – by B.[174] The lover in Naṟ. 166, tells his beloved that his love for her is greater than the sea, in the sense that it is as limitless as the sea.[175] In Aiṅ. 184, the beloved says that "his friendship" with her is for her greater than the sea. In Kuṟ. 3, she uses three elements – the earth, the sea and the sky – for the three dimensional aspects of her love for him: the earth for length and breadth, the sea for depth and the sky for height. The beloved tells, in Ak. 128, her companion that her passion (kāmam) is more on tides than the sea itself, and overflows its limits.[176] Naṟ. 397 expresses the love of the beloved for her lover in an extremely exquisite manner: The girl is afraid that if she were to be born in the next birth otherwise than a human being, she might perchance forget her lover – her kātalaṉ! The poems in which the lover and the beloved, or the companion speaking about the beloved, say that any separation would mean their death, may be considered in this context: e.g. Kuṟ. 168 – L; Naṟ. 79,117; Kuṟ. 334 – B; Naṟ. 19,183 – C. In Kuṟ. 305, the beloved compares the passion to fire which burns up into the marrow (Comp. SS 8:6ef). Again she compares her passion that overflows her controlling power (niṟai), to the floods in Ganges that overflow the banks: Naṟ. 369. Passion (kāmam) is compared to a power like in SS 8:6cd.

---

[174] For the translation of poems Naṟ. 166,397 and Kuṟ. 3, see the appendix.

[175] Theoretically speaking, this statement could be a general statement taken over by the lover. For the first person possessive pronoun before the word *kātal* is not there in the text. But the climactic structure of the poem and the life-context implied in the text of the poem as well as the indication in the colophon show that the lover is speaking of his love and not of love in general. The imported image, i.e. the sea, has the advantage of the three dimensional aspects for comparison.

[176] Again one may argue for this statement being a general reflection, since here too the possessive pronoun is not used with *kāmam*. But the two past participles and the verb used in the text, besides the context, clarify that she is talking about her passion which is on high tides.

The sapiential comment in 8:7cd, where wealth is rejected in preference to love, has many parallels in Tamil poems: e.g. Kuṟ. 267: The lover says that anyone who knows how death (personified as Kūṟṟam, comp. Mot in 8:6cd) comes upon without mercy, will not part with a beloved like mine, even if the wealth of the whole world were offered all together (comp. SS 8:7 which speaks but of all the wealth of his house!).[177]

F. **Fertility Symbolism**

The fundamental similarity between the SS and the Tamil akam poetry seems to lie in the fertility symbolism pervading all throughout the poems. In other words, the power of fertility in man and woman, esp. the latter, is at the basis of the whole corpus of love poems in both literatures.

If we examine the similes and metaphors used for the beloved in the SS, we see that almost all of them refer to mother-symbols, or to imagery of fecundity.[178] Among similes, we may mention: mare (1:9ab), lotus (2:2b – image of fecundity), Tirzah and Jerusalem (6:4 – mother symbols), palm tree and clusters (7:8-9 – imagery of fecundity), and among metaphors, vineyard (1:6e – place of fertility), crocus of plain and lotus of valley (2:1ab – flowers as imagery of fecundity), a garden (4:12-5:1 – place of fertility), vineyard (8:12a), palm-tree and fruit-stalks (7:9bc) – both imagery of fecundity or fertility; round bowl (7:3a – a container – image of maternal womb), a wall, door and tower (8:9-10 – container and opening). In a particular way in this connection should be mentioned the symbolical expressions of fertility about the vineyard and the pomegranates in blossom: vineyard in blossom (2:15 – where the vulnerability is a clear indication; 6:11; 7:13), and expressions about fruits in gardens or vineyards (4:13,16; 8:11-12) which are directly connected with fertility. The mention of the arrival of the spring time with flowers and fruits, with harvest song and the song of turtle-dove as the season for love-making denotes certainly the fertility symbolism. We may add that it is this symbolism that allots the prominent place in the description of the beloved to her breasts which are the physical signs of fecundity.[179]

In Tamil akam poems, "most of the Tamil images are natural objects or phenomena that evoke fertility in some way."[180] In fact, the attitude

---

[177] Cf. also Aiṅ. 147 spoken by the companion, and Naṟ. 234 by the mother of the maid. The mother says that even Uṟantai (the capital city of Chola Kingdom) and Vañci (the capital city of the Chera Kingdom) cannot be an equal price to her daughter.

[178] See Landy, F., *Paradoxes*, 61-133 for a detailed study on this point.

[179] That female breasts represent fertility is perhaps the most universal symbolism in all love literatures. This point needs no proof; cf. the images of Ashtarte, Anath, Diana, etc., in different cultures.

[180] Hart, G. L. III, *Poets*, 8.

towards fertility seems to have suggested and ruled most of the similes and metaphors, especially the uḷḷuṟai uvamams of the poems. The language of love-relationship in Tamil turns around the fertility of the woman – which is a sacred power residing in her but in her breasts and vulva in a special way.[181] This sacred power of the woman is brought into reality by the action of the male – which action in a sense destroys the physical integrity of the woman. On this idea are based the numerous references to the triad of similes, or better uḷḷuṟai uvamams, namely the flower – girl, the bee or insect – young man, and the pollen – fecundation: See Naṟ. 176,399; Kuṟ. 21,211,220,239,265,306; Ak. 21,71, etc. "One of the most common occurrences of the sexual symbolism of ruined flowers in Tamil is the description of how plants are mutilated by the wheels of the hero's chariot as he comes at night to meet his beloved":[182] See esp. Kuṟ. 37,112,179,180; Ak. 8,12,78,148. This symbolism can fittingly be compared to SS 2:15.

The fertility symbolism pervades poems of all regions: in poems of kuṟiñci – the triad of flower, bee and pollen, and the ruined plants and flowers which contain also the uripporuḷ of neytal; in poems of pālai – the barrenness and "chaos" caused by the separation symbolized by the emaciated animals, dried up plants and faded flowers; in poems of mullai – the re-union of the lovers symbolized by the revival of nature, esp. of vegetation by rain.[183]

It is not surprising, then, that the similes and metaphors, selected and used for describing the beloved in general, and her organs in particular, are all connected with objects of fertility, like flowers, etc. Naturally the female organs directly connected with the two essential acts of motherhood – childbearing and lactation – are regarded as beautiful and ideal when they are broad and good-sized.[184]

G. **Love and Divinity**

One of the most striking features of the SS, is that in it God does not speak, nor is deity even mentioned.[185] The supposed mention of the abbreviated name of Israel's God in 8:6ef is highly improbable and there

---

[181] Hart, G. L. III, *Poems*, 97ff et passim.

[182] Ib., 264.

[183] For the application of this fertility symbolism for Mullai - Pālai poems, see the articles of Dubianski, M., *JTamS* 17 (June 1979), 88-103 and *JTamS* 19 (1981)., 15-18. The marutam poems do not *seem* to be directly connected with fertility symbolism.

[184] See under "portrait of the beloved", esp. breasts and vulva. This ideal of beauty and symmetry of form were also found in the Aegean islands even as early as 15th century BC, as suggested by some marble figurines discovered there, see Nadarajah, D., *Women in Tamil*, 30.

[185] Cf. Trible, P., *God and the Rhetoric*, 145.

the particle is only a sign of superlative.[186] The lack of explicit mention of God or his intervention in SS, does not mean atheism nor lack of interest in theology. The sages who preserved the collection were concerned about the empirical world. "Human sexual love, portrayed in the Song of Songs, was a crucial, strategic aspect of creation with which humankind must deal responsibly." [187] The male-female relationship is the gift of the created order. The Song displayed a lesson in mutual love and expressed the importance of fidelity. "The Song of Songs describes the human attempt to come to terms with sexual love – part of the natural and social world." [188]

The situation is exactly the same in Tamil akam poetry. God is not mentioned in relation to sexuality and its purpose.[189] As pointed out earlier, god belongs to karupporuḷ in akam grammar. Perhaps the only god who has something to do with love-affair is the god Murukaṉ, but he is only a "divine" type for human lover, cf. Naṟ. 82. He is not the author of what is called love between male and female.

The word *kaṭavuḷ* (god) appears of course in Tamil akam poems, not as creator, but perhaps as witness of love-affair.[190] In phrases like *kaṭavuṭkaṟpu*, i.e. divine chastity (Kuṟ. 252; Ak. 184), *kaṭavuḷ eḻutiya pāvaiyiṉ*, like a statue made by god (Ak. 62), etc. the word *kaṭavuḷ* (god), is used to denote something of excellence or a superhuman being (analogous to the use of *yah* in SS 8:6ef). This does not mean that the Tamils of classical period were atheists. They believed that gods inhabited in trees and on mountains. But they have not made any *causal* connection between god and the love-sentiment.[191]

The explanation lies in the approach of the old Tamils – at least the poets of akam poetry to sexual love. The Tamils accepted the seen world

---

[186] Pope, M. H., *Song*, 670-671 for discussion. See also above on "the Power of Love".

[187] White, J. B.., *A Study*, 133.

[188] Ib., 134. See also Grelot, P., *Le couple humain dans l'Écriture*, Paris 1962, 65-71; Id., *Man and Wife in Scripture*, Herder 1964, 76-84.

[189] Cf. Ramanujan, A. K., *Poems of Love*, 239.

[190] Aravaanan, K.P., *JTamS* 20 (1981), 100-120. See esp. Varadarajan, E. S., "Paḻantamiḻar Kaṭavuḷ Vaḻipāṭu", *JAU*, VIII, 3 (1939), 193-248; David, H. S., "The Earliest Stage of Tamil Religion", *TC*, IX, 4 (1961), 395-401. There are poems in which the girl prays that the god may not punish her lover for breaking his oaths: Naṟ. 358; Kuṟ. 87. God is worshipped during marriage ceremony: Ak. 136. In Ak. 282 the girl prays to the family god for the coming of the marriage day.

[191] The poems on veṟiyāṭṭayartal (frenzied dance of Murukaṉ's priest) *might seem* to imply causal relation between love and god, but it is not so. The real causal connection implied in these poems is between the love-*sickness* and the god Murukaṉ, which is believed to be cured by offering sacrifices to him by his priest *Vēlaṉ*. The real author of this situation of the girl is not Murukaṉ, but the man from the hill country, namely the lover. There is certainly a deep and subtle irony in all these poems: e.g. Naṟ. 34; Ak. 388.

and were satisfied with the joys of the living present. The concrete appealed to the Tamil mind much more than the abstract. They were optimists, and they did not regard the joys available in the created world as sinful and therefore to be renounced. This does not mean that the Tamils of ancient days were hedonists, or they indulged in sexual licence. On the contrary, they had a very refined and balanced sense of justice, social order and also sexual life. That is why they could develop poetry of the most realistic type.[192] The sexual love and the male-female relation, etc. belong to the order of the visible real world and they are gifts of the created order. The order of the created universe was usually called by the Tamils, *Ūḻ* (Destiny). It is not the blind fate. For, fatalism does not and cannot go along with optimism. The Tamils therefore considered the sex-urge and attraction as the command of *Ūḻ* – in this case the sexuality, *Pāl*. This idea comes out clearly in Kuṟ. 229: The wayfarers, seeing a young couple that has eloped from home, address the *Pāl* and praise it that it has united these two in a natural union – these two who, as small children, used to play and even quarrel together!

That sexual urge, attraction and love have to be dealt with responsibly is inculcated by the lady companion who represents the family-social consciousness.

H. **Literary Techniques**

Besides the similarity between the SS and the Tamil akam poems in the level of literary genre, i.e. in the sense of dramatic monologues, there are two literary techniques which are analogous in these two collections of love poems and they are worth mentioning at least briefly.

1. *Apostrophe and Messenger Theme*

The figure of speech called apostrophe is used sometimes by people who are emotionally charged.[193] This literary technique may naturally be expected in love-monologues or even in dialogues as "asides". In SS, this technique of apostrophe seems to be employed in two poems, once by the beloved and once by the lover.

In SS 4:16, after listening to the praises of the lover, the beloved addresses the North wind and the South wind and asks them to blow

---

[192] Cf. Srinivas Iyengar, P. T., *History*, 154-155, esp. 612-613. See Thirunavukkarasu, K. D., "The Ethical Philosophy of the Ancient Tamils", *Bull. ITC* (July-Dec. 1973), 42-50.

[193] Oxford Advanced Learner's Dictionary of Current English defines apostrophe: passage in a public speech, in a poem, etc. addressed to a particular person who may be dead or absent. Cf. also Shipley, J. T., *Dictionary*, 18.

over her garden so that its fragrance may spread everywhere.[194] Thus they too become participants in the love-affair of the lovers.

In SS 8:11-12, the lover narrates about the vineyard of Solomon, etc., and suddenly he addresses Solomon and tells him that his own vineyard (i.e. his beloved) is before him and wealth is nothing for him in comparison to his beloved! This addressing of Solomon may be classified as apostrophe since he is not present then and there in front of the speaker.

Messenger theme is present in a poem in which a love partner sends a messenger to the other partner to tell him or her how much she or he loves the other one. This is one of the literary techniques to express the deep emotions. In the dream-poem (SS 5:2-6:3), towards the middle of it (5:8) the beloved tells solemnly the daughters of Jerusalem to find and tell her lover that she is sick with love.

Apostrophe is frequently used in Tamil akam poems.[195] According to the calculation of the present writer, this technique of apostrophe (including those which contain the messenger theme) is used some thirty-three times in this proportion:

the beloved:	14
the lover:	8
the lady companion:	9
the wayfarers:	1
the mother of the maid:	1[196]

The beloved addresses the heavy rain, which has become an obstacle to the night rendezvous with the lover, and tells that it has no pity on the lonely women: Kuṟ. 158. The lover asks the bee, which has smelt countless flowers, whether there is any flower at all which is as fragrant as the hairs of his beloved: Kuṟ. 2. The lady companion accuses the bright moon that it is an impediment for the clandestine meeting of the lovers near the house garden: Kuṟ. 47. In these apostrophes will naturally be revealed the love sentiments corresponding to the regions: e.g. Kuṟ. 163 – an apostrophe to the sea – pining or iraṅkal, i.e. the uripporuḷ of neytal.

---

[194] SS 5:1de, where the companions and lovers are addressed and are invited to eat and drink, and to get drunk, need not necessarily be an apostrophe. It is possible that concretely there were other couples who joined them.

[195] Varadarajan, M., *The Treatment of Nature*, 356-388; Id., "A Type of Apostrophes", in *PTICSTS*, 91-96.

[196] The proportion is interesting. The beloved naturally holds the first place. The companion who participates very intimately (cf. Ak. 12) in the emotions of the lady love comes next. Then follows the lover — note that the difference between him and the lady companion is just by one poem. The most emotionally charged character in Tamil akam poetry is the beloved!

There are a few poems with the messenger theme and through them the speaker expresses the sentiments and emotions. In Naṟ. 54, the beloved sends the crane as messenger to her lover to tell *its* sea-ford-land-owner about her lonely state. The female companion sends a similar message through a bee: Kuṟ. 392. Naṟ. 196, spoken by the beloved, asking the moon to show where her lover has gone and hidden himself is similar in sentiments to SS 5:8. The maidens of the SS and the Tamil akam poems are very much alike!

2. *Flash-back*

Flash-back is a literary technique by which past events can be brought in connection with the present emotions. For example, a scene may be introduced in which the speaker can report his or her experiences that happened in dream or phantasy.[197]

In SS, this literary technique *seems* to have been used in 3:1-5; 4:8-11; 5:2-6:3; 6:11-12; 8:1-5ab.

In Tamil poetry, such flash-backs are found, for example, in poems where the lover or the beloved narrate a past experience in a context which is at present different: Ak. 39 – by the lover; Ak. 205 – by the beloved. One may mention in this connection also the many cases of dream-narratives in Tamil poems: e.g. Naṟ. 87; Kuṟ. 30 – B; Kuṟ. 147; Aiṅ. 324,418; Ak. 39 – L. Note that the lover in SS, has no dream experience like the one of Tamil poems.

I. **Cultural Elements**

Between the SS, and the Tamil akam poetry, there are certain cultural elements which appear similar or analogous. Some of them have already been mentioned in passing, but for the sake of completeness, a few are recalled and commented on briefly.

1. *Equality of Sexes*

The SS is a clear testimony to the equality of sexes at least in the sphere of love-life. "Significantly, the man and woman are 'toe to toe' in their assertive acts and expressive words, a sexual equality which might equally bespeak the *comradeship of peasant lovers* not yet encumbered by children or the *companionship of upper-class lovers* whose affluence and education encourage feminist consciousness."[198] One is struck even by the superiority of the female partner with regard to sobriety, initiative and responsible handling of the situations. The equality and mutuality of

---

[197] Cf. Sundaramoorthy, G., *Early Literary*, 161-162.
[198] Gottwald, N. K., *The Hebrew Bible*, 549.

the woman with the man cannot be contested as far as the SS is concerned.[199] "Love is harmony. Neither male nor female asserts power or possession over the other."[200]

In Tamil akam poetry, the equality of sexes is revealed in a very balanced and refined way. Though in the outside world and activity, the man may assert his strength and superiority, in love-life he acknowledges the equality of the other partner. The Tamil beloved is also sober, takes initiative to further the relationship of love but always with responsibility. The rôle of the lady companion here is unparalleled. There is no question of superiority of the male over the female, nor that of preference of male child to a female. On the contrary, Aiṅ. 257 says that a hill man prayed to god and obtained a girl who is precious – no such testimony is available for obtaining a male one.[201]

2. *Fixing the Rendezvous*

Love relationship is a personal involvement, begins at one definite moment, and develops as a secret affair till in due time it becomes consummated in permanent union. This process is clearly implied, if not revealed, in SS 1:5-6; 2:16-17; 8:13-14.[202] In some poems, we have evidence that one of the two parties fixes the place of tryst: in 1:7-8, the girl asks and the boy fixes the place; in 4:16 the girl suggests and in 5:1 the boy accepts; 6:11-12 and 8:13-14 appear to be meetings already fixed; 7:11-14 is clear in the beloved's suggestion of the rendezvous.

That love relationship starts as a secret affair according to Tamil poetry is shown already by the name *kaḷavu*.[203] This relationship is fostered in successive secret meetings. The theme of the heroine or her friend suggesting an appropriate place for a rendezvous is present in many poems but made explicit not so frequently:[204] e.g. Kuṟ. 113,114,141,142, etc. Usually it is the companion who suggests or does the arrangements: e.g. Naṟ. 285,323; Kuṟ. 113. Sometimes the beloved herself may suggest: Kuṟ. 141. But the present writer knows no case in Tamil akam poetry in which the girl asks for a rendezvous and the boy fixes it, as in SS 1:7-8.[205]

---

199 Trible, P., *God and the Rhetoric*, 145.

200 Ib., 159.

201 Plllay, K.K., *Social History*, 372, 387 et passim; Balasubramanian, C., *The Status of Women*, 6.

202 Cf. Falk., M., *Love Lyrics*, 93.

203 *kaḷavu* does simply mean "secret" and does not mean in itself "illicit". Because stealing takes place in secret, the word later began to denote stealing and illicit action.

204 Hart, G.L. III, *The Poems*, 216-217, 219, etc.

205 There are cases of shepherd girl fixing a rendezvous for a shepherd boy and that only in Mullaikkali: see Millaikkali. 8, esp. 10,16. There are also cases in which the boy explicitly asks for rendezvous, e.g., Naṟ. 213.

3. *Elopement*

Elopement is one of the ways in which the lovers overcome the hindrances to their love-meetings and become united permanently. Whether elopement was a reality among the Hebrews, is not clear from the SS itself. But there are certain poems which suggest such elopements — at least as intentions of the speaker: e.g. 1:4; 2:8-13; 4:8-11. SS 2:14 fits in very well in one of such elopements as life context.

Elopement is mentioned in Tamil love poems quite a few times. It is either the boy or the lady companion that suggests the elopement as an ultimate recourse for permanent union: e.g. Naṟ. 149; Kuṟ. 297,343 – the lady companion; Naṟ. 82 – the lover is inviting the beloved.[206] The beloved, while eloping with her lover, meets in the arid land some wayfarers and sends through them to her mother the news about her decision to go with him: Aiṅ. 385.

4. *Kissing in Public*

In Hebrew culture, the lovers do not kiss each other in public. At least, this is what is implied in SS 8:1 where the female speaker claims that *if* her lover were to be in reality her brother she would kiss him in public without being despised.[207] This would make SS 1:2a clear that the kisses from his mouth which the beloved wishes to have, can be given to her only in secret rendezvous.

Kissing between lovers existed in Tamil culture.[208] From the description in the poems which speak of the nectar of the mouth of the beloved, "one can infer that the habit of kissing existed in Tamilnadu. There is not, however, a single description about kissing in public throughout the vast literature of love poems in Tamil."[209]

5. *Bride-price*

Paying bride-price in some form, e.g. ornaments or gifts, seems to underlie certain of the poems in the SS: e.g. 1:11 – in which the lover says: "Bangles of gold we will make you, with spangles of silver" (M. H.

---

[206] This poem *seems* to be the lover's suggestion for elopement. But it may simply be taken also as an offer or request made to her to accept his courtship and become his wife.

[207] Falk, M., *Love Lyrics*, 122 writes; "This testifies to the intimacy presumably allowed to siblings in this culture".

[208] See above on "Sense of touch and love".

[209] Aravaanan, K.P., "Marriage – A Dravido-African", in *PFifICSTS*, Vol. II, sec. 8, 5. It may be added here that the Tamil word, now used for kiss, is the same word *muttam* as pearl in ancient Tamil: see Naṟ. 202:2 *Muttam* - pearl; also Aiṉ. 105:2. Could it be that the preciousness and rarity of both were the reason and aspect for the development of this word and its significance? *DED* accepts that the word *Muttam* means both and that the word is Tamil: nn. 4959-4960.

Pope). Also SS 8:7 apparently refers to such a custom: "If a man gave all the wealth of his house for love, they would be despised." [210] There may be some historicity to this custom of paying bride-price in accounts like Gen. 24.

Paying bride-price is, according to some scholars, one of the five patterns of marriage in Tamil culture.[211] This does not mean that the girl was bought for the price, but they were the gifts to the bride from the bridegroom. It is simply the development of the lover's gifts to his lady-love, symbolic at first and material afterwards: See Kuṟ. 1 – flowers; Kuṟ. 214 – leaf-garment; Naṟ. 80 – garlands; Naṟ. 300; Aiṅ. 193; Ak. 280 – bracelets and other costly gifts. This bride-price is called *pāciḻai vilai*, i.e. price of gold jewels for her in Ak. 90; or *taḻai vilai*, i.e. price for the leaves, in Aiṅ. 147, etc.[212] It is noteworthy that in Tamil akam poems, "there is no reference to payment of money to the bridegroom corresponding to the dowry of modern times." [213]

Conclusion

By now it will be clear that the similarities and analogies between the SS and the Tamil love poems are multiple and deep. The anonymity of the speakers in the poems gives to the sentiments expressed a permanent openness for universal application to and personalization by all lovers. The analogies in the levels of imagery, aesthetics, language-symbolism and esp. cultural elements draw the two groups of poems quite close. The experience and expression of various aspects of the one love-sentiment are delightful. The similarities and analogies between the characters in both literatures, esp. the beloved of the SS and the heroine of the Tamil poems are striking. Their centrality and their self-surrendering love are worth admiring for their endurance and daring!

---

[210] See discussion in Pope, M. H., *Song*, 675f and various interpretations.

[211] Manickavasagom, M. E., *TC*, XI, 4 (1964), 331-332; Balasubramanian, C., *The Status of Women*, 10 & 31; Pillay, K. K., *Social History*, 362.

[212] The commentator of Aiṅkuṟunūṟu, understands this phrase *taḻai vilai* in Aiṅ. 147 as euphemism for sexual intercourse. It may also simply mean "price for leaves", meaning the leaf-garment as sign of his love.

[213] Pillay, K. K., *Social History*, 362. It seems that the same may be said about the Hebrew culture too! See De Vaux, R., *Ancient Israel*, London 1965², 19-40; Tosato, A., *Il Matrimonio Israelitico*, AnBib. 100, Roma 1982, 95 on *mōhar* as probable "bride-price". Dowry system, it seems, did not exist.

CHAPTER 8.

DISSIMILARITIES BETWEEN THE SONG OF SONGS AND THE ANCIENT TAMIL LOVE POEMS

While showing the similarities between the Song of Songs and the ancient Tamil love poems, dissimilarities were also here and there pointed out. It would be useful, however, to speak of the differences which are rather important and which constitute the individuality and specificity of the two literary corpora.

A. **From the Literary Point of View**

From the literary point of view, there are at least two dissimilarities which seem important and worth noting, between the SS and the Tamil akam poems.

1. *Dialogues versus Monologues*

The SS contains comparatively a good number of dialogues vis-à-vis the monologues. According to the calculation of the present writer, there are eight dialogues out of altogether twenty-eight poems in the SS.[1] This amounts to some 28.5% of the whole collection. It may be recalled also that the dialogues find place in different life-situations.

Dialogues in the proper sense of the word are conspicuously absent in the early classical Tamil akam poems. All the poems in Aiṅkuṟunūṟu, Kuṟuntokai, Naṟṟiṇai and Akanāṉūṟu are only monologues. As it has been mentioned, dialogues are cited within the monologues: e.g. Ak. 390 (see appendix), but dialogues in the strict sense are not to be found. In the late classical akam poetry, i.e. in Kalittokai, there are a few – indeed very few cases of dialogues: e.g. Kuṟiñcikkali 28. Otherwise, they too are monologues, containing often within them, dialogues of the past: e.g. Kuṟiñcikkali – 1.

Even among monologues in SS and Tamil akam poetry, there is an important difference to be noticed: In the SS, there are ten monologues spoken by one of the love-partners directly to the other. That means, some 35.7% of the whole collection. Among the ten monologues addressed by one partner directly to the other, the distribution is five to

---

[1] See Part Three, Chapter 7, p. 154.

each one, i.e. 50%. If we compare the monologues, spoken by the love-partners in Tamil poems belonging to courtship, the girl very rarely addresses the lover directly and speaks to him.[2] Mostly the man does so. Such directly addressed poems too are not many.[3] This comparison shows that the beloved of the SS, is more forthright in her talks with her lover than the beloved in Tamil poetry!

2. *Poetic Conventions*

It cannot be affirmed with certainty that there were definite poetic conventions to be followed by the poets who composed the poems of the SS collection. The facts are there, however, which *seem to indicate* that poetic conventions were at least initiated: the fact that the lover and the beloved remain unindividualized – hence types; that the cultivated country side is favourable to love-relation; that civilized society or ambient is either unfavourable or dangerous, etc. The specific mention of "the daughters of Jerusalem", although it can be argued that this designation is too vague to be specific, seems to point out that the poetic conventions, if they ever existed in Hebrew love poetry, did not reach the perfect stage of getting rid of any hint whatever of specification. There is no ancient Hebrew grammar, similar to Tolkāppiyam in Tamil, that would give us informations and clarifications on this matter. One may with caution say that in Hebrew "akam" poetry, the poetic conventions seem to have at least begun.

In Tamil akam poetry, the poetic conventions have been well developed and clearly defined in the course of many centuries. The definitions and precisions, found in Tolkāppiyam with regard to poetic conventions, esp. for akam poetry are the result of long poetic tradition of many centuries.[4]

B. The Role of Nature

We have seen that the landscape and nature, esp. vegetation, constitute in the SS, a veritable foreground and background for the love-relationship of the lover and the beloved. But it must be admitted that "there is an insufficiency of data within the Song of Songs to construct a precise scheme of landscapes (if they are indeed present), together with the type of love which each might represent." [5] As it has

---

[2] See above on "Designations used for the hero", pp. 172-173.

[3] See "Portrait of the Beloved", p. 195.

[4] On this point, there can be no doubt. See for example, Srinivas Iyengar, P.T., *History*, 63-64, 69-70, et passim. Cf. also the discussion on conventions in Part Two, Chapter 6, pp. 148-149.

[5] Craigie, P.C., *SR* 8 (1979), 171.

been said above, unfortunately Hebrew literature has no ancient equivalent to the Tamil Tolkāppiyam to give us the scheme of landscapes and the corresponding manifestations of the experience of love, reflected through them. If we may use the terminology of the Tamil akam poetry to the SS, the uripporuḷ-correspondence (sentiments-correspondence) is indeed striking, but the aspects of mutaṟporuḷ (Spatio-temporal elements) and karupporuḷ (Avifauna etc.) are not so evident. No one can deny that Nature serves as the stage – at least to some extent – in SS, for the drama of human love. But there is no indication to affirm that the Nature is described in such a way that its participation in and reflection of human sentiments of love are evident from the poems themselves.[6]

In this respect, the Tamil akam poetry is far advanced and refined. The man and the girl in Tamil poetry view the Nature as participating, sympathizing and correspondingly reflecting their own emotions. The external world is brought into direct relationship with their individual feelings of joy, sorrow or expectation, etc.[7] Indeed, "the human elements are so fused with the pictures of Nature that one cannot think of the love-scenes apart from their fresh and lovely surroundings."[8] If we may use the terminology of dramaturgy, Nature in Tamil akam poetry is not only the stage for the drama of human love, but also the appropriate background screen, reflecting the human life-context through the depiction of animals, birds and even plants "experiencing" the same sentiments, and the sound and light systems affecting and aggravating the human emotions. In Tamil poetry, "Nature was the sympathetic scenery portrayed to match the drama of life. The scenery was changed to keep in harmony with the human sentiments that were dramatized."[9]

In love-life, the whole universe is involved: the space, the time, plants, birds and animals – all are involved in the love-life of the central figures, namely man and woman. Love experiences pervade in one way or other through all sectors of the universe in so far as they are turning round the man and woman. In Tamil akam poetry, it is the love-relationship of man and woman that gives value and meaning to Nature. That is why Nature is never the object of poetry for its own sake.

This anthropocentric conception of Nature explains well the interactions of the elements of Nature on the love-life of man, and the human sentiments on the presentation of Nature in poetry.

---

[6] Gordis, R., *Song*, 29.
[7] Cf. Varadarajan, M., *The Treatment of Nature*, 356.
[8] Ib., 404.
[9] Thani Nayagam, X. S., *Nature*, 178.

C. The Characters

In two points, there are dissimilarities between the SS and the Tamil akam poetry with regard to the main characters, namely in the designation of the beloved and the portraits of the lover and of the beloved.

1. *Designation of the Beloved*

Among the many designations of the beloved in the SS, there is one which is conspicuous – the designation "sister" (SS 4:9,10,12; 5:1,2), used altogether five times and always as an appellation. This particular designation of the beloved as sister is not at all found in Tamil poems nor even its equivlent.[10]

On the other hand, the beloved in the SS, is never once called "wife", and child-bearing does not come into view. "In fact, to the issues of marriage and procreation the Song does not speak."[11] Union of man and woman in love is the only objective of the poems of SS. The designation of the beloved by *kallāh,* i.e. bride in combination with *'ăḥôtî* seems not to exclude the purpose of marriage and permanent companionship.[12]

There are two terms in Tamil akam poetry which designate the wife, *Maṉaiyōḷ* and *Maṉaivi.* The first term occurs in akam poems altogether fifteen times, but only two references are relevant to our discussion, i.e. Naṟ. 77:6 and Ak. 394:10:[13]

(i) Naṟ. 77 is by the hero and belongs to kuṟiñci tiṇai poem and refers to his beloved. The word *maṉaiyōḷ* in this poem probably means "the girl who is at home." The significance of "the girl going-to-be my wife" is perhaps implied in the context.

---

[10] This designation of the beloved as "sister" has parallels in ancient Egyptian love songs. See White, J. B., *A Study*, 130. In this background, it is interesting to see the effect of double-entendre of this designation and the word-play in Gen. 12:10-20 and parallel narratives.

[11] Trible, P., *God and the Rhetoric*, 162.

[12] Cf. also the appellation, *ra'yātî* - companion.

[13] The other thirteen occurrences designate:

— the beloved of the man (7x): Naṟ. 100:7; Kuṟ. 164:5; Aiṅ. 81:5; 87:3; Ak. 166:10; 186:13; 396:15 – all by the prostitute in marutam poems.

— wife in general (2x): Aiṅ. 47:2; 48:2 – by the heroine referring to wife in general in marutam poems.

— the wife of a forest dweller: Naṟ. 336:5 – does not refer to the beloved.

— the beloved of the man, as wife (3x): Aiṅ. 410:2 – by the foster-mother of the girl referring to her after marriage; Ak. 14:14 – by the pāṇaṉ (bard); 224:11 – by the hero to his charioteer while returning from distant land – all the three poems belong to mullai. The latter two poems may or may not refer to the separation before marriage.

(ii) Ak. 394 is by the lady companion to the hero. The poem is a case of *tiṇaimayakkam,* namely the kuṟiñci uripporuḷ (i.e. union) occurring in mullai nilam (forest region). The companion is urging the hero to make the beloved the *maṉaiyōḷ,* i.e. to hasten to marry her and give her the status of the wife – the queen of the house, the *maṉaiyōḷ.*

The word *maṉaivi* occurs only once, in Naṟ. 121:11 in the sense of wife and refers to the beloved of the hero to whom the poem is addressed by the charioteer – hence in mullaittiṇai.

The designation of the beloved as wife during the courtship is very rare – indeed only these two cases. But that the final goal of the courtship is happy marriage and permanent companionship at home is clear at least from the poem spoken by the lady companion, Ak. 394. Naṟ. 82, by the lover to the beloved, shows through the simile of Murukaṉ and Vaḷḷi (standing for the lover and the beloved) that the lover wants to take her as wife.

Child-bearing is *not* seen *as an end* of the marriage in poems dealing with courtship. But it is accepted as a fact and mentioned as a source of joy and happiness in the poems of mullaittiṇai: See, for example, Aiṅ. 401-406, 408-410; Naṟ. 221, etc. In poems of marutam, the child (usually the poems mention the son – putalvaṉ) is an effective means of reconciliation between the guilty husband and the angry wife: cf. Kuṟ. 359. References to child-bearing, however, do not come in akam poetry for its own sake, but only in relation to the problems of love-relationship between the hero and the heroine. The theme of the greatness of children, their education, etc., are objects of puṟam poems.[14]

2. *Portraits of the Lover and the Beloved*

The beloved in the SS, is portrayed by the lover in somewhat detailed manner: 4:1-7 and 6:4-7 – both of them describe the beloved in downward sequence. The first one starts with a general statement on her beauty, comes as far down as her breasts and closes with the final total: "You are all fair, *ra'yātî* (my companion) blemish there is none in you." The second description starts also with a general statement on her beauty (6:4) and comes only as far as the cheeks, and there is no final total in 6:7.[15] The third one by the onlookers in 7:2-6 follows the upward sequence of the members of the beloved's body. No total statement is to be found either in the beginning or at the end of the description.

---

[14] Cf. Manavalan, A. A., "Caṅka Ilakkiyam", in *Tamiḻ Ilakkiyak*, 28.
[15] Cf. Watson, W. G. E., *Classical*, 352-355.

The beloved describes her lover (5:10-16) in downward sequence (like 4:1-7 about herself), starting with a general statement in the beginning (5:10) and closing with a total at the end (5:16b: "Everything of him is desirable"). The downward sequence, however, in this description is not consistent, because his mouth or palate comes after the legs. In general we can say that the description is built on the model of 4:1-7.[16]

In early classical Tamil akam poems, there is not a single description of the beloved by the lover (or for that matter by anyone) which attempts to describe all the parts of the body in downward or upward sequence. Each time only a few members of the body are described and they normally pertain to the uripporuḷ of the poem.[17] In fact, no poem follows any fixed order in describing the members of the body. The descriptions are discreet and sober, and they concentrate on the emotions evoked by the actions of those members of the body: e.g. the look, the speech, the embrace, etc. We may find examples of poems which start with a general statement in the beginning, e.g. Aiṅ. 255 (appendix), 256, or at the end, e.g. Ak. 390, but they do not come out as forcefully as in the SS 4:1-7. In this respect, there *seems* to be an attempt to follow a certain sequence in the late classical poems of Kalittokai: e.g. Kuṟiñcikkali, 19,20,22 and Mullaikkali, 8. For the description of women by parts, the list is more complete in Tirumurukāṟṟuppaṭai (lines: 12-41: description of heavenly maidens) and Ciṟupāṇāṟṟuppaṭai (lines: 13-31; description of the female dancers), but still without strict sequence. Only in Porunarāṟṟuppaṭai (lines: 25-47), the description of a female bard follows a strict sequence from head to foot and attempts to cover all the parts.[18]

The description of the members of the lover's body is not found in the classical akam poems.[19] The beloved never attempts, like the beloved of the SS, to describe in detail the limbs of her lover. In the Kuṟiñcippāṭṭu, there are ca. 20 lines describing the appearance of the lover (lines: 107-127). There, the description is mostly of his garlands and the flowers in them. The only members of his body receiving some descriptive elements, are his chest, hand, waist with a girdle and his feet with anklets. Other parts like head, eyes, etc. do not come under description. This is a significant difference between the SS and the Tamil love poems.

---

[16] Cf. Angénieux, J., *ETL* 42 (1966), 582-596.

[17] Manavalan, A. A., "Caṅka Ilakkiyam", in *Tamiḻ Ilakkiyak*, 42-43.

[18] See Chelliah, J. V. (trans.), *Pattuppāṭṭu: Ten Tamil Idylls*, SISSWPS, Madras 1962, 63 & 65. But this and the other two descriptions are found in poems belonging to Puṟattiṇai.

[19] See Part Three, Chapter 7 "Portrait of the Lover".

3. *Rendezvous between the Lover and the Beloved*

There is a marked difference between the SS, and the Tamil poems as regards the fixing of the rendezvous. In the SS, except in 1:8, it is the beloved who suggests the place of tryst: e.g. 7:12-13 – there is an explicit indication of the place. Moreover the encounter between the two partners is direct, either in reality or in phantasy.[20] In fact, both types of encounters are represented in the text: direct in 1:7-8; in dream or phantasy in 5:2-6:3. Be it what it may, the evident fact is that there is no intermediary who arranges the meetings.

The maids of Jerusalem do not play a rôle, strictly intermediary, even though once in dream (6:1), they are ready to help her in her search. Otherwise, they do not in any way work as intermediaries between the lover and the beloved.

In Tamil poems, the lady companion, the *tōḻi* is unique. More than the friend of the lover, she plays the go-between in the love-affair. The hero approaches her to plead with the beloved for him, she goes as a messenger to the girl, arranges for their meetings and even fixes different places at different times.[21]

D. **Idea of Love**

In the SS, marriage is not mentioned as a culmination of the love-relationship. If at all there might be something of a context of marriage, it could be in the poem, SS 3:6-11, which is spoken by a crowd of onlookers about the procession of a palanquin. Some authors consider this poem as a description of one of Solomon's wedding processions.[22] Solomon's name here, as elsewhere, may also be taken as an historical type for any bridegroom either royal or common. In any case, if this poem is a description of a wedding procession, it would be the only text in the SS, about marriage. It is not, however, certain that this wedding procession is the goal of the whole process of encounters between the lovers. We must say that the central position of the poem in the received text *seems* to indicate this purpose at least in the mind of the final redactor. Verse 8d seems to confirm this line of argumentation since there the fear of the night makes an allusion to some traditional beliefs of the Hebrews, i.e. "protecting the nuptial bed from evil spirits."[23]

---

[20] There are scholars who hold that all the encounters between the lover and the beloved are in dreams: e.g. the scholars who support the theory that the SS is a random collection of dream-experiences: See Part One, Chapter 1. Rabin, C., *SR* 3:3 (1973/4), 210, who holds that the lover speaks in the beloved's phantasy.

[21] See Part Three, Chapter 7. "The Characters" under "Persons of acquaintance".

[22] E.g. Gordis, R., *Song*, 20.

[23] Krauss, S., "Der richtige Sinn von 'Schrecken in der Nacht' HL III,8", in *Moses Gaster Eightieth Anniversary Volume*, 1936, 323-330. Compare Tob. 6:13-17; 8:1-3.

The Tamil akam poems extend the love-relationship of the man and the woman even after marriage. Already during the courtship, there is the idea that steps should be taken by the young man to make his love-relationship recognized by their parents and the elders of their villages. It is especially the lady companion who insists on this goal. For the lover and the beloved in their mutual attraction and longing, sporadic encounters and unions, forget this important aspect of their relationship. Hence she thinks of it, insists on it to the young man and when an occasion is given, reveals it to those responsible. According to the spirit of the kuṟiñci (and neytal) poems, the mutual love of a young man and a young lady culminates in the recognition by the society. The *ceremonial* marriage is only later introduction.[24]

Ak. 394 shows well that the courtship must end in public recognition and celebration of the union, and thus the girl should become the *maṉaiyōḷ* in the full sense of the word. The wording and the context of the poem leave no doubt as regards this purpose of the love-relationship. Similar exhortations are implied in all the poems of the lady companion urging marriage arrangements, i.e. poems of *varaivu kaṭāvutal*: e.g. Ak. 2, 12, etc. It is still more clear in those poems, in which she expresses her joy and satisfaction as she learns that the lover is coming with his parents and relatives to take the girl home as his wife: *varaivu malital*: e.g. Aiṅ. 218, 230, 300, etc.[25]

That wedded-family life is goal of love-affair is seen also in those mullaittiṇai poems in which either the foster-mother or the lady companion praise the happy married life of the couple: e.g. Aiṅ. 401-410 by foster-mother.

In some of the poems, spoken by the lover, the idea is present that the union by nature, *iyaṟkaippuṇarcci* leads to permanent state of husband and wife: Naṟ. 202; Ak. 221. Strangely but interestingly, the poems on *maṭalēṟutal,* show this intention on the part of the lover: See, for instance, Kuṟ. 14, in which the lover feels a little shy to ride on the palmyra horse, and make the people say that he is the husband (kaṇavaṉ) of that good girl.

That living together as husband and wife is the ideal to be reached through courtship is indicated and inculcated by the description of

---

[24] Manickam, V. Sp., *Tamil Concept*, 87-106: the author deals on the history of the introduction of rituals for marriage, the different symbols of married state, etc.

[25] Wedding ceremonies are described in two poems: Ak. 86,136. Both are poems of marutam and the wedding is recalled by the speaker. The important point of the poems is to recall the first-night experience by the lover. It is interesting to note that two groups of women play important rôles in wedding ceremonies: one of old women who have long experience and the other of women who have borne children. The latter pronounce the words of "Blessing". Compare Ps. 45.

animals and birds which appear in pairs in the karupporuḷ. They are so well "organized" and described according to uḷḷuṟai uvamam that they reflect the different stages of family ideal: e.g.

- bee gathering honey in flowers: courtship: Kuṟ. 239
- animals and birds in pairs in kuṟiñci and neytal: symbol for marriage: Naṟ. 322, 348
- animals in pairs with their little one(s) in pālai and mullai: reunion in family ideal:[26] Naṟ. 202; Ak. 34, 287, 304, 314, etc.

The absence of the motif of faithlessness and love quarrel in SS, constitutes a very important difference between the SS and the Tamil love poems. The marutam poems in Tamil have the motif of faithlessness of the husband whom the wife or the companion corrects. These poems bring to light the repentant return of the guilty but humble husband, and the "motherly" forgiving wife. The absence of this motif in SS "must be accidental, or the result of the editor's choice – the human emotion involved is ubiquitous and must have existed in ancient Israel."[27]

---

[26] See for example Aiṅ. 401 in the appendix.
[27] Gordis. R., *The Song*, 30.

CHAPTER 9.

CLASSIFICATION AND APPRECIATION OF THE SONG OF SONGS ACCORDING TO TAMIL RHETORIC

We shall treat this topic under three sections: A. Classification and appreciation of the similes in the SS according to Tamil rhetoric. B. Classification and appreciation of the metaphors in the SS according to Tamil rhetoric. C. Classification and appreciation of the individual poems in the SS according to Tamil akam grammar and categories.

A. **Classification and Appreciation of the Similes**

Simile is the most fundamental and universal imagery in human language. All the other items of imagery have developed from this and after this. So we begin with this imagery in our appreciation of the SS according to Tamil rhetoric.

1. *Concept of Simile (Uvamai) according to Tolkāppiyam*

We have already seen the general notion of uvamai as exposed by Tolkāppiyam.[1] There are four principles on which a comparison may be established (Tol. Por. Uvam. 276): viṉai (action), payaṉ (result), mey (body) and uru (colour).[2] We have seen also that there are five causes for establishing a comparison or using a simile (Tol. Por. Uvam. 279-280): of these five causes, three are objective: (i) Ciṟappu (excellence); (ii) Nalaṉ (goodness); (iii) Vali (strength); and two subjective: (i) Kātal (love or appreciation); (ii) Kiḻakkiṭu poruḷ (depreciation).

---

[1] See Part Two, Chapter 6, pp. 132-133.

[2] The word *Mey* is translated in different ways by different commentators. Pērāciriyar explains it by *vaṭivu*, i.e. shape, form. See Pārāciriyar, *Tolkāppiyam* - SISSWPS, 1975, 58. S. Ilakkuvaṉār renders *mey* by body, *Tholkāppiyam*, 218. G. Sundaramoorthy, on the other hand, by "quality", cf. *Early Literary*, 100. All commentators translate *uru* by "colour". Pērāciriyar explains *uru* by *vaṇṇam*, (*Tolkāppiyam*, 58) and by *niṟam*, (*Tolkāppiyam*, 59). It appears strange that the word *uru* whose primary meaning in Sanskrit is "shape, form, beauty" (*CDIAL*, n. 10803) has been taken to mean "colour" by the commentators (Cf. *DED*, n. 657 which gives the meaning of "colour" after "form, shape" for the word *uru*).

Tolkāppiyam lays down certain rules for the use of simile. Worth mentioning are the following ones:

– The object used as simile should be superior to the object described (Tol. Por. Uv. 278).

– Comparison may be established under more than one aspect (Tol. Por. Uv. 277).

– The whole and the part of the simile may be compared with the whole or the part of the object (Tol. Por. Uv. 281), i.e. the whole // the whole; the part // the part; the whole // the part; the part // the whole.

– Exaggeration is not desirable; it may, however, be permitted when showing the "greatness" (perumai) and the "smallness" (ciṟumai) (Tol. Por. Uv. 285).

– While expressing the "greatness" (perumai) and the "smallness" (ciṟumai), the eight *meyppāṭu* will be revealed through the similes (Tol. Por. Uv. 294). Meyppāṭu means, taste (cuvai), suggestion or indication (kuṟippu) according to Pērāciriyar.[3] We may render it by sentiment or emotion.[4] The eight meyppāṭu (Tol. Por. Mey. 251) that may be enhanced by the use of simile are: (i) Laughter (nakai); (ii) Weeping or lament (aḻukai); (iii) Despisedness or sense of disgrace (iḷivaral); (iv) Wonder or admiration (maruṭkai); (v) Fear or awe (accam); (vi) Excellence or fortitude (perumitam); (vii) Anger (vekuḷi) and (viii) Delight (uvakai).[5]

– The simile clarifies the object as regards the meyppāṭu (Tol. Por. Uv. 295).

– Traditional usage helps to see the aspect of comparison and the meyppāṭu (Tol. Por. Uv. 296).

– If the object (used as simile) appears with adjunct, the compared object may also follow suit, i.e. may have adjuncts (Tol. Por. Uv. 297).

– A comparison that denies the similarity between the object of comparison and the compared object, is allowed (Tol. Por. Uv. 308).

---

[3] Cf. Pērāciriyar, *Tol. Por. Comm.* 5.

[4] See what has been said in Chapter 6 under "Imagery", p. 131 and see also the corresponding notes 33, 34. The word *meyppāṭu* is compounded from *mey* — body, and *pāṭu* — a verbal noun (toḻiṟ-peyar) from *paṭu* which means, "to suffer, to endure..." and "to appear, to exhibit, to occur, to come to existence..." Hence *pāṭu* –"coming to existence, happening, experience; see *DED*, 3853. In the Chapter on Meyppāṭu, Tolkāppiyar speaks mostly about the emotions or feelings exhibited in the lovers, esp. in the beloved.

[5] Ilakkuvaṉār, S., *Tholkāppiyam*, 213 for the English terms, and 456-457 for comments. *Iḷivaral* is better rendered by "disgrace", cf. *DED*, 511. *Perumitam* may also be translated by "celebrity, nobleness, greatness", *DED*, 4411.

– Displaced simile,[6] may be allowed (Tol. Por. Uv. 310).

– Accumulation of similes is to be avoided (Tol. Pol. Uv. 311).

– Similes and the objects related to them may be placed in order. It is called *niral niṟai,* i.e. order in order (Tol. Por. Uv. 312).

2. *Classification of the Similes in the SS*

The purpose of the classification of the similes in the SS is to discover, (i) the principle or principles on which the similes are based or used, (ii) the objective cause that induced the speaker to use it, (iii) the subjective cause or motive why the poet used it, (iv) and lastly the meyppāṭu that is revealed through the use of a given simile.[7] In order to discover these aspects and to appreciate them, we shall bring all the similes found in the SS under two categories.

a) *Similes with adjuncts*: By similes with adjuncts (in Tamil *aṭai, aṭaimoḻi,* see Tol. Por. Uv. 297), we undestand the objects etc., used as similes which have some *explicit* qualificative that will indicate the aspect of comparison. These adjuncts may be:

(i) an adjective: e.g. dark, SS 1:5a.

(ii) a participle used as an adjective: e.g. looking forth, SS 6:10b.

(iii) a verbal expression: e.g. that stream down (*šeggālšû* – verb), SS 4:1f.

(iv) a noun phrase, i.e. a noun in construct state: e.g. thread of scarlet, SS 4:3a.

(v) a noun phrase in apposition: e.g. work of the hands of master workman, SS 7:2c.

(vi) a prepositional phrase: e.g. *among* the Pharaoh's cavalry. SS 1:9ab.

Out of altogether 58 cases of similes used [8] in the SS, 47 are classified as similes with adjuncts, basing the analysis on the rules of Tolkāppiyam. They are to be found in: SS.1:2b, 3a, 3b, 5ac, 5ad, 9ab; 2:2, 3ab, 9ab,

---

[6] "Displaced simile" translates the Tamil *taṭumāruvamam*, Ilakkuvaṉār, S., *Tholkāppiyam*, 222. Cīṉivācaṉ, R., *Caṅka Ilakkiyattil*, 31-33.

[7] Thus we shall apply to the similes of the SS the rules of Tol. Por. Uvamaviyal and Meyppāṭṭiyal (251-259) which give the eight meyppāṭu and their sources. For details, see Pērāciriyar, *Tol. Por. Commentary*, 1-18; Ilakkuvaṉār, S., *Tholkāppiyam*, 213-214 and 456-457. Tol. Por. Meyp. cūt. 260 also enumerates some thirty-two meyppāṭu, but they are given under different aspect of division. In reality, they can be more or less related and identified with those treated in cūts. 251-259.

[8] For the list of similes in the SS, see the "Table of Similes", pp. 72-74.

17c-f; 3:6c; 4:lef, 2ab, 3a, 3cd, 4a, 5a, 10c, 11c; 5:11bc, 12ab, 13ab, 15d; 6:4a, 4b, 4c, 5cd, 6ab, 7ab, 10b, 10c, 10d, 10e; 7:1cd, 2c, 4a, 5a, 5d, 9d, 10a; 8:1a, 6a, 6b, 6c, 6d, 10d, 14bc.

b) *Similes without adjuncts*: By simile without adjuncts is understood the comparison or use of a simile, where the basis of comparison is not explicitly stated by adjectives, etc. Tolkāppiyar advises us to put together the object of comparison and the compared object in order to discover the basis or aspect of comparison (Tol. Por. Uv. 282). There are cases in which the object and the simile are just joined by the particle *kĕ* and juxtaposed: e.g. SS 7:8b: The lover tells the beloved, "Your breasts are like clusters". No adjective, etc. explicates the aspect of similarity. If we put in the context of the poem, the two components side by side, "breasts" and "clusters", i.e. of fruits, we can see that the comparison is based on "form and colour".

Following the rules of Tolkāppiyam for analysis,we classify the following similes as similes without adjuncts: SS. 1:4d, 4e, 7e; 4:10d; 5:15c; 7:6a, 6b, 8a, 8b, 9e; 8:10b.

3. *Appreciation of the Similes in the SS*

If our analysis and classification of similes in SS according to the rules of Tolkāppiyam are accepted, the following comments are in order:

a) Exaggeration may be permitted, according to Tolkāppiyam, when the similes are used to show the greatness or bigness (perumai) and inferiority or smallness (ciṟumai): Tol. Por. Uv. 285. The following are exaggerations to show the greatness or bigness (perumai):

SS 4:4a – Tower of David for neck.
SS 6:10 – All three similes: dawn, moon, and sun.
SS 7:5ad – Towers for neck and nose.
SS 7:6a – Mount Carmel for head.
SS 7:8a – Palm tree for stature.
SS 8:6cd – Death and Sheol for the power of love and passion.
SS 8:10b – Towers for breasts.
SS 8:10d – Evening star for herself.

Exaggeration to show the inferiority or smallness (ciṟumai) is seen in:

SS 1:5 – Tents of Kedar for her body.
SS 1:7e – "the one veiled" (or "wandering one") for her condition(?).

b) The technique of *niral - niṟai,* i.e. order in order – namely similes and the compared objects being placed in order – is found in the following instances (Tol. Por. Uv. 312; cf. also *ib.,* 297):

SS 1:5 – dark: beautiful:: tents of Kedar: pavilions of Solomon.
SS 2:2 – lotus: brambles:: my companion: girls.
SS 2:3a – apple tree: trees of forest:: my lover: boys.

c) The exhibition of feelings (meyppāṭu) through the usage of similes is in the following proportion (Tol. Por. Meyp. 251-260 and Tol. Por. Uv. 295-296):

Feeling of delight: 27
Feeling of wonder: 12
Feeling of excellence: 7
Feeling of delight and wonder: 7
Feeling of excellence and delight: 1 (SS. 2:3ab)
Feeling of excellence and wonder: 1 (SS. 2:9ab)
Feeling of wonder and fear: 2 (SS. 6:4c, 10e)
Feeling of disgrace: 1 (SS. 1:7e).

Except the feeling of disgrace (SS. 1:7e), the others exhibit in combination with one another. In SS. 1:5ac, the sense of wonder seems to be combined with the sense of inferiority.

d) Among the subjective causes or motives that induced the poet for the selection and use of the similes, kātal, i.e. love or affection or appreciation pervades all through the poems of the SS, except in SS 1:5 "dark like the tents of Kedar" and in SS 1:7e, "like the one veiled" where the motive is depreciation, (Tol. Por. Uv. 279-280). Of the three objective causes, namely ciṟappu (superiority or excellence), nalaṉ (goodness or beauty), and vali (strength or heroism), the first two are found either singly or in combination more often than the third one.[9] The principles or foundations on which the similes are based are found in various combinations. Tolkāppiyam accepts that a comparison may be established under more than one aspect (Tol. Por. Uv. 277).

---

[9] Vali, i.e. strength or heroism is applied alone twice to the Lover (SS. 2:9ab; 2:17c-f) and twice to the power of Love (8:6c and d). It appears in combination with beauty four times (4:4a; 6:4c,10e; 7:5a) and refers to the Beloved; in combination with excellence four times and refers thrice to the Lover (2:3ab; 5:15d; 8:14bc) and once to the Beloved (7:8a).

B. Classification and Appreciation of the Metaphors

Metaphor results from simile by the work of an emotionally charged mind and mood reacting on the imagination. Simile is less emotionally charged and more intellectually formulated than the metaphor. We have already discussed this problem.[10] Here we shall speak of the concept of metaphor according to Tamil rhetoric.

1. *Concept of Metaphor (Uruvakam) according to Tamil Rhetoric*

We have dealt with this question very briefly above.[11] We shall however, make a few more clarifications on this point of metaphor.

Tolkāppiyam, as it was said already, does not treat of metaphor separately, but *seems* to include it in simile. There are two aphorisms in the chapter on simile which *seem* to indicate the direction in which metaphor developed from simile. Tol. Por. Uvam, cūt, 282 says: "If the basis of comparison is not pointed out, it can be known on having the objects put together in comparison." [12] This may be realized in two ways: (i) By using the comparative particle and thus explicating the simile, but without indicating the aspect of comparison through an adjunct (cf. supra on similes without adjuncts); (ii) By omitting altogether the comparative particle and juxtaposing the simile and the object. The latter case is technically called *uvamaittokai,* i.e. the comparative particle and aspect are understood: e.g. "your lotus-face", in which "lotus-face" is *uvamaittokai.* "Your lotus-like-face" would be explicit simile or *uvamaiviri.* Now Tol. Por. Uvam. 284 says also: "If the compared object is used as the object of comparison, it becomes an object of comparison without fault." [13] This aphorism is understood differently by Pērāciriyar and by Iḷampūraṇar. Pērāciriyar explains the aphorism as follows: If the object (e.g. face) becomes the simile for another object (e.g. lotus), it is also simile: e.g. "face-like-lotus", or "breast-like-bud", etc. According to Pērciriyar, this peculiar simile may also be made into an *uvamaittokai,* i.e. the comparative particle may be dropped and one phrase is formed: e.g. "face-lotus" (mukattāmarai), "breast-bud" (mulaimukai), etc.[14] Pērāciriyar makes an "apologetical" remark and says, "there are some who, mistakenly, take these similes (i.e. mukattāmarai, mulaikkōṅkam)

---

[10] See Part One, Chapter 3, pp. 74-76.

[11] See Part Two, Chapter 6, p. 134.

[12] Ilakkuvaṉār, S., *Tholkāppiyam*, 218; Pērāciriyar, *Tol. Por. Commentary*, 67-68.

[13] Ilakkuvaṉār, S., *Tholkāppiyam*, 219. In Tamil,
"Poruḷē uvamam ceytaṉar moḻiyiṉum
maruḷaṟu ciṟappiṉ aḵtu-uvamam ākum".
For commentary and discussion, see Pērāciriyar, *Comm.* 68-69.

[14] Pērāciriyar gives *mulaikkōṅkam* as example, although strictly speaking, it should be *mulaimukai.*

as metaphor.[15] By this he is referring to the opinion of Iḷampūraṇar, according to whom this contracted-inverted simile which amounts to the identification of the simile with the object, is metaphor.[16] Later grammarians define metaphor as the identification of the object and simile.[17] Here in our study we shall take the most simple definition of metaphor, i.e. where the object and simile are identified either explicitly or implicitly by the verb "to be" and where the comparative particle "like" is not used, we consider the expression as metaphor.[18] Accordingly, we can classify the metaphors in the SS according to the principles, causes and feelings (meyppāṭu) given by Tolkāppiyam for similes.

2. *Classification of the Metaphors in the SS*

There are some 33 cases of metaphors used in the SS. In the same way as with the similes, we may distinguish here too two types of metaphors: a) the metaphors with adjuncts, namely, metaphors qualified by adjectives, etc.; b) and the metaphors without such adjuncts:

a) *Metaphors with adjuncts*: They are found in SS. 1:6e, 13a, 14a; 2:1a, 1b; 4:12ab (three metaphors), 15 (two metaphors); 5:11a, 13c, 14a, 14c, 15a; 7:3a, 3c, 5c; 8:6e, 6f. In three other cases the use of metaphor is somewhat uncertain, namely, in SS. 4:6c, 6d; 8:12a. For all practical purposes, they may be considered metaphors and thus metaphors with adjuncts amount to 23.

b) *Metaphors without adjuncts*: They are ten: SS. 1:15c; 2:14a; 4:1c; 5;2d; 6:9a; 7:9b, 9c; 8:9a, 9c, 10a.

3. *Appreciation of the Metaphors in the SS.*

As regards the exhibition of feelings through the use of metaphors and the causes for their use, the following may be observed:

a) The exhibition of feelings is in the following proportion:

Feeling of delight: 15
Feeling of wonder: 5

---

[15] Ib., 69.

[16] For further discussion and clarifications, see Gnanasambandan, A. S., *Ilakkiyak Kalai*, 187-189; Id., *JTamS* 4 (1973), 1-12, esp. 7. Cīṉivācaṉ, R., *Caṅka Ilakkiyattil*, 81ff.

[17] Cīṉivācaṉ, R., *Caṅka Ilakkiyattil*, 82 quotes the definition of the author of Taṇṭiyalaṅkāram. He also gives, "āka, ākiya, eṉṉum, eṉappaṭum" as metaphorical particles: e.g. *muka-mākiya tāmarai* is an explicit metaphor; *mukattāmarai* is a metaphor without particle, i.e. *tokai uruvakam*, see p. 82. A subtle distinction *seems to be implied* between *mukam-pōṉṟa-tāmarai* (inverted simile) and *muka-mākiya-tāmarai* (metaphor with particle).

[18] See the second theory on metaphor, Part One, Chapter 3, pp. 75-76. For the list of metaphors, see "Table of Metaphors", pp. 76-77.

Feeling of excellence: 3 (4:15 - twice; 8:10a)
Feeling of excellence & delight: 2 (1:13a, 14a)
Feeling of excellence & wonder: 1 (5:11a)
Feeling of wonder & delight: 2 (7:5c, 9b)
Feeling of laughter or humour: 2 (8:9a, 9c)
Feeling of inferiority: 2 (2:1a, 1b)
Feeling of lament: 1 (1:6e)

b) Among the subjective causes or motives, *kātal* ranks first: 29 cases are induced by the motive of appreciation out of love. Of the other four cases of depreciation, two are out of modesty (SS 2:lab) and two are out of humour (SS 8:9ac). Of the objective causes, excellence or superiority (ciṟappu) and beauty or goodness (nalaṉ) are far more numerous than strength or heroism (vali). As for the similes, here too, the principles on which metaphors are based, are found in various combinations.

C. Classification and Appreciation of Individual Poems in the Song of Songs According to Tamil Akam Grammar and Categories

Before classifying the individual poems in the SS according to Tamil akam categories, a few preliminary remarks are in order: No one can pretend to find in the SS. *identical* categories as in the Tamil akam anthologies. But an effort to find *similar* categories and appreciate them according to one's own native literary types is not *per se* excluded. "Since love is the same anywhere, the reactions and forms of expression of love-lyrics everywhere will resemble each other." [19] The universality of love as an emotion and an experience is one of the main reasons why the attempt is worth the try! There is an indirect invitation from the part of the Hebrew love-songs, i.e. the lack of strict literary conventions or of fixed categories in Hebrew poetic tradition. Hence the Hebrew love-poems stand always open for being classified according to sentiments, which, fortunately, are the essential keys (uripporuḷ) for classifying also the Tamil poems.[20]

Our attempt to classify the individual poems in the SS, will folow the rules and directions laid down by Tolkāppiyam. Here are the most important and relevant ones:

---

[19] Gordis, R., *Song*, 32.
[20] See the discussion on the importance of uripporuḷ, i.e.the particular aspect of love, pp. 118-119.

1. *Those who may speak*

In Ceyyuḷ-iyal, Tolkāppiyar gives directions to poets as regards the people who may give expressions in love-affair. There are persons who may speak during the courtship, and some others who may speak during the period of wedded love, and some others in both.

a) Those who may speak in the period of courtship, are: (1) pārppāṉ (seer); (2) pāṅkaṉ (friend); (3) tōḻi (female companion); (4) cevili (foster-mother); (5) kiḻavaṉ (hero or lover); (6) kiḻatti (heroine or beloved); see Tol. Por. Cey. 501.[21] Wayfarers or onlookers (kaṇṭōr) may also give expression (Tol. Por. Cey. 505) during the secret love. They speak to or with the hero and the heroine.[22]

b) Those who may speak during the period of wedded love are; (1) pāṇaṉ (minstrel); (2) kūttaṉ (male dancer); (3) viṟali (female dancer); (4) parattai (concubine or "harlot"); (5) aṟivar (the learned); (6) kaṇṭōr (onlookers or wayfarers) along with those who have the right to speak in the period of secret love (Tol. Por. Cey. 502), namely those mentioned in Tol. Por. Cey. 501. It is to be observed that the onlookers may speak in both periods.

2. *Courtship or Kaḷavu without Tōḻi*

In general, according to the Tamil akam grammar, courtship or kaḷavu progresses with the help of the friend of the hero and of the companion of the heroine. But the case is not excluded in which kaḷavu or love-meeting takes place without any intermediary. According to Tol. Por. Kaḷaviyal 119, in love-meeting, the hero and the heroine may themselves become their messengers, i.e. to express their love

---

[21] For translation, see Ilakkuvaṉār, S., *Tholkāppiyam*, 242; for commentary see Pērāciriyar, *Tol. Per. Comm.* 399-401; Kuḻantai, P., *Tolkāppiyam-Poruḷakikāram*, Erode 1968, 56. The meaning of pārppāṉ is disputed among scholars. For our purpose, the dispute has no significance. *Pārppāṉ* is a respectable person in the society of those times (cf. Tol. Por. Ceyy. 502).

[22] This aphorism – Tol. Por. Ceyy. 505 – is interpreted in many ways: (i) Pērāciriyar and Pulavar Kuḻantai think that the onlookers (kaṇṭōr) may speak to the hero and the heroine when they elope together. They do not speak to them individually. As an afterthought to the aphorism, they include also the foster-mother to whom the onlookers may speak: see Pērāciriyar, *Tol. Por. Comm.* 403-404; Kuḻanti, P., *Tolkāppiyam*. 58-59. (ii) Iḷampūraṇar is of the opinion that the onlookers (or wayfarers) may speak to the mother, foster-mother, female companion of the beloved, and to the hero. He seems to overlook the phrase *kiḻattiyoṭu*, i.e. with the heroine! See his opinion cited in the commentary of Pērāciriyar, p. 403 in a note. (iii) Nacciṉārkkiṉiyar says that onlookers may speak to foster-mother, the hero and the heroine. He takes *oṇṭoṭi mātar* as singular referring exclusively to foster-mother. See his opinion cited in the commentary of Pērāciriyar in the same note on p. 403.

relationships, to fix the tryst, etc.[23] In such cases of love-meeting without the help of a female companion, the heroine is to fix the meeting place, as she knows the place suitable for such meeting (Tol. Por. Kaḷ. 120). Place of rendezvous may be fixed for night or for day. The night tryst may be fixed and may take place as follows: (i) In the initial stage of courtship, the meeting takes place in the premises of the house of the heroine at such distance as to hear the speech of the people in the house; (ii) In course of further stages of courtship, the meeting may take place inside the house: See Tol. Por. Kaḷ. 131.[24] The day-tryst takes place outside the house and its premises, but the way to the place should be known to the heroine (Tol. Por. Kaḷ. 132).

The SS and the love-affair spoken of in it, seem to fall under this category of courtship without the help of a female companion.

3. *Manifestations and Expressions of Emotions in Kaḷavu*

Tolkāppiyam gives the list of emotions that are manifest in the lovers during the courtship. The most important ones are:

a) In kaḷavu, the following features are natural and common to both the hero and the heroine (Tol. Por. Kaḷ. 100):

1) Ardent desire
2) Brooding
3) Pining
4) Consoling oneself
5) Breaking the limit of modesty
6) Suspecting others as if they knew their love-affairs[25]
7) Forgetfulness (forgetting games, etc.)
8) Swooning and confusion[26]

b) The above mentioned sentiments will find expression in the following ways (Tol. Por. Kaḷ 101):

1) Addressing: i.e. apostrophe and esp. personification[27] of usually irrational beings

---

[23] See Naccinārkkiniyar, *Tolkāppiyam - Poruḷatikāram - Kaḷaviyal*, 147. Kuḻanti, P., *Tolkāppiyam*, 130-131. It must be recalled that the previous aphorism Tol. Por. Kaḷ. 118 says, "the lady-love has not the habit of making expressions about her ardent love in the presence of her lover if we examine the love-code..." Exceptions may occur (?).

[24] Naccinārkkiniyar, *Tol. Por. Kaḷ.*, 154-155; Kuḻantai, P., *Tolkāppiyam*, 152-153.

[25] The phrase used here *nōkkuva ellām avaiyē pōṟal*, may also mean, "delusion of seeing actions of their partner everywhere"; see Ilakkuvaṉār, S., *Tholkāppiyam*, 176, who includes this possible understanding in his translation of the aphorism.

[26] Naccinārkkiniyar, *Tol. Por. Kaḷ.*, 13-15; Kuḻantai, P., *Tolkāppiyam*, 120-121.

[27] In Tamil grammar, it is called *ilakkaṇai*, see Gnanasambandan, A.S. *Ilakkiyak Kalai*, 191-193. The German term, "Anrede" translates the Tamil *muṉṉilaiyākkal* of Tolkāppiyam.

2) Requesting them to pay heed to one's words
3) Expressing great desire or admiration
4) Understanding the situation of the other partner
5) Explaining the reason for pining
6) Explaining one's own situation
7) Making assurances [28]

c) In Meyppāṭṭiyal, Tolkāppiyar enumerates the exhibitions of feelings of the heroine in love-making (Tol. Por. Meyp. 260-272). Though most of them affect or refer to the heroine, a few of them are applicable also to the hero: e.g. indulging in praises (Pārāṭṭu eṭuttal: Tol. Por. Mey. 264), and having joy on seeing (Kaṇṭa vaḻi uvattal: Tol. Por. Mey. 265) are applicable to both.[29]

d) Another occasion where both the lover and the beloved may express their sentiments, is when they think of the past experience and narrate, i.e. flash-back narration (Tol. Por. Akat. 43). According to Tol. Por. Akat. 44, such expressions also form the theme of literature on aspects of love.[30]

4. *When may the Hero - the Lover speak?*

It would be too long to enumerate and comment on all the occasions in which the lover may, according to Tolkāppiyam, give expression to his sentiments. Those occasions which refer to Kaṟpiyal may be left out here.[31] Among the occasions of speech during the courtship, those which concern the speech of hero to the female companion, need not be taken into consideration.[32] Here below is the enumeration of occasions in kaḷavu, when the hero may speak either to himself or to the beloved:

---

[28] Naccinārkkiniyar, *Tol. Por. Kaḷ.*, 15ff and Kuḻantai, P., *Tolkāppiyam*, 117-119, take this aphorism as referring only to the hero's expressions. As S. Ilakkuvanār says, "but in the original text there is nothing to suggest such views. So they are to be considered as themes common to both the lover and the loved", *Tholkāppiyam*, 177, foot-note. The present writer is inclined to agree with S. Ilakkuvanār, except for the last theme, i.e. making assurances, for which examples for heroine are not found in the *existing* anthology poems!

[29] Kuḻantai, P., *Tolkāppiyam*, 407, 410.

[30] Naccinārkkiniyar, *Tolkāppiyam - Poruḷatikāram - Akattiṇaiyiyal*, 101 on cūt. 43-44; Kuḻantai, P., *Tolkāppiyam*, 269-271. According to these commentators, these two aphorisms refer to separation, i.e. pālai. The second rule, according to them, refers especially to the heroine and her companion. But once again, the original text does not give any indication about pālaittiṇai. Hence these may be applied to all situations. See the translation in Ilakkuvanār, S., *Tholkāppiyam*, 160, which is general.

[31] In the SS, except perhaps 3:6-11, there is no poem belonging to Kaṟpiyal.

[32] In the SS, there is no poem in which the lover speaks to any female companion of the beloved.

a) In Tol. Por. Akat. 41, six occasions, mostly in relation to elopement, are given, in which the hero may speak. Of these four are to be noted:

1) When the parents are not favourable to the love-affair
2) When the season or opportunities are not favourable
3) When the hero and the heroine have to pass through the desert
4) When he decides to elope with her [33]

b) Tol. Por. Kaḷ 102, enumerates altogether 24 actions or occasions during which or in which the lover may speak. Of these, the following are pertinent to our study:

1) Making physical touches
2) Making caresses
3) Having the chance embracing [34]
4) Expressing the playful difficulties created by the heroine
5) Having the meeting
6) Having the enjoyment
7) Rejoicing over the enjoyment
8) Wailing on separation [35]

c) There are five more occasions, enumerated in Tol. Por. Kaḷ 103, in which the lover may speak. Of these the following two are worth mentioning:

1) While pining on account of the intense love
2) When he gets occasion to meet and be with his beloved.[36]

5. *When may the Heroine — the Beloved speak?*

As may be expected, Tolkāppiyam devotes more aphorisms for the occasions of the heroine's expressions than for those of the hero. Besides

---

[33] Translation in Ilakkuvaṉār, S., *Tholkāppiyam*, 158-159; commentary, in Nacciṉārkkiṉiyar, *Tol. Por. Akat.*, 86; Kuḻanti, P., *Tolkāppiyam*, 250-253 with examples.

[34] This is according to S. Ilakkuvaṉār. This phrase (iṭam peṟṟut-taḻāal) is understood differently by Nacciṉārkkiṉiyar and P. Kuḻantai.

[35] Translation, Ilakkuvaṉār, S., *Tholkāppiyam*, 177-178. Commentary, Nacciṉārkkiṉiyar, *Tol. Por. Kaḷ.*, 18ff; Kuḻantai, P., *Tolkāppiyam*, 110, 114-117, 121-123. "Rejoicing over enjoyment" and "wailing on separation" are applicable to both the lover and the beloved; cf. Kuḻantai, P., *Tolkāppiyam*, 122.

[36] Ilakkuvaṉār, S., *Tholkāppiyam*, 178; Nacciṉārkkiṉiyar, *Tol. Por. Kaḷ.*,. 39ff; Kuḻantai, P., *Tolkāppiyam*, 111, 160-163.

the occsions of speech common to the hero and the heroine as mentioned above, Tol. Por. Kaḷ. 107-113, 123 and Tol. Por. Poruḷiyal 210 enumerate the occasions in which the heroine may speak. Eliminating those occasions which do not concern us here for our study, we may point out the following ones as relevant:[37]

a) Tol. Por. Kaḷ. 107, mentions ten occasions. The following ones are pertinent:

1) When she fails to meet him at both day and night trysts
2) At the act of welcoming him as a guest
3) At the act of shedding the annoying modesty
4) At the act of refusing the marriage other than the one she expected.

b) Tol. Por. Kaḷ. 108-110, mention occasions in which the beloved may speak without offending her feminine modestry(nāṇ) and simplicity or feigned ignorance(maṭaṉ): e.g. in the union through the female companion.

c) In Tol. Por. Kaḷ 111 are enumerated 36 occasions of heroine's expressions, among which are important:

1) Being hidden and seeing him, i.e. seeing him without being noticed
2) When she bemoans his departure
3) In her over-joy on having him
4) When trying to prevent the marriage with somebody else
5) When the marriage with her lover is approaching
6) When the secret love is being known
7) When she is closely guarded by her relatives
8) To describe his nature and great qualities when occasion needs it
9) When the feeling of love or passion abounds
10) When his caresses increase and multiply

d) Tol. Por. Kaḷ. 112 gives the following:

1) At the time of his separation, having the marriage postponed: e.g. by narrating her dreams about him, etc.
2) At his unexpected arrival and meeting with her family members

[37] For complete translation, enumeration, etc. see Ilakkuvaṉār, S., *Tholkāppiyam,* 179-182, 186, 205. Commentary, etc. see Nacciṉārkkiṉiyar, *Tol. Por. Kaḷaviyal,* 47-94, 149-150, 297-300.

e) According to Tol. Por. Kaḷ. 113, the following are also themes on love:

1) If the lady love goes to the place where her lover is
2) If she says that she will go to him on her own decision

f) Tol. Por. Kaḷ. 123: The lady love tells her companion about her secret love-affair so that she may in turn reveal it to the parents.

g) Tol. Por. Poruḷiyal 210 speaks of occasions in which both the beloved and her companion may speak. There are eight such occasions of which seven are applicable to both and one exclusively to the female companion:[38] e.g. when some one other than the lover is trying to demand the beloved in marriage (notumalar varaivu), either the lady love or the girl friend may speak out to prevent it. But it is only the female companion who tells the lover to come either at night or in the day to meet the girl.

6. *Classification and Appreciation of the Individual Poems*

In classifying the individual poems in the SS, according to Tamil categories, we shall follow the directions of the above rules of Tolkāppiyam, and use a combined method of Tamil commentators for the akam anthologies, i.e. we shall give the indication of the speaker or speakers, the theme or love aspect (tiṇai), poetic situation or Sitz im Leben (tuṟai), and feeling (meyppāṭu) of the poem.[39] We shall cite rules of Tolkāpiyam, pertaining to the situation and then a few parallel or analogous poems, ideas, situations, etc. from Tamil anthologies, and point out some differences. If needed, several possibilities are suggested, e.g. SS 3:1-5.

Poem 1 – SS 1:2-4:

What she said:

Tiṇai: Kuṟiñci

Tuṟai: Expressing great desire and praise for the lover by way of "direct-indirect speech" (muṉṉilaip – puṟamoḻi).

Tol. Por. Kaḷ. 101: Naṉṉayam uraittal

Tol. Por. Kaḷ. 111: When the feeling of passion abounds (kāmam ciṟappiṉum).

[38] See Kuḻantai, P., *Tolkāppiyam*, 207 for this specification.

[39] Commentators on Tamil akam anthologies do not follow the same method of indications of speaker, tiṇai, tuṟai, etc. Hence we shall adopt the best from every commentator. "He" refers to the hero and "she" to the heroine.

Feeling: Delight (uvakai)

v.2: kisses and caresses: comp. Kuṟ. 299, 399, 401; Aiṅ. 361 (see appendix).

v.3: perfumes: Kuṟ. 198 reference to the sandal paste of the lover. lover's name: cf. Aiṅ. 367 – the female companion says that the girl's life is mingled with the name of her lover.
"maidens love you": comp. Naṟ. 25 – *taṇṭāk-kāṭci.*

v.4: suggestion of elopement: cf. Kuṟ. 297, 343.
royal fiction: comp. Ak. 32.

In Tamil akam poems the female companion counsels elopement, whereas in SS, the beloved herself *seems* to suggest it.

Poem 2 – SS 1:5-6:

What she said to Jerusalem girls:

Tiṇai: Kuṟiñci

Tuṟai: Explaining the reason for pining.
Tol. Por. Kaḷ. 100: Suspecting others as if they knew their love-affair.
Tol. Por. Kaḷ 101: Melivu viḷakkuṟuttal
Tol. Por Kaḷ. 111: When the secret love is being known (Kaḷavu aṟivuṟiṉum)

Feeling: Wonder (maruṭkai) out of change, and excellence (perumitam).

v.5: dark complexion and beauty: Kuṟ. 27; Aiṅ. 146.
staring of the girls: comp. Naṟ. 149 for similar situation.[40]

v.6: watching the vineyard: cf. Naṟ. 213, 351 – similar situation.
anger of the brothers: cf. Kuṟ. 123.

In Tamil poems, watching the millet field is spoken of, whereas in SS, watching the vineyard is mentioned.

Poem 3 – SS 1:7-8:

What she asked and what he replied:

Tiṇai: Kuṟiñci in mullai, i.e. tiṇaimayakkam(?).

---

[40] Nacciṉārkkiṉiyar says that the beloved is not afraid of women's gossip and she boldly reveals her secret love: *Tol. Por. Akat.*, 99 — commentary and example of this poem for Tol. Por. Akat. 42. Iḷampūraṇar cites this poem and says that the beloved is agreed to elope with the lover. See the citation and reference in the commentary (Tamil) on Naṟṟiṇai ad locum on Naṟ. 149. Both these situations fit SS 1:5-6.

Tuṟai: Fixing the rendezvous – Kuṟiyiṭam peyarttal.

Tol. Por. Kal. 119: Courtship without go-betweens.

Tol. Por. Kaḷ. 132: Day-tryst outside the house or its premises – here in pasture land.

Tol. Por. Kaḷ. 102: has an "et cetera" (piṟavum) by which are implied such cases as enquiring the way, the profession, etc.[41]

Feeling: Disgrace (iḷivaral) out of weakness.

v.7: the beloved asks for a day-tryst: comp. Naṟ. 213 (by the hero)

v.8: the lover gives directions how and where to meet him: comp. Naṟ. 102. For a shepherd boy asking for the rendezvous and the girl indicating it, see Mullaikkali, 8, esp. 10, 16.

Difference: In Tamil, it is the boy who always asks for the rendezvous, whereas in SS 1:7 it is the girl who asks for it!

Poem 4 – SS 1:9-14:

What he said and what she replied:

Tiṇai: Kuṟiñci

Tuṟai: Expressing mutual desire and admiration.

Tol. Por. Kaḷ. 101: Naṉṉayam uraittal or Nalam pārāṭṭal

Tol. Por. Kaḷ 102: Rejoicing over union (peṟṟavaḻi makiḻcci)

Tol. Por. Kaḷ. 111: In her over-joy on having him (peṟṟavaḻi malital)

Feeling: Delight

v.9: the mare amidst cavalry: its majestic and attractive look: comp. Kuṟ. 286; Ak. 130.

v.11: ornaments – gifts as bride-price: comp. Aiṅ. 185, 193; Ak. 280.

vv.12-14: the beloved describes the union in "direct-indirect speech" (muṉṉilaip – puṟamoḻi). For similar idea of sleeping on the breasts of the beloved, comp. Ak. 44, 69, etc.

Poem 5 – SS 1:15-17:

What he said and what she replied:

Tiṇai: Kuṟiñci

Tuṟai Expressing mutual admiration and joy.
Rules as above for SS 1:9-14.

---

[41] Nacciṉārkkiṉiyar, *Tol. Por. Kaḷ.*, 31ff; Kuḻantai, P., *Tolkāppiyam*, 132.

Feeling: Delight and excellence (perumitam).

v.17: description of the watch-hut: comp. Naṟ. 194 (see appendix), 276, 351; Ak. 308 (see appendix). Interesting to note that in SS, cedars and cypresses are mentioned and they are costly wood – while in Naṟ. 351, the sandal wood is mentioned – a costly wood – and the hide of tiger.

Poem 6 – SS 2:1-3:

What she said, what he replied and what she responded:

Tiṇai: Kuṟiñci

Tuṟai: Expressing mutual admiration in "direct-indirect speech".
Rules as above for SS 1:9-14.

Feeling: Delight

vv.1-2: beloved compared to flower: comp. Kuṟ. 159, 226; Ak. 290.

v.3: shade and sweetness of the lover: comp. Naṟ. 1, 172; Kuṟ. 288.

Poem 7 – SS 2:4-7:

What she said to Jerusalem girls:

Tiṇai: Kuṟiñci

Tuṟai: Expressing extreme passion (kāmam mikka kaḻipaṭar kiḷavi).
Tol. Por. Kaḷ. 100: Swooning and confusion (mayakkam)
Tol. Por. Kaḷ. 111: When passion abounds (kāmam ciṟappiṉ).

Feeling: Lament and anxiety because of possible loss (Tol. Por. Meyp. 253).

v.4: amorous look: comp. Ak. 48, esp. 180; mutual look: Ak. 130.

v.5: love-sickness: comp. Ak. 22, 52, 128.

v.6: love-embrace: Naṟ. 28, 199; Kuṟ. 318, 368; Ak. 32, 58 (see appendix); Kuṟiñcikkali: 18.

v.7: adjuring not to disturb the union: cf. Kuṟ. 107, 157.[42]
Difference: Raisin cakes and apples as strengthening materials for love sickness have no parallel or anology in Tamil poems.

---

[42] For Kuṟ. 157, the introductory colophon says that the heroine was disturbed from the love-embrace by the occurrence of menses. But in the poem, there is no indication thereof whatever.

Poem 8 – SS 2:8-13:

What she said about him:

Tiṇai: Kuṟiñci in mullai – Tiṇaimayakkam
Tuṟai: Explaining one's own situation.

Tol. Por. Kaḷ. 101: Tannilai uraittal

Tol. Por. Kaḷ. 111: Seeing him without being seen (maṟaintu avaṉ kāṇṭal) and when she is closely guarded by her relatives.

Tol. Por. Akat. 41: When he decides to elope with her (oṉṟiya tōḻiyoṭu valippiṉum).

Feeling: Excellence (perumitam) and delight.

v.8: obstacles on the way: comp. Naṟ. 51, 104; Ak. 18, 122.
v.9: waiting for the lover: comp. Ak. 58 (see appendix).
vv-11-13: arrival of spring: the season of union or reunion of lovers: comp. Naṟ. 69, 224 (appendix), 243; Kuṟ. 220, 254 – by heroine; Naṟ. 242; Aiṅ. 420, 484, 494 – by hero.

The trees and plants in blossom, and the birds are from the geographical and climatic conditions of both groups of love poems.

Poem 9 – SS 2:14:

What he said to her:

Tiṇai: Pālai in kuṟiñci
Tuṟai: (i) Elopement: expressing great desire.

Tol. Por. Akat. 15: elopement belongs to kuṟiñci and also to pālai (since separation from the family).

Tol. Por. Akat. 41: When they have to pass through the desert.(oṉṟāc-curattum)

(ii) Day-tryst: expressing great desire and admiration.

Tol. Por. Kaḷ 101: Naṉṉayam uraittal

Tol. Por. Kaḷ. 132: Day-tryst outside the premises of the house, e.g. amidst rocks and clefts, as here.[43]

Feeling; Delight (uvakai).

Sweetness of the voice: comp. Naṟ. 209; Aiṅ. 185; Ak. 3, 9, 54, 109.

[43] See Kuḻantai, P., *Tolkāppiyam*, 152 for this precision.

Poem 10 – SS 2:15:

What she said:

Tiṇai: Kuṟiñci

Tuṟai: Revealing the secret love at the occasion of marriage-proposal from outsiders (aṟattoṭu niṉṟatu).

Tol. Por. Kaḷ. 111: When trying to prevent the marriage with someone else (vēṟṟu varaivu variṉ atu māṟṟutaṟ-kaṇṇum)

Tol. Por. Kaḷ. 112: When the marriage is being delayed.

Tol. Por. Poruḷ 210: Expressing the desire for marriage and revealing the secret love at the arrival of outsiders for marriage.[44]

Feeling: Lament at the thought of possible loss.

Similar situation described in Tamil poems: comp. Kuṟ. 171; Ak. 107, esp. by way of uḷḷuṟai uvamam.

The listeners of SS 2:15 are not known from the poem. It could be either the lover and his friends, or even the companions of the beloved. In Tamil poems, it is always the female companion to whom the beloved reveals (Tol. Por. Kaḷ. 112).

Poem 11 – SS 2:16-17:

What she said to him:

Tiṇai: Kuṟiñci

Tuṟai: Rejoicing over enjoyment.

Tol. Por. Kaḷ. 111: On having him, in her overjoy (peṟṟavaḻi malitam).

Feeling: Delight

Poem 12 – SS 3:1-5:

What she said (to Jerusalem girls?)

Tiṇai: Kuṟiñci

Tuṟai: (i) If the poem is taken as a dream narrative, it is "pining during the postponement of the marriage by narrating dreams about him," i.e. Kaṉavu nalivuraittal: Tol. Por. Kaḷ. 112.

---

[44] Ib., 207.

(ii) If the poem is taken as a narrative of a past fact of the girl's audacious action, it falls under "the girl goes to the place where her lover is," i.e. kāmak – kiḻavaṉ uḷvaḻip – paṭutal: Tol. Por. Kaḷ. 113.

Feeling: Lament and delight one after the other.

(i) If the poem is taken as a dream, comp. Kuṟ. 30 (appendix)

(ii) If it is taken as a fact:

v.1: sleeplessness: comp. Kuṟ. 6, 28, 243; Aiṅ. 142.

v.2: searching: comp. Kuṟ. 31 (appendix), esp. 322.

v.3: asking others: comp. Kuṟ. 75 (appendix).

Poem 13 – SS 3:6-11:

What the onlookers said:

Tiṇai: Mullai

Tuṟai: Maṉai maruṭci

Tol. Por. Ceyyuḷ. 502 holds that the onlookers may speak in kaṟpiyal also.[45]

Feeling: Wonder (maruṭkai) and admiration. Tol. Por. Meyp. 255 gives four sources of wonder: newness (putumai), bigness (perumai), smallness (ciṟumai) and change (ākkam). Of these four, the first two are to be found in this poem.

In Tamil poems, (i) the maṉai maruṭci, i.e. wondering at the family life of the lovers (or as here the marriage), is spoken either by the foster-mother or by the female companion, whereas here, the onlookers speak.[46]

(ii) the wedding procession as such is nowhere described. Hence poems of parallel descriptions are not available.

Poem 14 – SS 4:1-7:

What he said to her:

Tiṇai: Kuṟiñci

Tuṟai: In praise of her beauty.

Tol. Por. Kaḷ. 101: Tannilai uraittal and nalam pārāṭṭal.

Feeling: Delight and wonder

---

[45] Pērāciriyar, *Tol. Por. Ceyy.*, 401.

[46] We could suppose theoretically that v. 6 is spoken by one person, e.g. foster-mother or female companion, and vv. 7-10d is given as response. Both of them call to the Jerusalem girls to look in vv. 10e-11.

v.1: eyes: comp. Naṟ. 82 (appendix), 101, 160, 185; Kuṟ. 62, 70, 71 (appendix), 101 (appendix); Ak. 62, 140.

hair: comp. Kuṟ. 286.

v.2: teeth: comp. Naṟ. 198; Aiṅ. 380; Ak. 21,27, etc.

v.3: mouth: comp. Aiṅ. 255 (appendix); Ak. 3, 27, 29, 335.

vv.5,7: breasts and the whole body: comp. Kuṟ. 116, 132, 143, 147; Aiṅ. 106, 174, 176, 185 (appendix); Ak. 212, 390.

For a more systematic description of the beloved in Tamil poems, see Kuṟiñcikkali: 20. In Tamil poems, the neck and cheeks are not described.

Poem 15 – SS 4:8-11:

What he said to her:

Tiṇai: Kuṟiñci

Tuṟai: Ardent desire, admiration and invitation.

Tol. Por. Akat. 41: When he decides to elope with her.

Tol. Por. Kaḷ. 101: Tannilai uraittal.

Tol. Por. Kaḷ. 103: While pining on account of intense love (parivuṟṟu meliyiṉum).

Feeling: Delignt

V.8: difficulties for the meeting: comp. Naṟ. 11, 36, 98; Ak. 162.
invitation to come: comp. Naṟ. 82 (appendix); Kuṟ. 379.

v.9: ravishing of the heart: comp. Naṟ. 95, 160, 284; Kuṟ. 40, 129, 132 (appendix), 184, 280; Aiṅ. 171, 172, 191; Ak. 73, 141, 390.

v.10: caresses and embrace: comp. Kuṟ. 286; Ak. 389.

v.11: lips: cf. Kuṟ. 14, 206, 267; Ak. 335.

vv.10-11: perfumes: comp. Naṟ. 140.

For the description of the beloved's mouth and lips, see esp. Pālaikkali 3:13-14.

Poem 16 – SS 4:12-5-1:

What he said, what she replied and what he responded:

Tiṇai: Kuṟiñci

Tuṟai: Day-tryst and mutual praise and desire.

Rules as above for SS 2:1-3.

Tol. Por. Kaḷ. 101: muṉṉilaiyākkal (apostrophe and personification).

Feeling: Wonder and delight.

vv.12-15: Nalam pārāṭṭal, i.e. expressing praise and desire.
v.13: sweetness of the beloved: comp. Naṟ. 3
v.14: perfumes and spices: cf. Kuṟ. 286.
v.16: apostrophe of the winds and "direct-indirect speech" (muṉṉulaip – puṟamoḻi) to the lover.
joy of expectation: comp. Ak. 58 (appendix).
indication of day-tryst: comp. Ak. 360.
5:1: having the enjoyment – peṟṟavaḻi makiḻcci (Tol. Por. Kaḷ. 102).

Poem 17 – SS 5:2-6:3:

What she said:

Tiṇai: Kuṟiñci

Tuṟai: Dream-narrative: kaṉavu nalivuraittal.
Tol. Por Kaḷ 112: While the marriage is being delayed, pining is expressed by narrating dreams about him.

Feeling: Lament out of loss (iḻavu) and suffering (acaivu): Tol. Por. Meyp. 253.

v.2: dream: comp. Naṟ. 87; Kuṟ. 30 (appendix); Aiṅ. 234.
arrival of the lover, drenched in dew: comp. Naṟ. 182; Aiṅ. 206 (appendix); Ak. 102 (appendix), 272.
v.4: lover trying to open the door: comp. Kuṟ. 244, 321.
v.6: following the lover: comp. Naṟ. 56, 64, 107, 153; Kuṟ. 153, 334, 340; Aiṅ. 295, 334; Ak. 128.
v.7: watchmen: comp. Naṟ. 98, 132, 255; Kuṟ. 375; Ak. 122, 162.
v.8b: love-sickness: cf. Ak. 22, etc.
messenger-theme: cf. Naṟ. 54.
vv.9-16: description of lover's nature, etc. when occasion demands (iyaṟpaṭa moḻital: Tol Por. Kal. 111): comp. Kuṟ. 299; Ak. 82.
6:2-3: cf. Kuṟ. 130.

Poem 18 – SS 6:4-7:

What he said to her:

Tiṇai: Kuṟiñci

Tuṟai: Expressing praise and desire
Tol. Por. Kaḷ. 101: Naṉṉayam uraittal or Nalam pārāṭṭal.

Feeling: Delight and wonder.

v.4: beautiful like cities: comp. Naṟ. 39.
awesome: comp. Naṟ. 146, 155.

v.5: eyes: comp. Naṟ. 8, 16, 75, 77, 82 (appendix).

v.6: teeth: comp. Naṟ. 9, 179.
In Tamil poems, cheeks are not described.

Poem 19 – SS 6:8-10:

What he said:

Tiṇai: Kuṟiñci

Tuṟai: Expressing praise and admiration
Tol. Por. Kaḷ. 101: Naṉṉayam uraittal and Neñcoṭu pulattal.

Feeling: Wonder and excellence (perumitam).

v.9: uniqueness of the beloved: comp. Naṟ. 8; Kuṟ. 337; Aiṅ. 257; Ak. 109.

v.10: like the dawn: comp. Naṟ. 356.
like the moon: comp. Naṟ. 62.
awesome: comp. Naṟ. 9; also Kuṟiñcikkali: 20.

The listener of this poem is not known. It is most likely his own heart. Hence we have said: neñcoṭu pulattal, i.e. speaking to his heart.

Poem 20 – SS 6:11-12:

What he said:

Tiṇai: Kuṟiñci

Tuṟai: Narrating his past experience with the beloved.
Tol. Por. Akat. 43: Thinking of what happened: flash-back (nikaḻntatu niṉaittal).
Tol. Por. Kaḷ. 132: Day-tryst outside the premises of the house.
Tol. Por. Kaḷ. 102: Expressing the playful difficulties created by the heroine (iṭaiyūṟu kiḷattal). One such difficulty is created when the beloved comes behind the lover and blindfolds him.[47]

---

[47] For our enigmatic poem, SS 6:11-12, this life situation seems to fit very well. The day-tryst was fixed in the walnut grove. The lover arrives there. The beloved who was waiting for him, comes unnoticed from behind and blindfolds him. He is surprised and thrilled. This he narrates by way of flash-back. Such situation belongs to the period of courtship also: see Naccinārkkiṉiyar, on Tol. Por. Kaḷ. 102 in *Tol. Por. Kal.*, 20.

Feeling: Delight.

For a similar situation: comp. Aiṅk. 293.[48]

Poem 21 – SS 7:1-6:

What the onlookers said, what she replied and what they responded:

Tiṇai: Kuṟiñci

Tuṟai: In praise of her – Nalam pārāttal.

> Tol. Por. Akat. 40 enumerates the occasions when the onlookers may speak in kaḷavu to the lover and the beloved. Tol. Por. Ceyy. 505-507 are also in agreement. But it should be emphasized that the onlookers in Tamil akam poems do not describe or admire the beauty of the beloved so much *in detail* as in SS 7:1-6, although in their sympathy and appreciation of the couples, they may refer to the beauty of the beloved and the parts of her body *per transennam*.

Feeling: Wonder and delight.

Compare Naṟ. 133, in which the beloved cites the words of other women who described her upper arms, eyes, vulva and locks of hair. In Naṟ. 324 (see appendix) the onlookers dscribe the beloved's body, hair and feet. Compare also Kuṟ. 165; Ak. 131; Kuṟiñcikkali 19 – these are, however, descriptions by the lover.

v.1cd: There is a reference to a female dancer between two camps and this dancer is used by the beloved as a simile to herself. If this refers to woman-dancer or women dancers who go along with armies and entertain the warriors in the camps, this has also a cultural correspondence in ancient Tamil society: see Puṟam. 11, 12, 29, 69, which mention the dance of women (viṟaliyar) in camps. If the Shulamite were to be taken as one such dancer, it would be interesting to compare this description in SS 7:2-6 with Porunaṟṟuppaṭai lines 155ff where the description of a viṟali, i.e. female dancer is given.[49]

In Tamil akam poems, neither the neck nor the nose is described.

---

[48] See the explanation and application of this rule to the situation, in *Aiṅkuṟunūṟu:* Mūlamum Paḻaiyavuraiyum, 131. Iḷampūraṇar takes this poem as referring to courtship whereas Nacciṉārkkiṉiyar takes it as referring to wedded love: see ib.

[49] For different translations, and interpretations of 7:1cd see Pope, M. H., *Song*, 601-604.

Poem 22 – SS 7:7-10:

What he said to her:

Tiṇai: Kuṟiñci

Tuṟai: Making caresses and rejoicing over enjoyment.

Tol. Por. Kaḷ. 102: Mey toṭṭup-payiṟal, poy-pārāṭṭal and peṟṟavaḻi makiḻcci.

Feeling: Wonder and delight.

v.8: breasts: comp. Kuṟ. 62,71 (appendix), 101 (appendix); Ak. 32.

v.9: caressing – almost coition: comp. Ak. 58, 320, 330.

v.10: sweetness and honey of the mouth: comp. Kuṟ. 14, 206, 286; esp. Pālaikkali 3.

Poem 23 – SS 7:11-14:

What she said to him:

Tiṇai: Kuṟiñci

Tuṟai: Day-tryst – Pakaṟkuṟi nērtal.

Tol. Por. Kaḷ. 120: Beloved can fix the rendezvous.

Tol. Por. Kaḷ. 131: The night tryst may take place outside the house but in the vicinity.

Tol. Por. Kaḷ. 132: The day-tryst may take place in the cultivated country side, the way to which is known to her.

Feeling: Delight

vv.12-13: fixing the tryst: comp. Naṟ. 102, 156, 285, 323; Kuṟ. 198; Aiṅ. 290 (appendix); Ak. 30, 80, 92, 240.

v.14: enjoying together in the place of rendezvous: comp. Naṟ. 259.

Poem 24 – SS 8:1-5c:

What she said to herself – a wishful thinking.

Tiṇai: Kuṟiñci

Tuṟai: Expressing extreme passion (kāmam mikka kaḻipaṭar kiḷavi).

Tol. Por. Kaḷ. 100: Breaking the limit of modesty (nāṇu varai iṟattal)

Tol. Por. Kaḷ. 111: When passion abounds.

Tol. Por. Meyyp. 264: Indulging in speeches devoid of feigned ignorance.

Feeling: Lament out of loss: Tol. Por. Meyp. 253.

v.2: bringing the lover inside the house as guest: comp. Naṟ. 215, 254, 276; Ak. 340, 350.[50]

The whole poem is a speech in phantasy. The girl addresses her lover and expresses her wishful thinking. Then she imagines the embrace of the lover, and she adjures the Jerusalem girls not to disturb her – the girls who comment about lovers' embrace – all in phantasy!

Poem: 25 – SS 8:5d-7:

What she said to him:

Tiṇai: Kuṟiñci

Tuṟai: Expressing great desire or love.

Tol. Por. Kaḷ. 100: Ardent desire (orutalai vēṭkai)

Tol. Por. Kaḷ. 101: Expressing it (Naṉṉayam uraittal)

Tol. Por. Kaḷ. 112: When the marriage is delayed (varaiviṭai vaitta kālattu)

Feeling: Excellence (perumitam).

v.5d-f: under the apple tree: comp. Naṟ. 96, 172, 187, 227; Kuṟ. 266, 299.

v.6: power of love: cf. Naṟ. 166 (appendix), 369; Kuṟ. 3 (appendix), 95, 305; Aiṅ. 184

v.7: riches will not buy love or equal it: Naṟ. 234; Kuṟ. 267; Aiṅ. 147.

Poem 26 – SS 8:8-10:

What they said and what she replied:

Tiṇai: Kuṟiñci

Tuṟai: Saying that she is too young and replying that she is of age (maṭamai kūṟiyatum paruvam eytiyamai kūṟiyatum).

Tol. Por. Kaḷ. 114: Saying that the heroine is not of age.

Tol. Por. Kaḷ. 101: Tannilai uraittal, i.e. explaining one's situation.

Feeling: Excellence (perumitam).

Some questions to be clarified:

a) who are the speakers of vv.8-9?

Possibilities: 1) the brothers of the beloved;

2) the elder sisters of the beloved;

---

[50] Cf. "Guest-fiction" above, Chapter 7, p. 181.

3) some others who address the beloved as "our sister." [51]

"The common view has been that the speakers are the angry brothers of 1:6." [52]

According to Tol. Por. Kaḷ. 137, the father or the brothers of the beloved do not speak directly, but their words may be cited by the beloved or the female companion.[53] It is the female companion who says in Tamil tradition, that the beloved is not yet of age for love-making: Tol. Por. Kaḷ. 114. see Naṟ. 379.

b) Who is the speaker of v.10?

Certainly it is the sister of the speakers of vv.8-9, i.e. the beloved. According to Tamil akam grammar, such protest that the beloved is of age, comes from the lover and not from the beloved herself: e.g. Aiṅk. 256, or others: e.g. Ak. 7 – foster-mother; cf. Ak. 315 by the mother: See Kuṟ. 337 (appendix) by the lover. However, one may apply Tol. Por. Kaḷ. 101 and take v.10 as the explanation of her own situation by the beloved – as tannilai uraittal.

Poem 27 – SS 8:11-12:

What he said:

Tiṇai: Kuṟiñci

Tuṟai: Expressing admiration and praise.
Tol. Por. Kaḷ. 101: Naṉṉayam uraittal and Muṉṉilaiyākkal.

Feeling: Excellence (perumitam).

v.12: uniqueness of the "vineyard", i.e. the beloved: comp. Naṟ. 16,52; Kuṟ. 267, 280, 300.
– Solomon is addressed by apostrophe (Anrede).

Poem 28 – SS 8:13-14:

What he said to her and what she said to him:

Tiṇai: Kuṟiñci

---

[51] For discussion. see Pope, M. H., *Song*, 678-683.

[52] Ib., 681.

[53] If the poem were to be adapted to Tamil akam grammar, then vv. 8-9 could be the words of the female companion or companions. Or we could even take vv. 8-9 as a citation of the words of her brothers by the beloved.

Tu̱rai: Day-tryst – Pakar̠kur̠i

Tol. Por. Kaḷ. 132: Day-tryst in a garden or a grove.

Tol. Por. Poruḷ. 212: The hero may come to the day-tryst together with his servants (iḷaiñar – servants). This may allow the presence of "friends" in v.13.

Feeling: Lament (because of her not talking): Tol. Por. Meyp. 253.

v.13: request to talk: comp. Nar̠. 204.

v.14: the beloved tells him to go away – to escape!

Conclusion

As may be seen from what has been said above, most of the individual poems in the collection of the Hebrew love lyrics, i.e. the Song of Songs, can be adapted and classified according to the akam situations and categories prescribed by the rules and directions of Tolkāppiyam. The few exceptions, (e.g. SS 2:7; 3:6-11; 7:1-6; 8:8-10) we have noted are also important in that they show the specificity and originality of the Hebrew culture in which these poems were composed and which they reflect.

GENERAL CONCLUSION

European scholars, who were interested in Dravidology and Tamilology, have expressed the wish that enthusiastic, skilled and devoted interpreters of the akam poetry of two milleniums ago, come forward to convey "something of its beauty and riches in all the main world languages."[1] Xavier S. Thani Nayagam, who was foremost among the Tamil enthusiasts to work in order to meet this need, insisted that "Tamil research should have a twofold end in view, one to vitalise the studies at home, another to create interest and further research abroad."[2] The present study has tried to convey "something of the beauty and riches" of Tamil akam poetry in special reference to the SS – the Hebrew love poetry par excellence – and thus to create interest and further research particularly among biblical scholars. A considerable amount of materials has been collected, presented, analysed and compared in this study.

The separate presentation of both the corpora of love poems prepared the ground for bringing them close to each other. The comparison between them has shown that they are very analogous – even similar – almost "sisters". One gets the impression that a deeper and more elaborate analysis might bring to light more affinities and closer ones!

Interestingly enough, these two groups of love poems are similar also in that they played a formative rôle in the mystical love literature in their respective ambients — the SS among the Jews and Christians, and the Tamil akam poetry among the Śaiva and Vaiṣṇava mystics. Both of them not only inspired mystical love poems, but also served as models by supplying literary expressions and techniques on the level of language symbolisms and by lending a ready set of imagery which could easily be transferred to mystical level. The namelessness of the characters as idealized types in those poems and the functional openness of the language symbolism of both corpora have been useful for the mystics to compose their poems. One important difference between the SS and Tamil akam poems in this field is that the SS itself has been and still is interpreted as a collection of mystical love poems, whereas the Tamil

---

[1] Zvelebil, K., *TC*, X, 2 (1963), 30.

[2] Thani Nayagam, X. S., *Research in Tamil Studies: Retrospect and Prospect*, Jaffna 1980, 14.

akam poems are not. In recent years, however, there has been some effort or attempt to interpret and apply some of the ancient Tamil akam poems themselves to the level of mystical love.[3] Since the characters in these love poems are nameless and idealized types, these poems are more universal than the poems of either Śaiva or Vaiṣṇava mystics. Some poems, chosen at random,[4] may be cited as examples: Aiṅk. 203, 207, 208, 209, 210, 244, 322, 325, 326, 327, 359, 457; Kuṟ. 228, 240, 249, 274, 288, 361, 376, 388; Naṟ. 53, 68, 221, 236, 397; Ak. 82, 128.

There are certain elements of Hebrew poetry which seem to have analogies also in Tamil poetry and invite further explorations: e.g. the "word-sense-unit theory" of Hebrew metre may be compared with the sense-unit nature of the structure of one line in Tamil akaval metre. Similarly the Hebrew repetitive parallelism seems to have an analogous feature in Tamil poetry: e.g. compare SS 4:8a-d with Kuṟ. 4,23.

The analysis and comparison of the language of the Hebrew and Tamil akam poetry in this study has shown the genuine worth and beauty of human love between man and woman — a love which many waters cannot quench nor can floods drown (SS 8:7ab). For, "Kātal tāṉum kaṭaliṉum peritē" (Naṟ. 166:10), i.e. love is greater than the sea!

---

[3] Hirudayam, I., *Entaiyar Iṟaivaṉ*: God of our Fathers, Aikiya Ālayam, Madras 1977, Vol. I, 191-192. Earlier to this work, a mystical commentary on the Kāmattuppāl of Tirukkuṟaḷ appeared: Arulappa, R., *Thiruvalluvar a Mystic – God the Bridegroom*, Madras 1976.

[4] Besides the poems of Kuṟuntokai (3,23,25,40,102,118,126,290) cited and interpreted by I. Hirudayam, see the note above.

Appendix I

POSSIBLE LITERARY DEPENDENCE OF SS ON TAMIL AKAM POETRY?

A suggestion to this effect was first put forward by C. Rabin in an article,[1] on which P. C. Craigie commented by expressing his evaluation of Rabin's opinion.[2] Thus the present discussion originated. My intention is simply to focus the discussion and possibly to carry it a small step further by making it more relevant and precise in reference to and in the light of the foregoing comparative study.

A. C. Rabin's Position and P. C. Craigie's Reaction

C. Rabin formulates his position as follows: "It is thus possible to suggest that the Song of Songs was written in the heyday of Judaean trade with South Arabia and beyond (and this may include the lifetime of King Solomon) by someone who had himself travelled to South Arabia and to South India and had there become acquainted with Tamil poetry. He took over one of its recurrent themes, as well as certain stylistic features. The literary form of developing a theme by dialogue could have been familiar to this man from Babylonian-Assyrian sources (where it is frequent) and Egyptian literature (where it is rare). He was thus prepared by his experience for making a decisive departure from the Tamil practice by building what in Sangam poetry were short dialogue poems into a long work, though we may possibly discern in the Song of Songs shorter units more resembling the Tamil pieces. Instead of the vague causes for separation underlying the moods expressed in Tamil poetry, he chose an experience familiar to him and presumably common enough to be recognized by his public, the long absences of young men on commercial expeditions." [3]

P. C. Craigie, in his turn, expresses his evaluation about C. Rabin's opinion: "In the early periods of both the Hebrew and Tamil traditions, there is evidence of the composition of secular love poetry, and the poetry of each tradition bears some similarity to that of the other... It is my contention that the similarities which have been summarized in the preceding paragraph do not indicate, nor need they imply, any kind of historical interrelationship between the Hebrew and Tamil traditions." Concerning the evidences adduced by C. Rabin, P. C. Craigie says: "The general religious and literary data presented in Rabin's study (e.g.

---

[1] Rabin, C., "The Song of Songs and Tamil Poetry", *SR* 3:3 (1973/4), 205-219. Id., (Indian Connections of the Ct), *Sefer Baruch Kurzweil* (Tel Aviv 1974s) (Hebrew), 264-274.

[2] Craigie, P. C., "Biblical and Tamil Poetry: Some further Reflections", *SR* 8 (1979), 169-175.

[3] Rabin, C., *SR* 3:3 (1973/4), 216.

Rabin, 210-14) must be seen as less important in any hypothesis of a particular and historical nature. The evidence is less important in that it is simply one part of a large spectrum of similarity between the Hebrew and Tamil traditions which does not require historical explanation. On the other hand, particular data (e.g. philological arguments, Rabin, 207-09) retain importance for an historical hypothesis, though the basis of the hypothesis is now considerably reduced. If this is a fair analysis, then Rabin's hypothesis has been weakened, but by no means disproved."[4]

B. **Assessments and Problems**

C. Rabin suggests that the SS already as human love poem could have been influenced by the contact with Tamil love poetry inasmuch as the author would have taken over one of its recurrent themes, as well as certain stylistic features (p. 216). He admits the possibility of discerning shorter units or poems in the SS similar to Tamil poems. In fact, smaller units are admitted by all those scholars who hold that the SS is an anthology of human love poems. Rabin thinks that the causes for separation underlying the moods expressed in Tamil poetry are vague. But the causes for long absences underlying the moods in Tamil akam poetry are as real as the commercial expeditions of the Jews.[5]

All the parallels and similarities adduced by P. C. Craigie in his article may perhaps weaken the conclusion of C. Rabin about the influence of Tamil poetry on the SS for the use of love themes to express *religious* longing of man for God. He says: "The general religious and literary data presented in Rabin's study (e.g. Rabin, 210-14) must be seen as less important in any hypothesis of a particular and historical nature". The *religious data* may be seen as less important.[6] But when we pin-point our discussion only to the level of the SS as collection of human love poems,[7] the data presented in Rabin's study in pp. 210-14 cannot be seen as less important. On the contrary, they are to be taken seriously inasmuch as the three features mentioned by Rabin "set the Song of songs apart from ancient oriental love poetry." (p. 210) Naturally, when these features "do not recur in the same measure and not in this combination," (p. 210) they call for an explanation at least. P. C. Craigie admits, however, that the "particular data (e.g. philological arguments, Rabin, 207-09), retain importance for an historical hypothesis" (pp. 174-75).

In the general context of our discussion, C. Rabin accepts that the Indus Valley culture was Dravidian (and Tamil?)[8] and that there was trade connection or some type of contact between the Hebrews and the Tamils via Babylonia and

---

[4] Craigie, P. C., *SR* 8 (1979), 174-175.

[5] See for instance, Tol. Por. Akat. 11, which refers to two types of voyages — by foot and by ship. Cf also Tol. Por. Akat. cūt. 25-34, which give more specifications. See Nacciṉārkkiṉiyar, *Tol. Por. Akat.*., 25 for commentary Cf. esp. such poems as Ak. 5,151,155; Kuṟ. 63, etc.

[6] In fact, in pp. 210-214, C. Rabin does not give general religious data, but only literary data are given.

[7] P. C. Craigie himself considers "the Song to be an anthology of (initially secular) love poetry", p. 171, note 4.

[8] Rabin, C., *SR* 3 (1973/4), 208 with notes 20ff on pp. 218-219 with bibliography.

Arabia.[9] Parting from these hypotheses, we may enunciate the most important problems connected with our discussion:

1. Whether the Indus Valley culture was Dravidian — and more precisely Tamil.

2. Whether there was a continuity of contact between the Tamils and the Hebrews, either commercial or otherwise.

3. Could the Tamil akam poetry have influenced the SS?

Here below the data for and against for answering these questions are presented briefly:

1. *Whether the Indus Valley Culture was Dravidian — and More Precisely Tamil*[10]

It is *almost* certain that the Indus Valley culture is pre-Aryan and non-Aryan.[11] Whether it is Dravidian or not, depends mainly and, even exclusively, on the results of the decipherment of the Indus Valley script. At this level, there are differences of opinion among the specialists. B. B. Lal would suggest a *tertium quid,* i.e. the Indus language could have been a language which is neither Sanskrit nor Dravidian but one which is since dead![12] But most of the scholars are making efforts to decipher the script and to find affinity with one of the known languages. Those who formulate a hypothesis that the Indus Valley script is Dravidian, arrive at it by way of *argumentum per exclusionem.*[13]

---

[9] Ib., 205-210.

[10] A good treatment of this question with ample bibliography may be conveniently found in Victor, M., *Tamil-Islamic*, Vol. I, 153-167 with notes 228-233 and bibliography 234ff. In addition one may consult Joseph, P., "The Harappa Script – A Tragedy in Timing", TC, XI, 4 (1964), 295-307; Cornelius J. T., "The Graffiti on the Megalithic Pottery of South India and Dravidian Origin", *TC*, XII, 4 (1966), 287-301 with bibliography. Parpola, A., "The Indus Script Decipherment – the Situation at the End of 1969", *JTamS*, II, 1 (1970), Part I, 89-109, with bibliography; Joseph, P., "Harappa Script Decipherment – Rev. Heras and his Successors", *JTamS*, II, 1 (1970), Part I, 111-134, with bibliography; Clauson, G.-Chadwick, J., "The Indus Script Deciphered?", *JTamS*, II, 1 (1970), Part I, 135-148; Burrow, T., "Dravidian and the Decipherment of the Indus Script", *JTamS,* II, 1 (1970), Part I, 149-156; Mahadevan, I., "Dravidian Parallels in Proto-Indian Script", *JTamS*, II, 1 (1970), Part I, 157-276 with rich bibliography; Lal, B. B., "Some Observations on Harappan Script", in *India's Contribution to World Thought and Culture*, Vivekananda Rock Memorial Committee, Madras 1970, 189-202; Thani Nayagam, X. S., *Tamil Humanism*: Jaffna, 1972, 1-8; Xavier, J. T., "The Original Language of Hinduism – Sanskrit or Proto-Dravidian?", in *PFifICSTS*, Vol. I, sec. 1, IATR, Madras 1981, 11-27.

[11] Cf. Joseph, P., *TC*, XI, 4 (1964), 299. On this point, there seems to be unanimity among the scholars.

[12] Cf. Lal, B. B., "Some Observations.., in *India's Contribution*, 202.

[13] The argumentation is well presented by P. Joseph: See *TC*, XI, 4 (1964), 300.

Decipherment and research on the basis of this Dravidian hypothesis seem to elucidate the Indus Valley script-riddle.[14] According to A. Parpola and I. Mahadevan, the language of the Indus Valley was Dravidian, more precisely proto-Dravidian.[15] In a recent article, J. T. Xavier has brought some clarification on another aspect, i.e. "the original language of Hinduism was Proto-Dravidian and not Sanskrit."[16] It must be immediately added that the Dravidian hypothesis has not been accepted by all paleographists and Dravidologists, and some of them even deny that the decipherment of the Indus Valley script has been convincingly carried out at all.[17] T. Burrow is not convinced that the Indus script belongs to Dravidian.[18] Much has to be done before one can certainly say that the Indus Valley script belongs to Proto-Dravidian. It seems, however, that Dravidian-hypothesis enjoys a certain amount of probability among those who are working at it.[19] Among the Dravidian languages, old Tamil is the only one which is chronologically nearer to the Indus script and one may expect that it preserves the roots of the words better than the others.[20]

2. *Whether there was a Continuity of Contact Between the Dravidians (or Proto--Tamils) and the Hebrews*

Two kinds of contact may be considered here in relation to our question: commercial and linguistic.

a) *Commercial Contact*

There are indications that the Indus Valley dwellers were maintaining commercial contact with outside world and esp. with Western Asia, namely Mesopotamia, Arabia, etc.[21] The Indus Valley culture came to an end ca.1900 BC[22] and the people who occupied that region were scattered, and some of them

---

[14] Interesting studies have been published on this question. The articles of A. Parpola and I. Mahadevan are worth mentioning. See note above.

[15] Cf. Parpola, A., *JTamS*, II, 1 (1970), 91-94. For a short but clear account of how H. Heras, Finnish Team and Soviet Team of scholars came to same conclusion and what are the differences, etc. see Joseph, P., *JTamS*, II, 1 (1970), 111ff. Mahadevan, I., *JTamS*, II, 1 (1970), 157ff accepts this hypothesis and works further on the decipherment.

[16] Xavier, J. T., "The Original", *PFifICSTS* Vol. I, Sec. 1, 12. This point was already touched by A. Parpola in his article, pp. 92-93, 96ff, et passim.

[17] Cf. Clauson, G.-Chadwick, J., *JTamS*, II, 1 (1970), 135-148.

[18] Cf. Burrow, T., *JTamS*, II, 1 (1970), 149-156.

[19] Joseph, P., *JTamS*, II, 1 (1970), 129-130 indicates what has to be still done in this field.

[20] Cf. Thani Nayagam, X. S., *Tamil Humanism*, 4. In pp. 1-8, he claims that there was a continuity both of territorial and possibly chronological nature between Indus Valley civilization and South Dravidian-Tamil civilization.

[21] Rabin, C., *SR* 3 (1973/4), 205-209; Crown, A., "Some Contacts and Comparisons between the Ancient Near East and the Indus Valley Civilization", in *PSICSTS*, Vol. II, IATR, Madras 1971, 379-386.

[22] Joseph, P., *JTamS*, II, 1 (1970), 130, note 10.

migrated towards the South and settled in the Southern peninsula.[23] The maritime connection of the Dravidians of the South continued at least from ca.700 BC onwards with Babylon.[24] J. Kennedy even holds that Dravidian traders had their settlements in Babylon.[25] The same author tells us that two non-Aryan Indian chiefs came to Armenia, founded the town of Vishap and set up a temple with idols, which they worshipped in India.[26] Indications are that these settlers were Dravidians and the gods were Dravidian deities.[27] This commercial contact of the Dravidians with the West Asian countries, Palestine included, fits well in the larger context of the commercial activities of the Dravidians with other countries like Greece and the Roman Empire.[28]

b) *Linguistic Contact*

In the larger context, the Proto-Dravidian language and to some considerable extent old Tamil – *seem* to have affinity with very ancient languages of the West: e.g. with the Etruscan language,[29] and more interestingly

---

[23] Mahadevan, I., *JTamS*, II, 1 (1970), 242-243. See also Khaire, V., "Tamil, The Language of the Pre-historic Maharashtra", *JTamS*, 17, (1979), 14-25; *JTamS*, 17, (1979), 78-83.

[24] In detail, see Victor, M., *Tamil-Islamic*, Vol. I, 86-104; Kennedy, J., "The Early Commerce of Babylon with India – 700-300 BC", *JRAS* 30 (1898), 241-288.

[25] Ib., 270.

[26] Kennedy, J., "The Indians in Armenia, 130 BC - 300 AD", *JRAS* 36 (1904), 309-314.

[27] Ib., 312; see also Srinivas Iyengar, P. T., *History*, 202-205; Panikkar, K. M., *India and the Indian Ocean*, George Allen & Unwin Ltd., London 1951², 24-25 for evidences that the Dravidians of the South had commercial contact with Mesopotamia, Egypt and Red Sea regions.

[28] See Rathnavel, L. K., "The Indian Circumnavigators of the Past", *JTamS*, V, 4 (1973), 24-32. The author mentions an epigraph at DER-EL-BAHRI in Egypt which mentions people who came from Pāṇṭiya kingdom and migrated to the Nile basin, cf. p. 29; Mahadevan, I., "Origin of the Tamil Script', in *Origin, Evolution and Reform of the Tamil Script*, 11 for evidence that the Tamil merchants – Cāttaṉ and Kaṇaṉ – at least visited the Roman trading station at Quesir-al-qadim on the Red Sea coast of Egypt. For the trade between Greece and South India, from the time of Ptolemy Philadelphus (283-246 BC) to Cosmas Indicopleustos (c. 543 AD) with documentary evidences, see Eliki Laskarides-Zannas, "Greece and South India", in *PFifICSTS*, Vol. I, sec. 6, IATR, Madras 1981, 25-33. See esp. *Anōnymou Periplous tēs Erythras Thalassēs*, paras. 54-62 which are about the Dravidian South India. See further, Zvelebil, K., "The Yavanas in Old Tamil Literature", in *Charisteria Orientalia praecipue ad Persiam pertinentia*, (eds.) F. Tauer et alii, Československá Akademie Véd, Praha 1956, 401-409; Margabandhu, C., "Ancient Seaports of South India – their Trade Relationship with the Western World during the First Century BC to the Second Century AD", in *Sri Dinesacandrika Studies in Indology*, Shri D. C. Sircar Festschrift, (eds.) B. N. Mukherjee et alii, Sundeep Prakashan, Delhi 1983, 185-202. For trade between South India and Roman Empire, see Sewell, R., "Roman Coins found in India", *JRAS*, 36 (1904), 591-637; Sanford, E. M., "Roman Avarice in Asia", *JNES*, 9 (1950), 28-36; Cimino, R. M.-Scialpi, F. (eds.), *India and Italy*, Exhibition-Catalogue, IsMEO, Rome 1974, esp. 17-27.

[29] Konow, S., "Etruscan and Dravidian", *JRAS*, 36 (1904), 45-51. It seems that this affinity between Dravidian and Etruscan cannot be maintained any longer.

with the Sumerian language.[30] That Tamil has lent quite a few words to Greek and Latin is accepted by many linguisticians.[31] To some extent, Tamil seems to have made its way even into Greek literary works. One example may be the Greek Farce included in "The Oxyrhynchus Papyri Part III", which seems to contain conversations in Tamil.[32]

In the narrower context of linguistic connection between Dravidian language (Proto-Dravidian and/or Tamil) and Hebrew, the following may be mentioned:

(i) In general: There is no doubt that the Tamil names (or Dravidian names) of certain commercial goods have been taken into the Hebrew language. The following words are said to be Tamil loans into Hebrew, found in the Bible:[33]

tukkiyyîm: 1 Kgs. 10:22; 2 Chr. 9:21 – tōkai. see Kuṟ. 26:2; 347:3; Naṟ. 396:5; Aiṅk. 74:1 etc.[34]

qôp -qôpîm: 1 Kgs. 10:22; 2 Chr. 9:21 – kapi.[35]

---

[30] Sathasivam, A., "The Dravidian Origin of Sumerian Writing", in *PFICSTS*, Vol. II, IATR, Madras 1969, 673-697; Muttarayan, L. K., "Sumerian: Tamil of the First Caṅkam", *JTamS*, VII, 4 (1975), 40-61.

[31] Legrand, F., "Tamil Loan Words in Greek", *TC*, III (1954), 36-45. The author argues for the Dravidian and even old Tamil origin of about 17 Greek words, of which 12 could have come into Greek only "through daily contact with another population, whose language they amalgamated partly into their own", p. 45. The author even opines that there was a Dravidian settlement along the Mediterranean shores. Rathnavel, L.K., *JTamS*, V, 4 (1973), 30-31: He gives a list of six words in Greek which belong to the terminology of navigation and which, he claims, are loan words from Tamil. Gnani Giri Nadar, K. C. A., *Latin Words of Tamil Origin*, Madurai 1981; Id., *Greek Words of Tamil Origin*: An Etymological Lexicon, Madurai 1982; Id., *A Statement in Tamilo-European Linguistics*, Madurai 1982. I have yet to see the reactions of Greek and Latin linguisticians about these works. In the last one, the author states the linguistic principles and laws on which his research is based. He has presented his works for the perusal and comments of the linguisticians.

[32] Panikkar, K. M., *India and the Indian Ocean*, 26. More in detail, Mativanan, I., *Kirēkka Nāṭakattil Tamiḻ Uraiyāṭal*, Cennai 1978. The author discusses more than 40 sets of phrases which are, according to him, Tamil sentences or phrases. For the text of the Greek Farce, see *The Oxyrhynchus Papyri: Part III*, (eds.) B. P. Greenfell & A. S. Hunt, London 1903, 41-57 under "Farce and Mime".

[33] Bibliography: Rabin, C., "Rice in the Bible", *JSS*, XI, (1966), 2-9; Id., "Loanword Evidence in Biblical Hebrew for Trade between Tamil Nad and Palestine in the First Millenium BC", in *PSICSTS*, Vol. I, IATR, Madras 1971, 432-440; Id., *SR* 3:3 (1973/4), 206-209. Joseph, P., "Algummim or Almuggim of the Bible", *TC*, VI, 2 (1957), 133-138; Id., "Romance of Two Tamil Words", *TC*, VIII, 3 (1959), 201-207; Id., "Indian Ivory for Solomon's Throne", *TC*, IX, 3 (1960), 271-280; Id., "Ophir of the Bible: Identification", *TC*, X, 3 (1963), 48-70. Greenfield, J. C.-Mayrhofer, M., "The 'algummīm/'almuggīm – Problem reexamined", in *Hebräische Wortforschung*, Festschrift Walter Baumgartner, VTS 16, Leyden 1967, 83-89.

[34] Joseph, P., *TC*, VIII, 3 (1959), 204-207; Rabin, C., *SR*, 3:3 (1973/4), 206-207. Kennedy, J., *JRAS* 30 (1898), 254-256 denies Dravidian origin to this word, as well as for almuggim/algummim, and qoph (ape).

[35] Joseph, P., *TC*, VIII, 3 (1959), 202-203.

pannag: Ez. 27:17 – kampu.[36]
mĕsukkān: Is. 40:20 – musukkattai.[37]
bûṣ: 1Chr. 15:27 – pancu.[38]
'almuggîm: 1 Kgs. 10:11 etc. – akil.[39]

(ii) In particulsr: The following words in SS are Tamil loans:

nērdĕ: SS 1:12; 4:13.14 – the BDB suggests that this word might have come from Sanskrit *naladâ* through Persian *nârdîn*. But it is almost certain that it is the Tamil word narantam: cf. Kuṟ. 52:3; Ak. 266:4; Porunarāṟṟuppaṭai – line 238; DED 3604; cf. CDIAL 7073; cf. Akkadian *naradu*; Greek *nardos*; Hebrew *nērd*.[40]

'ahālôt: SS 4:14 cf. also Ps. 45:9; Prov. 7:17 – The BDB again searches in Sanskrit for the word. But it is again from the Tamil akil: cf. Naṟ. 282:7; Kuṟ. 286:2; etc. DED 13; CDIAL 49.[41]

karkom: SS 4:14 – probable.[42]

qāneh: SS 4:14 – probably from Tamil kaṉṉal (sugar-cane) cf. DED 1414.

3. *Could the Tamil Akam Poetry have Influenced the SS?*

With all that has been said so far, one cannot still answer the question for certain whether the Tamil akam poetry could have influenced the SS, before solving some other problems which are connected with our question, namely:

a) The date of the SS, at least, the date of its compilation, has to be fixed.

b) The date of the early literary output in Tamil akam poetry.

c) Among the literary and cultural similarities between both corpora, how many cannot be explained by having recourse to the similar literary products of the immediate neighbours of the Hebrews.

d) Whether these particular similarities, not explicable with neighbouring literatures, are peculiar to Tamil akam poetry.

---

[36] Rabin, C., "Loanword", in *PSICSTS*, Vol. I, 435 and notes.

[37] Ib., p. 436.

[38] Ib.

[39] Joseph, P., *TC*, VI, 2 (1957), 138. This etymology from Tamil is not considered by J.C. Greenfield and M. Meyrhofer, "The 'algummīm" in *Hebräische*, 83-89 where its etymology is, according to them, to be sought in Ugaritic. The very identification of the tree is not certain.

[40] Rabin, C., "Loanword", in *PSICSTS*, Vol. I, suggests that neerd (SS 1:12) might come from Tamil *nhaaNal*, cf. 436-437. But it seems to me that *narantam* is the Tamil word that has given *nard*. It is to be noted that *narantam* is mentioned together with akil, and āram, i.e. sandal wood, in Porunarāṟṟuppaṭai, line 238.

[41] Rabin, C., "Loanword", *PSICSTS*, Vol. I, 434; Id., *SR* 3:3 (1973/4), 209.

[42] Rabin, C., "Loanword", *PSICSTS*, Vol. I, 437.

The present writer is of the opinion that most of the smaller units in SS must have been written during the period when the wisdom movement was enjoying its golden age, i.e. much after the return from the Exile and just before or even during the Hellenistic period. This seems to be confirmed by the small proportion of these poems vis-à-vis other types of writings in the Bible and by the reluctance with which it was received by the Jews among the books of the Bible.

The date of the early literary output in Tamil akam poetry must have started at least – most probably even before – ca. 5th century BC. This seems to be confirmed indirectly by the highly developed literary conventions represented by the poems of the extant anthologies, some of whose poems belong already to the 3rd or even 4th century BC.

Without claiming to have studied the two other questions in detail, it may be said that there are certain features in SS which are closely similar to Tamil akam poetry and which are not explicable by having recourse to the neighbouring literatures. Besides those which have been mentioned by C. Rabin,[43] we may adduce, for instance, the use of the towns Tirzah and Jerusalem as simile for the beauty of the girl and the idea that female beauty is awe-inspiring. These ideas may be claimed as peculiar to Tamil akam poetry where they occur so many times.[44] However, it must be admitted that deeper and more elaborate studies must be carried out before giving a positive answer. In any case, an a priori negative answer has no chance. On the contrary, the *possibility* of the influence of Tamil akam poetry on SS seems to be on a firmer ground.

---

[43] Rabin, C., *SR* 3:3 (1973/4), 210-211.
[44] See Part Three, Chapter 7 for details and citations.

APPENDIX II

SELECTIONS FROM THE ANCIENT TAMIL LOVE POEMS

Here below are given some 36 Tamil poems in English translation from different anthologies of love poems. These are only samples from the early classical poems. They have been selected in such a way that they can be compared with different poetic units in the Song of Songs. Kalittokai has not been represented here for the simple reason that it is considered as late classical poetry. The speakers are indicated simply as "he" for the hero, "she" for the heroine, etc. Selections have been made to represent different tiṇais. For the marutam, only one sample is given.

Selections from Aiṅkuṟunūṟu

1. What she said to her companion:

> Listen, dear friend, bless you!
> Sweeter than the milk
> mixed with honey from our garden
> is in his land
> the left-over water low in the pits covered with leaves
> muddied by animals
> after they have drunk. (Aiṅk. 203).

Author: Kapilar
Tiṇai: Kuṟiñci
Tuṟai: In praise of the hero and his land
Speaker: Heroine or Talaivi
Listener: Companion of the heroine
Sense: The least in *his* land is better than the best in *our* house!

2. What her companion said to her at his earshot:

> Look there, dear friend, bless you!
> Like the sentinel of this rainy hill stands he,
> with a glistening, garland-like sword wet with drops,
> his big anklets covered round with moss,
> his striped waist-cloth drenched in cold dew! (Aiṅk. 206)

Author: Kapilar
Tiṇai: Kuṟiñci
Tuṟai: Pointing out to the presence of the hero at the place of night-tryst
Speaker: Lady companion
Listener: Heroine – and the hero who stands near the house garden
Sense: Daring all the dangers on the way, the hero has come to meet his Beloved
Comparison: SS 5:2ff

3. What he said to his friend:

> The darling-young daughter of the hill-chief is she,
> in complexion like the heavenly dames on mountains,
> in beauty, wonder-inspiring,
> with blossomed breasts,
> her mouth being red and
> her chest full of beauty spots –
> She it is! (Aiṅk. 255)

Author: Kapilar
Tiṇai: Kuṟiñci
Tuṟai: In praise of his Beloved
Speaker: Hero, i.e. talaivaṉ or lover
Listener: Pāṅkaṉ or the friend of the hero
Comparison: SS 4:1-5

4. What her companion said at hero's earshot:

> Much better than the righteous-good king
> are certainly the parrots of the field:
> For, they are watched and chased
> by the kuṟiñci-girl
> with flower-smelling long hair. (Aiṅk. 290)

Author: Kapilar
Tiṇai: Kuṟiñci
Tuṟai: Hinting at the place of day-tryst
Speaker: Companion
Listener: Heroine – also the hero who stands near the house garden
Sense: Meeting the heroine at night is not possible – so better come to the millet field, where she will be chasing parrots.
Comparison: SS 7:11-14: Rendezvous in the cultivated country side, i.e. in the garden. Notice also that the hero is called king – which is similar to the poetic fiction in SS 1:4,12.

5. What she said to herself:

> My heart has gone with the man of the hill;
> will it ever come back?
> Or will it remain with him
> where it wants to live?
> On his mountain,
> peacocks, fleeing from the torches of millet-field owners,
> and running like girls playing ball,
> disturb and cause pain to little birds
> that are in the stubble of the grain field. (Aiṅk. 295)

Author: Kapilar
Tiṇai: Kuṟiñci
Tuṟai: Pining after the Lover
Speaker: Heroine speaking to herself

Sense: My heart has found its peaceful habitation in him but left me in doubt and pain
Uḷḷuṟai uvamam: Peacocks and the little birds in the field.

6. What he said to the heroine's companion:

Young maiden is she;
her teeth are like the shining pearls
from the ford of Koṟkai
with neytal-flowers of swinging petals;
red coral is her mouth;
she wears pretty bangles, well shaped;
her speech is sweet like the sounding of the strings in the harp. (Aiṅk. 185)

Author: Ammūvaṉār
Tiṇai: Neytal
Tuṟai: In praise of the Beloved
Speaker: Hero
Listener: Lady companion
Comparison: SS 4:2-3.

7. What she said to her companion:

Listen, my friend, bless you!
Are they not capable at all -
those numerous birds in that rocky land,
to tell him there:
"We are living together with our beloveds,
how could you live separated from yours?" (Aiṅk. 333)

Author: Ōtalāntaiyār
Tiṇai: Pālai
Tuṟai: Complaint against the birds
Speaker: Heroine
Listener: Lady companion

8. What he said to her:

O young maid,
who are making a garland
out of the summer-pātiri full-petalled flowers
that grow near the sandy ford of forest river bank,
more furious than the eyes are your breasts,
more furious than the breasts are your broad upper arms! (Aiṅ. 361)

Author: Ōtalāntaiyār
Tiṇai: Pālai
Tuṟai: In praise of the Beloved during elopement
Speaker: Hero
Listener: Heroine
Comparison: The technique of comparison in SS 1:2-3 is similar to that of this poem.

9. What the foster-mother said about them:

Like a deer and a mother doe
with their young one in the middle,
lay he and she
with their son between them:
Their lying together was so sweet and beautiful!
Neither on this earth surrounded by blue seas
nor in the world above
is such a thing easy to obtain. (Aiṅk. 401)

Author: Pēyaṉār
Tiṇai: Mullai
Tuṟai: Joyful comment or announcement
Speaker: Foster-mother
Listener: Mother of the heroine
Sense: Happy union in the family life with a child is incomparable.

10. What she said to him:

You, man of the village with abundant income,
in whose fields the female water-fowl,
with sweet voice and white forehead,
lives together with its relatives,
you are behaving like small children.
Those who see you, my dear,
will they not laugh at you? (Aiṅk. 85)

Author: Ōrampōkiyār
Tiṇai: Marutam
Tuṟai: Correction and acceptance
Speaker: Heroine
Listener: Hero
Sense: Behave in a mature way
Uḷḷuṟai uvamam: The female water-fowl which lives with its relatives symbolizes the heroine who lives with her relatives, i.e. the lady companion.

Selections from Kuṟuntokai

11. What she said to her companion:

Wider than the earth, indeed,
higher than the sky,
more unfathomable than the vast waters
is this love of mine for the man
of the mountain slopes
where bees make rich honey
from the black-stalked kuṟiñci flowers. (Kuṟ. 3)

Author: Tēvakulattār
Tiṇai: Kuṟiñci
Tuṟai: In praise of love between herself and her lover

Speaker: Heroine
Listener: Lady companion
Sense: In all the three dimensions, love is immeasurable
Uḷḷuṟai uvamam: Rich honey produced by bees signifies the love relation wrought by destiny or *Ūḻ*.
Critical notes: – this love of mine: lit. friendship, i.e. love relationship
– three *um* to denote superiority
– twice *ē* and once the particle *aṉṟu* to denote certainty
Comparison: SS 8:5-7, esp. v.6.

12. What she said to her companion:

Do listen, my friend, bless you!
That one capable of telling lies that seem true,
lay close to me and embraced me at night
in the false dream that lied like truth.
Confused I woke up and caressed the bed
thinking that he was there!
To be pitied am I,
who am certainly alone
like the kuvaḷai-flower
that has been made to suffer by the bee. (Kuṟ. 30)

Author: Kaccippēṭṭu Naṉṉākaiyār
Tiṇai: Kuṟiñci
Tuṟai: Kaṉavu nalivuraittal, i.e. dream narration
Speaker: Talaivi, i.e.Heroine
Listener: Tōḻi, i.e. Companion
Simile: Kuvaḷai flower that has been made to suffer stands for the maid who suffers from love sickness. The bee stands for the lover.
Comparison: SS 3:1-5; 5:2-6.

13. What she said to her companion:

Nowhere did I find him, that man of nobility.
Neither at the festivals of warriors
nor among the dances of girls!
Now, even I am a dancer
and that noble man,
who has made these bangles, carved from the shining conch,
slip from my hands,
he is a dancer too. (Kuṟ. 31)

Author: Ātimantiyār (a poetess)
Tiṇai: Kuṟiñci
Tuṟai: Revealing the secret love affair (Aṟattoṭu niṉṟatu)
Speaker: Talaivi
Listener: Tōḻi
Theme: Searching and not finding
Comparison: SS 5:2-6

Notes: "That man of nobility" and "that noble man" are two designations which are almost equal to epithets of royal status: Compare the "royal fiction" in SS 1:4,12.

14. What he said:

You want nectar, she it is!
You want wealth, she it is!
The young maiden,
  of pretty – heaving – huge breasts with beauty spots,
  of broad upper arms
  and of thin waist,
the daughter of those who dwell
  in the forests on the hills. (Kuṟ. 71)

Author: Karuvūr Ōtañāṉiyār
Tiṇai: Kuṟiñci (or Pālai according to the colophon)
Tuṟai: In praise of the Beloved (or postponement of the journey)
Speaker: Talaivaṉ, i.e. Hero or the Lover.
Listener: Either his friend or his own heart

Notes: Nectar translates *maruntu,* lit. medicine, i.e. the medicine for immortality. It may signify also medicine for passion or the pain caused by passion.

Comparison: SS 7:7-10.

15. What she said to the messenger:

Did you really see?
Or did you just hear from someone who saw?
Tell me, I pray,
I want to know only "one thing" –
  the coming of my lover –
from whose mouth did you hear it?
May you receive as gift
the city of Pāṭali, full of gold,
on the bank of River Cōṇai
where elephants with white tusks bathe. (Kuṟ. 75)

Author: Paṭumarattu Mōcikīraṉār
Tiṇai: Mullai
Tuṟai: In praise of the messenger
Speaker: Talaivi
Listener: Messenger, i.e. Pāṇaṉ
Theme: Eagerly waiting for the lover
Comparison: SS 3:3

Note: The different stages of testimony are to be noticed: seeing, hearing from another and speaking.

16. 'What he said:

The entire world surrounded by vast oceans,
the scarcely achievable precious land of the gods –
These two are worth nothing,
if weighed with the day,
on which I clasp the upper arms of the young maid,
with the painted eyes like flowers
with the body like gold
with the striped vulva! (Kuṟ. 101)

Author: Parūu Mōvāyppatumaṉār
Tiṇai: Kuṟiñci
Ṭuṟai: In praise of the Beloved
Speaker: Lover
Listener: Either the companion of the Beloved or his own heart.
Notes: – *tōḷ-māṟupaṭutal* is an euphemism for sexual enjoyment, here translated by "clasp the upper arms."
– the entire world and the land of the gods represent all the pleasures available in them.
– four organs or parts of the Beloved are mentioned as sources of pleasure.

Comparison: SS 7:7-10.

17. What he said to his friend:

A girl of dark complexion is she:
Ever ready to embrace,
desirable in beauty,
with delicately bulging breasts
and long flowing hairs!
How can I forget her and be at rest?
In her look is such longing
as in the look of a new-born tender calf
that longs to see its mother
whose udders are ready to flow! (Kuṟ. 132)

Author: Ciṟaikkuṭiyāntaiyār
Tiṇai: Kuṟiñci
Tuṟai: Response or explanation to the condition
Speaker: Talaivaṉ
Listener: Friend or Pāṅkaṉ
Simile: cow for the hero and the new-born calf for the heroine
Comparison: SS 4:8-11, esp. v.9 on look.

18. What he said:

Listen, you Dream!
You disturbed me from the sweet sleep

by pretending to give to me
the girl of orderly hair like the petals of summer patiri-flowers,
of pretty dark complexion
and with fine jewels,
and woke me up.
Will not the separated lovers despise you? (Kuṟ. 147)

Author: Kōpperuñcōḻaṉ
Tiṇai: Pālai
Tuṟai: Dream-narration
Speaker: Lover
Listener: Dream: Apostrophe or personification.

19. What she said to her companion:

The man from the land of high hills,
where pepper grows on the slopes
and the monkeys in gangs eat tender leaves,
is such a sweet one!
Could then even the so-called sweet land of the gods
be as sweet as the most unsweet things
resulting from his relation with me? (Kuṟ. 288)

Author: Kapilar
Tiṇai: Kuṟiñci
Tuṟai: In praise of the Lover
Speaker: Talaivi
Listener: Tōḻi
Theme: Even the most unpleasant things caused by the love relation is more pleasant than the heaven.
Uḷḷuṟai uvamam: The monkeys which eat pepper leaves together with tender leaves symbolize the heroine who undergoes sweet and painful experiences.
Note: The word "sweet" is repeated in contrast to the "unsweet".

20. What he said to her companion:

Breasts have indeed blossomed,
her hairs have grown long and are flowing down,
her white teeth have come up in perfect line,
some beauty spots have shown up already in her body.
I know, I have been suffering because of her.
But she does not yet know it,
she – the only daughter of wealthy parents.
What shall become of her? (Kuṟ. 337)

Author: Potukkayattuk Kīrantaiyār
Tiṇai: Kuṟiñci
Tuṟai: Kuṟaiyirattal, i.e. pleading

Speaker: Talaivaṉ
Listener: Tōḻi
Theme: The girl is of age for marriage
Comparison: SS 8:8-10.

Selections from Naṟṟiṇai

21. What she said to her companion:

> Give up, my friend,
> the idea of sending a messenger to him,
>   however good he might be!
> Don't be sad that he is far away.
> What is the use of his friendship to us,
>   whom he left to suffer like this?
> As the juice in the sandal tree of small leaves
> slowly flows down to cause the tree to dry up,
>   when its bark is torn off by the ignorant hill-dwellers
>   who wear dresses of tree-fibres,
> so my mind and heart have gone over to him, my friend,
> and there is nothing left in my body.
> Even if he comes,
> he will not be a medicine for my sickness.
> Let the Lover be where he is – let him not come.
> Here let not our relatives notice
> our amorousness and the sufferings
> caused to us by such thoughts! (Naṟ. 64)

Author: Ulōccaṉār
Tiṇai: Kuṟiñci
Tuṟai: Lament out of love and passion
Speaker: Beloved
Listener: Companion
Note: The absence of the Lover can cause death to the Beloved, but his presence is like the medicine. Notice the similes, and the metaphor of the medicine.

22. What he said to her:

> You, maid of the hill country,
>   who have pretty bamboo-like upper arms
>   that can heal my love sickness and debility
>   and who walk beautifully,
> will you come with me,
>   as Vaḷḷi loved Murukaṉ and went away with him,
> to my village, where
>   in a forked way amidst tall nāka trees a wild boar,
>   with red mud on its body
>   was caught in a trap and was torn to pieces
>   by hunting dogs,
>   but its flesh was rescued by the forest dwellers?

The brilliance of your form shines in your eyes
and that is why I cannot look at you! (Naṟ. 82)

Author: Ammaḷḷaṉār
Tiṇai: Kuṟiñci
Tuṟai: In praise of the Beloved and speaking out the intention.
Speaker: Talaivaṉ
Listener: Talaivi
Simile: Murukaṉ and Vaḷḷi – from mythology
Uḷḷuṟai uvamam: The wild boar that was caught and whose flesh was rescued stands for Talaivi who is suffering from love sickness.
Comparison: SS 4:8-11, esp. vv.8-9

Notes: – Muruku puṇarntu iyaṉṟa Vaḷḷi: lit. Vaḷḷi who joined or had intercourse with Murukaṉ. – hence "as Valli loved and went away"
– Niṉ uruvu kaṇ eṟippa: Two possible translations:
(i) Your form shines in your eyes and I cannot look at.
(ii) Your form shines so brilliantly in my eyes that I cannot look at it.

23. What she said to her companion:

Do not complain, my friend, that
although you are very dear to me
as if one life were divided into two
and were set in you and me,
I have not told you
why the brightness of my body is fading away
like a lamp burning at midday
why the sheen of my forehead is going out
like the moon swallowed by the Snake,
but now you have seen it,
and I tell you now:
As I was guarding the millet field with ripe ears of corn
there came a young man
who wore a garland on his head,
anklets on his feet,
and garland on his chest,
and embraced me from the back with his cool hands.
From then on, my heart is thinking only of his action
and this is the sickness I am suffering from. (Naṟ. 128)

Author: Naṟcēntaṉār
Tiṇai: Kuṟiñci
Tuṟai: Revelation of the secret love
Speaker: Talaivi
Listener: Tōḻi

Similes: a lamp that burns dimmly at midday and the eclipsed moon for the fading beauty of the girl's body and of her forehead.

24. What he said to her:

Like gold, indeed, O maiden, is your shining body,
and like sapphire, your fragrant dark hair;
Like flowers are your pretty painted eyes
and like bamboos, your well shaped upper arms.
Whenever I see them,
I feel extremely happy like those perfect in family bliss.
Besides, our son, with golden anklets
has learned to play about.
I have no work anywhere else to do.
Above all, my love for you is greater than the sea!
If you come to think of it,
why should I part with you at all? (Naṟ. 166)

Author: Anonymous
Tiṇai: Pālai
Tuṟai: Assurance to the Beloved
Speaker: Talaivaṉ
Listener: Talaivi
Theme: Ideal of family life achieved. Hence nothing to seek for elsewhere. Thus assures the hero that he is not going to part with her for earning wealth.
Comparison: SS 8:7.

25. What her companion said;

Listen, I pray, my friend:
What recompense can we make at all
to the male elephant, that,
with proboscis dragging on the earth
and with very strong tusks,
walks along, embracing its mate who has by her side
the big-mouthed little calf,
and to the green little parrots?
For, they did not destroy the fields
nor steal away the ripe ears of millet corn,
when we left the watch-hut alone on the rock
and went to play with the man of the hill country
in the thick of the forest
where even monkeys do not frequent! (Naṟ. 194)

Author: Marutaṉiḷanākaṉār
Tiṇai: Kuṟiñci
Tuṟai: Reminds that the heroine is kept at home
Speaker: Lady companion
Listener: Beloved (who is addressed)
Lover (who stands unseen and listens)
Uḷḷuṟai uvamam: Family of elephants – a model for the Lover to imitate.
Suggestion or iṟaicci: Not possible to meet anymore in the fields, so come to marry her.
Comparison: SS 1:15-17 – rendezvous in the watch-hut.

26. What she said to her companion:

His love for me is genuine
and he indeed is a great man.
Besides, the early dew season has set in to indicate
that the late dew season is soon to arrive.
Kurā buds have blossomed
and the sweet early summer is already there.
On branches of flowers, black cuckoos with red eyes
call to each other in sweet voice:
"Lovers in embrace,
keep on embracing."
But what shall I say about him
who assured me saying, "I will never leave you"
and yet after all such assurance, went away
to a distant country through the barren lands
where the ponds are dry and without water,
the ways are long and forked and full of dangers? (Naṟ. 224)

Author: Pālai Pāṭiya Peruṅkaṭuṅkō
Tiṇai: Pālai
Tuṟai: Lament and longing at the arrival of spring or early summer.
Speaker: Beloved
Listener: Companion
Notes: – kurā buds: bottle flowers
– in the first two lines there might be an irony implied in view of the assurances of the hero.
Comparison: SS 2:10-13. The arrival of spring and the revival of vegetation are parallel. Notice also the birds: the turtle dove and cuckoos are parallel.

27. What her companion said:

"Like a kuṟiñci flower,.
that blossomed just this morning
on the high mountain, is her body.
Like flowers from a large fountain, put side by side,
are her eyes cool and eye-brows dark.
Like that of a peacock is her beauty.
Like that of a red-striped parrot is her speech.
Her upper arms are large.
Like that of a statue is her form;
such is this girl"
With loving heart and in many ways
so praises the mother and never forgets this maid
whose fragrant hairs do not fail to be scented with oil. (Naṟ. 301)

Author: Pāṇṭiyaṉ Māṟaṉvaḻuti
Tiṇai: Kuṟiñci
Tuṟai: In praise of the Beloved
Speaker: Companion

Listener: To herself, but the lover being within earshot.

Notes: Kuriñci – strobilanthes (genus)
flowers from fountain – blue water lily
oil (for scenting the hairs) – akil oil

Comparison: SS 7:2-6.

28. What he said to himself:

The sea-waves have become still;
The sea-shore grove is at peace from cold wind;
The hooter with its mate
hoots frightfully in the lonely dark squares
in the large streets of this sandy old village;
The demons wander about in this midnight.
Desirous to caress the yellow spotted breasts
of the young pretty maiden,
with large bamboo-like upper arms
and beautiful like the statue,
I lie here sleepless at this moment
when even the fishes sleep!
What will become of me? (Nar. 319)

Author: Viṉaittoḻil Cōkīraṉār
Tiṇai: Neytal
Turai: Musing to oneself
Speaker: Talaivaṉ

29. What they said:

Alas for the mother!
What will become of her – she will suffer and wear out!
For she was very fond of her daughter,
whose body is like gold.
Her father's forest swarms with elephants of matured tusks,
and he has in his hands spears shining as if oiled.
As she was once rolling the ball with her feet
in her father's spacious house,
so now is she running around in the stony tract,
with her delicate spongy feet,
while her few beautiful hairs flow in the air. (Nar. 324)

Author: Kayamaṉār
Tiṇai: Pālai
Turai: What they said who saw them in the arid tract
Speaker: The onlookers
Comparison: SS 7:1-6.

30. What she said to her companion:

The day fixed for his return is past;
My upper arms are pining.

By seeing always towards the long dry barren ways,
my eyes have lost the power to see;
My mind has abandoned me alone, and is in confusion.
Love-sickness has gone to extreme.
Evening has arrived.
What shall become of me?
Truly, I am not afraid of dying;
but that in the next birth,
if I were to be born otherwise than as human being,
I might by chance forget my lover –
This is what I am afraid of! (Naṟ. 397)

Author: Ammūvaṉār
Tiṇai: Pālai
Tuṟai: Lament
Speaker: Beloved
Listener: Lady companion
Theme: Desire not to forget the lover for ever.

Selections from Akanāṉūṟu

31. What she said:

O man of hill country, where in winter
 it rains heavily with sweet thunders,
 all living beings sleep at midnight,
 the fathers of hill-dwelling maidens,
  with pretty jewels and fragrant hairs,
 have searched for sleeping place during the chase
 but returned home to sleep on the bed of tiger-hide.
When I am separated from you,
I suffer whenever I think of you.
When I wait long for you outside,
 during the night, while all sleep,
 at the cold and unfriendly north wind,
 in our garden, and stand embracing a tree
 and pondering over your return –
Such standing and waiting is sweeter than
 embracing your breast so as to press
 my well shaped heaving breasts many times
 and to surround you with my arms wearing shining bangles. (Ak. 58)

Author: Maturai Paṇṭavāṇikaṉ Iḷantēvaṉār
Tiṇai: Kuṟiñci
Speaker: Beloved
Listener: Lover
Sense: Eager expectation is sweeter than the actual embrace
Comparison: SS 2:4-7.

32. What he said to her:

"If men, thinking that the real wealth is
not to live with the sweet heart,
but to earn wealth,
and following this meaningless reasoning
and stubborn will,
dare go through the stony ways on the mountains,
where there is no water,
and where warriors like tigers,
wearing anklets, sleep in the public squares
of their ancient village,
and where trees are all burnt and black,
they will always regret that,
without embracing in unquenchable love
and sqeezing the garlands,
on their large chest and blossoming breasts,
with garland of pearls,
the beauty of women with pretty forehead,
faultless ideal words, mouth like red-coral,
arms with shining bangles and artistically made jewels,
was lost once for all
and none will ever give it back again"
Thus you say and suffer unrelieved pain –
You, young and pretty maid,
with dark body like the tender shoots of iṇṭai
that sprouts in rainy season,
with thin waist and vulva with cusps,
decorated with the girdle of gold coins;
How can I possibly think of parting with you,
you – who are so precious to me? (Ak. 75)

Author: Maturai Pōttaṉār
Tiṇai: Pālai
Tuṟai: Postponement of the journey
Speaker: Talaivaṉ
Listener: Talaivi

33 What she said to her companion:

In his country,
the summer west wind blows flute music
through the shining holes made by beetles
in swaying bamboos;
the sweet sound of the cool waters of the stream
makes the beat of many concert drums;
the low voices of a herd of deer
play the brass trumpets;
the bees on the flowering mountain slopes
are the lutes;

the female monkeys as spectators look on in wonder
the peacock sway and strut happily amidst bamboos
like a dancing woman entering a festival stage.
My friend, there were many who saw him,
as he stood, with a garland of flowers on his chest,
by the side of the entrance of the ripe millet field,
carefully choosing an arrow,
and holding in hand a strong, well shaped bow,
and asked us which way the elephant he was hunting,
had gone.
But, of all those who looked at him,
why is it that I alone,
lying on my bed in the thick-dark-night,
my eyes streaming with tears,
feel my arms grow lean? (Ak. 82)

Author: Kapilar
Tiṇai: Kuṟiñci
Tuṟai: Revelation of the secret love: aṟattoṭu niṟṟal
Speaker: Beloved
Listener: Companion

34. What she said to her companion:

My friend,
The man of that land where,
the forest dweller, strong like a lion,
in his watch-hut in the millet field,
having drunk toddy, was hilarious
and his wife whose long dark hairs,
scented with sandal oil,
were being dried by gentle breeze,
and who, having arranged
the long hairs with her fingers,
sang kuṟiñci music on the mountain slope;
A valiant male elephant,
not eating the millet ears that he had plucked,
nor moving from his position,
fell slowly asleep in that music;
He, having painted his chest with sandal lotion,
wearing on his chest and head garlands
where bees went round singing,
and holding a spear in his right hand,
came, without being noticed by the watchmen,
and opening the door that was not bolted
and entering slowly inside the house,
embraced my upper arms and caressed me,
and thus relieved me from the painful sickness,
spoke to me sweet words and went away.

Because he has not deigned to come today,
how is it that we see pallor in my forehead,
surrounded by dark hairs of pleasant sight,
so that our affair has become the gossip of the village? (Ak. 102)

Author: Cēntaṅkūttaṉ (Maturai Iḷampālāciriyaṉ)
Tiṇai: Kuṟiñci
Tuṟai: The lover at earshot; the Beloved speaks to her companion.
Uḷḷuṟai Uvamam: The male elephant sleeping at the music of the forest woman stands for the hero, who is lost in love for the heroine but forgot to do what he should, i.e. to make arrangements for marriage.
Comparison: SS 5:2-6 – the night visit.

35. What her companion said to him:

O man of the land where,
white clouds, like the smoke of a potter's kiln,
surround and cover the glistening mountains;
sheets of rain and hail beat down at night,
and wash the deep cuts of the male elephant
that was wounded in a fight with a tiger
and was slowed in its walk;
at dawn a pure water fall
roars down with a flood of water;
Why should you come at night at all?
If you come during the day,
you can pass your time with us in the watch-hut,
raised by our hot-tempered father,
whose spear never misses the mark,
on the rocky cleft too high for elephants to reach.
There with us you can chase parrots,
from the tiny-grained millet,
You can sleep on the pillow of soft hairs,
full of many fragrant, bright, pollen-filled
water lilies, taken from the spring,
gushing forth on the rocky slopes;
And then at dusk you can return
to your own pleasant town of black-stalked kuṟiñci,
like a great elephant that has stealthily eaten its fill
in a field carefully guarded by watchmen. (Ak. 308)

Author: Picirāntaiyār
Tiṇai: Kuṟiñci
Tuṟai: Rendezvous proposed during the day
Uḷḷuṟai uvamam: The elephant who comes and eats its fill and goes away stealthily stands for the hero.
Theme: Dangers on the way at night.
The watch-hut seves as the place of union.
Comparison: SS 1:15-17; 7:11-14.

36. What he said:

Oh! Is it perhaps the best life
to sell the salt produced in salty-land
and go along, in paths full of dust,
with a group of salt merchants,
who take with them thick sticks!
With her long curly hairs flowing freely,
and delightful large vulva beautifully covered
with a dress of tender leaves,
she walked along, swaying when and where to sway,
and, calling, "O people of the village,
Salt shall be exchanged
for equal measure of paddy.
Don't you want to buy?"
sold it in all the streets.
We stopped her a little and said:
"You, who have beautiful curved belly
and bamboo-like upper arms,
We don't know the price of that 'salt'
that 'lives' in your body"
She looked at me in bewilderment,
with her large painted-dark eyes,
and retorted: "Who are you who stop us?"
Saying so, she moved a little with a blossoming smile.
She had a few white, orderly beautiful bangles.
Yes, to that young maid of many qualities,
my heart lost itself! (Ak. 390)

Author: Ammūvaṉār
Tiṇai: Neytal
Tuṟai: In praise of the Beloved
Note: The words "salt" and "lives" are used in double-entendre. They refer to erotic pleasure.
Speaker: Lover
Listener: Friend or he speaks to himself.

Appendix III

GLOSSARY OF TAMIL TERMS

1. These are mostly grammatical and literary terms.
2. The list is very selective and so not exhaustive.
3. Words are arranged according to Tamil alphabetical order.

Akam	love, literature or poems on love.
Akattiṇai	behaviour in love life.
Akattiṇaiyiyal	chapter on mutual love and its situations.
Ampal	publicity of love-affair in close quarters.
Alar	wide pubblicity of love-affair or gossip in the village.
Iṭantalaippāṭu	meeting of lovers.
Iṟaicci	suggestion implied in the words.
Uvamai	simile, comparison.
Uvamaittokai	a phrase having the object and simile but without the comparative particle.
Uvamaviyal	chapter on simile.
Uḷḷuṟai uvamam or uvamai	ambient "allegory", suggestive simile, built by the native elements.
Uripporuḷ	love-aspect pertaining to the particular region.
Uruvakam	metaphor
Uvakai	joy, rejoicing.
Ūṭal	love-quarrel.
Eḻuttatikāram	chapter on phonetics in Tolkāppiyam.
Karupporuḷ	native elements of a region.
Kaḷavu	secret love-affair.
Kaḷaviyal	chapter on aspects of premarital love-affair, i.e. courtship.
Kaṟpu	chastity, wedded love-life.
Kaṟpiyal	chapter on aspects of wedded love.
Kātal	love
Kātalaṉ	lover
Kātali	beloved
Kāmam	love that manifests itself very strongly, passion.
Kuṟiñci – a region	mountainous and hilly region.
– love-aspect	union of lovers.
– literary	poems on this aspect of love.
Kuṟippupporuḷ	meaning implied in the words used in the poem.
Kaikkiḷai	unrequited or unreciprocated love.
Cuṭṭu	demonstrative, meaning hinted at indirectly.

Collatikāram	chapter on morphology in Tolkāppiyam.
Ceyyuḷ	prosody and rhetoric
Ceyyuḷiyal	chapter on prosody & rhetoric
Talaivaṉ	chief, i.e. hero or lover.
Talaivi	lady love, heroine, beloved.
Tiṇai	class, division, region, behaviour – code.
Tiṇaimayakkam	intermingling of region or behaviour in love-life.
Tuṟai	life-situation, poetic context within a tiṇai.
Tokai	anthology, lit. compound.
Tōḻi	female companion of the heroine or beloved.
Neñcam	heart, mind.
Neñcaṟi-cuṭṭu	the demonstrative pronoun which the heart understands.
Neytal – a region	sea-coast land.
– love-aspect	pining
– literary	poems on this aspect of love.
Pacalai	pallor, sallowness resulting from love-sickness.
Pāṅkaṉ	friend of the hero or lover.
Pālai – a region	dry and waste land.
– love-aspect	separation
– literary	poems on this aspect of love.
Puṇarcci	union, meeting, intercourse.
Puṇarcci (Iyaṟkaip)	union through destiny.
Puṇarcci (Uḷḷap)	union of hearts.
Puṇarcci (Kāmap)	union of love, physically manifesting.
Puṇartal	union, meeting, etc.
Puṟam	affairs other than akam, i.e. heroism in war, etc.
Puṟattiṇai	behaviour in war, etc.
Puṟattiṇaiyiyal	chapter or treatise on situations outside love-life.
Peruntiṇai	mismatched or unnatural love.
Poruḷ	that which is essential, matter of literature, meaning.
Poruḷatikāram	chapter on literary theory.
Poruḷvayiṟpirivu	separation for earning wealth.
Poḻutu	time, period, season.
Poḻutu (Perum)	season
Poḻutu (Ciṟu)	time of the day
Maṭalēṟutal	riding on palmyra-leaf-horse.
Marapu	tradition
Marapiyal	chapter on poetic or literary tradition.
Marutam – a region	water-logged land, riverine tract.
– love-aspect	love-quarrel.
– literary	poems on this aspect of love.
Mutaṟporuḷ	first elements, basic elements.
Mullai – a region	forest region
– love-aspect	patient waiting
– literary	poems on this aspect of love.
Meyppāṭu	psychic feelings, exhibiting such feelings.
Meyppāṭṭiyal	chapter on psychic feelings, etc.
Muṉṉilaippuṟamoḻi	direct-indirect speech.

BIBLIOGRAPHY

1. **Song of Songs**

1. Bibliographies on the text of the Song of Songs, Versions, Grammars (Hebrew, Ugaritic and Phoenician) and Lexica are not included here. They are taken for granted.

2. Only books and articles that are cited or referred to either in the text or in the notes, are given in this bibliography.

3. Alphabetical order is followed for the authors, and chronological order is kept for their works — either books or articles.

Albright, W. F., "The Earliest Forms of Hebrew Verse", *JPOS* 2 (1922), 69-86.

———, "Archaic Survivals in the Text of Canticles", in *Hebrew and Semitic Studies Presented to Godfrey Rolles Driver*, (eds.) W. Thomas & W. D. McHardy, Oxford 1963, 1-7.

Alonso Schökel, L., "Genera litteraria", *VD* 38 (1960), 3-15.

———, *Estudios de Poética Hebrea*, (ed.) J. Flors, Barcelona 1963.

———, *The Inspired Word*: Scripture in the Light of Language and Literature, trans. F. Martin, Herder & Herder, 1965.

———, *El Cantar de los Cantares*, Los Libros Sagrados, Vol. X, 1, Ediciones Cristiandad, Madrid 1969.

———, "Poésie hebraïque", *DBS*, Vol. VIII, cols. 47-90, (eds.) Létouzey & Ané, Paris 1972.

Angénieux, J., "Structure du Cantique des Cantiques", (En chants encadrés par des refrains alternants), *ETL* 41 (1965), 96-142.

———, "Les trois Portraits du Cantique des Cantiques", (Étude de critique littéraire), *ETL* 42 (1966), 582-596.

———, "Le Cantique des Cantiques en huit chants à refrains alternants", *ETL* 44 (1968), 87-140.

Aristotle, *The Poetics*, in *Aristotle XXIII*, Eng. trans. W. H. Fyfe, William Heinemann Ltd., London 1982.

Audet, J. P., "Le sens du Cantique des Cantiques", *RB* 62 (1955), 197-221.

———, "Love and Marriage in the Old Testament", *Script* 10 (1958), 65-83.

Avishur, Y., "Addenda to the Expanded Colon in Ugaritic and Biblical Verse", *UF* 4 (1972), 1-10.

Berger, P. R., "Zu den Strophen des 10 Psalms", *UF* 2 (1970), 7-17.

Bettan, E., *The Five Scrolls*, A Commentary on the Song of Songs, Ruth, Lamentations, Ecclesiastes & Esther, Cincinnati 1950.

Bloch, R., "Midrash", *DBS*, Vol. V, cols. 1263-1281.

Bossuet, J. B., *Libri Salomonis*, Proverbia, Ecclesiastes, Canticum Canticorum, Sapientia, Ecclesiasticum, Apud Jo. Baptistam Albritium Hier, F., Venetiis 1732.

Brenner, A., *Colour Terms in the Old Testament*, JSOT, Supplement Series-21, Sheffield 1982.

Briggs, C. A., *The Book of Psalms*, A Critical and Exegetical Commentary, Vol. I, ICC, Edinburgh 1907.

Brown, S. J., *Image and Truth: Studies in the Imagery of the Bible*, Catholic Book Agency, Rome 1955.

Budde, K., "The Song of Solomon", *The New World*, III, (Boston 1894), 56-77.

———, "Was ist das Hohelied?", *Preussische Jahrbücher* 78 (1894), 92-117.

———, *Die Fünf Megillot*, Das Hohelied erklärt: KHAT, XVII, Freiburg 1898.

Buzy, D., "La composition littéraire du Cantique des Cantiques", *RB* 49 (1940), 169-194.

———, "Un chef-d'oeuvre de poésie pure: le Cantique des Cantiques", dans *Memorial Lagrange*, Gabalda, Paris 1940, 147-162.

———, "L'allégorie matrimoniale de Jahvé et d'Israël et le Cantique des Cantiques", *Vivre et Penser - RB* 52 (1944), 77-90.

———, "Le Cantique des Cantiques", *L'Ann. Théo.* 8 (1947), 1-17.

———, *Le Cantique des Cantiques*, La Sainte Bible, Tome VI, (eds.) L. Pirot & A. Clamer, (eds.) Létouzey & Ané, Paris 1951.

———, "Le Cantique des Cantiques: Exégèse allégorique ou parabolique?", in *Mélanges Jules Lebreton I, RSR* 39 (1951-52), 99-114.

Byington, S. T., "A Mathematical Approach to Hebrew Metres", *JBL* 66 (1947), 63-77.

Caminade, P., *Image et Métaphore*, Un problème de poétique contemporaine, Collection Études Supérieures, Bordas 1970.

Cantwell, L., "The Allegory of the Canticle of Canticles", *Script.* 16 (1964), 76-93.

Casanowicz, I. M., *Paronomasia in the Old Testament*, Dissertation, Boston 1894.

Ceresko, A. R., "The Chiastic Word Pattern in Hebrew", *CBQ* 38 (1976), 303-311.

———, "The Function of *Antanaclasis* (mṣ' "to find"//mṣ' "to reach, overtake, grasp"), in Hebrew Poetry, Especially in the Book of Qoheleth", *CBQ* 44 (1982), 551-569.

Childs, B. S., *Introduction to the Old Testament as Scripture*, Fortress Press, Philadelphia 1982^3.

Cicognani, L., *Il Cantico dei Cantici*: Un Melodramma antichissimo, (ed.) Fratelli Bocca, Torino 1911.

Collins, T., *Line-Forms in Hebrew Poetry*, Rome 1978.

Cothenet, E., "L'interprétation du Cantique des Cantiques", *L'ami du Clergé* 73 (1963), 529-540 & 545-552.

Craigie, P. C., "Biblical and Tamil Poetry: Some further Reflections", *SR* 8 (1979), 169-175.

Crenshaw, J. L., "A Liturgy of Wasted Opportunity", *Semitics I* (1970), 27-37.

Cross, F. M., "Prose and Poetry in the Mythic and Epic Texts from Ugarit", *HTR* 67 (1974), 1-15.

Dahood, M. J., "Ugaritic Studies and the Bible", *Greg.* 43 (1962), 55-79.

———, "Hebrew - Ugaritic Lexicography - II", *Bib.* 45 (1964), 393-412.

Dahood, M.J. *Ugaritic-Hebrew Philology*, An. Or. - 17, PIB, Rome 1965.
———, "Hebrew-Ugaritic Lexicography - IV", *Bib.* 47 (1966), 403-419.
———, *Psalms I, 1-50*, AB. 16, Garden City NY 1966.
———, "A New Metrical Pattern in Biblical Poetry", *CBQ* 29 (1967), 574-579.
———, "Hebrew-Ugaritic Lexicography - V", *Bib.* 48 (1967), 421-438.
———, "The Phoenician Contribution to Biblical Wisdom Literature", in *The Rôle of the Phoenicians in the Interaction of Mediterranean Civilizations:* Papers presented to the Archaeological Symposium at the American University of Beirut, March 1967, (ed.) W. A. Ward, Beirut 1968, 123-148.
———, "Comparative Philology Yesterday and Today", *Bib.* 50 (1969), 70-79.
———, "Ugaritic-Hebrew Syntax and Style", *UF* 1 (1969), 15-36.
———, *Psalms III,101-150*, AB.17A, Garden City NY 1970.
———, "Ugaritic-Hebrew Parallel Pairs", in *Ras Shamra Parallels*, (ed.) L. R. Fisher, Vol. I, An. Or. - 49, PIB, Roma 1972, 71-382.
———, "UT, 128 IV 6-7,17-18 and Isaiah 23:8-9", *Or* 44 (1975), 439-441.
———, "Third Masculine Singular with Preformative *t*- in Northwest Semitic", *Or* 48 (1979), 97-106.
———, "Ugaritic-Hebrew Parallel Pairs", in *Ras Shamra Parallels*, (ed.) S. Rummel, Vol. III, An. Or. - 51, PIB, Roma 1981, 1-206.
Delitzsch, F., *Das Hohelied*: untersucht und ausgelegt, Leipzig 1851.
———, *Commentary on the Song of Songs and Ecclesiastes*, trans. M. G. Easton, Edinburgh 1877.
De Vaux, R., *Ancient Israel*, Its Life and Institutions, trans. J. McHugh, Darton, Longman & Todd, London 1965[2].
Driver, G. R., "Hebrew Notes on 'Song of Songs' and 'Lamentations'", in *Festschrift Alfred Bertholet*, (ed.) W. Baumgartner et alii, Tübingen 1950, 134-146.
Driver, S. R., *An Introduction to the Literature of the Old Testament*, International Theological Library, Edinburgh 1913[9].
Dubarle, A. M., "L'amour humain dans le Cantique des Cantiques", *RB* 61 (1954), 67-86.
———, "Bulletin de theologie biblique: Le Cantique des Cantiques", *RScPhilT* 38 (1954), 92-102.
Eco, U., *Semiotics and the Philosophy of Language*, Indiana University Press, Bloomington 1984.
Eissfeldt, O., *The Old Testament: An Introduction*, trans. P. R. Ackroyd, Harper & Row Publishers, Paperback, New York 1976.
Eitan, I., "La répétition de la racine en hébreu", *JPOS* 1 (1921), 171-186.
Erbt, W., *Die Hebräer*, Kanaan im Zeitalter der hebräischer Wanderung und hebräischer Staatengrundungen, Leipzig 1906.
Ewald, H., *Die poetischen Bücher des Alten Bundes*, Vandenhoeck und Ruprecht, Göttingen 1839.
———, *Die Salomonischen Schriften*, Vandenhoeck und Ruprecht, Göttingen 1867.
Exum, C., "A Literary and Structural Analysis of the Song of Songs", *ZAW* 85 (1973), 47-79.
———, "Asseverative *'al* in Canticles 1,6?", *Bib.* 62 (1981), 416-419.
Eybers, I. H., "Some Examples of Hyperbole in Biblical Hebrew", *Semitics* 1 (1970), 38-49.
Falk, M., *Love Lyrics from the Bible*, A Translation and Literary Study of the Song of Songs, (ed.) David M. Gunn, The Almond Press, Sheffield 1982.

Feuillet, A., "Le Cantique des Cantiques et la tradition biblique", *NRT* 74 (1952), 706-733.
———, *Le Cantique des Cantiques*: Etude de théologie biblique et réflexions sur une méthode d'exégèse, Lectio Divina, Les Editions du Cerf, Paris 1953.
———, "La formule d'appartenance mutuelle (II,16) et les interprétations divergentes du Cantique des Cantiques", *RB* 68 (1961), 5-38.
Fisch, H., "The Analogy of Nature: A Note on the Structure of the OT Imagery", *JTS* 6 (1955), 161-173.
Fitzgerald, A., "Hebrew Poetry", in *Jerome Biblical Commentary*, G. Chapman, London 1968.
Fitzmyer, J. A., "*L*^{e} as a Preposition and a Particle in Micah. 5,1 (5,2)", *CBQ* 18 (1956), 10-13.
Fox, M. V., "Scholia to Canticles", *VT* 33 (1983), 199-206.
Freehof, S. B., "The Song of Songs: A General Suggestion", *JQR* 39 (1948-49), 397-402.
Gaster, T. H., "Canticles i.4", *Exp.T.* 72 (1960/61), 195.
Gebhardt, C., *Das Lied der Lieder*: übertragen mit Einführung und Kommentar, Philo Verlag, Berlin 1931.
Gelin, A., "Genres littéraires dans la Bible", *DTC, Tables Générales I* cols. 1790-1794, (eds.) B. Loth & A. Michel, Paris 1951.
Geller, S. A., *Parallelism in Early Biblical Poetry*, Harvard Semitic Monographs-20, Missoula Mont. 1979.
Gerleman, G., *Ruth/Das Hohelied*, BKAT, Neukirchen-Vluyn 1963.
Gevirtz, S., "On Canaanite Rhetoric: The Evidence of the Amarna Letters from Tyre", *Or* 42 (1973), 162-177.
Gilbert, M., Recension of *Song of Songs*, by M. H. Pope, *NRT* 101 (1979), 422.
Ginsburg, C. D., *The Song of Songs and Coheleth*, Two Volumes in One, The Library of Biblical Studies, (ed.) H. M. Orlinsky, Ktav Publishing House, New York 1970, First Published 1857.
Glück, J. J., "Paronomasia in Biblical Literature", *Semitics* 1 (1970), 50-78.
Gollancz, H., *The Targum to "The Song of Songs"*, Luzac & Co., London 1908.
Good, E. M., "Ezekiel's Ship: Some Extended Metaphors in the Old Testament", *Semitics* 1 (1970), 79-103.
Gordis. R., "The Asseverative *kaph* in Ugaritic and Hebrew", *JAOS* 63 (1943), 176-178.
———, *The Song of Songs and Lamentations*, Ktav Publishing House, Inc., New York 1974. (Revised and Augmented Edition).
Gordon, C. H., "New Directions", *BASP* 15 (1978), 59-66, (Naphtali Lewis Festschrift).
———, Recension of *Song of Songs*, by M. H. Pope, *JAOS* 100 (1980), 354-357.
———, "Asymmetric Janus Parallelism", *Eretz-Israel* 16 (1982), 80-81 (English Summary).
Gottwald, N. K., "Song of Songs", *IDB*, Vol. IV, 420-426.
———, *The Hebrew Bible – A Socio-Literary Introduction*, Fortress Press, Philadelphia 1985.
Gray, G. B., *The Forms of Hebrew Poetry*, Prolegomenon by D. N. Freedman, Ktav Publishing House, New York 1972.
Gray, J., *The Legacy of Canaan, VTS*, V, E. J. Brill, Leiden 1957.

Greenstein, E. L., "Two Variations of Grammatical Parallelism in Canaanite Poetry and Their Psycholinguistic Background", *JANES* 6 (1974), 87-105.
Grelot, P., *Le couple humain dans l'Écriture*, Lectio Divina-31, Édition du Cerf, Paris 1962.
———, *Man and Wife in Scripture*, trans. R. Brennan. Herder & Herder, 1964.
———, "Le sens du Cantique des Cantiques", *RB* 71 (1964), 42-56.
Grill, S., *Die Symbolsprache des Hohenliedes*, Heiligenkreuz 1970².
Grossberg, D., "Noun/Verb Parallelism: Syntactic or Asyntactic", *JBL* 99 (1980), 481-488.
Haller, M., *Die Fünf Megilloth*, HAT, Tübingen 1940.
Hamp, V., "Zur Textkritik am Hohenlied", *BZ:NF* 1 (1957), 197-214.
Hanson, P. C., *Allegory and Event*, SCM Press Ltd., London 1959.
Haran, M., "The Graded Numerical Sequence and the Phenomenon of 'Automatism' in Biblical Poetry", *VTS* 22 (1972), 238-267.
Hirschberg, H. H., "Some Additional Arabic Etymologies in Old Testament Lexicography", *VT* 11 (1961), 373-385.
Holladay, W. L., "Form and Wordplay in David's Lament over Saul and Jonathan", *VT* 20 (1970), 153-189.
Honeyman, A. M., "*Merismus* in Biblical Hebrew", *JBL* 71 (1952), 11-18.
Horst, F., "Die Kennzeichen der hebräischen Poesie", *TRu.NF* 21, Heft 2 (1953), 97-121.
Jastrow, M., *The Song of Songs*: Being a Collection of Love Lyrics of Ancient Palestine, Philadelphia 1921.
Joüon, P., *Le Cantique des Cantiques*, Gabriel Beauchesne & Cie, Paris 1909².
Kaddari, M. Z., "A Semantic Approach to Biblical Parallelism", *JJS* XXIV (1973), 167-175.
Kosmala. H., "Form and Structure in Ancient Hebrew Poetry (A New Approach)", *VT* 14 (1964), 423-445.
———, "Form and Structure in Ancient Hebrew Poetry (A New Approach)", *VT* 16 (1966), 152-180.
Kramer, S. N., "The Biblical 'Song of Songs' and the Sumerian Love Songs", *Expedition* 5 (1962), 25-31.
Krašovec, J., *Der Merismus im Biblisch-Hebräischen und Nordwestsemitischen*, Biblica et Orientalia-33, Rome 1977.
Krauss, S., "Die 'Landschaft' im biblischen Hohenliede", *MGWJ*. 78 (1934), 81-97.
———, "Die richtige Sinn von 'Schrecken in der Nacht' HL III,8", in *Occident and Orient – Moses Gaster Eightieth Anniversary Volume*, (ed.) B. Schindler, London 1936, 323-330.
Krinetzki, L., *Das Hohe Lied*: Kommentar zu Gestalt und Kerygma eines alttestamentlicher Liebeslied, Patmos, Düsseldorf 1964.
———, "'Retractationes' zu früheren Arbeiten über das Hohe Lied", *Bib.* 52 (1971), 176-189.
Kselman, J. S., "Semantic-Sonant Chiasm in Biblical Poetry", *Bib.* 58 (1977), 219-223.
Kugel, J. L., *The Idea of Biblical Poetry: Parallelism and its History*, Yale University Press, New Haven & London 1981.

Kuhl, C., "Das Hohelied und seine Deutung", *TRu.NF* 3 (1937), 137-167.
———, "Formen und Gattungen", *RGG.II*, cols. 996-999.
Kuhn, G., "Erklärung des Hohen Liedes", *NKZ* 37 (1926), 501-510 & 521-572.
Kurz, G., *Metapher, Allegorie, Symbol*, Vandenhoeck & Ruprecht, Göttingen 1982.
Landsberger, F., "Poetic Units within the Song of Songs", *JBL* 73 (1954), 203-216.
Landy, F., "The Song of Songs and the Garden of Eden", *JBl* 98 (1979), 513-528.
———, "Beauty and the Enigma: An Inquiry into Some Interrelated Episodes of the Song of Songs", *JSOT* 17 (1980), 55-106.
———, *Paradoxes of Paradise*: Identity and Difference in the Song of Songs, (ed.) D. M. Gunn, The Almond Press, Sheffield 1983.
Le Déaut, R., "À propos d'une définition du midrash", *Bib.* 50 (1969), 395-413.
———, "Apropos a Definition of Midrash", *Interpr.* 25 (1971), 259-282.
Lerch, D., "Zur Geschichte der Auslegung des Hohenliedes", *ZTK* 54 (1957), 257-277.
Loewenstamm, S. E., "The Expanded Colon in Ugaritic and Biblical Verse", *JSS* 14 (1969), 176-196.
"Longinus", *On the Sublime*, in *Aristotle XXIII*, W. Heinemann Ltd., London 1982.
Longman, T., "A Critique of Two Recent Metrical Systems", *Bib.* 63 (1982), 230-254.
Loretz, O., *Das althebräische Liebeslied*: Untersuchungen zur Stichometrie und Redaktionsgeschichte des Hohenliedes und des 45 Psalm, AOAT 14/1.
Lundbom, J. R., *Jeremiah: A Study in Ancient Hebrew Rhetoric*, SBL Dissertation Series-18, Missoula 1975.
Lys, D., *Le plus beau chant de la création*, Lectio Divina-51, Les Éditions du Cerf, Paris 1968.
Mac Cormac, E. R., *Metaphor and Myth in Science and Religion*, Duke University Press, Durham NC 1976.
Mannucci, V., *Sinfonia dell'Amore Sponsale*, Torino 1982.
Marcus D., "Animal Similes in Assyrian Royal Inscriptions", *Or* 46 (1977), 86-106.
May, H. G., "Some Cosmic Connotations of Mayim Rabbîm, Many Waters", *JBL* 74 (1955), 9-21.
McClellan, W. H., "The Elements of Old Testament Poetry", *CBQ* 3 (1941), 203-213 & 321-336.
McCown, C. C., "Solomon and the Shulamite", *JPOS* 1 (1920), 116-121.
McKay, J. W., "Helel and the Dawn-Goddess", A re-examination of the Myth in Isaiah XIV 12-15, *VT* 20 (1970), 451-464.
Meek, T. J., "Canticles and the Tammuz Cult", *AJSL* 39 (1922), 1-14.
———, "The Song of Songs and the Fertility Cult", in *A Symposium on the Song of Songs*, (ed.) W. H. Schoff, 1924, 48-79.
———, "The Structure of Hebrew Poetry", *JRel.* 9 (1929), 523-550.
———, *The Song of Songs*: IB., Vol. V, Abingdon Press, Nashville 1956.
Miller, M. P., "Midrash", in *IDBSup*, Abingdon, Nashville 1976., 593-597.

Miller, P. D., "Animal Names as Designations in Ugaritic and Hebrew", *UF* 2 (1970), 177-186.

Moran, W. L., "taqtul – Third Masculine Singular?", *Bib.* 45 (1964), 80-82.

Moulton, R. G., *The Literary Study of the Bible*: An Account of the Leading Forms of Literature Represented in the Sacred Writings, Isbister and Company, London 1896.

———, *Biblical Idyls*, The Modern Reader's Bible, The Macmillan Company, New York & London 1910.

Muilenburg, J., "A Study in Hebrew Rhetoric: Repetition and Style", *VTS* 1 (1953), 97-111.

———, "The Linguistic and Rhetorical Usage of the Particle *Kî* in the Old Testament", *HUCA* 32 (1961), 135-160.

Müller, H. P., *Vergleich und Metapher im Hohenlied*, Orbis Biblicus et Orientalis-56, Universitätsverlag Freiburg-Schweiz, Vandenhoeck & Ruprecht, Göttingen 1984.

Murphy, R. E., "The Structure of the Canticle of Canticles", *CBQ* 11 (1949), 381-391.

———, Recension of *Canticum Canticorum Salomonis*, by A. Bea, *CBQ* 15 (1953), 501-505.

———, "Recent Literature on the Canticle of Canticles", *CBQ* 16 (1954), 1-11.

———, *The Book of Ecclesiastes and the Canticle of Canticles* with a Commentary, Paulist Press, Pamphlet Bible Series-38, New York 1961.

———, "Canticle of Canticles", in *Jerome Biblical Commentary*, G. Chapman, London 1968.

———, "Form-Critical Studies in the Song of Songs", *Interpr.* 27 (1973), 413-422.

———, "Song of Songs", in *IDBSup*, 836-838.

———, "Towards A Commentary on the Song of Songs", *CBQ* 39 (1977), 482-496.

———, "Interpreting the Song of Songs", *BTB* 9 (1979), 99-105.

———, "The Unity of the Song of Songs", *VT* 28 (1979), 436-443.

———, "A Biblical Model of Human Intimacy: the Song of Songs", *Concilium*, XIV, 1 (1979), (The Family in Crisis or in Transition), 61-66.

Ohly, F., *Hohelied-Studien*, Grundzüge einer Geschichte der Hohenliedauslegung des Abendlandes bis um 1200, Franz Steiner Verlag, GMBH, Wiesbaden 1958.

Origène, *Homélies sur le Cantique des Cantiques*, Sources Chrétiennes - No. 37 bis, Introduction, traduction et notes de O. Rousseau, Les Éditions du Cerf, Paris 1966².

Parente, P. P., "The Canticle of Canticles in Mystical Theology", *CBQ* 6 (1944), 142-158.

Paul, S. M., "Mnemonic Devices", in *IDBSup*, 600-602.

Payne, D. F., "A Perspective on the Use of Simile in the Old Testament", *Semitics* 1 (1970), 111-125.

Peeters, L., "Pour une interprétation du jeu de mots", *Semitics*, 2 (1971/72), 127-142.

Phipps, W. E., "The Plight of the Song of Songs", *JAAR* 42 (1974), 82-100.

Pope, M. H., *Song of Songs*, AB:7C, Garden City NY 1977.
Pouget, G.-Guitton, J., *Le Cantique des Cantiques*, Études Bibliques, J. Gabalda, Paris 1948.
Rabin, C., "The Song of Songs and Tamil Poetry", *SR* 3:3 (1973/4), 205-219.
Rankin, O. S., "Alliteration in Hebrew Poetry", *JTS* 31 (1930), 285-291.
Renan, E., *Le Cantique des Cantiques*, (ed.) C. Lévy, Paris 1884[5].
Ricciotti, G., *Il Cantico dei Cantici*, Società editrice internazionale, Torino 1927.
Ricoeur, P., *The Rule of Metaphor* (La Métaphore vive), Trans. Czerny et alii, University of Toronto Press, Toronto 1984.
Robert, A., "Le genre littéraire du Cantique des Cantiques", *RB* 52 (1943-44), 192-213 – *Vivre et Penser*, III Serie 1943-1944, J. Gabalda, Paris 1944.
———, "La description de l'Époux et de l'Épouse dans Cant. V, 11-15 et VII, 2-6", in *Mélanges É. Podechard*, Facultés Catholiques, Lyon 1945, 211-223.
———, "Littéraires (Genres), in *DBS*, Vol. V, cols. 405-421.
Robert, A.-Tournay, R.-Feuillet, A., *Le Cantique des Cantiques*: Commentaire, Études Bibliques, J. Gabalda & Cie, Paris 1963.
Robinson, T. H., "Some Principles of Hebrew Metrics", *ZAW* 54 (1936), 28-43.
———, "Basic Principles of Hebrew Poetic Form", in *Festschrift Alfred Bertholet*, (eds.) W. Baumgartner et alii, J. C. B. Mohr, Tübingen 1950, 438-450.
———, "Hebrew Poetic Form: The English Tradition", *VTS* 1 (1953), 128-149.
———, *The Poetry of the Old Testament*, Gerald Duckworth & Co., London 1969[4].
Roth, W. M. W., "The Numerical Sequence x/x + 1 in the Old Testament", *VT* 12 (1962), 300-311.
———, *Numerical Sayings in the Old Testament: A Form-Critical Study*, *VTS*, Vol. XIII, Leiden 1965.
Rowley, H. H., "The Meaning of 'the Shulamite'", *AJSL* 56 (1939), 84-91.
———, "The Interpretation of the Song of Songs", in *The Servant of the Lord and Other Essays*, London 1952, 182-234; revised edition, Oxford 1965, 195-246.
Sadgrove, M., "The Song of Songs as Wisdom Literature", in *Studia Biblica 1978* (I. Papers on OT and Related Themes), Sixth International Congress on Biblical Studies, (ed.) E. A. Livingstone, (Oxford 3-7 April 1978), JSOT Supplement Series-11, Sheffield 1979, 245-248.
Sarna, N. M., "The Mythological Background of Job. 18", *JBL* 82 (1963), 315-318.
Saydon, P. P., "Assonance in Hebrew as a Means of Expressing Emphasis", *Bib.* 36 (1955), 36-50 & 287-304.
Schmidt, N., *The Message of the Poets*, 1911.
Schonfield, H. J., *The Song of Songs*, The New American Library, New York 1959.
Schoville, K. N., "Song of Songs", in *Encyclopaedia Judaica*, Vol. 15, (eds.) C. Roth & G. Wigoder, Encyclopaedia Judaica, Jerusalem 1971, cols. 144-150.
———, *The Impact of the Ras Shamra Texts on the Study of the Song of Songs*, University Microfilms, Inc. Ann Arbor, Michigan 1972.

Scott, R. B. Y., "Secondary Meanings of *'aḥar*, after, behind", *JTS* 50 (1949), 178-179.

Segert, S., "Problems of Hebrew Prosody", *VTS* 7 (1960), 283-291.

Shea, W. H., "The Chiastic Structure of the Song of Songs", *ZAW* 92 (1980), 378-396.

Shipley, J. T. (ed.), *Dictionary of World Literary Terms*, George Allen & Unwin Ltd., London 1970.

Slotki, I. W., "Forms and Features of Ancient Hebrew Poetry", *JMEOS* 16 (1931), 31-49.

———, "Antiphony in Ancient Hebrew Poetry", *JQR* 26 (1935/36), 199-219.

Smith, G. A., *The Early Poetry of Israel in its Physical and Social Origins*: "The Schweich Lectures 1910", London 1912.

Soggin, J. A., *Introduction to the Old Testament*, SCM Press Ltd., revised edition, 1980.

Soulen, R. N., "The *Wasfs* of the Song of Songs and Hermeneutic", *JBL* 86 (1967), 183-190.

Stephan, S. H., "Modern Palestinian Parallels to the Song of Songs", *JPOS* 2 (1922), 199-278.

Stuiber, A., "Die Wachhütte im Weingarten (Vgl-Ct. 1,5 Vg)", *JbAC* 2 (1959), 86-89.

Teselle, S. M., *Speaking in Parables: A Study in Metaphor and Theology*, Fortress Press, Philadelphia 1975.

Tosato, A., *Il Matrimonio Israelitico*, An. Bib. - 100, Biblical Institute Press, Roma 1982.

Tournay, R. J., "Bulletin bibliographique", *RB* LX (1953), 414-417.

———, "Bulletin bibliographique", *RB* LXII (1955), 284-286.

———, *Qunad Dieu parle aux hommes le langage de l'amour*, Cahiers de la Revue Biblique-21, J. Gabalda & Cie, Paris 1982.

Trible, P., "Depatriarchalizing in Biblical Interpretation", *JAAR* 41 (1973), 30-48.

———, *God and the Rhetoric of Sexuality*, Fortress Press, Philadelphia 1978.

Tromp, N. J., "Wisdom and the Canticle", in *La Sagesse de l'Ancien Testament*, (ed.) M. Gilbert, Journées Bibliques Lv. 1978, Bib. ETL-51, Leuven-Gembloux 1979, 88-95.

Tsumura, D. T., "Literary Insertion (AXB Pattern) in Biblical Hebrew", *VT* 33,4 (1983), 468-482.

Ullendorff, E., "The Contribution of South Semitic to Hebrew Lexicography", *VT* 6 (1956), 190-198.

Vaccari, A., *La Cantica*, La Sacra Bibbia: I Libri Poetici-2, Casa editrice Adriano Salani, Firenze 1959.

Van Dijk, H. J., "Does Third Masculine Singular Taqtul exist in Hebrew?", *VT* 19 (1969), 440-447.

Vawter, B., "Apocalyptic: Its Relation to Prophecy", *CBQ*, 22 (1960), 33-46.

Vogt, E., "Einige hebräische Wortbedeutungen", *Bib.* 48 (1967), 57-74.

Watson, W. G. E., "Shared Consonants in Northwest Semitic", *Bib.* 50 (1969), 525-533.

Watson, W.G.E., "More on Shared Consonants", *Bib.* 52 (1971), 44-50.
———, "Gender-Matched Synonymous Parallelism in the OT", *JBL* 99 (1980), 321-341.
———, "A Note on Staircase Parallelism", *VT* 33 (1983), 510-512.
———, *Classical Hebrew Poetry*: A Guide to its Techniques, JSOT Supplement Series-26, JSOT Press, Sheffield 1984.
Webster, E. C., "Pattern in the Song of Songs", *JSOT* 22 (1982), 73-93.
Wellek, R.-Warren, A., *Theory of Literature,* Penguin Books 1970.
Wheelwright, P., *Metaphor and Reality*, University of Indiana Press, Bloomington 1967³.
White, J. B., *A Study of the Language of Love in the Song of Songs and Ancient Egyptian Poetry*, SBL Dissertation Series-38, Scholars Press, Missoula 1978.
Wilkinson, L. P., "Onomatopoeia and the Sceptics", *ClasQ* 36 (1942), 121-133.
Wittekindt, W., *Das Hohelied und seine Beziehungen zum Istarkult*, Orient-Buchhaldlung Heinz Lafaire, Hannover 1925.
Wright, A. G., "The Literary Genre Midrash", *CBQ* 28 (1966), 105-138 & 415-457.
Würthwein, E., "Zum Verständnis des Hohenliedes", *TRu.NF.* 32 (1967), 177-212.
———, *Die Fünf Megilloth*, HAT-18. Mohr, Tübingen 1969.
Yoder, P. B., "A - B Pairs and Oral Composition in Hebrew Poetry", *VT* 21 (1971), 470-489.
Young, D. W., "The Ugaritic Myth of the God ḤŌRĀN and the Mare", *UF* 11 (1979), 839-848.
Young, G. D., "Ugaritic Prosody", *JNES* IX (1950), 124-133.

2. **Tamil Literature**

I. *Primary Sources*

A. *Grammars*

1) Tolkāppiyam:

Tolkāppiyam: Eḻuttatikāram, Iḷampūraṇar Urai, SISSWPS, Madras 1974.
Tolkāppiyam: Collatikāram, Cēṉāvaraiyar Urai, SISSWPS, Madras 1980.
Tolkāppiyam: Poruḷatikāram (Akattiṇaiyiyal, Puṟattinaiyiyal), Nacciṉārkkiṉiyar Urai, SISSWPS, Madras 1975.
Tolkāppiyam: Poruḷatikāram (Kaḷaviyal, Kaṟpiyal, Poruḷiyal), Nacciṉārkkiṉiyar Urai, SISSWPS Madras 1977.
Tolkāppiyam: Poruḷatikāram (Meyppāṭṭiyal, Uvamaviyal, Ceyyuḷiyal, Marapiyal), Pēräciriyar Urai, SISSWPS, Madras 1975.[5]
Tolkāppiyam: Poruḷatikāram, Kuḻantai Urai, Vēlā Patippakam, Erode 1968. The commentator has rearranged the traditional sequence of the treatment.
Tholkāppiyam (in English) – With Critical Studies, trans. S. Ilakkuvaṉār, 'Kuṟaḷ Neṟi' Publishing House, Madurai 1963.

2) *Kaḷaviyal* (Iṟaiyaṉār Akapporuḷ), Nakkīraṉār Urai, SISSWPS, Madras 1953.

3) *Nampiyakapporuḷ* (Akapporuḷ Viḷakkam), Nāṟkavirāca Nampi, (ed.) K. R. Kōvintarāca Mutaliyār (with notes and commentary), SISSWPS Publication No. 338, Madras 1943.

B. *Texts with Commentary*

1) Eṭṭuttokai: The Eight Anthologies:

Naṟṟiṇai, (ed.) Pinnattur A. Narayanasamy Iyer, SISSWPS, Madras 1976.

Kuṟuntokai, (ed.) P. V. Cōmacuntaraṉār, SISSWPS, Madras 1978.

Aiṅkuṟunūṟu (Mūlamum Paḻaiyavuraiyum), (ed.) U. V. Cāminātaiyar, Cāminātaiyar Nūlnilaiyam Pub., Madras 1980.[6]

Kalittokai, (ed.) Cempiyaṉ, Comm. Caktitācaṉ Cupramaṇiyaṉ, Aṉpu Veḷiyīṭu, Pondicherry 1958.

Akanāṉūṟu: Poems 1-120, (eds.) N. M. Venkatasamy Nattar & R. Venkatasalam Pillai, SISSWPS, Madras 1954[3].

Akanāṉūṟu: Poems 121-300, (ed.) P. V. Cōmacuntaraṉār, SISSWPS, Madras 1976.

Akanāṉūṟu: Poems 301-400, (eds.) N. M. Venkatasamy Nattar & R. Venkatasalam Pillai, SISSWPS, Madras 1951.

Puṟanāṉūṟu, (ed.) U.V. Cāminātaiyar, Madras 1956[5].

Kuṟuntokai Viḷakkam: Poems 1-101, (ed.) R. Irākavaiyaṅkār, Aṇṇāmalai Palkalaik-kaḻakam, 1956[2].

Kuṟuntokai (An Anthology of Classical Tamil Love Poetry), trans. M. Shanmugam Pillai & David E. Ludden, Koodal Publishers, Madurai 1976.

2) Pattuppāṭṭu: Patippu: Āciriyak-kuḻuviṉarāl pala piratikaḷai oppunōkki, paricōtittu veḷiyiṭap peṟṟatu, New Century Book House Private Ltd., Madras 1981.

Pattuppāṭṭu: Ten Tamil Idylls, trans. J. V. Chelliah, SISSWPS, Madras 1962.

C. *Dictionaries and Concordance*

Kazhagam Tamil Dictionary, SISSWPS, Madras 1964.

Lifco Tamil, Tamil-English Dictionary, The Little Flower Company, Madras 1968.[2]

Burrow, T.-Emeneau, M. B., *A Dravidian Etymological Dictionary*, Clarendon Press, Oxford 1984[2].

Turner, R. L., *A Comparative Dictionary of the Indo-Aryan Languages*, Oxford University Press, London 1973[2].

Winslow, M., *A Comprehensive Tamil and English Dictionary*, Asian Educational Services, New Delhi 1984.

Index des mots de la littérature tamoule ancienne, 3 Vols., IFI, Pondichéry 1967-1968-1970.

II. *Secondary Sources*

Adaikalasamy, M. R., *Tamiḻ Ilakkiya Varalāṟu*, SISSWPS, Madras 1981[7].
Alexander, P. C., "Asoka and the Spread of Buddhism in Cheranadu", *TC* I,2 (1952), 125-131.
Aravaanan, K. P., *Kavitaiyiṉ uyir, uḷḷam, uṭal*, Pari Nilaiyam, Madras 1976.
———, *Aṟṟaināḷ Kātalum Vīramum*, Pari Nilaiyam, Madras 1978.
———, "Marriage - A Dravido-African Cultural Comparative Study", in *PFifICSTS*, Vol. II, sec. 8, IATR, Madras 1981, 1-10.
———, "Mara Vaḻipāṭu", *JTamS* 20 (1981), 100-120.
Arokiaswami, M., *The Classical Age of the Tamils*, University of Madras, 1972.
Arulappa, R., *Thiruvaḷḷuvar a Mystic - God the Bridegroom*, Madras 1976.
Arumugha Mudaliar, S., "The Antiquity of Tamil and Tolkāppiyam", *TC* II (1953), 340-361.
Balakrishna Mudaliyar, N. R., *The Golden Anthology of Ancient Tamil Literature*, Vol. II, SISSWPS, Madras 1959.
Balasubramanian, C., "The Age of Kutunthokai", in *An Insight into Tamilology*: Tamiḻiyal - Ōr Akanōkku (Dr. T. E. Gnanamurthy 61st Birthday Commemoration Volume), (eds.) R. Chandrasekaran & K. P. Ganesan, Kovai 1972, 121-133.
———, *The Status of Women in Tamilnadu during the Sangam Age*, University of Madras, 1976.
Baskaran, K., "Plants and Tamil Culture", *JTamS* 12 (Dec. 1979), 58-62.
Bharathi, S. S., "The Age of Tholkappiam", *JAU*, VI, 2 (Jan. 1937), 121-138.
———, "The Age of Tholkappaim", *JAU*, VI, 3 (May 1937), 216-229.
———, "Tholkappia Araichi - Ullurai", *JAU*, VIII, (Oct. 1938), 35-41.
Caldwell, R., *A Comparative Grammar of the Dravidian or South-Indian Family of Languages*, revised and edited by J. L. Wyatt & T. Ramakrishna Pillai, Oriental Books Reprint Corporation, New Delhi 1974[3].
Chatterji, S. K., "Old Tamil, Ancient Tamil and Primitive Dravidian", *TC*, V, 2 (Apr. 1956), 148-174.
Chellappan, K., "Towards a Theory of Tamil Aesthetics with Special Reference to Sangam Poetry and Cilappatikāram", in *PFifICSTS*, Vol. I, sec. 3, IATR, Madras 1981, 1-5.
Chidambaranatha Chettiar, A., *Advanced Studies in Tamil Prosody*: Being a History of Tamil Prosody up to the 10th Century AD, Annamalai University, Annamalainagar 1943, Repr. 1955, 1957.
———, "Introduction to Tamil Poetry", *TC*, VII, 1 (Jan. 1958), 56-75.
Cīṉivācaṉ, R., *Caṅka Ilakkiyattil Uvamaikaḷ*, Aṇiyakam, 1973.
David, H. S., "The Earliest Tamil Poems Extant", *TC*, IV, 1 (Jan. 1955), 90-98.
———, "The Kutunhthokai Anthology", *TC*, VII, 4 (Oct. 1958), 323-349.
———, "The Earliest Stage of Tamil Religion", *TC*, IX, 4 (Oct.-Dec. 1961), 395-401.
———, "The Place of *Tolkāppiyam* in Ancient Tamil Literature", in *PFICSTS*, Vol. II, IATR, Madras 1969, 19-37.

Dubianski, A. M., "An Analysis of the *Mullai-Pālai* Fragment of Ancient Tamil Poetry", *JTamS* 17 (June 1979), 88-103.
———, "A Motif of Messenger in the *Mullaittiṇai*", *JTamS* 19 (June 1981), 15-18.
Emily (Sr.), "Akattiṇaiyum Ati-uṉṉata Caṅkītamum", *Thozhan* 24 (May-June 1983), 170-178.
Gnanasambandan, A. S., *Akamum Puṟamum: Akam*, Pari Nilaiyam, Madras 1956.
———, *Ilakkiyak Kalai*, SISSWPS, Madras 1964[4].
———, "Tolkappiyar's Concept of Uvamai", *JTamS* 4 (Dec. 1973), 1-12.
Hart, G. L. III, *The Poems of Ancient Tamil*: Their Milieu and their Sanskrit Counterparts, University of California Press, 1975.
———, *Poets of the Tamil Anthologies*: Ancient Poems of Love and War, Princeton University Press, Princeton 1979.
Hirudayam, I., *Entaiyar Iṟaivaṉ*: God of our Fathers, Vol. I, Aikiya Alayam, Madras 1977.
Jesudason, C., "A Study of Kabilar, the Sangam Poet", *TC*, III (1954), 18-35.
Kailasapathy, K., *Tamil Heroic Poetry*, Oxford University Press, London 1968.
Kalidos, R., *History and Culture of the Tamils*: From Prehistoric Times to the President's Rule, Vijay Publications, Dindigul 1976.
Kanakasabhai, V.., *The Tamils Eighteen Hundred Years Ago*, SISSWPS, Madras 1966 Repr.
Kandaswamy, S. N., "The Age of *Tolkāppiyam*", *JTamS* 20 (Dec. 1981), 37-71.
Kothandapani Pillai, K., "Vada Venkatam", *TC*, IX, 1 (Jan.-Mar. 1961), 65-92.
Krishnan, K. G., "Origin of the Tamil Script", in *Origin, Evolution and Reform of the Tamil Script*, Seminar Papers, The Institute of Traditional Cultures, Madras 1983, 15-19.
Kumaraswamy, R.-Meenakshinathan, E., "Ethno-medical Studies on Thoyyil Painting in Sangam Period", in *PFifICSTS*, Vol. II, sec. 13, IATR, Madras 1981, 33-38.
Kurucāmi, M. R. P., *Tamiḻ Nūlkaḷil Kuṟippup Poruḷ*, Tamiḻpputtakālayam, Cennai 1980.
———, "Uḷḷuṟaiyum Iṟaicciyum", in *Aintām Ulakat Tamiḻ Māṉāṭu, Maturai, 1981: Viḻā Malar*, Madras 1981, 168-172.
Mahadevan, I., "Tamil Brahmi Inscriptions of the Sangam Age", in *PSICSTS*, Vol. I, IATR, Madras 1971, 73-106.
———, "Origin of the Tamil Script", in *Origin, Evolution and Reform of the Tamil Script*, Madras 1983, 7-14.
Mahadevan, K., "Refractions in Akam Poetry", in *PFifICSTS*, Vol. I, sec. 7, IATR, Madras 1981, 17-20.
Manavalan, A. A., "Caṅka Ilakkiyam", in *Tamiḻ Ilakkiyak Koḷkai*, (eds.) S. V. Subramanian & V. Veerasami, IITS, Madras 1975, 25-64.
Manickam, V. Sp., *The Tamil Concept of Love*, SISSWPS, Madras 1962.
———, *Tamiḻk Kātal*, Pari Nilaiyam, Madras 1980[3].
Manickam, V. T., *Marutam*: An Aspect of Love in Tamil Literature, Tēmā Publications, Karaikudi 1982.

Manickavasagom, M. E., "Patterns of Early Tamil Marriages", *TC*, XI, 4 (1964), 329-338.

Manikkam, N., "Mutal, Karu, Uri – Ōr Āyvu", *Tamilkkalai*, I, 2 (June 1983), 22-29.

Manuel, M., "The Use of Literary Conventions in Tamil Classical Poetry", in *PFICSTS*, Vol. II, IATR, Madras 1969, 63-69.

Marr, J. R., *The Eight Tamil Anthologies*: With special reference to Purananuru and Patirruppattu, Unpublished Ph.D. Thesis, University of London, 1958.

Marutanāyakam, P., "Tolkāppiyamum Mēlaināṭṭuk Kavitaiyiyalum", *Tamilkkalai*, I, 4 (Dec. 1983), 1-14.

Meenakshisundaram, T. P., "The Theory of Poetry in Tolkāppiyar", *TC*, I, 2 (June 1952), 104-113.

Mīṉāṭcicuntaram, K., "Caṅka Ilakkiyam – Kaṟpaṉai Marapu", in *PFifICSTS*, Vol. III, IATR, Madras 1981, 520-527.

Muttuk Kaṇṇappaṉ, T., *Caṅka Ilakkiyattil Neytal Nilam*, Atipattar Patippakam, Cennai 1978.

Nadarajah, D. (Mrs), "The Gloriosa Superba in Classical Poetry", *TC, XI, 3* (July-Sept. 1964), 280-290.

———, "The Mullai and the Tuḷaci as Symbols of Chastity", in *PFICSTS*, Vol. I, IATR, Madras 1968, 314-319.

———, *Women in Tamil Society: The Classical Period*, Faculty of Arts, University of Malaya, Department of Indian Studies Monograph Series - No. 15, Kuala Lumpur 1969.

———, "The Tamil Ideals of Female Beauty", in *PSICSTS*, Vol. II, IATR, Madras 1971, 34-40.

Narasimhaiah, B., *Neolithic and Megalithic Cultures in Tamilnadu*, Sundeep Prakashan, Delhi 1980.

Natarajan, A. D., "An Introduction to the Traditional Doctrine of Love", in *PFICSTS*, Vol. II, IATR, Madras 1969, 70-87.

Parthasarathi, J., "The Love Poetry of Old Tamil: A Literary Appreciation", *AUJRL*, XIX, Pt. II (July 1971), 17-54.

Periyakaruppan, I., "Oppiyal Nōkkil Meyppāṭu", in *PFifICSTS*, Vol. III, IATR, Madras 1981, 127-133.

Pillay, K. K., "The Brahmi Inscriptions of South India and the Sangam Age", *TC*, V, 2 (Apr. 1956), 175-185.

———, *A Social History of the Tamils*, Vol. I, University of Madras, 1975[2].

Puvarakam Pillai, A., "Neytal", in *Naṟṟiṇaic Coṟpoḻivukaḷ: 22.2.1942*, SISSWPS, Madras 1975[4], 72-112.

Rajamanickam, M., "Saivism in the Pre-Pallava Period", *TC*, V, 4 (Oct. 1956), 328-339.

———, "Kuṟiñcikkali", in *Kalittokaic Coṟpoḻivukaḷ: 9,10 March 1940*, SISSWPS, Madras 1970[5], 39-69.

Ramachandran, K. S., *Archaeology of South India: Tamil Nadu*, Sundeep Prakashan, Delhi 1980.

Ramanujan, A. K., *The Interior Landscape*, Peter Owen, London 1970.

———, *Poems of Love and War*: From the Eight Anthologies and the Ten Long Poems of Classical Tamil, Columbia University Press, New York 1985.

Rasanayagama, Y. (Mrs), "Physico and Poetic Tradition in Tamil Literature of the Tholkāppiyam and Sangam Periods", in *PFifICSTS*, Vol. I, sec. 7, IATR, Madras 1981, 29-45.

Sambamoorthy, L., "The Psychological Symbolism of *Paalai* in *Ḱutunhthokai*", in *PSICSTS*, Vol. II, IATR, Madras 1971, 25-33.

Samy, P. L., "Kurinjci", *TC*, IV, 2 (Apr. 1955), 132-139.

———, *Caṅka Ilakkiyattil Ceṭikoṭi Viḷakkam*, SISSWPS, Madras 1967.

———, *Caṅka Ilakkiyattil Puḷḷiṉa Viḷakkam*, SISSWPS, Madras 1976.

———, "Common Names and Myths of the Flora and Fauna in Dravidian and Indo-Aryan Languages", in *PFifICSTS*, Vol. II, sec. 8., IATR, Madras 1981, 43-53.

———, *Ilakkiya Āyvu: Aṟiviyal*, Cekar Patippakam, Cennai 1982.

Sankaran, C. R., "Tolkāppiyar and the Science of Phonemics", *TC* IX (1961), 117-130.

Sēnāthi Rājā, E. S. W., "The Pre-Sanskrit Element in Ancient Tamil Literature", *JRAS* XIX (1887), 558-582.

Shankar Raju Naidu, S., "A Comparative Study of Tamil and Nagari Alphabets", *TC*, IX, 1 (Jan.-Mar. 1961), 33-42.

Shanmugam, R., "The Background Myth in Sangam Poetry", in *PFifICSTS*, Vol. I, sec. 7, IATR, Madras 1981, 11-15.

Singaravelu, S., *Social Life of the Tamils: The Classical Period*, Kuala Lumpur 1966.

Siromoney, G., "Origin of the Tamil-Brahmi Script", in *Origin, Evolution and Reform of the Tamil Script*, Madras 1983, 21-29.

Somasundaram Pillai, J. M., *A History of Tamil Literature*: With Texts and Translations from the Earliest Times to 600 AD, Annamalainagar 1968.

Srinivas Iyengar, P. T., *History of the Tamils*: From the Earliest Times to 600 AD, C. Coomaraswamy Naidu & Sons, Madras 1929.

Subbiah, A., "Is the Tamil Alphabet System an Adaptation?", *JTamS*, 3 (Sept. 1973), 64-74.

Subramanian, N., "The Avifauna of the Tamil Country", *TC* 12 (Oct.-Dec. 1966), 259-268.

———, "The Avifauna of the Tamil Country", *Supplement TC*, XII, 4 (Oct.-Dec. 1966), 1-16.

Subramoniam, V. I., "The Dating of Sangam Literature", in *PTICSTS*, IFI, Pondichéry 1973, 75-86.

Sundaramoorthy, G., *Early Literary Theories in Tamil in Comparison with Sanskrit Theories*, Sarvodaya Ilakkiya Pannai, Madurai 1974.

Sundararaj, T., "Rise and Fall of Koṟkai", *JTamS* 19 (June 1981), 55-63.

Thani Nayagam, X. S., *Nature in Ancient Tamil Poetry*: Concept and Interpretation, Tamil Literature Society, Tuticorin 1952.

———, "The Ethical Interpretation of Nature in Ancient Tamil Poetry", *TC* I (1952), 186-196.

———, "The Tamils said it all with Flowers", *TC* II (Apr. 1953), 164-175.

———, "Apperception in Tamil Literary Studies", in *PFICSTS*, Vol. II, IATR, Madras 1969, 120-128.

———, *Tamil Humanism: The Classical Period*, Bunker Memorial Lectures 1972, Jaffna College, Jaffna 1972.

———, "Tolkāppiyam – The Earliest Record", *JTamS* 1 (Sept. 1972), 61-70.

Thani Nayagam, X. S., *Research in Tamil Studies: Retrospect and Prospect*, Chelvanayakam Memorial Lectures, Thanthai Chelva Memorial Trust, Jaffna 1980.

Thirugnanasambandhan, P., "A Study of Rasa – Tholkāppiar and Bharata", in *PFICSTS*, Vol. II, IATR, Madras 1969, 10-18.

Thirunavukkarasu, K. D., "The Ethical Philosophy of the Ancient Tamils", *Bull.ITC* (July-Dec. 1973), 42-50.

Thiyagarajan, D. (Mrs), "Symbolism in Tamil Literature", in *An Insight into Tamilology*, Kovai 1972, 140-149.

Vaiyapuri Pillai, S., "History of Tamil Language and Literature", *TC*, III, 3-4 (1954), 331-358.

————, *History of Tamil Language and Literature*, New Century Book House, Madras 1956.

Varadaraja Iyer, E. S., "The Kuṟiñji Girl", *JAU* XVII (July 1952), 144-152.

Varadarajan, E. S., "Palantamiḻar Kaṭavuḷ Vaḻipāṭu", *JAU* VIII 3 (June 1939), 193-248.

Varadarajan, M., *The Treatment of Nature in Sangam Literature*, SISSWPS, Madras 1957.

————, *Ōvac Ceyti*, Pari Nilaiyam, Madras 1963[4].

————, *Ilakkiyat Tiṟaṉ*, Pari Nilaiyam, Madras 1965[2].

————, "Literary Theories in Early Tamil - Eṭṭuttokai", in *PFICSTS*, Vol. II, IATR, Madras 1969, 45-54.

————, "A Type of Apostrophes in Sangam Literature", in *PTICSTS*, IFI, Pondichéry 1973, 91-96.

Vasuki, M., "Variety of Hair-Dos in Ancient Tamil Nadu", *JTamS* 9 (June 1976), 50-58.

Vellaivaranan, K., *Tolkāppiam: Tamiḻ Ilakkiya Varalāṟu*, Annamalai Palkalaikkaḻakam, 1957.

Venkatachalam Pillai, R., "Presidential Address", in *Akanāṉūṟṟuc Coṟpoḻivukaḷ: 15.12.1940*, SISSWPS, Madras 1977[3], 1-38.

Venkatarajulu Reddiar, V., *Kapilar*, Madras University Tamil Series No. 5, University of Madras, 1936.

Victor, M., *The Tamil-Islamic Cultural Encounter in Cīṟāppurāṇam*, Vol. I, Unpublished Dissertation in Pontificia Universitas Gregoriana, Rome 1985.

Zvelebil, K., "Tentative Periodization of the Development of Tamil", *TC*, VI, 1 (Jan. 1957), 50-55.

————, "Tamil Poetry 2000 Years Ago", *TC*, X, 2 (Apr.-June 1963), 19-30.

————, "The Brahmi Hybrid Inscriptions", *ArOr* (1964), 545-575.

————, "From Proto-South Dravidian to Old Tamil and Malayalam", in *PSICSTS*, Vol. I, IATR, Madras 1971, 54-72.

————, *An Introduction to Tamil Classical Prosody*, Hoe & Co., Madras 1972.

————, *The Smile of Murugan*, Leiden/Brill 1973.

————, *The Tamil Literature*, Handbuch der Orientalistik-zweite Abteilung 2, Band 1, Abschnitt, E. J., Brill, Leiden/Köln 1975.

3. **Other Works**

Amalorpavadass, D. S., (ed.) *Indian Christian Spirituality*, NBCLC; Bangalore 1982.

Burrow, T., "Dravidian and the Decipherment of the Indus Script", *JTamS*, II, 1 (May 1970), 149-156.

Cimino, R. M.-Scialpi, F. (eds.), *India and Italy*, Exhibition organized in collaboration with the Archaeological Survey of India and the Indian Council for Cultural Relations, Is.MEO, Rome 1974.

Clauson,G.-Chadwick, J., "The Indus Script Deciphered?", *JTamS*, II, 1 (May 1970), 135-148.

Cornelius, J. T., "The Graffiti on the Megalithic Pottery of South India and Dravidian Origin", *TC*, XII, 4 (Oct.-Dec. 1966), 287-301.

Crown, A. D., "Some Contacts and Comparisons between the Ancient Near East and the Indus Valley Civilization", in *PSICSTS*, Vol. II, IATR, Madras 1971, 379-386.

Dhavamony, M., "Problematica dell'Inculturazione del Vangelo oggi", *Stromata* XLI (1985), 253-272.

Eliki Laskarides-Zannas (Mrs), "Greece and South India", in *PFifICSTS*, Vol. I, sec. 6. IATR, Madras 1981, 25-33.

Fabricius, B. (ed.), *Der Periplus des Erythräischen Meeres von einem Unbekannten, Anonymou Periplous tēs Erythras Thalassēs*, Verlag von Veit & Comp., Leipzig 1883.

Gnani Giri Nadar, K. C. A., *Latin Words of Tamil Origin*: An Etymological Dictionary, Madurai 1981.

———, *Greek Words of Tamil Origin*: An Etymological Dictionary, Madurai 1982.

———, *A Statement in Tamilo-European Linguistics*, Madurai 1982.

Greenfell, B. P.-Hunt, A. S. (eds.), *The Oxyrhynchus Papyri*, Part III, "Farce and Mime", London 1903, 41-57.

Greenfield, J. C.-Mayrhofer, M., "The algummîm/almuggîm – Problem reexamined", in *Hebräische Wortforschung*, Festschrift Walter Baumgartner – VTS-16, Leyden 1967, 83-89.

Joseph, P., "Algummim or Almuggim of the Bible", *TC*, VI, 2 (1957), 133-138.

———, "Romance of Two Tamil Words", *TC*, VIII, 3 (July-Sept. 1959), 201-207.

———, "Indian Ivory for Solomon's Throne", *TC*, IX, 3 (1960), 271-280.

———, "Ophir of the Bible: Identification", *TC*, X, 3 (July-Sept. 1963), 48-70.

———, "The Harappa Script – A Tragedy in Timing", *TC*, XI, 4 (Oct.-Dec. 1964), 295-307.

———, "Harappa Script Decipherment – Rev. Heras and his Successors", *JTamS*, II, 1 (May 1970), 111-134.

Kennedy, J., "The Early Commerce of Babylon with India – 700-300 BC", *JRAS* 30 (1898), 241-288.

———, "The Indians in Armenia, 130 BC - 300 AD", *JRAS* 36 (1904), 309-314.

Khaire, V., "Tamil, The Language of the Pre-historic Maharashtra", *JTamS* 17 (June 1979), 14-25.

———, "Tamil, The Language of the Pre-historic Maharashtra", *JTams* 17 (Dec. 1979), 78-83.

Konow, S., "Etruscan and Dravidian", *JRAS* 36 (1904), 45-51.

Lal, B. B., "Some Observations on Harappan Script", in *India's Contribution to World Thought and Culture*, Vivekananda Rock Memorial Committee, Madras 1970, 189-202.

Legrand, F., "Tamil Loan Words in Greek", *TC*, III (1954), 36-45.

Mahadevan, I., "Dravidian Parallels in Proto-Indian Script", *JTamS*, II, 1, Part I (May 1970), 157-276.

Margabandhu, C., "Ancient Sea-ports of South India, their Trade Relationship with the Western World during the First Century BC to the Second Century AD", in *Sri Dinesacandrika Studies in Indology*, Shri D. C. Sircar Festschrift, (eds.) B. N. Mukherjee et alii, Sundeep Prakashan, Delhi 1983, 185-202.

Mativāṇaṉ, I., *Kirēkka Nāṭakattil Tamiḻ Uraiyāṭal*, Tāynāṭu Patippakam, Cennai 1978.

Muttarayan, L. K., "Sumerian: Tamil of the First Caṅkam", *JTamS* VII, 4 (Dec. 1975), 40-61.

Panikkar, K. M., *India and the Indian Ocean*: An Essay on the Influence of Sea Power on Indian History, George Allen & Unwin Ltd., London 1951[2].

Parpola, A., "The Indus Script Decipherment – the Situation at the End of 1969", *JTamS*, II, 1, Part I (May 1970), 89-109.

Rabin, C., "Rice in the Bible", *JSS* XI (1966), 2-9.

———, "Loanword Evidence in Biblical Hebrew for Trade between Tamil Nad and Palestine in the First Millenium BC", in *PSICSTS*, Vol. I, IATR, Madras 1971, 432-440.

Rathnavel, L. K., "The Indian Circumnavigators of the Past", *JTamS*, V, 4 (Dec. 1973), 24-32.

Roest Crollius, A. A., "Inculturation and Incarnation. On Speaking of the Christian Faith and the Culture of Mankind", *Bull.Secr.n-Chr.* 38 (1978), 134-140.

Sanford, E. M., "Roman Avarice in Asia", *JNES* 9 (1950) 28-36.

Sathasivam, A., "The Dravidian Origin of Sumerian Writing", in *PFICSTS*, Vol. II, IATR, Madras 1969, 673-697.

Sewell, R., "Roman Coins found in India", *JRAS* 36 (1904), 591-637.

Xavier, J. T., "The Original Language of Hinduism - Sanskrit or Proto-Dravidian?", in *PFifICSTS*, Vol. I, sec. 1, IATR, Madras 1981, 11-27.

Zvelebil, K., "The Yavanas in Old Tamil Literature", in *Charisteria Orientalia praecipue ad Persiam pertinentia*, (eds.) F. Tauer et Alii, Československá Akademie Véd, Praha 1956, 401-409.

Index of Names

Index of Texts

(Selective)

Index of Subject

TIPOGRAFIA POLIGLOTTA DELLA PONTIFICIA UNIVERSITÀ GREGORIANA
PIAZZA DELLA PILOTTA, 4 - ROMA